Self-Speaking in Medieval and Early Modern English Drama

Subjectivity, Discourse and the Stage

Richard Hillman

First published in Great Britain 1997 by
MACMILLAN PRESS LTD
Houndmills, Basingstoke, Hampshire RG21 6XS and London
Companies and representatives throughout the world

A catalogue record for this book is available from the British Library.

ISBN 0–333–62899–3

First published in the United States of America 1997 by
ST. MARTIN'S PRESS, INC.,
Scholarly and Reference Division,
175 Fifth Avenue, New York, N.Y. 10010

ISBN 0–312–17552–3

Library of Congress Cataloging-in-Publication Data
Hillman, Richard, 1949–
Self-speaking in medieval and early modern English drama :
subjectivity, discourse, and the stage / Richard Hillman.
p.   cm.
Includes bibliographical references and index.
ISBN 0–312–17552–3 (cloth)
1. English drama—Early modern and Elizabethan, 1500–1600—History
and criticism.   2. Subjectivity in literature.   3. English drama—To
1500—History and criticism.   4. English drama—17th century-
-History and criticism.   5. Drama, Medieval—History and criticism.
6. Self in literature.   7. Discourse analysis, Literary.   I. Title.
PR658.S79H55 1997
822.009'353—dc21   97–6895
                                                          CIP

This book is printed on paper suitable for recycling and made from fully managed and sustained forest sources.

10   9   8   7   6   5   4   3   2   1
06   05   04   03   02   01   00   99   98   97

Printed and bound in Great Britain by
Antony Rowe Ltd, Chippenham, Wiltshire

Aux amitiés, et aux idées, qui franchissent les frontières
and
To the memory of two kind colleagues, lost in successive
years:
E. J. Devereux and James F. Woodruff

Contents

Acknowledgements

My foremost material debt is to the Social Sciences and Humanities Research Council of Canada for a research grant extending over the several years during which I have been engaged on this project. I am also happy to thank the organizers of the Waterloo International Conference on Elizabethan Theatre, Lynne Magnusson and Ted McGee, for inviting me to deliver a paper on *The Spanish Tragedy* that subsequently appeared in *The Elizabethan Theatre XV* (ed. A. L. Magnusson and C. E. McGee [Toronto: Meany, 1997]) and, with permission, is incorporated here in slightly revised form. Colette Quesnel, whose friendship is generous beyond measure, has collaborated with me on a translation of Marie de Gournay's 'Préface', excerpts from which appear in Chapter 7. Thanks are further due to four colleagues at other institutions who offered a platform for versions of work first published here: Joseph Black (Centre for Reformation and Renaissance Studies, Victoria University in the University of Toronto), Gwendolyn Davies (Acadia University), Barbara Garner (Carleton University), and A. Elizabeth McKim (St. Thomas University). Arthur F. Kinney (The University of Massachusetts, Amherst) and François Rigolot (Princeton University) were kind enough to provide useful comments on early versions of parts of the book. Françoise Guichard-Tesson helped me on the subject of mirrors. I profited from some good talk about silence with Christina Luckyj (Dalhousie University). Colleagues at the University of Western Ontario who generously answered questions or provided a sounding-board for ideas include Peter Auksi, Kathryn Brush, Angela Esterhammer, Richard Firth Green, Catherine Grisé, Elizabeth D. Harvey, M. Elizabeth Revell, Nicholas Watson, and Lynn Wells. Gratitude of a special kind goes to my colleague and spouse, Kristin Brady, whose insight, advice, and support cross all boundaries.

Note on Texts and References

Shakespeare is cited from *The Riverside Shakespeare*, gen. ed. G. Blakemore Evans (Boston: Houghton Mifflin, 1974), Chaucer from *The Riverside Chaucer*, gen. ed. Larry D. Benson, 3rd ed. (Boston: Houghton Mifflin, 1987). Except where indicated, Biblical references are taken from the Geneva version. For Early Modern playwrights apart from Shakespeare, I have opted for accessibility over consistency (even in the matter of modern *versus* old spelling) by citing sound individual editions, where available. I have omitted the square brackets used by some editors to signal departures from the copy-text. Abbreviated speech headings in play-texts have been expanded. The standard MLA abbreviations are employed for the works of Shakespeare and for books of the Bible. At the risk of rebuilding Babel, but partly for the sake of dramatizing our universal inscription within that on-going construction project, I have included the original versions of non-English texts cited, generally accompanied by the standard published translation. Where no such translation exists (and occasionally as a matter of preference), I have supplied my own (with the collaboration, in the case of Marie de Gournay, of Colette Quesnel). Regrettably, the new edition of *The Towneley Plays* by Martin Stevens and A. C. Cawley (Oxford: Oxford UP for The Early English Text Society, 1994) did not become available in time to be used in the preparation of this book.

1

Introduction

This is a book about the discursive practices associated with what I will call 'self-speaking' on the English stage, from that stage's Medieval origins to the closing of the theatres in 1642. More particularly, my concern is with the representation of subjectivity, and this means, to some extent, talking about subjectivity itself. For in the course of tracing across several centuries those dramatic techniques whose *raison d'être* is the production of a fictional interiority – besides what are generally called 'soliloquies',[1] they include various kinds of monologues, asides, and even silences – one can hardly help engaging a question of daunting scope and current scholarly controversy: the nature of the Early Modern (and earlier) subject. Yet I am also concerned to keep my distance from this question. Quixotically, no doubt, I plan to analyse theatrical effects in the light of current subject theory, but without treating them as a conduit to the more elusive sectors of lived experience.

I am therefore free, I take it, to confine myself to a narrow segment of literary history, albeit one with some claim to the status of a discrete tradition. By contrast, the proposition that a particular discursive phenomenon supplies not merely an 'episteme' but a virtual snapshot of the contemporary 'self' as actually experienced by human beings would surely call for testing across both historical and cultural boundaries. Projects along such lines, moreover, require more than theorizing, however stimulating – as it often is, for example, in Ken Frieden's *Genius and Monologue* (1985). Adventurously yoking rhetorical and philosophical analysis, Frieden extrapolates modes of consciousness from monologues of all kinds over a wide range of Western cultures (although he is strangely reticent about ancient Greek and Roman drama).[2] The approach yields some benefits on a correspondingly large scale, including a framework within which my own more restricted study fits quite comfortably: 'Ever since Plato's philosophical biography, literary texts have confronted the tensions between monologue as prayer (dialogue with God) and as solitary contemplation (dialogue with oneself)' (16).

Such a perspective makes for some particular points of contact with my readings of the Medieval religious drama.

I remain persuaded, however, that before we can draw conclusions about the history even of English subjectivity, we must, as David Aers puts it, 'learn more about the economic and social realities encountered and made by the peoples of late medieval England, and a lot more about their diverse experiences of community and individual identity' (17). Thus encouraged, I appropriate the freedom to focus on texts independent of their socio-historical connections and to allow those texts to make sense freely in relation to each other and to broader signifying patterns. Obviously, those patterns come from somewhere – somewhere human; moreover, they derive their signifying capacity from an audience's responses, which in turn will be conditioned by a multitude of cultural, contextual, and individual variables. Some of the latter are known or may be inferred; others must remain out of intellectual reach. In resisting, on the one hand, the consolidation of such elements into a rigid outline of developing human consciousness while, on the other hand, drawing upon recent scholarship concerned with subject-formation, I am cognizant of operating in a shifting middle-ground – at once no-man's-land, everyman's, and Everyman's.

In recent years, large but selective questions have been raised about the traditional figuration of Western cultural history, in which the Renaissance and its literature have featured prominently. The essentialist humanism in the claim of Jacob Burckhardt that the Renaissance discovered 'the full, whole nature of man' (2: 303) – a claim that Paul Delany could still take as a 'starting-point' (11) for his 1969 study of British autobiography in the period – has been widely debunked, even as Burckhardt's nineteenth-century structuring of history has been enlisted, beginning with Stephen Greenblatt, to validate a supposed 'radical change in consciousness' (*Self-Fashioning* 161).[3] But it is chiefly as part of the neo-Marxist and anti-formalist strain within poststructuralism, as sponsored most notably by Michel Foucault, that scholars of English literature including Catherine Belsey and Jonathan Dollimore have joined Greenblatt in promoting a re-historicizing, in terms of political, cultural, and economic power relations, not merely of texts but of the modes of thinking that produced them. This critical trend, whose productions may be loosely grouped under the rubrics of New Historicism and Cultural Materialism, has often run parallel with the concerns of feminist critics, who have focused on issues of gender within the discourses of the period. Despite significant divergences – in particular, between some feminist criticism and some New Historicism – it is possible to speak of these various theoretical approaches as sharing a common outlook, based on a single pivotal concept. That concept is a revolutionary notion of subjectivity – namely, the idea that, as Dollimore puts it, 'human identity is more constituted than constitutive' ('Subjectivity' 54). This idea poses a radical challenge to the essentialist view of the 'self' current since at least the nineteenth century, when the modern discipline of literary criticism had its origin. The particular focus on the Renaissance (or, as current usage prefers, the Early Modern period – a time whose idea has come) stems from the argument that the very notion of a human subject with the capacity to 'identify with the "I" of an utterance' (Belsey, *Tragedy* 15) is a product of modern ideologies just beginning to make themselves felt during this era. This position has substantially displaced earlier arguments (based on very different theoretical premises) that the Western European 'individual' or 'self' dates from around the twelfth century.[4]

Not that the new outlook has gone unchallenged, as my subsequent discussion will illustrate, but it has probably succeeded in overturning long-standing assumptions about characterization – especially in drama, which was the most widely and variously practised genre in England over the period, as well as the one most directly concerned with the fictional representation of human beings. While the influence on Renaissance drama of traditional character-types from a variety of sources has long been recognized, criticism of character has until quite recently depended largely on such concepts as development, unity, and consistency – in short, on mimesis as a principle of characterization. On the surface, at least, this is in keeping with Hamlet's famous advice to the Players that to represent persons and actions on stage is to 'hold . . . the mirror up to nature' (*Ham.* 3.2.22), although it is bothersome that the law of universal true reflection lends itself equally to the purposes of E. M. W. Tillyard (in *The Elizabethan World Picture*) and of Foucault: 'théâtre de la vie ou miroir du monde, c'était là le titre de tout langage [the theatre of life or the mirror of nature, that was the claim made by all language]' (*Les mots* 32; *Order* 17). And as Marie-Luce Demonet points out in her exhaustive analysis of Renaissance language theories, to accept transparent correspondence as the basis of representation is to ignore 'les avatars inquiétants du miroir [the disturbing manifestations of the mirror]' that produce distortion and manipulation, half-truth and untruth: for finally, mirrors 'sont rien moins que transparents, et c'est leur opacité même qui leur permet de réfléchir le monde [are not transparent at all, and it is their very opacity that permits them to reflect the world]' (Demonet 247).[5] What does it really mean, then, to hold the mirror up to *human* nature, especially if that nature – perhaps in a way that Hamlet himself epitomizes – is merely a discontinuous stream of artificial, provisional constructs?

In propounding such a view in her influential study, *The Subject of Tragedy*, Belsey has frequent recourse to the soliloquy,[6] which, she considers, 'shows evidence of its own [Medieval] genealogy, rendering precarious precisely the unified subjectivity which it is its project to represent' (44). The soliloquy seems an obvious focus for her approach: if there is any aspect of the dramatic experience which foregrounds the formation and presentation of the 'self', it is surely that notably artificial exercise, ubiquitous on the Early Modern stage, whereby characters do what persons as a rule do not – that is, speak alone in a more or less sustained fashion, and usually in blank verse. Yet Belsey's large claim for the soliloquy's 'project' looms indistinctly through the very humanist mists she aims to dispel, while her sketchy 'genealogy' is no substitute for a systematic examination of the convention as an evolving phenomenon of literary representation. Ultimately, in linking 'the subject's imaginary interiority' to the 'formal development of the soliloquy' (48), Belsey merely deems 'imaginary' what had generally been reckoned to be substantial.

To take representational effects for granted is effectively to assume the priority of the concept of interiority – however that concept is understood – at the expense of the discourses in which it is embodied. When Frieden makes observations similar to Belsey's, he more prominently foregrounds the artificial – 'Dramatic soliloquies develop together with the evolving representation of English individuality' (111) – and the linguistic: 'the "I" comes into conscious existence through languages of inwardness' (17). The latter view reflects, by way of the linguistics of Émile Benveniste, a poststructuralist perspective that is later made explicit: 'The absence of the traditional subject turns out to mean that, from another standpoint, language itself is the subject' (187). In Frieden's analytical practice, however, poststructuralism is a property of postmodern texts, and the subjectifying function of language is rarely explored as such – almost never within soliloquies. In setting the current controversies regarding subjectivity against the stage-techniques of Renaissance drama, I have consistently found the soliloquy (together with various allied modes of discourse) presenting itself as in need of rethinking in its own right, but in terms that frankly acknowledge the status of all 'subjectivity effects' in drama as linguistic, or more broadly semiotic, constructs. Perhaps improbably, then, my starting point is closer than either Frieden's or Belsey's to the conclusion of Raymond Williams:

> . . . there is no formal equivalence between presumed psychological content, of a subjective kind, and a mode of writing centred on a single and isolated speaker. The 'soliloquy', to put it another way, is not 'inner speech' in any defining or exclusive sense. The degrees of address, over a range from 'self-discoursing practice' to indirect and direct monologue of more outward kinds, control much more variable and complex relations, which the modern private / public dichotomy cannot construe; indeed often literally cannot read.
>
> (55)

It is thus necessary to re-confront fundamental assumptions about what such forms of self-representing discourse are and do. The relatively small body of traditional criticism concerned with the soliloquy as a dramatic technique has tended to take for granted its role as 'a mode of human expression' (Clemen, *Soliloquies* 6) and therefore the presence of a 'self' to be 'revealed'.[7] All soliloquies, however diverse, thus become variations on a single theme. The same is true, paradoxically, according to the diametrically opposed materialism of Franco Moretti, a major (if not always acknowledged) influence on New Historicists and Cultural Materialists. For him the Shakespearean tragic soliloquy, at least, uniformly manifests the 'stupefied perception that cultural paradigms, abruptly defaulting, are no longer capable of ordering and guiding the word' (71). In the place of a stable self, this view offers a subjectively inert 'poetic' mode, non-'constructive' and divorced from the dramatic context (70–1) – truly, in Bakhtinian terms, monologic. This is effectively to renew a venerable idea of the soliloquy as '*Ruhepunkt* [resting-point]' (Müller 333), to which Lessing, for one, opposed the view that 'auch jeder innere Kampf von Leidenschaften, jede Folge von verschiedenen Gedanken, wo eine die andere aufhebt, eine

Handlung sei [each inner struggle of passions, each sequence of different thoughts, where one sequence cancels out the other, is also an action]' (cited Müller 333). To allow at once for the self as a variable construct and for the dialogic potential of dramatic monologue is to reopen the closed systems of both Clemen and Moretti.

To restake my 'middle ground', the mere fact that my concern is not the socio-historical subject but its representation in drama involves me, however unwillingly, in a *parti pris*. In assuming the possibility of discussing the two ideas separately, I allow for a complex, variable, and conceivably disjunctive relation between them. I also avow a concern with texts as objects, even aesthetic objects, worthy of attention and interest in themselves. Such biases exclude me automatically from New Historicism and Cultural Materialism – the very schools that have had most to say about subjectivity in Medieval and Early Modern drama. Yet I hasten to stress my distance from their most persistent and polemical detractor on this point,[8] Richard Levin, despite his useful insistence on convention in representation ('Bashing' 77–8), as well as some persuasive results of his aggressive 'common sense'. In fact, I sometimes see in Levin's more negative argumentative tactics a constructive value of which he himself seems unaware.

This is strikingly the case with one rhetorical question that displays an especially high proportion of rhetoric to interrogative content. Here Levin is explicitly throwing down the empirical gauntlet to Belsey, Dollimore, Greenblatt, Jonathan Goldberg, and Anthony Easthope – that is, to all who promote versions of what he calls the 'Bourgeois Humanist Subject' as a product of early capitalist (seventeenth-century) society:

> Have they ever known anyone, outside a mental institution, who believed that she generated herself or the world, or that he was completely free to choose and act without any conditions or constraints, or that she had no internal or external conflicts, and was entirely independent of all other persons and things, or that he could make words mean whatever he wanted, and created history all by himself, and was attached (loosely speaking, of course) to a self-contained phallus?
>
> ('Bashing' 79)

Levin's intent, obviously, is to caricature by agglomerating and exaggerating the attributes with which the 'modern' subject –

supposedly 'unthinkable' in previous eras (Levin, 'Unthinkable Thoughts') – has been credited. But it seems to me that he hits his head on the nail, with productive reverberations.

For if Levin's question were put (probably minus the phallus) to a townsperson of virtually any social caste in fifteenth-century England, the answer might well be, 'No, I have never known such a person, but this exactly describes the Holy Trinity, whom I have often seen impersonated in our pageants'. To take an instance nearly at random, here is God's opening account of himself from the first York pageant, The *Fall of the Angels*:

Ego sum Alpha et O: vita, via, veritas, primus et nouissimus

> I am gracyus and grete, God withoutyn begynnyng,
> I am maker vnmade, all mighte es in me;
> I am lyfe and way vnto welth-wynnyng,
> I am formaste and fyrste, als I byd sall it be.
> . . . .
> . . . I am maker vnmade and most es of mighte,
> And ay sall be endeles and noghte es but I . . .
>
> (Beadle, ed. 1–10)

Levin's flippant reference to a mental institution points precisely, of course, to another form of the same impersonation, thereby again opening a door instead of closing one. In particular, it invites the psychoanalytical argument – which I will be actively putting to use – that such psychosis is not so much aberrant as profoundly revelatory.

Ironically, the detailed correspondence between the image of the supreme being on the Medieval stage(s) and the 'Bourgeois Humanist Subject', as tendentiously characterized by Levin, tends fundamentally to undercut the historicist claims he is bent on frontally assaulting. Despite Foucault's insistence on the idea of 'l'homme [man]' as 'une invention récente [a recent invention]' *not* due to the 'accès à l'objectivité de ce qui longtemps était resté pris dans des croyances ou dans des philosophies [the entry into objectivity of something that had long remained trapped within beliefs and philosophies]' (*Les mots* 398; *Order* 386–7), any idea of God entails the projection of human imaginings; it therefore demonstrates at least the collective human capacity to conceive of the qualities so attributed, even if humanity prefers to renounce the privilege of possessing them. The codification of such projections by theology, transmitted to Medieval drama largely through the homiletic tradition, does not alter their origin or diminish their potential to reflect it theatrically. Indeed, the cycle, morality, and saints' plays represent divinity in human guise with an immediacy and dynamism beyond the reach of other forms of religion-inspired art, however 'humanized' the depictions of the latter. Without falling back on outmoded theories about progression from sacred ritual to pageants outside the church walls, we may still legitimately see the cycle drama, in particular, as putting into bodily form and motion the stained-glass images, minutely prescribed texts, and abstract figurations of ecclesiastical representation. And when it comes to impersonating the deity, the same typological thinking that unites, say, the shepherds of contemporary Wakefield with those of ancient Palestine would insist on the literal presence of the actor within the role. This is to emblematize, however unwittingly, the truly 'unthinkable' inversion – man as the creative father of God – whose containment depends on the symbolic structure as an article of faith.

It is hardly surprising that, with the advent of iconoclastic Protestantism, such impersonation became attached to the doctrinal, political, and social subversiveness now attributed to the traditional religious drama; hence, the official injunctions that divine beings and mysteries cease to be 'counterfeyted or represented'.[9] After the early flurry of Protestant polemical plays – many of them by John Bale, whose zeal allowed him to make divinity his mouthpiece – English dramatists became decidedly chary, in contrast with their Continental counterparts, about broaching Biblical subjects at all.[10] No post-Henrician plays bring God on stage (Craik 50) – a shift paralleled in Protestant-influenced French practice (Lebègue 165). Thus the Calvinist convert Théodore de Bèze, in reworking material from *Le mistère du viel testament* into his *Abraham sacrifiant* (1550), eliminated God as a character and heaven as a setting.[11] (On the other hand, Satan was introduced, habited as a monk – a prototype of Marlowe's Mephastophilis.)

Evidently, the 'unthinkability' of modern ideas of the subject makes a promising starting point for examining the history of the subject's theatricality. And by this route, ironically, much of the work done with dramatic texts by New Historicists and Cultural Materialists may be reclaimed. This is thanks to their focusing of attention on character – arguably the most fundamental issue of dramatic practice – in a way free from traditional mimetic and illusionist biases, such as Levin himself, despite his allowances for stylistic convention, continues to display.[12] As for the equally formidable biases of the recent historicist schools, I share the more circumspect scepticism that currently seems easier to find among Medievalists: Lee Patterson, for instance, as well as Aers. Patterson identifies the New Historicist / Cultural Materialist view as the latest version of a long-standing tendency to treat the Middle Ages 'as an all-purpose alternative to whatever quality the present has wished to ascribe to itself' (Patterson 8). At the same time, his insistence on the pervasive Medieval 'dialectic between an inward subjectivity and an external world that alienates it from both itself and its divine source' (8) scrupulously leaves open the possibility of a changing concept of subjectivity. It is perhaps more remarkable that Aers, despite his well established historicist and materialist credentials, so forthrightly criticizes unsubstantiated claims about the 'construction of the subject' (17) that flow from the same general perspective. Regrettably, the 'economic and social realities' to which he directs attention remain elusive. In any case, they are beyond the scope of this enquiry, even if they necessarily hover on its margins.

I

I am far from suggesting that my approach will exclude theoretical constructs. First and fundamentally, I remain committed to intertextual analysis of the kind theorized and applied in my 1992 book, *Intertextuality and Romance in Renaissance Drama*. I continue to pursue this approach in an experimental spirit, which my sense of the risk involved – essentially, that of intellectual irresponsibility – helps to keep current. I like to think that most of the forms such irresponsibility might take in this study are venial, but there is one potential exception, involving as it does my second major theoretical orientation. For in this same experimental spirit I draw – heavily though not extensively – on the subject-formation theory of Jacques Lacan. Here I am aware of a definite and more substantial risk, which goes to the heart of my project.

The problematic relation of psychoanalytic theory generally to pre-modern subjectivity – unquestionably a valid concern – is at once focused and blurred by various pronouncements of Lacan himself. At times, he effectively aligns himself, albeit in characteristically enigmatic fashion, with the prevailing historicist view of the subject. That is, the origin of the 'modern' subject is situated at the juncture in European intellectual history announced by Descartes, 'Cogito, ergo sum [I think; therefore, I am]' (even if it took Romanticism to consolidate the transcendental 'I' [Ragland-Sullivan 9]). Thus, according to Serge Cottet, whose article appears in a valuable collection produced by some of Lacan's closest collaborators,

> C'est en effet sous l'égide du cogito cartésien que Lacan s'inscrit lorsqu'il annonce: 'Le sujet, le sujet cartésien, est le présupposé de l'inconscient'.
> [Indeed, it is under the aegis of the Cartesian *cogito* that Lacan inscribes himself when he declares: 'The subject, the Cartesian subject, is the precondition of the unconscious'.]

> (Cottet 14)

Like such New Historicist / Cultural Materialist figures as Dollimore (*Tragedy* 173–4), not to mention more traditional historians of human self-consciousness, Lacan explicitly accords a sort of transitional precocity to Montaigne. Implicitly, however, as I will be arguing when I take up this point more fully in Chapter 4, Montaigne is credited with intuiting, rather than inaugurating, a subjectivity presumed to be transhistorical. Elsewhere, certainly, as when he deals with classical Greek tragedy (*Séminaire 7* 285 ff.; trans. Porter 243 ff.), Lacan freely projects his ideas across large historical spaces. So do many responsible interpreters and adapters, such as Anthony Wilden (esp. 164–5) and Michel Beaujour – the latter actually treating Lacan's approach to the unconscious as 'une variante du projet humaniste de la Renaissance [a variant of the humanist project of the Renaissance]', insofar as both 'vise[nt] manifestement la démystification, la dépossession, l'exorcisme [clearly aim at demystification, dispossession, exorcism]' (209). In fact, it is difficult to find, in the vast and sprawling discourse that comprises Lacan's thought, more than a few historical claims, and they are hardly so prominent or sustained as to justify foregrounding this element.

To judge from the summary of Ellie Ragland-Sullivan, Lacan actively promoted a view of the evolution of the subject from Medieval times, when 'outward, objective concentration on meeting the ritual obligations of this life . . . precluded any sense of interiority' (Ragland-Sullivan 7), to Renaissance Humanist / secularist doubts,

which 'awakened the beginnings of a personal and individual "I",
sensible of a divinity withdrawing its transcendent presence from
human affairs' (7–8). The next cultural turn was to scepticism,
embodied in Montaigne, as 'the Renaissance subject withdrew from
a critique of issues themselves to an examination of the criteria by
which issues could be discussed at all' (8). Such an account, by
gathering Lacan firmly into the fold of historicist subject-theory,
tends to preclude any pre-Early Modern application of his ideas.
But this is, in my view, a more coherent and reductive narrative
than can reasonably be extrapolated from the whole body of Lacan's
writing. Even in his basic definition of subjectivity in terms of 'le
sujet cartésien, qui apparaît au moment où le doute se reconnaît
comme certitude [the Cartesian subject, who appears at the moment when doubt is recognized as certainty]' (*Séminaire 11* 116;
Concepts 126), Lacan invokes Descartes less as a point of chronological reference than as a marker for the presence of the unconscious.

Obviously, however, to stress the transhistorical range of Lacanian
theory in practice, as it were, entails a fundamental problem for a
study that, while claiming not to deal with the historical status of
the subject, nevertheless purports to document historically contingent discursive practices. In confronting this dilemma, I find highly
sensible the approach of Paul Smith, who argues for the historicization of the subject '[b]y way of an emphasis on the possibility
that the processes described by Lacan might be regarded as a set of
continuous and changing re-articulations or re-formations of subjectivity' (Smith 77). There is further encouragement in the fact that
those processes, as Smith points out, precisely entail a differentia-
tion between the subject and a 'someone' on the basis of the presence of the unconscious, which is understood as a function of
language (Smith 71). Smith is himself concerned with 'life' rather
than 'art', but his formulation makes a valuable reminder that the
historical records of textual representation, grounded as they are
in language, provide documentation of the 're-articulations or re-
formations of subjectivity' beyond (and apart from) the evidence
bearing on actual existences.

It may further help to make clear that – unlike, I take it, most
traditional practitioners of psychoanalytic criticism – I make no claim
to be exploring the psychology of character. Indeed, to do so on a
Lacanian basis would involve a crucial distortion of his post-
Freudian revisionism:

C'est en effet en réaction à un glissement progressif de la psychanalyse freudienne vers la psychologie, et notamment vers une 'orthopédie du moi', que Lacan réinterprète l'inconscient freudien d'une façon qui fait valoir le sujet comme divisé par son propre discours.
[It is indeed in reaction to a progressive slippage of Freudian psychoanalysis towards psychology, and notably towards an orthopaedics of the ego, that Lacan reinterprets the Freudian unconscious so as to emphasize the subject as divided by his own discourse.]

(Cottet 14)

There is a fundamental distinction between Lacan's 'inconscient sans profondeur [unconscious without depth]' – a formulation that fits neatly with much dramatic self-speaking – and

toute conception qui verrait dans l'inconscient une zone d'ombre, opacité muette, et comme le sanctuaire d'où le sujet véritable, enfermé dans la prison de l'intériorité, trouverait son salut.
[any conception that would see in the unconscious a zone of shadow, mute opacity, and a sort of sanctuary where the true subject, enclosed within the prison of interiority, would find its salvation.]

(Cottet 13)[13]

It is this latter form of self-conception, 'quelque peu romantique [somewhat romantic]' (Cottet 13) and resoundingly Burckhardtian, that New Historicists and Cultural Materialists attribute to the Bourgeois Humanist Subject. Yet the religious lexis – 'sanctuaire', 'la prison de l'intériorité', 'salut' – establishes continuity, rather than a break, with the Christian idea of the soul within the body, hence with the pre-Early Modern subject of, for instance, Belsey and Dollimore. From this perspective, Lacan sought to cut through not only the modern investment of subjectivity with psychological depth but also the precursor mystery of interior presence – even if, as Beaujour points out, he simultaneously experienced 'la fascination du mystère [the mystery's fascination]', as manifested especially 'par un vertigineux syncrétisme dans les métaphores, empruntées à bien des domaines du "sacré", y compris les sacremens chrétiens [by a dizzying syncretism in metaphors drawn from a good many

domains of the "sacred", including the Christian sacraments]" (210).
Ultimately, this is only to say, with Lacan himself, that there is no
escape from the symbolic order as the producer of subjectivity, given
that 'la sémiotique occidentale est inséparable, dans son origine,
des débats qui entourèrent, lors de la Réforme, la question de
l'eucharistie: "symbole" ou "présence réelle"? [the Western semiotic is inseparable, in its origin, from the debates that, during the
Reformation, surrounded the question of the eucharist: "symbol" or
"real presence"?]' (Beaujour 210).

At any rate, Lacanian subject-theory is not psychology, at least in
the ordinary sense, but a semiotic system, a text, at once free and
bound (according to intertextual principles) to interact with other
texts. It will do so in differing ways according to any number of
ideological pressures and conditions of reception, which we may
(but need not) distinguish as 'contexts'. In my book on intertextuality,
which involved the collocation of texts (including 'contexts') with
which an English Renaissance subject might conceivably have been
familiar, I proposed the concept of a grid of intertextual coordinates
as a means of constructing a hypothetical reader / auditor and
keeping this receptive entity, if not honest, at least at arm's length
from the critic. Once such coordinates are extended to include a
frankly anachronistic (or otherwise alien) discursive system, that
entity no longer becomes a plausible historical construct; the fiction of
arm's length, as a costume for a critical stance, becomes wholly transparent. It does not necessarily, however, cease to be sustainable or
useful, and, once again, history as such is not my business here.
Still, paradoxically, the tentative arrogation of such ahistorical freedom may pay historical dividends by developing links between
some of Lacan's fundamental ideas and discourses of subjectivity
that were very much present to contemporary audiences (if not
always seen for what they were). The door is opened to such an
exploration by the fundamental fact that, as Patterson resonantly
puts it, 'Medieval anthropology defined the subject as desire' (8).

While the peculiar linguistic event that is the dramatic soliloquy
has not received sustained study to date as a site of subject-
production, there has been much attention in recent years to the
functioning of language in the production of identity in both fact
and fiction (and often with a view to breaking down the barrier
between them). It is perhaps his concern with the constructive force
of language that lends greatest trenchancy to Greenblatt's exploration of Renaissance 'self-fashioning' – an idea that he himself traces

to Burckhardt (*Self-Fashioning* 161) and that Delany had already developed (though quite differently) from the same source:

> A more novel feature of Renaissance individualism, I would argue, lies ... in the emergence of men who are able to imagine themselves in more than one role; who stand as it were outside their own personalities; who are protean.
>
> (Delany 11)

Delany's account is resoundingly essentialist: even in Medieval psychomachia, 'the essence of [man's] personality remains intact'; the Hamlet-like 'new man' (11) is produced when 'his core of selfhood splits and his very identity becomes doubtful' (12). Linguistic effects are, consequently, derivative rather than determinant. Still, there is a closer match with the narrative of non-essentialist subjectivity propounded by Dollimore than the latter's attack (*Tragedy* 178–9) would seem to allow, and, disappointingly, Greenblatt ignores Delany instead of engaging him. Nor, despite citing it approvingly, does Greenblatt fully pursue the implications of Gorgias' contention that 'through the power of language men construct deceptions in which and for which they live' (Greenblatt, *Self-Fashioning* 215).[14] Despite his historicist allegiance, however, Greenblatt does at one point in *Renaissance Self-Fashioning* allow into play Lacan's concept of the deceptive discourse of the subject. This is, tellingly, with regard to a theatrical instance, and his rationale for doing so comes close to my own, although I will later be taking issue with this application of the idea:

> ... I would propose that there is a deep resemblance between the construction of the self in analysis – at least as Lacan conceives it – and Othello's self-fashioning. The resemblance is grounded in the dependence of even the innermost self upon a language that is always necessarily given from without and upon representation before an audience. I do not know if such are the conditions of human identity, apart from its expression in psychoanalysis, but they are unmistakably the conditions of theatrical identity.
>
> (244–5)

In negotiating the notoriously difficult terrain of literary subjectivity and language, I have found stimulating and illuminating guidance in the recent book of Edward Burns, *Character: Acting and Being on the Pre-Modern Stage*, an analytical history of the classical tradition of rhetorical character-depiction and what he takes to be its Renaissance derivatives.[15] While our emphases differ substantially, our interests largely converge, and, in a sense, my entire study may be taken as a gloss on his reading of the single text that virtually all writers on subjectivity agree to be paradigmatically Early Modern – namely, *Hamlet*: 'The gap between signs and things is the space in which interiority operates in this play, . . . it looms as a divorce between action and being' (Burns 150). It is precisely this gap that I will address in terms of Lacan's link between language and subjectivity, as well as (secondarily) by way of speech-act theory.

Such transhistorical procedures are certainly not mandated by Burns, however, and my conclusions will be only partially compatible with his historical ones. For Burns considers the dramatized 'loss of fixed subjecthood' (168) to be a localized (mainly Shakespearean) and transitional phenomenon, which involves a 'retreat from "character"' (154) as rhetorically produced in the classical tradition, and which defines an unstable vacuum shortly to be filled by ideas of essential interiority – first Puritan, then Romantic. Seductive as this teleological scenario is – and despite the support it receives from New Historicist / Cultural Materialist narratives – I believe that it underrates the self-exposing tendencies of self-speaking rhetoric throughout the Early Modern period, the sense of self-absence *in suspension*, and misses the plays' frequent intimations that the experience of such self-absence amounts to the only essential subjectivity. The very notion of 'an almost subjectless utterance' (154) – Burns's view of Hamlet's rhetorical destination in his most famous soliloquy – buys into what Lacan and Jacques Derrida would agree in branding the Western metaphysics of presence.

Much the same critique applies, from my point of view, to two further books on the conception and representation of the self in the most 'personal' poetic form of the period – works, I hasten to add, that I have also found eminently (though more sporadically) useful. These are Anne Ferry's *The 'Inward Language': Sonnets of Wyatt, Sidney, Shakespeare, Donne* (1983) and Joel Fineman's *Shakespeare's Perjured Eye: The Invention of Poetic Subjectivity in the Sonnets* (1986). Despite her non-dramatic focus, Ferry (almost inevitably) introduces her argument with reference to Hamlet's negotiation of the dichotomy between 'being' and 'seeming'. Fineman's concluding chapter contains some stimulating if cryptic comments on the 'remarkable subjective density' achieved by Shakespearean tragic heroes 'because they enact in their actions their loss of self-presence' (Fineman 303). This process recapitulates that which Fineman traces in the *Sonnets*, whereby Shakespeare produces 'a genuinely new poetic subjectivity' (15). Both authors also briefly consider, as have several others (e.g., Burns 130–1; Delany 12–13; Trilling 24–5), the implications for self-formation of a commonplace Renaissance motif – that of the mirror, the *sine qua non* of self-fashioning.

Perhaps strangely (and quite fortuitously, since her book appeared when mine was all but complete), my ideas are more broadly compatible with those of Katharine Eisaman Maus, who, in *Inwardness and the Theater in the English Renaissance* (1995), pursues a more rigorously historical line and, while she does not disallow psychoanalytic approaches, finds them 'dispensable' (31). She, too, begins with Hamlet's claim to inward substance but quickly moves on to correlate a range of theatrical phenomena with 'the far-reaching political, religious, and economic realignments that constitute the English Reformation' (15). Although she is interested in some of the same texts – both dramatic (*The Spanish Tragedy, Doctor Faustus, Richard III*) and non-dramatic (Foxe's *Acts and Monuments*) – she does not anticipate my focus on self-speaking as a discursive category, much less one with Medieval roots. Nor does she question the simply reflective relation between representation and reality – the enabling premise of both Old and New Historicist enquiry. On the current tendency to deny Renaissance human beings anything like inwardness in the modern sense, however, Maus is refreshingly sceptical, and her scepticism opens the door to textual analysis that often complements mine. Moreover, she usefully stresses the mimetic value, in representing subjectivity, of the very inadequacy of representation. Theatre, in her analysis, qualifies as 'a form of display that flaunts the limits of display', often with respect to 'a personal inwardness withheld or withholdable from others' (210). Such a view was anticipated a few years earlier in theoretical terms closer to my own (though from a more remote perspective – that of 'us', the spectators) in Barbara Freedman's application of poststructuralism generally, and particularly of Lacan, to Shakespearean comedy:

... theater offers a perspective glass by means of which our look is revealed as always already reflected, defined by the exchange of signifiers that displace as they place us in the symbolic. . . . both psychoanalysis and theater stage the circuitous routes through which we find ourselves as lost as the only viable form of self-knowledge.

(72)

Freedman, it should be noted, posits a subject that is not so much transhistorical as endowed with a specific historical itinerary: 'Shakespearean drama stages the unseen space of our being which Freud later discovers there' (29).

II

Despite Freedman's theatricalization of the Lacanian 'mirror stage' (31–3, 52–6) and the valuable work done by Frederick Goldin some thirty years ago on the Medieval troubadour's self-mirroring interaction with the image of his beloved – despite even Foucault in *Les mots et les choses* (translated as *The Order of Things*) – the motif of the mirror appears to me to possess greater complexity and symbolic potency than have yet been critically recognized. This under-recognition may be related to the received history of subjectivity, to judge from Rodolphe Gasché: 'Although it is true that the Augustinian notion of *reditus in se ipsum* – a return upon and into oneself constituting the medium of philosophy – prefigures the modern concept of reflection, the philosophy of reflection is generally considered to have begun with Descartes's *prima philosophia*. . . . With the ego as *cogitans* becoming its own *cogitatum*, a major paradigm of reflection, and of the ensuing philosophy, is set forth' (17).[16] Yet that the precedent of Augustine merits glossing, rather than glossing over, is amply apparent from the work of Goldin and confirmed by Beaujour's theorized history of autobiography, which actually posits the mirror as a vital emblem of continuity: '[l]a métaphore maîtresse de l'autoportrait moderne, qui fut d'abord celle de l'encyclopédie médiévale, sera donc le miroir dont la fonction réfléchissante est mimée dans l'énoncé symétrique: *moi par moi* [the metaphorical matrix of the modern self-portrait, which was first that of the Medieval encyclopedia, would thus be the mirror, whose reflective function is mimicked in the symmetrical pronouncement: *myself by myself*]'. That continuity, moreover, extends to the inextricability of 'self' and Other: 'l'Autre (Inconscient, ami mort, lecteur ou Dieu) reste le juge et garant de ce que l'écrivain rassemble et distribue [the Other (Unconscious, dead friend, reader, or God) remains the judge and guarantor of what the writer brings together and distributes]' (36).

The centrality of the Other in my understanding of self-speaking will become evident in the ensuing chapters. And if the inclusion of 'unconscious' in Beaujour's list appears problematic in Early Modern terms, given the standard interdependence of 'self' and outward image in contemporary formulations, it is possible to glimpse such a dimension behind the very faculty that characteristically mediates the Other's more concrete manifestations – that is, conscience. Arnaud Tripet, in what seems to me an important commentary on Petrarch, both insists on the external derivation of the self-image, as conveyed by 'le regard d'autrui – le miroir [the gaze of others – the mirror]', and posits conscience as, in effect, the internal repressive mechanism required to keep this reflective system in place:

Dès que la conscience entre en jeu, l'être se fait soumission à un ordre qui le dépasse et le détermine tout à la fois. . . . Dans la mesure où elle tente d'accorder ses vues avec le sujet dont elle émane, d'accompagner des opérations dictées du dedans, elle s'obscurcit, cesse d'être ce qu'elle est, devient aveuglement, opinion erronée. Instrument qui permet de devenir ce qu'on est, de le redevenir, la conscience fait pièce à une liberté qui serait initiative ou rayonnement du *moi*. Elle garantit l'être contre la tentation de se constituer par lui-même une essence à travers sa libre activité, l'empêche de s'égarer hors de la voie qui lui est déjà tracée, par le donné de sa nature sociale.

[From the point where conscience comes into play, being submits itself to an order which at once exceeds and determines it. . . . Insofar as conscience tries to attune its views to those of the subject from which it issues, to accompany functions dictated from within, it obscures itself, ceases to be what it is, becomes blindness, erroneous opinion. As an instrument that permits one to become, or re-become, what one is, conscience checks any liberty that would be an initiative or extension of the *ego*. It guarantees being against the temptation to constitute an essence by itself through its free activity, preventing it from straying from the way which is already set out for it by the premise of its social nature.]

(25)

'Conscience' itself, moreover, is a term (hence a concept) whose specialized religio-moral sense tends suggestively to slide, in the Middle Ages and Renaissance, into the more general meaning of 'inward knowledge, consciousness' (*OED* I). (Both meanings still coexist in French usage.)

To foreground the mirror, therefore, is at once to recapitulate the remark, cited above, of Hamlet, the self-speaker *par excellence*, and to mark as self-evasive (and therefore self-productive) the conclusion of his most famous soliloquy, namely, that 'conscience' – the word is especially slippery here – 'does make cowards of us all' (3.1.82). A major intersection is thereby also signalled with Lacan's schema for the constitution of subjectivity. As a central strategy, I explore the implications, both for and through soliloquy, of Renaissance uses of the idea of the mirror, in conjunction with that of the book – also a standard (and similarly slippery) metonymy for identity and one that likewise intersects with the Lacanian paradigm. For Lacan figures the infant's induction into subjectivity according to a double process involving not only the well-known mirror-stage but also a subsequent entry into the exchange-relations of the symbolic order – that is, into language.

In the ensuing chapters, I will flesh out (if that is the appropriate term) these paradigmatic events in the course of applying them to the construction of the dramatic subject. For introductory purposes, it is sufficient to establish that the mirror-stage (which, in fact, 'never "occurs" at all' [Wilden 174]) entails the infant's joyous identification with its own image as an ideal of perfect union – an ideal which, however, is simultaneously exposed as unrealizable.[17] The second event re-figures Freud's Oedipal complex: the prohibitive *Nom du Père* [Name of the Father] – I keep the French so as to keep the pun on '*non*' – shatters the mother-infant dyad, which had preserved the infant's self-conception (the double meaning is functional here) within the imaginary register. This alienating process is similarly figured by Lacan in visual terms, this time as 'aphanisis' ('fading') – a term (adapted from Ernest Jones [Lacan, *Séminaire 11* 189]) that I find indispensable:

le sujet apparaît d'abord dans l'Autre, en tant que le premier signifiant, le signifiant unaire, surgit au champ de l'Autre, et qu'il représente le sujet, pour un autre signifiant, lequel autre signifiant a pour effet l'*aphanisis* du sujet. D'où, division du sujet – lorsque le sujet apparaît quelque part comme sens, ailleurs il se manifeste comme *fading*, comme disparition.

(*Séminaire 11* 199)

[the subject appears first in the Other, in so far as the first signifier, the unary signifier, emerges in the field of the Other and represents the subject for another signifier, which other signifier has as its effect the *aphanisis* of the subject. Hence the division of the subject – when the subject appears somewhere as meaning, he is manifested elsewhere as 'fading', as disappearance.]

(*Concepts* 218)

Finally, the confusion that sometimes, in discussions of Lacan's thought, surrounds the relation between the two primal subjectifying occasions – they are sequential yet mutually imbricated – may be much diminished by keeping in mind the particularly clear formulation of Marc Strauss:

Pour que le Stade du miroir opère, il faut qu'à ce miroir l'Autre donne un cadre, cadre qui ne peut être d'images qui se renverraient l'une l'autre à l'infini, mais est d'ordre symbolique. C'est l'architecture dans l'Autre qui ordonne, organise le monde imaginaire auquel le sujet s'aliène comme Moi, donnant leurs règles et leurs limites à ses jeux, qu'ils soient de prestance, de rivalité, de parade amoureuse.

[In order for the mirror-stage to function, the Other must supply a frame for that mirror, a frame which cannot be made up of images that would reflect one another to infinity but which is of the symbolic order. It is the architecture within the Other that gives order to, organizes, the imaginary world in which the subject alienates himself as ego, giving his games their rules and their limits, whether they have to do with a commanding appearance, competition, or mating behaviour.]

(Strauss 62)

Lacan's mirror-stage, at least, has received attention as a paradigm for some non-dramatic Medieval and Renaissance discourses of the self. In her study of the text-as-self in lyric poetry, Mariann Sanders Regan poststructurally recasts and develops the insights of Goldin, which derived both from the dynamic relation between the soul and God, according to Augustine (Regan 61; Goldin 207–58), and from the paradigmatic experience of Narcissus:

He has discovered the *moi*, a body whose form and climate are distinguishable from every other, and an inner life whose events are invisible to everyone else, revealing its existence to a consciousness newly awakened by pain and desire.

(Goldin 31)

Regan's theoretical supplement includes Lacan's central concept (59–60), as well as a perspective on language itself, particularly as it functions within the courtly love tradition. Her summary roughly anticipates my approach to dramatic self-speaking:

Language leaps to Source but lapses, caught in two motions like the self. For even while they seem haunted by Presence, metaphor and metonymy can certify absence, their own inadequacy and duplicity.

(30)

To turn to more explicitly religious eroticism, the remarkable Lacanian affinity of certain Medieval theological treatments of mirror-imaging has been fruitfully explored by Sarah Beckwith (41–5). Her focus is on the processes of self-construction, involving identification and (mis)recognition vis-à-vis the divine present-absence, that are entailed in late Medieval mysticism, especially as designed for and practised by female subjects. Beckwith lays stress on the ideological implications of the double-functioning of the Incarnation as a mirror:

a potentially fluxive relationship is re-presented as a dyadic one of one-to-one imagery identification which encloses and contains a potential otherness in the image of the same. The identification, mimesis, resemblance, never achieves the identity with its creator which is its goal; and it is this gap, this permanent alienation, which perpetuates the mystical desire as it explores the profundity of its own lack of and distance from its creator.

(Beckwith 45)

Since Christ, in his dual nature, 'represents the problematic relationship between spirit and matter, finite and infinite in Medieval Christianity' (Beckwith 44), the mystic's negotiation of identity vis-à-vis that image combines in proto-Lacanian fashion the two functions of the mirror – as emblem of the ideal and as reminder of its unattainability – that dominate in Western tradition through the Medieval period.[18]

Beckwith's perspective, which is grounded in the tenets of Augustinian Platonism, may be extended beyond the Middle Ages. For the mystical tradition associated with such figures as Richard Rolle and Nicholas Love (translator into English of the influential *Meditationes Vitae Christi* in 1410) feeds – if not directly, at least by way of common Augustinian roots – into the emphasis of Reform theologians on an intensely personal relation with God, and the mirror-image continues to play a key authorizing and descriptive role. Thus St Paul's words figuring the imperfect knowledge of God – 'Nowe we see in a glass, euen in a darke speaking: but then (shal we see) face to face' (*Bible* [Bishops'] 1 *Cor.* 13:12) – not only 'echo and re-echo in medieval theological writings' (Beckwith 42), inevitably with discursive overtones,[19] but also constitute a favourite text of Jean Calvin.[20]

A particularly striking, because subtextual, use occurs in the first book – 'De Cognitione Dei Creatoris [Of the Knowledge of God the Creatour]' – of Calvin's *Institutio Christianae Religionis* [*The Institution of Christian Religion*], where the effect is to insist on the distance between man and God:

> hominem in puram sui notitiam nunquam pervenire constat, nisi prius Dei faciem sit contemplatus, atque ex illius intuitu ad se ipsum inspiciendum descendat.
> [it is certaine, that man neuer commeth vnto the true knowledge of himselfe, vnlesse he haue firste beholden the face of God, and from beholdinge thereof do descende to loke into himselfe.]
>
> (32; trans. Norton fol. 1)

Even Thomas Norton's Elizabethan translation falls short of capturing the subjunctive force of the conditional verbs (though it comes closer than modern English can do); in any case, the image of descent draws attention to the weak links in this chain of signification. Along the same lines, Ulrich Zwingli's application of the Biblical passage goes so far as to derive the fundamental unknowability of the soul from its presumptive resemblance to the divine:

> Noch so wir got an im selbs nach siner gestalt nie gesehen habend, mögen wir ie nit wüssen, wie unser seel im glich sye der substantz und ires wesens halb, dann die seel sich selbs nach der substantz und wesen gar nit erkent.

[Now we have never seen God as he is in himself. Therefore we can never know in what respect our soul is like him in its substance and essence. For the soul does not even know itself in its substance and essence.]

(344; trans. Bromiley 61)

In its context, this view is far from, say, the scepticism of Montaigne's 'Apologie de Raimond Sebond [An Apologie of *Raymond Sebond*]' (2:115–317 [Bk. 2, Ch. 12]; trans. Florio 2:125–326). Yet Zwingli's ensuing injunctions to trust in God arise out of an analogous depreciation of human understanding – a standard Protestant preoccupation, after all. Typically, an emphasis on the obstacles, both inherent and contingent, to true spiritual self-imaging coexists intimately with confidence in the 'authority coming . . . directly to the individual, from God' (Burns 168). It is on that confidence that Burns, for one, founds his understanding of the seventeenth-century 'discourse of the self' associated with the 'purity of pure religion' (168). Yet radical Protestantism insists on the irremediably corrupting effects of the fall – effects pointedly extending, for Luther and Calvin, to language,[21] with which even human vessels of divine grace must clothe the Word. And, of course, deciding when such a discourse reflected such purity proved to be far from an easy matter – a point abundantly clear from Maus's exploration of the idea of ' "inward truth" in early modern England' by way of 'transcendental religious claims' (27).

Compelling as the theological tradition is, I prefer to ground my application of the mirror and the book in the more wide-ranging work of Herbert Grabes, who has compendiously documented the ubiquity and multiplicity throughout the Middle Ages and Renaissance of those intertwined symbols.[22] I approach the soliloquy and its discursive analogues as involving, not merely self-reflection, as in mystical meditation, but a wide variety of forms of 'mirror-talking'. Indeed, my concern with this metaphor will lead me beyond the drama *per se* – notably, to the mirroring mechanisms featured in Robert Henryson's *The Testament of Cresseid*, as well as to the dramatic monologues of *The Mirror for Magistrates*, which may be seen as integrating *de casibus* tragedy with the model of the speech from the scaffold.

In pursuing the motif of the book, I will be engaging an already large and growing critical discourse associated with the historicist schools and beginning, it seems, with Greenblatt, who sketches a development over the Early Modern period from the '*presence* in the written word of [presubjective] identity' to seventeenth-century texts in which 'the inner life is *represented* in outward discourse' (*Self-Fashioning* 86–7). Greenblatt's successors have tended to focus on the development of the figure of the author, especially the literary author. As Greenblatt's emphasis indicates, however, to take up the book as a medium and emblem of subjectivity is to be strongly drawn to religious paradigms, and this is no less true if one's starting point is theatrical representation. Certainly, Greenblatt, like others, follows this route in the contrary direction – from self-writing to drama – as the distinction between presentational and representational presages, although he reads the soliloquies of Hamlet as exemplifying the prior mode: 'words that claim not access to the inner life but existence as the inner life' (*Self-Fashioning* 87). As in Dollimore's narrative of subjectivity, Montaigne comes into play at this point, but for Greenblatt the essayist's practice is backward-looking ('last brilliant flowering' [87]), not forward-looking. Compelling and important as the collocation of Hamlet and Montaigne appears to be, I will be taking issue with the views of both Greenblatt and Dollimore in considering the radical re-figuration of the self-as-book propounded in the *Essais*.

III

To foreground language as preceding and governing pre-modern subjectivity – at least on stage, whatever the off-stage situation – is to direct attention to early linguistic theories. Here I wish to take up the emphasis of Terence Cave on the myth of Babel, which rises from relative dormancy to prominence in the early Renaissance and reaches the zenith of its artistic and intellectual vogue in the sixteenth century.[23] Although the myth surfaces less frequently in England than on the Continent, it may serve to define a powerful epistemological current beneath the waves of subjectifying textuality within post-Medieval English drama. Building (as it were) on Derrida's reading of the Babel myth (in 'Des Tours de Babel') and fortified by his more recent affirmation, 'La babelisation n'attend … pas la multiplicité des langues [Babelization does not … wait for the multiplicity of languages]' ('Apories' 313; *Aporias* 10), I align myself with Cave's view that the Early Modern hermeneutics of Babel anticipate poststructuralism's problematization of the processes of signification: 'The consequences of Babel, the uncertainties of the "logocentric" model (according to which language is presumed to have a natural and, ultimately, a supernatural grounding), were as pervasive then as now' (xvi).[24] In this respect, the Early Modern period largely recuperated the outlook typified by Augustine, for whom the episode of that 'ciuitas, quae appellata est confusio [city, which was called Confusion]' (*De Civitate Dei* 48:504 [Bk. 16, Ch. 4]; *City of God* 312), amounted to a second fall, entailing the alienation of the sign from its divinely established signified, with the result of rendering speech ephemeral and the unitary truth of Scripture subject to multiple and imperfect interpretation.[25] It is, of course, for this reason that Biblical commentary, as Richard II laments in attempting to fix his self-image in the mirror of God, can 'set the word itself / Against the word' (*R2* 5.5.13–14). Humanism's 'great feast of languages' tends to resolve into purloined 'scraps' (*LLL* 5.1.36–7), which ultimately go to feed the New Philosophy. Francis Bacon, like Montaigne (and perhaps following him [Villey 92–4]), directly attacks the illusion of control over words, making this the origin of the most pernicious Idols of all – those of the Marketplace: 'Credunt enim homines rationem suam verbis imperare; sed fit etiam ut verba vim suam super intellectum retorqueant et reflectant [For men believe that their reason rules over words, but it also happens that words twist and turn back their force upon the understanding]' (*Novum Organum* 170 [Aphorism 49]).

Even to formulate the problem on the level of the sign may be seen as buying into the process by which, according to one of Foucault's more intertextually liberating theses, Christian exegetical tradition used dialectic to contain the pagan mystery configured within its own typological structure – namely, that good and evil relate to each other, not as simple contraries, but as reciprocal images of co-present difference and identity: 'Mais si le Diable, au contraire, si l'Autre était le Même? . . . Si le duel se déroulait dans un espace de miroir? [But if, on the contrary, the Devil, the Other, were the Same? . . . If the duel were taking place in the space of a mirror?]' ('Prose' 444).[26] The principle that 'le simulacre ne détermine pas un sens [the *simulacrum* does not determine a meaning]' but 'est de l'ordre de l'apparaître dans l'éclatement du temps [belongs to the category of appearing in the bursting forth of time]' (450) would constitute the *simulacrum*'s myth of simultaneous origin and repression in the moment when the builders of Babel suddenly recognized each other, hence themselves, as Other through their speech

– the veil simultaneously lifted and put in place. The divine decree setting in motion typology's interplay of 'Fabula et Fatum [Story and Destiny]' would thus qualify not only as 'l'énonciation première d'où ils viennent, ... cette racine que les Latins entendent comme parole, et où les Grecs voient l'essence de la visibilité lumineuse [the primal pronouncement from which they come, ... that root which the Latins understand as speech and where the Greeks see the essence of luminous visibility]' (450), but as Lacan's *Nom du Père*. Certainly, Derrida extends the significatory reach of the name 'Babel' beyond double 'confusion' (that of tongues and that of the architects) to 'le nom de Dieu comme nom de père [the name of God as name of father]':

> En donnant son nom, un nom de son choix, en donnant tous les noms, le père serait à l'origine du language [*sic*] et ce pouvoir appartiendrait de droit à Dieu le père. Et le nom de Dieu le père serait le nom de cette origine des langues. Mais c'est aussi ce Dieu qui, dans le mouvement de sa colère ... annule le don des langues, ou du moins le brouille, sème la confusion parmi ses fils et empoisonne le présent (*Gift-gift*).
> [In giving his name, a name of his choice, in giving all names, the father would be at the origin of language, and that power would belong by right to God the father. And the name of God the father would be the name of that origin of tongues. But it is also that God who, in the action of his anger ..., annuls the gift of tongues, or at least embroils it, sows confusion among his sons, and poisons the present (*Gift-gift*).]
> ('Des Tours de Babel' 210–11; trans. Graham 166–7)[27]

The acknowledged consequences of Babel had profound implications for pre-modern subjectivity. As Cave puts it, 'the desire to penetrate to the will of God ... necessitates a movement through human intentions; an opacity, which is directly consequent upon the difference of language, inserts itself between the desire and its *telos*' (Cave 81); yet, by a circular process that comes close to a Lacanian formulation of 'desire' in general, 'the opacity and ambiguity of fallen language are not simply an inert barrier: they are the means by which desire is aroused, appetite provoked, and the pursuit set in motion' (Cave 102). Whatever the potential spiritual benefits, such potent 'opacity' could hardly remain unconflicted. Hence, perhaps, the obscure menace associated with Babel in Boccaccio's *De Casibus Virorum Illustrium* (21–2 [Bk. 1, Ch. 3]). Especially as embellished in *The Fall of Princes* (Lydgate's adaptation of a free French translation), not only does this fall recapitulate the first one, multiplying the serpent like the tongues themselves, but it is also fascinating and ever-present – embodied in ruins within the eternal landscape of romance:[28]

> For to this day touchyng the grete myht
> Off this tour, which Babel yit men call,
> Men fro ful ferr may han therof a syht,
> For it surmountith othir touris all.
> Off which[e] werk thus it is befall,
> Off serpentis and many a gret dragoun
> It is now callid cheeff habitacioun,
>
> That no man dar, as ferr as thei it see,
> For wikkid heir and for corrupcioun,
> Bi a gret space and bi a gret contre
> Approche no neer that merueilous dongoun,
> So venymous is that mansioun
> And so horrible, no man dar approche,
> Lik to a mounteyn bilt off a craggi roche.
>
> (1.1135–48)

The concept of a double fall intersects with Lacan's scenario of the induction into subjectivity. Kaja Silverman, speaking of the mirror-stage, evokes mankind's knowledge of sin and loss of Paradise: 'it is only "natural", after all, that the first self-confrontation on the part of a mutilated subject should involve both a compensatory vision of plenitude and coherence, and a sense of exclusion from that vision' (Silverman 191). By the same token, the account of Elizabeth Grosz casts Lacan's second stage as a fall into the symbolic order, reversing the apparent balance of power between speaker and speech:

> the subject no longer constitutes language or functions as its master, but conversely, is constituted as a subject by language. . . . the signifier subverts the subject's intentions and undermines the possibility of communication. . . . The subject cannot be considered the agent of speech; it is (through) [sic] the Other (i.e. the unconscious) that language speaks the subject. The subject is the effect of discourse, no longer its cause.
>
> (Grosz 97–8)

By way of a variety of Renaissance discourses, I will be extending the dynamic of the mirror to this latter fall, which enacts the principle that to appear in the field of the Other is to disappear through aphanisis. My broad direction may be indicated by returning to Richard II, whose acute awareness of the self-contradictoriness of the 'word' as filtered through human intentions coincides with his shattering of the looking glass, which shows him to himself as he no longer feels himself to be – that is, *not* as 'the very book indeed / Where all my sins are writ' (4.1.274–5) with unambiguous clarity. In the analysis of Fineman, insofar as the looking-glass figures 'the mirror of language on which depends his ideal image of himself' (304), language itself, as in the *Sonnets*, becomes – or rather, in my view, is revealed as – 'something corruptingly linguistic rather than something ideally specular, . . . something duplicitously verbal as opposed to something singly visual' (15).[29] The 'self' – a royal one – is so un-'fashioned' as to produce an illusion of presence through absence, the discursive equivalent of Milton's 'darkness visible'. To adapt Paul Zumthor, it is as if this 'grand rhétoriqueur', the poetic voice of a royal persona, suddenly emerges as his own auditor, who 'ne perçoit qu'un Autre méconnaissable, lui-même, émietté dans les débris d'un miroir [perceives only an unrecognizable Other, himself, dispersed in the debris of a mirror]' ('Carrefour' 335). That Richard's fall is felt to involve a gain in self-knowledge and human stature – to the point of finally tipping him into the category of subjectified 'tragic hero' (or 'realized person' [303] in Fineman's essentialist phrase) – may be related to Augustine's idea of the compensation entailed in the difficulty of interpreting Scripture. Such compensation is predominantly moral – the chastening of pride – but it also involves a sort of thickening of the substance of the interpreter, as he is 'spoken' by his text:

> Between the polarities of hunger and possession, the movement towards an authentic understanding is indicated. The deferment of an ultimate revelation is essential to the proper working of human cognition: tension is inherent in the reading process.
>
> (Cave 82)

From this perspective, there would be a loss involved in the attainment of 'plenitude' as envisaged in Erasmus's ideal of a reader's submissive absorption of (and by) the sacred text, for this 'depends on the total transparency of the self, the elimination of the

congenital obscurity or opacity of fallen man and fallen language'
(Cave 86). Augustine would appear to agree, opining that truly to
hear God speak requires the silencing of all mortal speech, the
abolition of earthly signification (Borst 2.1:393). Yet Erasmus and
Augustine both made texts their life's work, and the latter, the
most sceptical of the church fathers concerning the relation of language to spirituality, was drawn with potent nostalgia to a linguistic ideal of human perfection: 'selbst Augustin, der der menschlichen
Sprache am wenigsten traute, gestand doch der ursprünglichen
Menschennatur die höchste Sprachkraft zu [even Augustine, who
placed the least trust in human language, nevertheless granted to
original human nature the highest power of speech]' (Borst 2.1:404).[30]

According to patristic tradition, the dispersal of language at Babel
found compensation in the gift of tongues at Pentecost (*Acts* 2:4–
11). No doubt, in broad exegetical and philosophical terms, the
affirmation of Marcia L. Colish is justified:

> The medieval confidence that Babel had been redeemed in the
> gift of tongues was the immediate context in which men of this
> period judged, understood, and pressed into service the symbolic
> forms of human discourse.
>
> (3–4)[31]

Yet all in all, Augustine's treatment of the consequences of the
second fall combines the familiar dynamic of *felix culpa* with the
imperfect nature of such consolation. The joyous prospect of dis-
seminating the Word among nations is mitigated by the rhetoric of
spiritual struggle and reward. In the case of this fall, too, the terrible punishment of pride opens into a divine promise at once glorious, mysterious, and daunting:

> et per linguas diuisae sunt gentes dispersaeque per terras, sicut
> Deo placuit, qui hoc modis occultis nobisque inconprehensilibus
> fecit.
> [and the nations were divided according to their languages, and
> scattered over the earth as seemed good to God, who accom-
> plished this in ways hidden from and incomprehensible to us].
> (*De Civitate Dei* 48:505 [Bk. 16, Ch. 4]; *City of God* 313).[32]

Paul himself had gone on from '[n]ow we see in a glasse, euen in
a darke speaking' to an equivocal discussion of speaking in tongues

– a spiritual gift that, even while betokening perfect communication with God, frustrates the functioning of language in this world; for, 'except ye vtter words that haue significacion, how shal it be vnderstand [sic] what is spoken? for ye shal speake in the ayre' (1 *Cor.* 14:9). Paul comes close to identifying such an unfallen discourse with an inaccessible core of unitary selfhood:

> For he that speaketh a *strange* tongue, speaketh not vnto men, but vnto God: for no man heareth him: howbeit in the spirit he speaketh secret things.
>
> (14:2)

Such a private self, flawlessly reflecting the divine presence yet unintelligible to mankind – at once transfiguring and confirming the fall into languages – appears miraculously to transcend the framework of signification, the 'cadre' of the Lacanian mirror-stage. And it thereby acquires disruptive potential, even a certain menace, for those who define themselves through the struggle to understand and disseminate the divine word.[33] In a telling anticipation of his imposition of silence upon women five verses later,[34] Paul enjoins, 'if there be no interpreter, let him kepe silence in the Church, *which speaketh languages*, and let him speake to him self, and to God' (14:28). Those continuing to labour under the significatory burden become the divinely authorized communicators, the Lord's true *subjects*, still desiring. In an elision, if not a veritable undoing, of the history of Babel, Paul insists that 'God is not *the autor* of confusion, but of peace' (14:33). It makes a matching lacuna that, unlike the gift of tongues at Pentecost, the episode of the Tower – action eminently suited to the stagey predilections of the genre, as the dramatization in *Le mistère du viel testament* (1:257–72) tends to confirm – was not included (according to the extant evidence) in any cycle's treatment of Biblical history.[35]

Notes to Chapter 1

1. On the formal and popular definitions of 'soliloquy', see Williams 40–5, whose discursive analysis of modes of dramatic dialogue and monologue, brief as it is, represents an important methodological advance over previous approaches. Still, I differ fundamentally in recuperating the original (Augustinian) notion of 'talking aloud to oneself' (40) without, I trust, buying into the 'conventions of "natur-

alist" drama', which Williams sees as the only alternative to the actor's 'talking *to* . . . an audience' (44). He is doubtless reacting against the school of naturalistic representation typified by Sprague, *Shakespeare and the Audience* (62–90), and Joseph (102–3). The question of whom soliloquizers address was handled with considerable finesse in the early part of this century by Arnold (esp. 2–3 and 133–4), who described the practice of addressing soliloquies to the air as marking 'a step nearer subjectivity' (134).

2. This limitation is more apparent by comparison with Burns (1–6,18–38) on the classical concepts of 'character' and 'ethos'. Classical monologues have been valuably analysed from a technical point of view by Arnold and esp. Leo.

3. See Patterson 7 and Hieatt, who notes the irony of rehabilitating Burckhardt's 'whipping boy of a book, long reproached for its unbalanced view of the transition from the Middle Ages' (25).

4. Bynum (82–109) usefully summarizes (and refutes) such arguments, whose generally essentialist flavour may be gathered from Hanning's readings of chivalric romance in terms of the 'pursuit of self-fulfilment' (233), as well as Oppenheimer's more recent claim that the thirteenth-century invention of the sonnet initiated portrayal of the hitherto-ignored '"self", in the modern sense of a personality in conflict' (9).

5. See also Demonet's sceptical conclusion concerning Foucault's 'lyrique [lyric]' account of language in the sixteenth century as 'cet univers de fusion totale entre les mots et ce qu'ils représentent, où tout est signe, où tout se ressemble [that universe of complete fusion between words and what they represent, where everything is a sign, where everything resembles everything]' (Demonet 577).

6. This material was subsequently gathered as 'Subjectivity and the Soliloquy' for an anthology of criticism on *Mac*.

7. Thus 'reveal' is repeatedly used by Arnold (11,13). Even Dahl, who exhaustively analyses certain syntactic patterns in the soliloquies of Shakespeare (while usefully drawing attention to Medieval and Renaissance analogues), can refer to a linguistic phenomenon as 'the outcome of natural situations and of the state of the character's emotions' (205). That this outlook has Romantic roots is evident from Lamb's remarks on dramatic language as an imperfect means of conveying 'the inner structure and workings of mind in a character' (219); that it has life in it yet appears from the recent book of Newell, who actually seeks to enlist Belsey in support of 'the special ability of a soliloquy to suggest the hidden self of the speaker' (182n9).

8. The issue of subjectivity does not figure prominently in the increasingly crowded field of anti-New Historicist critique – not even for Bradshaw, despite his premise that 'the "Essentialist Humanist" is an ideological fiction' (2).

9. From the decree of the Diocesan Court at York in 1576 (cited Gardiner 78).

10. See Craig, *Drama* 363–77; even the official censorship of religious plays in Paris in 1548 calls attention to their general persistence throughout France (Lee 371).

11.   For a detailed account of the adaptation, see Wallace xxxvii–xlix; the play attracted Arthur Golding as a translator.

12.   On the other hand, to privilege presentational style is to produce a sort of anti-aesthetic hierarchy – witness Shepherd, who condemns mimetic tendencies in the characterization of Shakespeare's Titus Andronicus on the Brechtian grounds that

> the plenitude suppresses questions about what constitutes the human subject. . . . In place of a critical relationship with a split subject, the audience is offered a view into the non-problematic, depoliticised subjectivity of the central fictional character; and this view feels satisfyingly full because everything is expressed.
>
> (83)

13.   Lacan himself differentiates his project from that of psychology in terms of the subject's relation to the Other (*Séminaire 11* 188; *Concepts* 206–7).

14.   Behind this position lies that Sophist's 'aesthetic of the irrational' (Untersteiner 191), based on a denial of Being and extending to a proto-poststructuralist concept of the impossibility of pure or stable signification. The connection between language and the irrational in Gorgias' thought, as developed by Untersteiner, appears particularly congruent with Lacanian theory.

15.   The poststructuralist abolition of essential selfhood has made for a minor renaissance in this field. See also Desmet, although her concentration (following Kenneth Burke) on identification as a rhetorical function places her approach at a greater distance from my own.

16.   I hasten to add that Gasché's approach to Derrida in terms of 'the philosophy of reflection' is fascinating and persuasive on its own terms.

17.   See Lacan, 'Le stade du miroir' ('The Mirror Stage'); perhaps the best of many explications is by Ragland-Sullivan 16–30.

18.   With regard to the Middle Ages and the Augustinian background, Goldin's treatment of this dualism remains unsurpassed, and I am indebted to it. See also Beaujour 35.

19.   The Bishops' *Bible* closely translates the Vulgate's 'per speculum in aenigmate', while the Geneva version collapses the two metaphors, eliding the discursive allusion: 'For now we se through a glass darkely: but then shal we se face to face'. Augustine's commentaries stress the double metaphor:

> justus in hac peregrinatione vivens, ad speciem quoque perducitur post speculum et aenigma, et quidquid erat ex parte, ut facie ad faciem cognoscat, sicut et cognitus est.
> [the just man . . . is led on, after the stages of 'the glass', and 'the enigma', and 'what is in part', to the actual vision, that, face to face, he may know even as he is known.]
>
> (*De Spiritu et Littera* col. 231 [Ch. 28, Sect. 49];
> *On the Spirit and the Letter* 104)

Nunc uero *in* hoc *speculo*, in hoc *aenigmate*, in hac qualicumque similitudine quanta sit etiam dissimilitudo, quis potest explicare? [But now, who can explain how great is the unlikeness also, in this glass, in this enigma, in this likeness such as it is?]

(*De Trinitate* 50a:490 [Bk. 15, Ch. 11]; *On the Trinity* 210]

Cf. Colish 329–30 on language and sight in Dante.

20. I have found useful the survey of allusions to the *Corinthians* passage in *A Dictionary of Biblical Tradition in English Literature* 308–9.

21. See Dubois 52–6.

22. See also Curtius 336, Soellner 416n25, and Beaujour's discussion of the mirror-book connection (34 ff.). On the mirror in relation to classical, Medieval, and Renaissance language-theory, see Demonet 247–74.

23. Dubois provides a stimulating overview of the Renaissance fascination with Babel. This fascination, which ranged across the arts and sciences, extending in France to plays on the subject (Craig, *Drama* 364), naturally figured among theorists of language (see Demonet *passim*).

24. This point emerges clearly from Dubois's study of sixteenth-century language theories. See Steiner 57 ff. for a useful consideration of Babel as a second fall from the perspective of translation theory (the primary focus also of Derrida in 'Des Tours de Babel'). Such a fall is presumed by what Desmet terms the 'Burkean vision of identification after Babel, where we may be embroiled in malice and lies' (164); she concludes that '[i]n the domain of rhetoric, the price of identification is the knowledge that we are in Babel after the fall' (167). On the ramifications of the Babel myth world-wide, the monumental survey of Borst is invaluable.

25. Borst (2.1:391–404) offers the most thorough analysis of Augustine's evolving views. See also Goldin 223–33 on the 'word' in the *De Trinitate*, including its capacity to mirror the divine Word in a way that 'precedes language' (227).

26. Such a view would seem to allow for a complex semiotic dynamic within Medieval typology, as is by no means inconsistent with Kristeva's account of the Medieval symbol as having 'une fonction d'échappement au paradoxe [a function of escaping paradox]' because 'dans sa "logique" deux unités oppositionnelles sont exclusives [within its "logic", two opposing units are exclusive]' ('Le texte clos' 116; 'Bounded Text' 38).

27. A similar Lacanian reading of the Babel myth, but from a theological perspective, was proposed by Bost (218–27) in the same year.

28. The embellishment draws on Jeremiah's prophecy concerning Babylon, whose identification with Babel will be discussed in Chapter 4:

Et erit Babylon in tumulos,
Habitatio draconum, stupor et sibilus,
Eo quod non sit habitator.

(*Jer.* 51:37 [Vulgate])

On Boccaccio's treatment of the Tower episode in proto-Romantic tragic terms – to the point of blurring the issue of divine punishment and ennobling Nimrod – see Borst 3.1:962–3.

29.   Regan (223–52) perceives in the *Sonnets* a struggle to preserve 'that timeless dual unity, I-and-thou' (246).

30.   Beaujour addresses this paradox in a structural analysis of the *Confessions* (284). Cf. Dubois 17–92 on 'la mythologie du verbe [the mythology of the Word]' in the sixteenth century.

31.   Colish nevertheless documents in Dante a more acute sense of the consequences of Babel (263–5,328–9), which are grotesquely figured in some forms of verbal expression in hell (320). Bost (151–6) observes that Dante's Nimrod is condemned 'au soliloque [to soliloquy]' (155).

32.   Such a rationale is still far from the celebration of linguistic diversity in itself by Jérôme Cardan in the sixteenth century (Dubois 118–19) – a secular version of *felix culpa*.

33.   Borst characterizes Paul as 'tief besorgt [deeply anxious]' (1:220). Cf. Calvin's use of Babel symbolism to condemn attempts to know God directly – that is, without passing through Christ as intermediary (Bost 147).

34.   'Let your women kepe silence in the Churches: for it is not permitted vnto the[m] to speake: but *they oght* to be subiect, as also the Law saith' (1 *Cor.* 14:34).

35.   In representing Babel, the European theatre generally lagged behind the visual arts. Apart from the French *Mistère*, a comprehensive fifteenth-century compilation of Old Testament dramatizations, Rothschild (lxxxiv–lxxxv) can cite only one Medieval dramatic treatment (in Spanish). By contrast, there are numerous surviving visual representations, especially from the fourteenth and fifteenth centuries. While the episode is not prominent in the twelfth-century French revival of symbolic art documented by Mâle, the latter records (161) its pairing with Pentecost on Italian frescoes as early as the sixth century. Commentary supports this figural function, with the apostles sometimes cast specifically as builders of the church (a reason, perhaps, for the predominance of scenes of building over scenes of the fall). This is the reading, e.g., of the *Hortus Deliciarum* of Harrad of Hohenbourg, a twelfth-century encyclopedia of spiritual history reminiscent, in its broad outline, of a dramatic cycle. Similarly reminiscent is the pattern of thirty-eight large miniatures, including both Pentecost and the building of Babel, in the fourteenth-century *Bedford Missal (Book of Hours)* (British Library Add. MS 18850). On representations and commentary throughout the Middle Ages, see Harrad of Hohenbourg 1: figs. 26–30 and 2:51; Réau 2.1:120–2; Vandekerchove 67–70; and Kirschbaum 1:236–7.

2

'I am Alpha and Omega': By-passing Babel

Given that this quotation from *Revelation* (1:8) figures most commonly during the Middle Ages in the iconography of Christ as Doomsday judge (Aurenhammer 1:1–2), its recurrent and specialized use in the cycle drama is remarkable.[1] It serves to initiate the self-introductory soliloquies of the deity in the first pageants of all four extant cycles, as well as in the second and final Chester plays (*Adam* and *The Judgement*, respectively).[2] In keeping with the Corpus Christi framework, the portrayals of creation have the task of establishing the eternal divine presence within temporality, and they consistently do so in terms drawn from the Biblical vision of the end. It is the same point made by including the formula in artistic representations of the seasons (Kirschbaum 1:1).

Bound up with the mystery of divine time is that of the tripartite divine nature – another aspect of some iconographical applications of 'alpha and omega' (Aurenhammer 1:1). The preamble to *Revelation* distinguishes between God the Father and God the Son; it then records the alphabetical self-definition of the 'Almightie' (1:8). When the vision proper commences, the 'Sonne of man' (1:13) repeats the formula. This mystery of the Trinity the cycle plays are also concerned to implicate – and explicate – at the outset:

> *Ego sum alpha et oo, principium et finis. . . .*
> I am þe trewe Trenyté
>   Here walkyng in þis wone.
> Thre personys myself I se
>   Lokyn in me, God alone:
> I am þe Fadyr of Powsté;
>   My Sone with me gynnyth gon;
> My Gostis grace in magesté
>   Weldyth welthe up in hevyn tron.
> (*The Creation of Heaven; The Fall of Lucifer*
>   [N-Town], Spector, ed. 1–21)

There is, moreover, a quasi-generic factor that makes the alpha-and-omega text especially adaptable to introducing God in the cycle pageants: these words constitute, in fact, the first self-spoken *revelation* of the inclusive divine nature in the New Testament,[3] hence the first speech that lends itself to recasting as such a soliloquy. From this perspective, it is especially striking to find, standing out in metadramatic relief, the concept that I take to underlie the mode of soliloquy beginning with the earliest English drama. The line, 'Thre personys myself I se', distinctly marks the speaker as regarding his own image – as in a mirror.

Inevitably highlighted by such a verbal gesture, even if unaccompanied by action, is the physical incarnation of the godhead in the actor, and by this route we are returned to the divine mystery at the core of a drama constructed, by whatever evolutionary processes, around the Corpus Christi celebration.[4] The typological functioning of the cycles, according to which diachronically organized 'historical' occasions acquire synchronic significance on the level of God's eternal plan – the advancing plot-line simultaneously tracing a circle, at once complete and uncompleted – is grounded in the dynamic relation between the actors and their roles. In itself, that relation comprises the conjunction and disjunction of imperfect human imagining and divinely revealed truth, of then and now, of there and here. The signifying mechanism thereby deployed is important to recognize as pervasive – not just a source of local effects, like Mak's 'sothren tothe' (England and Pollard, eds 215) in the second Wakefield Shepherds' Play[5] – and as extending to language at a basic level. The vernacular scripts, whose wide variety of forms and styles gives the impression of exuberant invention, accept their 'fallen' relation to Scripture and yet, being informed by the divine spirit, are contained by its letter – that is, within the first and last letters of the creating Word. Behind the portrayals of a failure of communication between man and God – one consequence of which is that the devil's side notoriously gets the 'best' lines – lies the promise of a transcendent unity of discourse as guaranteeing that creation's fundamental coherence, in accordance with Julia Kristeva's concept of the 'pratique sémiotique cosmogonique [semiotic practice of cosmogony]' ('Le texte clos' 116; 'Bounded Text' 38) proper to the Medieval symbol.[6]

Such a promise might have been more difficult to sustain had the cycles included the story of Babel. Obviously, given the uncertain influences on the dramatization of Biblical material, not to mention the spotty records, one can hardly build an argument on any episode's omission. However, the staging of the Pentecost antitype, redeeming linguistic multiplicity in service to the divine Word at the threshold of post-Scriptural history, effectively defines a figural gap, which, in turn, focuses a fundamental point about the dramatic use of language and its relation to subjectivity.[7] For language in the Medieval drama remains wholly God's – or the devil's, which here amounts to the same thing, given the supporting role of evil within the divine scheme. The many monologues that, in effect, ventriloquize the divine Word are merely the most obvious manifestations of a broad underlying principle, according to which all human discourse derives significatory transparence from its positive or negative relation to that transcendent authority. Hence, while Adam and Eve fall into shame, seeing themselves naked, no longer the right likeness of God, neither their speech nor that of their descendants suffers from Augustine's 'diseases of fallen language – plurality, ambiguity, obscurity' (Cave 82). God has a monopoly of mirrors in these texts, and other characters who image themselves in language are viewed by the audience in the light of their conformity or opposition to him.

From Foucault's perspective in 'La Prose d'Actéon', it might be said that to foreground the myth of Babel would dangerously enable the free-play of mutual mirroring by which 'l'Autre' reveals itself as 'le Même' (444). By the same token, to stage Pentecost without Babel, so that it looks forward but no longer backward – or backward only into an empty space – is to truncate the very signifying mechanism that pre-conditions typology on the levels of both discourse and temporality:

Un pareil signe est à la fois prophétique et ironique: tout entier suspendu à un avenir qu'il répète à l'avance et qui le répétera à son tour en pleine lumière; il dit ceci puis cela, ou plutôt il disait déjà, sans qu'on ait pu le savoir, ceci et cela. En son essence il est simulacre, – disant tout simultanément et simulant sans cesse autre chose que ce qu'il dit.
[Such a sign is at once prophetic and ironic: suspended in its entirety from a future that it repeats in advance and that will, in turn, repeat it in full light; it says this, then that, or rather it has already been saying this and that without our being able to know it. In its essence, it is *simulacrum* – saying everything simultaneously and simulating unceasingly something other than what it says]'

(Foucault, 'Prose' 450)

It would be tempting to take the cycle drama's by-passing of Babel as signalling in Lacanian terms that humanity, as represented on the Medieval stage, remains in the mirror-stage of psychological development, not yet inscribed in the symbolic order. Certainly, the pervasively dyadic structure of the universe portrayed, on the level no less of moral oppositions than of figural relations, is suggestive of the imaginary register – a point confirmed by the iconographic underpinnings of dramatic structure and method, given that '[i]nsofar as traditional symbolism depends upon visual resemblances, Lacan would relegate it to the Imaginary' (Wilden 232).[8] Nor – with the qualified exceptions I will be citing – do the plays display a Lacanian dynamic of psycho-discursive exchange relations. Yet the *Nom du Père* that conditions such relations in Lacanian theory is irresistibly identifiable with the Prime Mover of the entire project, the very transcendental signifier that here appears to block the passage of a 'fixed symbolic code' into a means of 'communication', which is the 'central aspect of the Symbolic order' (Wilden 230,232). Then there is Lacan's fundamental premise (as previously mentioned) that '[p]our que le Stade du miroir opère, il faut qu'à ce miroir l'Autre donne un cadre . . . d'ordre symbolique'. The divine creation itself would thus become, like the cathedrals containing the church's symbolic objects and the transactions involving them, 'l'architecture dans l'Autre qui ordonne, organise le monde imaginaire auquel le sujet s'aliène comme Moi [the architecture within the Other that gives order to, organizes, the imaginary world in which the subject alienates himself as ego]' (Strauss 62). Accordingly, the drama may be seen, not as defining a distinctively pre-modern subject, but as precipitating the Other(A) as God – the inverse of the process by which, arguably, Lacan himself dissolved God into the Other(A). Such a view accords with what Beaujour describes as Augustine's veritable abdication as speaking subject at the end of the *Confessions*:

> c'est l'allocution au Verbe qui produit l'étrange dérobade du dixième Livre, la 'disparition élocutoire' d'Augustin ayant lieu au moment même où celui-ci s'apprête à dire 'qui il est'. Mais dire 'qui je suis' relève de la folie du monde, que la connaissance de Dieu condamne. Le rhéteur Augustin doit surmonter la rhétorique, rejeter son vide et ses masques, pour se laisser envahir par le Verbe révélé auquel il s'adresse.
>
> [it is the address to the Word that produces the tenth Book's

strange withdrawal, Augustine's 'elocutionary disappearance' taking place just at the moment when he is preparing to say 'who he is'. But to say 'who I am' belongs to the madness of the world, which knowledge of God condemns. Augustine the rhetorician must rise above rhetoric, reject his emptiness and his masks, so as to let himself be invaded by the revealed Word to which he addresses himself.]

(284)

Whereas, for Lacan, the Other(A) is the unconscious at large, conceived discursively, the concretizing (through anthropomorphosis) of that fluid set of quasi-linguistic structures into the unitary Word produces a much narrower figure – that of the *surmoi* or superego, which is thereby rigidly identified with the *Nom du Père*. Every plot originating in such a discursive function effectively fantasizes the conversion of the *non* transmitted through original sin into the fatherly 'yes' to be spoken to the saved on Doomsday: 'Mi chosen childir, comes vnto me!' (*The Last Judgement* [York], Beadle, ed. 365). The origin and development of the superego, as first delineated by Freud, are usefully characterized by Silverman in terms of the father-figure and the mirror-image. Her account closely matches the dramatized relation between God and fallen man:

> ... the male subject internalizes along with the image of the father an image of his own distance from the father. That distance is expressed through the creation of a psychic construct which stands to one side of the ego, as a kind of ideal version of it. This ego ideal or superego functions throughout the history of the subject as the mirror in which the ego sees what it should be, but never can be.
>
> (Silverman 135)

Here the mirror serves, in a typically Medieval way, as an instrument of conscience, offering the reflection of an externally derived ideal, which the individual, with the best will in *this* world, must fail to measure up to. The numerous figures of ill-will and sin in the religious drama frankly invert this ideal image, often parodically; they may be seen as the repressed inverse of the idealization of the father, according to Lacan's provocative formulation:

Ce père imaginaire, c'est lui ... qui est le fondement de l'image providentielle de Dieu. Et la fonction du surmoi, à son dernier terme, dans sa perspective dernière, est haine de Dieu, reproche à Dieu d'avoir si mal fait les choses.

[It is this imaginary father ... which is the basis of the providential image of God. And the function of the superego in the end, from its final point of view, is hatred for God, the reproach that God has handled things so badly.]

(*Séminaire 7* 355; trans. Porter 308)

(This translation regrettably effaces the French's pointed reference, in 'fait les choses', to God as creator.)

The double self-modelling of the individual in terms of idealization and failure depends on the 'cadre' supplied by 'l'architecture dans l'Autre'. For identification with the father causes the child to feel ' "at home" in those discourses and institutions which define the current symbolic order ... he will "recognize" himself within the mirror of the reigning ideology, *even if his race and economic status place him in contradiction to it*' (Silverman 141, my emphasis). Yet the very concept of 'contradiction' suggests that, with the superego installed as the Other(A), the symbolic order *masquerades* as a stable field of fixed binary terms, conditioned by the assumption of unmediated signification, such as necessarily grounds manifestations of the divine Word. Such a system would naturally resemble Kristeva's economy of the restrictive and '*anti-paradoxal* [*antiparadoxical*]' ('Le texte clos' 116; 'Bounded Text' 38) Medieval symbol – an economy whose stock-in-trade is the deployment of oppositions between good and evil figures, whether Biblical derivatives, allegorical embodiments of moral qualities, or concretized principles of conscientious self-measurement (*bonus angelus, malus angelus*). All in all, Dollimore, eager to find forerunners of Early Modern 'decentred' subjectivity in morality-play depictions of 'man's divided nature' (Dollimore 164), would appear to be looking in the wrong place.

Yet according to the logic of psychoanalysis (as well as the formulation of Tripet introduced in the previous chapter), a process by which 'conscience' takes the place of the 'unconscious' would be fundamentally repressive, as indeed Foucault finds the dualism of Christianity to have been in a profound way ('Prose', esp. 444–5).[9] This might encourage us to look for slippage in the relation between sign and signified, points where the effects of Babel make themselves felt by hinting at subjectivity as elusive or fragmented – thickened by the 'opacity' of the language of the unconscious, rather than clarified by the divine Word. Only a very few such instances present themselves in the surviving religious drama; I will concentrate on two of these – one more extensive than the other, but both 'precociously' indicative of the potential of the spoken self to overflow the prescribed discursive channel.

I

Everyman is well known for departing from the standard psychomachic structure of the morality play in order to take its protagonist on an insistently linear journey towards death. Death, however, is far from taken for granted: in the 42-line soliloquy with which God opens the play (after the moral lesson is announced by the Messenger), death is first determined as mankind's punishment for sin within the divine plan, then imposed by God upon Everyman 'personally'. Despite its allegorical method, then, and its detachment from 'historical' material, this text also stands out among the morality plays for actively instating the cycle pageants' double temporal perspective – synchronic and diachronic. Certainly, there is no equivalent in the other extant non-cycle plays of the self-introductory soliloquy of God.

At the same time, this soliloquy differs radically from its cycle counterparts in its treatment of the mystery of the Trinity. In contrast with the usual concern to establish the transcendence of divinity – a stance that implicitly acknowledges the actor's position outside the role – God here begins by expressing perceptions and feelings in a surprisingly subjective mode: 'I perceyue, here in my maieste, / How that all creatures be to me vnkynde' (22–3). He then perceptibly shifts in voice and perspective from the wrathful Old Testament Father to the merciful Son, and finally to the judge of Doomsday:[10]

> Of ghostly syght the people be so blynde,
> Drowned in synne, they know me not for theyr God.
> In worldely ryches is all theyr mynde;
> They fere not my ryghtwysnes, the sharpe rod.
> My lawe that I shewed, whan I for them dyed,

> They forgete clene / and shedynge of my blode rede.
> I hanged bytwene two theues, it can not be denyed;
>
> . . . .
>
> I se the more that I them forbere
> The worse they be fro yere to yere.
>
> . . . .
>
> I profered the people grete multytude of mercy,
> And fewe there be that asketh it hertly.
> They be so combred with worldly ryches
> That nedes on them I must do iustyce.
>
> (25–61)

The doctrinal message is no different, of course, from that conveyed by the alpha-and-omega (and numerous similar) self-declarations elsewhere in the Medieval drama. The innovation takes place on the level of dramatic representation, and it has what might be termed subjectifying results.

It would be misleading to speak of 'psychological realism' in such a context, even if that context includes the late-Medieval humanization of divinity. Nevertheless, the speech conveys an impression of thought and emotion spontaneously unfolding in human time without the support of a fixed and stable identity. The effect may be conceived as an enfolding of the actor within the role, as if we are now watching a single entity rather than a double one with the speaker and his speech juxtaposed. Divinity is thereby brought down to earth, given that, as Demonet puts it, '[s]euls les anges parlent sans corps [only the angels speak without bodies]' (275). Despite the authority of the Word, which sets the action in motion and governs its meaning, these *words* are not felt to exist independently of their occasion, as a script perpetually awaiting enactment. Rather than 'se' nothing but his own transcendent nature, like the N-Town God, *Everyman*'s divinity, when he mirror-speaks, is made to 'perceyue' and 'se' *others*, multiple fallen images reflecting him incompletely and imperfectly.

By this means, monologue itself is effectively dialogized – decidedly before its time, to judge from Georges Gusdorf's opposition of monologue to modern discourses of 'connaissance de soi [self-knowledge]'. The latter supposedly depend on the '[r]upture . . . avec la tradition chrétienne [rupture with Christian tradition]' (30) effected by Montaigne:

Le monologue, le soliloque de l'introspection apparaît faux en
son principe, dans la mesure où il s'applique à une réalité sans
consistance, hypothétique et provisoire. Il faut, pour s'affronter
directement, que la personne prenne de soi à soi ses distances.
Elle se retrouve grâce à l'interposition d'un terme extérieur où
elle s'est inscrite. Connaissance en form de dialogue, incertaine et
problématique, comme partout où s'introduit la séparation, le
dédoublement.
[The monologue, the soliloquy of introspection appears false in
its premise, insofar as it applies to a reality without consistency,
hypothetical and provisional. It is necessary, in order to confront
himself directly, that the person consider himself-as-self at a distance. He finds himself again thanks to the interposition of an
exterior term in which he has inscribed himself – knowledge in
the form of dialogue, uncertain and problematic, as wherever
separation and doubling intervene.]

(136)

More immediately to my purpose, the play's technique implicates Lacan's distinction between being and signification, especially
as that distinction dovetails with the linguistic definition of subjectivity propounded by Benveniste: 'la capacité du locuteur à se poser
comme "sujet" [the capacity of the speaker to posit himself as "subject"]' (259; trans. Meek 224). This is Silverman's Lacanian application of Benveniste's now-virtually-standard concepts of le sujet de
l'énonciation (the speaking subject) and le sujet de l'énoncé (the subject of speech):

The speaking subject belongs to what Lacan would call the domain
of the real, but it can attain subjectivity or self-apprehension only
through the intervention of signification. Since signification results in an aphanisis of the real, the speaking subject and its
discursive representative – i.e. the subject of the speech – remain
perpetually dissimultaneous, at odds.

(196–7)

Such a view remarkably intersects with those Renaissance theoreticians of language who problematized the mirror – the traditional
(ultimately Platonic) emblem of the truthfulness of signification –
by way of individual intentionality:

le miroir se tourne pour montrer moins l'énoncé que la 'volonté' de l'énonciateur, distincte de la thélémie du premier inventeur des noms qui ne peuvent pas mentir.

[the mirror turns itself to show less what is spoken than the 'will' of the speaker, as distinct from the *thélémie*[11] of the first inventor of the names that cannot lie.]

(Demonet 274)

Arguably, then, in *Everyman*, re-creation comes out on top. Twice-fallen man slips into place as the creative father of God, who undergoes a version of Lacanian aphanisis, disappearing from the 'domain of the real' in becoming a speaking subject. What is more, God subsequently vanishes from the text as a source and guarantor of a discourse of presence, holding the mirror up to Everyman. The action represents the discourse of God as mediated – by Knowlege, by Confessyon; hence, it partakes in the flux of communication comprising the symbolic order. This pattern is radically initiated by the deputation of Death as 'myghty messengere' (63).

Death's function as the most powerful instrument of self-awareness is itself, of course, a commonplace in the Middle Ages and Renaissance (to say nothing of pre-Christian precursors). The moral and symbolism of *Everyman* were multiply pre-scripted – for instance, by Alanus de Insulis (Alain de Lille) in the eleventh century: 'memorare igitur novissima tui in libro scientiae' ['Remember then your final end, which is written in the book of knowledge'] (col. 118, B; trans. Evans 29). Alanus joins this 'book', by the way, to those of experience and conscience, and all three in turn are linked to the triple 'speculum in quo te debes videre [glass in which you should behold yourself]' to understand the miserable human condition – namely, 'Speculum Scriturae, speculum naturae, speculum creaturae [the mirror of Scripture, the mirror of nature, and the mirror of creation]' (col. 118, B–C; trans. Evans 29).[12] At the other extreme of the period, Walter Ralegh, in *The History of the World*, provides an especially resonant account in terms of the mirror-image: '[Death] holds a Glasse before the eyes of the most beautifull, and makes them see therein, their deformitie and rottennesse; and they acknowledge it' (396).[13]

But built into this idea, as befits death's introduction into the world as punishment for neglecting the divine Word, is the failure of communication between God and man, figured in the fallen state of language itself. This, too, Ralegh vividly brings out, with a conclusion that anticipates Lacan's (and Derrida's) understanding of signification:

> They neglect the aduice of God, while they enjoy life, or hope it; but they follow the counsell of Death, vpon his first approach. It is he that puts into man all the wisdome of the world, without speaking a word; which God with all the words of his Law, promises, or threats, doth not infuse. *Death* which hateth and destroyeth man, is beleeued; God which hath made him and loues him, is alwayes deferred.
>
> (396)

Nor is the message of mortality, self-alienating and therefore self-producing, absent from the Lacanian mirroring experience:

> l'homme se distingue en ceci des autres animaux qu'à considérer son image, il en lit la signification mortifère, puisqu'elle lui est foncièrement 'ravie'. Ce qui conduira Lacan à énoncer que 'le moi n'est toujours que la *moitié* du sujet'.
> [man is distinct from the other animals in this respect – that in considering his image, he reads its death-bearing signification, since it is fundamentally 'ravished' from him. This is what leads Lacan to state that 'the I is never more than half of the subject'.]
>
> (Léger 42)

The fall of language is insistently concretized in Everyman's personal account-book, which he has difficulty reconciling with the scripturally encoded Word. As is mandated by the invariably comic trajectory of eschatological drama before *Doctor Faustus*, the outcome is assured: the reckoning will become a 'crystall-clere' (898) reflection of the divine (a seamless uniting of the metaphors of the book and the mirror). But such a result conspicuously depends on the gift of grace ('Come, excellente electe spouse, to Iesu!' [894]), as well as on death's extraction of the purified soul from the incorrigible body ('Now thy soule is taken thy body fro' [897]). Prior to these events, which begin to take shape roughly half-way through the play, the governing pattern is Everyman's search for companions, who successively refuse or abandon him, in effect disappearing as the stable aspects of himself he took them for and fragmenting his illusion of wholeness. That pattern subjects him to (and subjectifies him by means of) a process of shifting signification.

Forced to negotiate the discursive vacuum produced by the withdrawal of the divine Word, to search for his true image in the face of the ultimate absence, Everyman is no longer where he speaks but where he is spoken. Moreover, the text's interechoing proverbs, commonplaces, and key spiritual terms comprise a signifying network that negates discrete identity. This effect becomes part of the character's allegorical inclusiveness, which, as in the morality plays generally, exists in tension with individualizing elements. Commonly, such tension is activated by a dialectic between the Mankind figure's successive allegiances to vice or virtue, conveyed through dialogue, and his stock-taking monologues. The latter tend to subsume situation-specific attitudes into universal commentary, as when the vice-besotted Humanum Genus in *The Castle of Perseverance* effectively views his image in the divine mirror ('In sowre swettenesse my syth I sende, / Wyth seuene synnys sadde beset' [1240–1]), then generalizes himself along with his vision: 'I se no man but þey vse somme / Of þese seuene dedly synnys' (1249–50). The other surviving texts offer no parallel to the subjectifying discursive conflict enacted within Everyman's soliloquies, in which glimpses of himself as, in effect, the victim of language's deceptive insubstantiality, of 'fayre wordes' that 'maketh fooles fayne' (379) in the guise of stabilizing identity, alternate with delusions of recapturing a 'lost' prelapsarian self through personalized acts of speech:

> It is sayd, 'In prosperyte men frendes may fynde,
> Whiche in aduersyte be full vnkynde'.
> . . . .
>
> To my kynnesmen I wyll, truely,
> Prayenge them to helpe me in my necessyte.
> . . . .
>
> I wyll go saye, for yonder I se them.
>
> (309–17)
>
> Lo, fayre wordes maketh fooles fayne;
> They promyse, and nothynge wyll do, certayne.
> . . . .
>
> All my lyfe I haue loued ryches;
> If that my Good now helpe me myght,
> He wolde make my herte full lyght.
> I wyll speke to hym in this dystresse.
>
> (379–91)

For Everyman, the cycle can be broken only with a shift from the mode of soliloquy to that of prayer; by God's grace (as mediated by Confessyon), Everyman is finally enabled to address the transcendent 'Myrrour of ioye' (591), which shows him to himself as 'a synner moost abhomynable' (595), with the request that 'my name be wryten in Moyses table' (596). Thus the Other is duly reinscribed as the superego. What remains remarkable, in the context of the Medieval drama, is to find the soliloquy, as a mechanism of self-alienation rather than self-affirmation vis-à-vis the divine presence, given such a run for its money, beginning with the voice of God himself.

II

Several factors combine to make *Everyman* a likely site for discursive instability. Especially from an intertextual perspective, this apparently tightly unified text reveals major tensions, not only internally, but also generically, beginning with its status as a printed translation (from a Dutch original) with no known performance history. The play stands in oblique relation to the tradition of English religious drama – a tradition which, diverse as it is now commonly acknowledged to be, is overwhelmingly consistent and coherent in its representational techniques. It is more surprising to find a related anomaly, albeit a more localized one, within a Biblical play, even if the 'cycle' of the N-Town manuscript is increasingly approached as itself heterogeneous.[14]

In structure, as in staging, the N-Town Passion Play is conspicuously anomalous – a long and sprawling sequence of pageants, intended for performance in two successive years, which was evidently an addition to the original cycle (Gauvin 56; Kahrl 59). David Bevington has remarked on the use of soliloquies at intervals throughout 'to offset scenes of tumultuous action' (Bevington, ed. 478). But the lamenting soliloquy of Mary over the news of Jesus' arrest occupies a privileged position at the conclusion of Part I. And on the discursive level, what stands out is the obtrusion of a language expressive of the unconscious, the slippage of the symbolic code into the communicative dynamic of the symbolic order.

The effect is heightened by comparison with the briefer soliloquized laments of Mary Magdalene (Spector, ed. *Passion Play* I.27,141 ff.[15]) and Peter (II.29,213 ff.), which are straightforward conscience-driven expressions of repentance: she for her sinful life, he for his denial of Christ. Each, in effect, looks into the mirror held up by God-as-superego and sees what the audience simultaneously recognizes as an accurate likeness – respectively, 'a wyckyd wrecche all wrappyd in wo' (I.27,142) and 'a synful creature' (II.29,220). This is the standard turn taken by the guilty in response to Christ's innocence, as when Mary Magdalene, in the Wakefield *Resurrection*, soliloquizes, 'It was my gylt he was fortayn, / And nothing his' (England and Pollard, eds 422–3).

By contrast, the spiritual state of the Virgin is itself transcendent, as the N-Town Magdalene confirms just before the key monologue: 'O, immaculate modyr, of all women most meke. / O devowtest, in holy medytacyon evyr abydyng' (I.28,149–50). Indeed, Roger Bacon credited Jesus' mother, alone among human beings, with the capacity to see directly in the Pauline sense, not in a mirror.[16] So when her lament for her son turns, albeit momentarily, to self-blame, she has lost sight of her image in the divine mind; she no longer experiences that fusion of the imaginary with the symbolic by which Christian ideology produces its (necessarily counterfeit) version of the 'pure plenitude or fullness' (Grosz 34) of the 'domain of the real'[17]:

> Wherefore þan xuld ȝe sofer þis gret peyn?
> I suppoce veryly it is for þe tresspace of me.
> And I wyst þat, myn hert xuld cleve on tweyn.
> (I.28,170–2)

Mary's very search for an explanation ('I suppoce') marks the intervention of signification between *le sujet de l'énonciation* and *le sujet de l'énoncé*, with the latter, figured as the 'hert' whose breaking is contingent, fading even as she speaks.

Of course, the divine image of Mary requires its own temporary eclipse by her human grief, of which the heart is a recurrent symbol. This access of humanity is the basis of the pan-European tradition of the *planctus Mariae*, on which several cycles, including that of N-Town, draw in providing laments for the Virgin at the foot of the cross.[18] The most sustained and 'personal' adaptation in monologue form occurs in a variant of the Chester *Passion Play* (Lumiansky and Mills, eds 241 ff.), where Mary feels herself going mad with grief, recalls the joys of motherhood, and twice wishes she could die – first, as an escape from sorrow, then in order to take her son's place. I will be proposing (in Chapter 7) that this speech significantly anticipates the subsequent staging of female madness as a means of encoding tragic subjectivity. However, the attitudes themselves lie well within the Marian convention.

The monologue of the N-Town Virgin, on the other hand, appropriates a radical freedom in the handling of the standard motifs – something made possible, perhaps, by its displacement forward to the occasion of Christ's arrest, a unique position for a Marian *planctus* within the drama or elsewhere (Taylor 624n2). Here Mary envisages dying from grief, not to free her son from his destiny or herself from pain, but as a proof of adequate feeling, hence of a subjective presence that suddenly eludes her. The heart becomes a site of aphanisis, enacting a transition, in Kristeva's terms, from symbol to sign:

> A! A! A! How myn hert is colde.
> A, hert hard as ston, how mayst þu lest
> Whan þese sorweful tydyngys are þe told?
> So wold to God, hert, þat þu mytyst brest!
> (I.28,161–4)

A few lines later, in a more daring psychologizing of formulaic tokens of humanity, the Virgin's grief is not only cut loose from its spiritual moorings but allowed to drift close to blasphemy. Among the other extant dramatic *planctus*, only in the Wakefield *Crucifixion* does Mary register a sense of her own betrayal; there she addresses Gabriel and quickly concludes, despite her inability to fathom the sorrowful turn of events, 'and yit I trow thi red' (England and Pollard, eds 442). The prayer of the N-Town figure gives way to insistent complaint, as she directly accuses God of breaking his promise to her and develops the innocence of Jesus in the personal terms of an idealizing mother. Not sinful man but God himself becomes guilty of perverse injustice:

> O Fadyr of hefne, wher ben all þi behestys
>   þat þu promysy[d] me whan a modyr þu me made?
> þi blyssyd sone I bare betwyx tweyn bestys,
>   And now þe bryth colour of his face doth fade.
>
> A, good Fadyr, why woldyst þat þin owyn dere sone xal sofre
>   al þis?
> And dede he nevyr aȝens þi precept, but evyr was obedyent;

And to every creature most petyful, most jentyl and benyng,
    iwys;
And now for all þese kendnessys is most shameful schent.
                                        (I.28,177–84)

The inevitable realignment of Mary with the divine will, marked by
the reversion of her discourse to the spiritual plane, follows immediately and without external prompting, but for these very reasons
it stands out as abrupt and artificial:

Why wolt þu, gracyous Fadyr, þat it xal be so?
    May man not ellys be savyd be non other kende?
ȝet, Lord Fadyr, þan þat xal comforte myn wo
    Whan man is savyd be my chylde and browth to a good
    ende.
                                        (I.28,185–8)

Moreover, although the mode of prayer, together with Mary's traditional role as intercessor for mankind, is pointedly recovered in
the next four lines with an address to the son in his divine aspect,
the final note remains ambiguously self-regarding, given what has
gone before: 'On all mankend now have þu pety – / And also
thynk on þi modyr, þat hevy woman' (I.28,191–2).
    It will take the experience of the crucifixion, as moralized by
Jesus himself and her comforters, Mary Magdalene and John, to
confirm the spiritual redirection of this Virgin's grief at the expense
of her subjectivity. Her sight of Jesus on the cross at first renews her
apostrophe to her heart as an emblem of inadequate feeling:

A, out on my hert – whi brest þu nowth?
    And þu art maydyn and modyr, and seyst þus þi childe
    spylle!
How mayst þu abyde þis sorwe and þis woful þowth?
    A, deth, deth, deth! Why wylt þu not me kylle?
                                        (II.32,97–100)

The subsequent address to Jesus stands out for its highly particular-
ized reproachfulness, tinged with sarcasm and redolent of self-pity:

O my sone, my sone, my derlyng dere!
    What! Haue I defendyd þe?

þu hast spoke to alle þo þat ben here,
And not o word þu spekyst to me.

To þe Jewys þu art ful kende:
þou hast forgove al here mysdede.
And þe thef þu hast in mende:
For onys haskyng mercy, hefne is his mede.

(II.32,133–40)

The effects of the ensuing instruction and consolation are evident, however, in Mary's less problematic effusion at the moment of Jesus' death: 'A, myn herte with peyn is pressyd – / For sorwe myn hert doth twynne!' (II.32,228–9). While John must intervene to reinforce the divine perspective, the heart and the grieving subject are now at least perfectly aligned.

A non-dramatic analogue sheds light on Mary's brush with blasphemy. Dorigen, in *The Franklin's Tale* of Chaucer, is given an extended monologue, beginning as prayer but quickly becoming complaint, about the rocks that threaten her husband's safe voyage home. In the standard complaint, unhappy circumstances are more or less personified as Fortune or elevated to the status of a safely pagan Fate. Here a Christian framework is established, within which the speaker conspicuously *falls* into a blinkered human perspective and language to match, setting her own 'wit' against – and thereby projecting her own 'confusion' upon – the divine wisdom:

Eterne God, that thurgh thy purveiaunce
Ledest the world by certein governaunce,
In ydel, as men seyn, ye no thyng make.
But, Lord, thise grisly feendly rokkes blake,
That semen rather a foul confusion
Of werk than any fair creacion
Of swich a parfit wys God and a stable,
Why han ye wroght this werk unresonable?
. . . .
It dooth no good, to my wit, but anoyeth.
Se ye nat, Lord, how mankynde it destroyeth?
. . . .
Which mankynde is so fair part of thy werk
That thou it madest lyk to thyn owene merk.
Thanne semed it ye hadde a greet chiertee

> Toward mankynde; but how thanne may it bee
> That ye swiche meenes make it to destroyen,
> Whiche meenes do no good, but evere anoyen?
>
> (865–84)

As with the N-Town Mary, self-speaking becomes a vehicle of self-delusion, as a virtuous woman's excess of earthly love plunges her into post-Babel signification. According to the Augustinian view of the world 'as a reflection of God's glory' (Beckwith 42), Dorigen ought to see in the rocks the essential goodness of the divine creation, reading nature like a holy book. Instead, she sees nothing but menace to herself, a self which she has made dependent on a mere 'creature'. And again according to Augustine (as cited by Chaucer's Parson), it is deadly sin 'whan the love of any thyng weyeth in the herte of man as muchel as the love of God, or moore' (*Parson's Tale* 366).[19]

Mary needs only to regard Jesus in his divine aspect in order to set herself straight. Dorigen is made to suffer precisely on the level of earthly love and precisely by means of her self-confinement within fallen language, unstable signification: she allows herself to be trapped into a 'rash promise' of infidelity, and the trap is sprung when the mysterious Clerk of Orléans makes the rocks appear to disappear. From this predicament she is released only by successive self-sacrifices on the part of her husband and her would-be lover. The ultimate power exercised by the Clerk reinscribes her within the transcendental discourse she had challenged:

> I woot wel clerkes wol seyn as hem leste,
> By argumentz, that al is for the beste,
> Though I ne kan the causes nat yknowe.
>
> . . . .
>
> To clerkes lete I al disputison.
> But wolde God that alle thise rokkes blake
> Were sonken into helle for his sake!
>
> (*Franklin's Tale* 885–92)

There are intriguing implications for the connection between soliloquy and subjectivity, particularly where women are concerned, in the intimation that Dorigen is punished at once for the content of her monologue and for its form – for her rejection of mediated speech, as well as of patriarchally mediated truth.

These issues may be revisited by way of the cycle treatments of the Sacrifice of Isaac, which, like the passion plays, show a parent struggling with the divinely mandated death of a son. There is, of course, a typological connection, as the texts are at pains to make clear, partly by developing the anguish of Isaac, as the Biblical account does not. Yet even in the version (that of the Brome manuscript) that pushes the pathetic potential of the situation to the limit, Abraham never questions the logic or coherence – that is, the significatory authority – of the divine will. He merely wishes, deferentially, that God had appointed a different sign for obedience: 'I had lever, yf God had be plesyd / For to a forbore all the good that I have' (Norman Davis, ed. 72–3). As with the serio-comic doubts typically assigned to Joseph before he is angelically enlightened, the human perspective is allowed full rein and extensive expression – on the condition of its containment. What here makes that containment an issue in itself is that it depends, not on dramatic irony, but on Abraham's internalized view (endorsed by Isaac himself) of man as God's dutiful creature: 'I love my chyld as my lyffe, / But ȝyt I love my God myche more' (81–2). Only, perhaps, in Isaac's sense of his mother's love for him and his loving wish to shield her from the facts – 'But, good fader, tell ye my moder nothyng; / Sey that I am in another cuntré dwellyng' (205–6) – is there a glimpse of a prospective grief that might resist such containment.

In fact, this element – a standard feature of the dramatizations – is pointedly contained even where it is carried furthest. In the Northampton *Abraham* (from a manuscript of Trinity College, Dublin), an anxiously doting Sara actually frames the action,[20] and Isaac virtually laments on her behalf:

> For of my modre, I wot wel, I shal be myst.
> Many a tyme haþ she me clipt and kyst,
>   But farewel nowe, for þat is do.
>
> She was wont to calle me hir tresoure and hir store;
> But farewel now, she shal no more.
>   (Norman Davis, ed. 213–17)

Here the *planctus Mariae* tradition not only helps to develop the typological significance but also, precisely because this is *not* Mary – or even a character who speaks for herself – reinforces the emotional weakness of the female as a justification for her marginal and indirect relation to the godhead. 'And if thei wil learne anie thing', adds Paul, after forbidding women to speak in church, 'let them aske their housbands at home' (1 *Cor.* 14:35). This Abraham sagely keeps Sara in ignorance until the happy outcome, then relates the whole story in a familiar and reassuring style, firmly turning her initial horrified reaction ('Alas, where was your mynde?' [345]) in a pious direction: 'My mynde? Vpon þe goode Lord on hy!' (346). The upshot is her submissive affirmation:

> Now blessid be þat Lorde souereigne
> . . . .
> And what þat euer he lust, I say not þeragayne,
> But his wille be fulfilled.
>
> (358–61)

On the traditional model of Adam and Eve, so resoundingly expressed by Milton, and as with the cycle portrayals of Noah and his wife, the woman is dependent for her vision of God on the particular 'him' who transmits the divine message. She is thus especially liable to slip into forms of self-regard, placing the human before the divine, as do, according to the Doctor who concludes the Brome *Abraham*, 'thys women that wepe so sorowfully / Whan that hyr chyldryn dey them froo, / As nater woll, and kynd' (Norman Davis, ed. 449–51). Thus the clear sight of God vouchsafed to chosen male instruments of his will is opposed to the mirror in which Eve idolatrously admires herself.

Notoriously, the classic psychoanalytical model of the superego (as of other things) concerns the 'male subject' (Silverman 135). The absence of an equivalent female dynamic matches the general dependence of female figures within the religious drama on a discourse of spirituality controlled by males. The pattern could not be clearer than in the single surviving text, the lengthy *Mary Magdalen* of the Digby manuscript, that is actually centred on a female character. In this romantically structured saint's life, Mary travels far and wide geographically, but the circular staging visually encloses her within a framework of spiritual signification. Similarly, her speech stays very much at home, keeping to the narrow channel defined by her relations with masculine figures of vice and virtue; she 'ventriloquizes' male voices, first of sin, then of sanctity. The frequent spoken interventions of the ascended Jesus mark her language (much of which takes the form of prayer) as now tuned to the same wavelength – all the more clearly because he sends his messages through angelic intermediaries. Moreover, the divine discourse that she faithfully mirrors is constituted as the essence, rather than a mere vehicle, of spirituality. Her instruction of the King of Marcyll (Marseilles) emphasizes true religion as a discourse, beginning with 'In principio erat verbum' (1483) and ending with the authority of Scripture (1521).

Among the cast of characters in the Christian story, as extrapolated from the Bible in the Middle Ages, the Virgin Mary has a special capacity to enable the exploration of alternatives to the patriarchal discourse of the superego. As the privileged bearer of the Word, she alone is exempt from the status of the female at a double remove from God – 'blessed . . . among women' (Luke 1:28), the exception that proves the rule. This point is indirectly made by the cycle plays of the Annunciation, which regularly incorporate a comic element emphasizing gender – like the Noah pageants, but inversely: it is Mary who receives the divine message, while Joseph has trouble getting beyond the 'natural' – fallen – reading of her pregnancy. Insofar, therefore, as the N-Town Mary strangely participates in the paradigm of female spiritual waywardness, momentarily disjoined from the transcendental discourse, she partially redeems that paradigm by activating the proto-tragic potential within the divine comedy – a potential elsewhere circumscribed within the limits of the planctus. Her act of self-speaking functions catalytically to transform the mirror of vanity, the emblem of illusory self-presence, into the subjectifying mirror of self-absence. The exceptional subjectivity-effect in the N-Town monologue reflects a rare willingness to give a dynamic voice to those contradictory discourses that define Mary by their intersection: divine / human, male / female, justice / mercy.

The last of these dichotomies leads to a final comment. Mary's propensity for turning grief inward is linked with her abrogation of the Old Law's call for vengeance, in contrast with her prefigurations, the bereaved mothers of the Slaughter of the Innocents. To this extent her position anticipates the dilemma of the Elizabethan revenger – a significant site for the evolving representation of subjectivity, as I will be arguing in Chapter 4. To find such an anticipation in such a context shows a paradox already emerging with regard to self-speaking and subjectivity. The numerous Medieval and Early Modern stagings of speech as an instrument of privilege, silence as an index of weakness, rub shoulders even in the earliest English drama with a contrary model, epitomized in the taciturn sufferings of the Word-made-flesh. That model mandates the potential of the soliloquy to mark a fall from a prelapsarian (and pre-linguistic) ideal into a painful state of vulnerability and fragmentation. Such a view particularly coincides, perhaps, with Kristeva's concept of the semiotic, as opposed to the symbolic – part of her challenge to traditional 'phallocentric' psychoanalysis.[21] But then, from any psychoanalytic perspective, the symbolic order hardly makes a cosy space.

III

The fugitive points of resistance offered by *Everyman* and the N-Town Mary to the prevailing prelapsarian discourse of Medieval religious drama demonstrate at least the availability of ideas of the instability of identity and of identity as constituted in and by language. This poses, surely, a *caveat* against setting limits to Medieval consciousness on the basis of dramatic representations of mankind (or Mankind). More specifically, to dramatize the alienation of the *sujet de l'énonciation* from the *sujet de l'énoncé* presupposes the capacity to 'identify with the "I" of an utterance', which Belsey, for one, altogether denies to the pre-modern subject. Patterson speaks persuasively of a Medieval 'dialectic between an inward subjectivity and an external world that alienates it from both itself and its divine source' (8). The dramatic instances point to such 'inward subjectivity', not merely as liable to alienation, but rather as, at the fundamental level, alienation itself. It is, however, late-Medieval non-dramatic literature (as well as non-literary texts), about which theorists of the Early Modern period have had relatively little to say, that most insistently foregrounds subjectivity. The very premises of mystical writing (as Beckwith demonstrates) and dream-vision hardly allow for doubt as to the sustained attention accorded within literate English Medieval culture (as opposed to a didactic drama aimed at a mainly popular audience) to the dynamics of self-representation – a process commonly foregrounding imagery of the mirror, the book, or both. And if this concern is pervasive in Chaucer generally, as Patterson proposes, it is inescapable in *Troilus and Criseyde*, which 'everywhere proclaims the fragmentation of subjectivity, both that of its protagonists and of its author' (Patterson 86). Although 'everywhere' includes a number of monologues, a study of the drama is not the place to survey such effects.[22] Nevertheless, for the remainder of this chapter I wish to consider a related fifteenth-century poem, Robert Henryson's *The Testament of Cresseid*, which not only deploys both mirror and book to illustrate the problematic production of identity as discourse but, thanks partly to its overtly supplementary status, actively comments on that process.

This commentary bears provocatively on the theatrical example just discussed. Again, a figure of female suffering (though one more along the lines of Mary Magdalene) must negotiate identity in relation to a transcendental discourse, but here that discourse, safely paganized, veers sharply towards the tyranny, in effect, of metaphysical presence. The *Nom du Père*, iconified as superego, looms forbiddingly at the very threshold of the symbolic order, forbidding access. Cresseid's abundantly self-moralized yet cut-and-dried fall thus becomes a matter of curtailed subjectivity. The immediate prelude to her formal testament shows her moulding the identities of herself and her former lover into the proverbial watchwords their names will become; her refrain is, 'O fals Cresseid and trew knicht Troylus!' (546). This is to enact the prophetic lament of her Chaucerian counterpart:

> Allas, of me, unto the worldes ende,
> Shal neyther ben ywriten nor ysonge
> No good word, for thise bokes wol me shende.
> (5.1058–60)

Criseyde's prophecy is ironically sandwiched between the narrator's disclaimer regarding Diomedes ('Men seyn – I not – that she yaf hym hire herte' [5.1050]) and his charitable refusal to blame 'this sely womman . . . / Forther than the storye wol devyse' (1093–4), since her 'name, allas, is publysshed so wide, / That for hire gilt it oughte ynough suffise' (1095–6). Henryson's narrator pointedly echoes this tolerance. As Chaucer 'wolde excuse hire yet for routhe' (1099), Henryson would 'excuse als far furth as I may / Thy womenheid, thy wisdome and fairnes' (87–8). But as his direct address suggests, this narrator is more personally involved in his subject, and his standpoint is correspondingly less stable. His contempt for Cresseid's sexual misdemeanour is extreme ('Sa giglotlike takand thy foull plesance!' [83]), yet he can present her as an innocent victim of Fortune ('nathing throw the gilt / Of the' [90–1]) and portray himself – with an irony intertextually enriched by the famous model of Gower's Amans – as a futile devotee of Venus. The uncompromising self-condemnation assigned to Cresseid (and reinforced in the narrator's final injunction to 'worthie wemen' [610][23]) issues strangely from a framing narrative that stresses her unjust persecution by the 'scornefull' (86) and 'wickit langage' (91) of men and goes well beyond Chaucer in questioning the facts. Indeed, the narrator applies the key moral term in doubting his precursor ('Quha wait gif all that Chauceir wrait was trew?' [64]) and displays even greater scepticism about the alternative 'quair' (61) purporting to recount Cresseid's fate:

> Nor I wait nocht gif this narratioun
> Be authoreist, or fenȝeit of the new
> Be sum poeit, throw his inuentioun.
>
> (65–7)

The poem thus moves from a perception of truth as elusive, variable, and subject to (de)formation within the discursive system – in effect, a recognition of language itself as fallen – to a ringing endorsement of the reductive labelling of the lovers: 'fals' and 'trew'. Such binarism, like the religious drama's oppositions of good and evil, recuperates a transcendental discursive unity. This text is at pains, however, to expose the hegemonic tendency of that discourse through the inability of Henryson to deliver what he first appears to offer – namely, Cresseid's testament in the sense of *her* story, which Chaucer simply bypasses, withdrawing from Criseyde in a haze of 'ruth'. Henryson begins as if by searching for the true Cresseid through that haze, but it turns out that truth 'belongs' elsewhere and defines Cresseid by opposition.

The helplessness of the narrator to control his linguistically pre-cast material is figured in the virtual assimilation of his original doubtful voice into the narrative of the supposed 'quair'. The transition is seamless, and the initial trappings of dream-vision are arguably strong enough (he takes up the book '[t]o brek my sleip' [61]) to cast what follows in a dream-like light. Hence, perhaps, the ventriloquized quality of the subsequent moralizing. But it is the central – highly functional – irony of the poem that a hardening of language and attitude, the subsumption of discourse by superego, also takes place within Cresseid's self-speaking.

In that Troilus' death at least implicitly precedes Criseyde's in the account of Chaucer, to tell the story of Cresseid's wretched end, with Troilus' entombing of her body, is logically to undo the hero's fall.[24] It is also to circumvent the vision of worldly vanity that Chaucer attributes to him once his spirit has ascended through the seven spheres to 'the pleyn felicite / That is in hevene above' (Chaucer 5.1818–19). From the vantage point of ultimate truth, Troilus gazes contemptuously at worldly pursuits and values, including love; his laughter at 'the wo / Of hem that wepten for his deth so faste' (1821–2) issues from the Christian 'domain of the real', prior to and beyond signification, and contrasts with a fallen human semiotics.

Henryson's Troilus is explicitly anchored in that of Chaucer, beginning with the same posture of wavering, hoping, and interpreting; he too is a prisoner of the doubtful signs of Cresseid's faithfulness:

> Of his distres me neidis nocht reheirs,
> For worthie Chauceir in the samin buik,
> In gudelie termis and in ioly veirs,
> Complyit hes his cairis, quha will luik.
>
> (57–60)

This Troilus, however, far from dying into an *éclaircissement* that subverts even his own terrestrial 'truth', is reborn through suffering as the noblest of lovers. From his worldly perspective, the sight of 'fals' Cresseid entails a flattering self-reflection; his version of his precursor's cosmic laughter is the unutterability of his feelings on hearing of her death: 'I can no moir; / Scho was vntrew and wo is me thairfoir' (601–2).

Even to manipulate language successfully, by imposing labels that stick, is to remain within it. Yet just as no emblem of containment rivals a tomb, there is no last word like an epitaph, and the one supplied by Troilus immortalizes Cresseid's fall from 'flour of womanheid' (608) to 'lipper' (609). His control over signification receives an echoing endorsement at the point of closure. The narrator concludes his closing address to 'worthie women' (Troilus' inscription is addressed to 'fair ladyis' [607]) with 'Sen scho is deid I speik of hir no moir' (616). Thus the successor poem superficially validates a non-Chaucerian vision of linguistic stability and truth in this world, even if the narrative door remains slightly ajar, given that Troilus' tomb-building and inscription-making themselves remain dependent on variable human words: 'Sum said . . .' (603).

In fact, despite the interpretations proffered by Henryson's character and his narrator, this is not the whole story as the poet portrays it. For he also makes Cresseid the conspicuous object of a multi-layered process of identity-construction, beginning with the gods' imposition of the visible identity of leper. Thus her conscientious self-reflections, which produce a subjectivity to match that image, culminating in her internalization of untruth as a function of gender, are displayed as derivative. In her last words prior to the testament *per se*, Cresseid engages in anticipatory ventriloquism by foreshadowing the antifeminist discourse of Troilus and the narrator; her broken syntax suggests the intrusion of their voices:

> Becaus I knaw the greit vnstabilnes,
> Brukkill as glas, into my self, I say –
> Traisting in vther als greit vnfaithfulnes,
> Als vnconstant, and als vntrew of fay –
> Thoucht sum be trew, I wait right few ar thay;
> Quha findis treuth, lat him his lady ruse;
> Nane but my self as now I will accuse.
>
> (568–74)

Such a perspective unconvincingly displaces the generalized perception of 'false worldes brotelnesse' (5.1832) at which Chaucer arrives by way of Troilus' vision. What finally emerges from Henryson's text is the inadequacy of the conventional mirror of conscience to the complexity of human situations, yet the tempting propensity all-round to adopt its images, when the fault may indeed lie – as the narrator initially affirmed – with Fortune, the emblem of divine power divorced from justice.

This point begins to take shape with Cresseid's complaint against Venus and Cupid after she has been rejected by Diomeid and welcomed home by her father Calchas, himself a violator of truth who cuts a more sympathetic figure in Henryson than elsewhere. Obviously, in blaming her ill-fortune on the gods, she fails to allow for her initial betrayal of Troilus; from this she could have expected nothing but misery, according to the moral laws of love-relations, as succinctly articulated by Genius in the *Confessio Amantis*: 'Fortune, thogh sche be noght stable, / Yit at some time is favorable / To hem that ben of love trewe' (Gower 8.2013–15). At the core of this principle remains, however, the commonplace of fortune's fickleness, and from there it is but a short step (one eventually

taken by Amans himself) to exalting eternal verities over terrestrial
vanities – that is, to the ultimate vision of Chaucer's Troilus. Despite her self-deception, Cresseid is right to recognize the powers of
earthly love as deceptive in themselves. To turn away from the
worship of Venus and Cupid would seem a necessary precondition
of spiritual cure. Moreover, the tenor and language of her monologue betoken incipient subjectivity along the lines of the N-Town
Mary. Cresseid, too, feels anger at a divine promise betrayed; her
transcendental identity similarly collapses into an acute experience
of forsaken humanity, as she accuses the gods of love:

> 3e causit me alwayis vnderstand and trow
> The seid of lufe was sawin in my face,
> And ay grew grene throw 3our supplie and grace.
> Bot now, allace, that seid with froist is slane,
> And I fra luifferis left, and all forlane.
>
> (136–40)

The immediate sequel to this first complaint forms a pointed
countermovement to the ascent of Chaucer's Troilus. Henryson
shows '[t]he seuin planetis, discending fra thair spheiris' (147) to
condemn the blasphemer to an earthly hell. Yet an extensive description of the double appearance of Venus, fitting the nature of
'all fleschelie paramour' (232), '[r]icht vnstabill and full of variance'
(235), vindicates Cresseid's perception. The narrator, still capable of
Chaucerian 'routh', exclaims against the 'wraikfull sentence' (329):
'O cruell Saturne, fraward and angrie, / Hard is thy dome and to
malitious!' (323–4). In this context, the identity imposed by the gods
involves both a literal and a figural deformation. Refusing her a
lapse into self-absence, which implies *their* absence, the gods force
their presence upon her. In a way that (as observed by Fox, ed. n.
to 348) ironically recalls Pandarus' advice to Criseyde not to hold
out against love until age brings an unpleasing reflection of herself,
Cresseid must continue to regard herself in love's mirror, but now
as anathema: 'than rais scho vp and tuik / Ane poleist glas, and hir
schaddow culd luik' (347–8).

Still, the divine condemnation has not been internalized. She is
initially capable not only of recognizing her transgression as fundamentally linguistic but of indirectly repeating it (with particular
point, if 'goddis' is taken as 'goddess', as it may be [Fox, ed. n. to
353, 357]):

> ... 'Lo, quhat it is', quod sche,
> With fraward langage for to mufe and steir
> Our craibit goddis; and sa is sene on me!
> My blaspheming now haue I bocht full deir;
> All eirdlie ioy and mirth I set areir.
> Allace, this day; allace, this wofull tyde
> Quhen I began with my goddis for to chyde!'
>
> (351–7)

Even as Cresseid leaves her sorrowing father to join the lepers, she preserves a distance between the image in the glass and a hidden, implicitly 'true' self: she 'wald not be kend' (380), with the result that '[s]um knew her weill, and sum had na knawledge / Of hir becaus scho was sa deformait' (393–4). And while her ensuing formal 'Complaint' (407 ff.) deploys her new appearance as a warning – 'O ladyis fair of Troy and Grece . . . in ȝour mynd ane mirrour mak of me' (452–7) – there is as yet no rhetoric of self-blame, of 'fals' and 'trew'. She makes herself a mirror only of 'fikkill' (469) fortune generally and worldly vanity at large. In fact, she comes remarkably close to combining the cosmic detachment acquired by the Chaucerian Troilus with the hortatory mode of Chaucer's explication: 'O yonge, fresshe folkes, he or she . . .' (5.1835) – an intertext pointing up the fact that, while Cresseid naturally addresses herself to women, she does not make vanity gender-specific.

What conspicuously causes Cresseid's subsumption by the misogynistically charged discourse of truth and falsehood – the effective transformation of the gods from emblems of arbitrary fortune into projections of the superego – is her doubly ironic encounter with Troilus. The primary irony lies in her interpretation of his lavish charity to her as evidence of his surpassing truth – 'Thy lufe, thy lawtie and thy gentilnes' (547). In the mirror of his perfection she sees herself as deserving her punishment, and this leads her to anticipate the narrator's use of her as moral exemplum. The fact, of course, is that Troilus does not recognize her, even if he recalls '[t]he sweit visage and amorous blenking' (503) of Cresseid as she was.

A second, deeper irony, insinuated through a digression into faculty psychology, is that Troilus has never loved the 'true' Cresseid:

> Na wonder was, suppois in mynd that he
> Tuik hir figure sa sone, and lo, now quhy:
> The idole of ane thing in cace may be

Sa deip imprentit in the fantasy
That it deludis the wittis outwardly,
And sa appeiris in forme and lyke estait
Within the mynd as it was figurait.

(505–11)

'Idole' is a technical term in the Aristotelian process outlined in this much-discussed passage,[25] but it is hard to take it as neutral, especially in company with 'fantasy' and 'deludis the wittis'. Nor, in Medieval moral terms, should the reader make allowance in Troilus' favour for the distorting effect of nostalgia. On the contrary, the mirror-theory of the Middle Ages included a connection between the operation of memory and the propensity of young lovers in the grip of sensuality – the state signalled by 'sweit visage and amorous blenking' – to fall prey, Narcissus-like, to an idolatrous image.[26] As Françoise Guichard-Tesson explains, with reference to Évrart de Conty's fourteenth-century commentary on *Les Échecs amoureux*, the young man looking in the mirror of memory ought to see

[l]'image même de sa condition, pourvu qu'il soit attentif; de son expérience passée, le miroir, symbole de sa lucidité et de son droit jugement . . . lui renvoie une image plus signifiante, qui lui permettra de se conduire plus sagement par la suite. . . .
   Mais le jeune homme est volontiers troublé par ses passions et la sensualité vient *déformer* l'image que lui renvoyait le miroir de la raison.
[the very image of his condition, provided that he pays attention; the mirror, symbol of his lucidity and of his true judgement . . . reflects to him a more meaningful image of his past experience, which will enable him to behave more wisely in the future.
. . .
   But the young man tends to be disturbed by his passions, and sensuality comes to *deform* the image which the mirror of reason was reflecting to him.]

(Guichard-Tesson 102, my emphasis)

If the encounter between Troilus and Cresseid involves deformity on both sides, the asymmetrical effects become all the more striking. In contrast with his Chaucerian namesake, looking into the truest mirror of all – that of death – this Troilus fails to draw from his vision a lesson regarding 'la vanité des biens temporels et de la gloire mondaine qui ont aussi peu de réalité que le reflet qui se joue dans le miroir [the vanity of temporal goods and of worldly glory, which have as little reality as the reflection that plays in the mirror' (Guichard-Tesson 103). Rather, he is confirmed in his image of himself as the eternal devotee of the shining lady. He remains the darling of the same gods that condemn Cresseid, and his self-image positively thrives on her containment within their language of cruelty. He does their dirty work even in causing Cresseid to erect a corresponding idol of himself as transcendental signifier. The poem ultimately displays – with the freedom permitted by substituting Saturn for God – a discursive tyranny, irrational and specifically patriarchal, which forecloses female signification, hence subjectivity, in the Father's multiple names of reason, justice, meaning, and – above all – the *selflessness* of 'true' love.

Notes to Chapter 2

1. The use of the formula in creation plays extends to Medieval German texts (Bartsch 268; Kretzmann 80). On its liturgical currency, see Cabrol *et al.* 1:24, where the account of symbolic uses (1:1–24) also points to the sort of magical overtones documented by Franz 1:351,430 and 2:95,482–3,508,587.

2. These significant soliloquies flaw Frieden's generalization, 'Early English drama makes soliloquy a concomitant of sin and separation from God' (133), although there are plenty of examples of the latter phenomenon. Frieden's connection between soliloquy and prayer remains broadly applicable, although the most actively subjectifying instance – that of the N-Town Mary (discussed below) – hardly illustrates his point about sin. Rather, perhaps, it backhandedly anticipates the effect he considers central in later drama: 'soliloquy appears as the device by which prayer can overcome the distance between human and divine realms' (133).

3. As opposed to the words of the Father concerning the Son in Matthew's account of Jesus' baptism (3:16–17) and in the story of the transfiguration (*Matt.* 17:1–8; *Mark* 9:2–8; *Luke* 9:28–36).

4. Woolf cites 'walkyng in þis wone' as 'a thoughtless use of a traditional alliterative collocation' (370n5) and the 'one tiny exception' to the rule that in his self-introductions in the cycle plays 'God never speaks of Himself as having a body' (107). In fact, this line pointedly recalls the Vulgate's 'Dum deambularet . . .' (*Gen.* 3:8), the foundation of a liturgical responsory incorporated into the twelfth-century

Ordo Repraesentationis Adae (Bevington, ed. n. to 1 S.D.), where it is followed by stage directions (386 S.D.) stressing God's corporeality; for a Medieval German analogue, see Bartsch 269 and Lehnen 308. More broadly, Woolf's view that the 'problem' of staging the Trinity is 'solved' by a purely symbolic presentational method (106–7) would disallow the interplay between ephemeral performance and sacred history that is central to the dramatic method of these texts. That interplay is also focused by the use of the term 'figura' for the actor playing God in the *Ordo*. I agree with Bevington that this points to 'a figural interpretation' implying the incarnation (n. to 1 S.D.), although I would stress that such symbolism is anchored in the dynamic of acting. Axton seems to miss this point in taking 'figura' to 'indicate that the actor is a mere cipher, not an impersonation of the Creator' (117). A useful overview of divine self-speaking in the cycles is provided by Diller 161–9.

5.   For the sake of consistency and simplicity, I cite the Towneley cycle (so called from the sometime owners of the MS) in the complete edition of England and Pollard, instead of extracting the 'Wakefield Pageants', which have been more recently edited by Cawley; nevertheless, as others have done, I refer to the entire cycle under the name of Wakefield, taking its provenance as proven (see Cawley xi–xvii).

6.   The English Medieval drama thus accommodates the contradiction that led some Renaissance thinkers in search of a ' "langue naturelle" [qui] part du Verbe pour retrouver le Verbe, celui de la création et celui de la fin: Alpha et Omega, la nostalgie des origines structure le désir des fins sous la forme de l'unité ["natural language" (that) departs from the Word in order to find the Word again, the Word of creation and of the end: Alpha and Omega, the nostalgia for origins structures the desire for endings in the form of unity]' (Dubois 38–9).

7.   There are Pentecost pageants in the N-Town, York, and Chester cycles; the descent of the Holy Spirit and the gift of languages are promised by Jesus in the Wakefield play of *The Lord's Ascension*, which is followed, however, by a MS gap (see England and Pollard, eds p. 366). Audiences at a Corpus Christi festival would have had the story fresh in mind, since Whitsunday came ten days before; indeed, Nelson (118) notes the post-Reformation expedient of re-associating plays with this still-acceptable holiday. On the dramatic effects sometimes employed to embellish Pentecost services, see Young 1:489–91.

8.   See Wilden's valuable discussion of symbolism in Lacan and psychoanalysis generally (229–37).

9.   Cf. Grosz: 'The *Autre* is the superego, which engenders the unconscious, . . . in so far as the id is subjected to repression' (74).

10.   I have written more generally elsewhere ('*Everyman*') about the play's treatment of identity and language, including the manipulation of divine voice(s) reminiscent of the cycle plays.

11.   Demonet adopts this term for the intentional (will-ful) function in language from the *Hypnerotomachia Poliphili* of Francesco Colonna (1499), where it is allegorically paired with *ratio* (Demonet 7). The conceptual evolution of *thélémie* is very much to the point:

Les définitions ordinaires du discours, chez les philosophes médiévaux, insistent sur l'"intention de signifier', condition indispensable pour que l'énoncé ait un sens. Cette approche théorique et austère est complétée par l'intervention de la volonté (thélémie) en tant que faculté participant à l'acte discursif. Nous avons pu voir que la volonté justifiait l'arbitraire dans la première nomination. . . . A la Renaissance, intention au sens logique et volonté au sens philosophique ont tendance à converger, formant ainsi la base d'une expression individuelle que l'on a attribuée aux humanistes. [Standard definitions of discourse in the Medieval philosophers insist on the 'intention to signify' as an indispensable condition if the utterance is to have meaning. This theoretical and austere approach is completed by the intervention of will (*thélémie*) as a faculty participating in the discursive act. We have been able to see that will justified the element of the arbitrary in original naming. . . . In the Renaissance, intention in the logical sense and will in the philosophical sense have a tendency to converge, thereby forming the basis of an individual expression, which has been attributed to the humanists.]

(Demonet 269)

12.   Bradley (112) considers this text a key influence on the mirror motif's application beyond spirituality in a narrow sense.
13.   On the mirror of death, see also Soellner 16 and 106.
14.   See Meredith vi, who extracts as a distinct entity (hence a counterpart of *The Passion Play*) those pageants dealing with the conception and early life of Mary.
15.   Spector divides the *Passion Play* into two parts (the standard modern practice) but maintains the numbering of its component pageants in relation to the entire cycle. My references specify part and pageant, then lines within pageants.

16.   nam rectitudo visionis Deo debetur: declinatio a rectitudine per fractionem, quae debilior est, angelicae naturae convenit: reflexiva visio, quae est debilior, homini potest assignari. . . . Et ideo cognitio hominis quantacunque sit perfecta, est debilior cognitione angelica ex hac causa, et merito dici potest specularis propter dictam similitudinem. Loquor de homine puro cum exceptione Beatae Virginis. . . . [for directness of vision belongs to God; deviation from the straight line through refraction, which is weaker, befits the angelic nature; reflected vision, which is weaker, may be assigned to man. . . . Therefore the perception of man, however perfect it may be, is weaker than the angelic perception for this reason, and rightly may be called a mirrored perception because of the similitude stated. I am speaking of the natural man with the exception of the Blessed Virgin. . . .]
          (*Opus Majus* 2:162–3 [5.1.3.2]; trans. Burke 2:579–80)

On Bacon's association of optical effects with divine grace, see Edgerton, *Perspective* 74–5.

17. Cf. Grosz: 'The Real cannot be experienced as such: it is capable of representation or conceptualization only through the reconstructive or inferential work of the imaginary and symbolic orders' (34).

18. The basic comparative survey of Taylor remains valuable; see also Diller 182–94.

19. I explore Dorigen's idolatry more fully, and in relation to *Tmp.*, in *Intertextuality* 124–35.

20. Sara also appears in *Le mistère du viel testament*; for a useful comparison of all the extant English and French versions, see Wallace xxxvii–lx.

21. See Kristeva, *Révolution*, whose first section ('Préliminaires Théoriques [Theoretical Preliminaries]') is available in English translation (*Revolution*). Despite some broad overlap, from time to time, between my discussion and Kristeva's adaptations of Lacan, I have not found it useful to pursue her approach to discourse analysis.

22. But see my *Intertextuality* 58–81 and 106–23.

23. Cf. the premonition of Chaucer's Criseyde that 'wommen moost wol haten me of alle' (5.1063).

24. Cf. the deferral of Troilus' death in *Tro*. In *Problem Plays* 17–53, I discuss Henryson's poem as mediating between Chaucer and Shakespeare.

25. See esp. Stearns 97–105, who, however, despite citing Augustine's *De Trinitate* on the deceptiveness and potential for carnality of this psychological mechanism, does not appear to detect irony at Troilus' expense.

26. On Medieval treatments of Narcissus as figuring 'the birth of self-consciousness through love', see Goldin 20–68. The Welle of Love, in *The Romaunt of the Rose*, is also the 'mirrour perilous' (de Lorris and de Meun 1600) of Narcissus.

3

Tudor Transitions and Ramifications

To approach self-speaking as a discursive function makes it easier to distinguish technical changes (and continuities) from broader stylistic developments such as 'realism', as well as from thematic trends, of which the most significant in the early Tudor period is, of course, secularization. Not that such issues have no bearing on the representation of subjectivity; indeed, secularization is the *raison d'être* of this chapter. But especially where movements appear to run parallel, to bundle them together can lead to blurred vision. Thus, while I would broadly endorse Freedman's psychoanalytically oriented overview of Early Modern secularization – an account that provocatively applies Nicholas of Cusa's figuration of God as a mirror – I am reluctant to allow such a cultural paradigm to subsume distinct discursive phenomena or, for that matter, to harden into a chronological progression. According to Freedman, 'As Renaissance games with the gaze become more complex and more internalized, God as the all-seeing other is displaced by the community as other, which in turn is displaced by an internalized other – whether soul, social conscience, or unconscious – as that point with which we can never merge' (20). Primarily concerned as she is with the audience's 'gaze', Freedman does not focus on this process in relation to theatrical discourses themselves. If we begin with those discourses, what emerges is a dynamic interplay among categories of 'otherness', which become rather more distinct than in Freedman's formulation. In the following pages, I pursue, under the aegis of sixteenth-century theatrical secularization, a highly intertextual exploration of some developments in self-speaking, including their implications for later drama.

I

Having enjoined man to view his miserable condition by means of the threefold mirror (of Scripture, nature, and creation) graciously held up to him by God, Alanus de Insulis, as cited in the previous chapter, indicates that alternative ways of regarding the self are liable to interpose. Another looking-glass, not under direct divine control and hence with a dangerous potential for misleading, lies closer to hand: 'In tua autem natura triplex resultat speculum, speculum rationis, sensualitatis et carnis [But in your own nature, a threefold mirror reflects back again: the glass of reason, the glass of the senses, and the glass of the flesh]' (col. 118, C; trans. Evans 29). The particular challenge lies in keeping the true image of reason paramount, when the distorting mirror of the senses is liable to show things backwards and that of the flesh threatens to turn them upside-down (col. 118, C–D; trans. Evans 29–30). Not surprisingly, there is basic agreement with the commentary of Évrart, as Guichard-Tesson observes (107), although Alanus' formulation remains more closely aligned with the Pauline text on seeing 'in a glasse, euen in a darke speaking', since it stresses not only reason's necessary mediation of the divine presence but also the obstacles to such mediation posed by the fallen human condition.

Paul's essential distinction between vision in this world and the next is adapted more explicitly, though with more provocative refinements, in Roger Bacon's late thirteenth-century treatise on optical science (in the *Opus Majus*):

> Et homo habet triplicem visionem, unam perfectam, quae erit in statu gloriae post resurrectionem; aliam in anima separata a corpore in coelo usque ad resurrectionem, quae debilior est; tertiam in hac vita, quae debilissima est, et haec est recte per reflexionem.
>
> [Man has a three-fold vision; one perfect, which will come in a state of glory after the resurrection; the second in the soul separated from the body in heaven until the resurrection, which is weaker; the third in this life, which is the weakest, and this is correctly said to be by reflection.]
>
> (2:163 [5.1.3.2]; trans. Burke 2:580)

On the same principle as Alanus, Bacon finds within mortality a corresponding hierarchy of perception ('visio'), ranging from true (in)sight to unthinking solipsism, when the beholder derives from his mirror-image no sense of himself as God's creature:

> scilicet recta in perfectis; fracta in imperfectis; et in malis et in negligentibus mandata Dei est etiam per reflexionem, secondum Jacobum Apostolum; nam comparantur viro consideranti vultum nativitatis suae in speculo.
> [namely, direct in those that are perfect; refracted in those that are imperfect; and in the evil and in those who neglect the commandments of God by reflection, according to the Apostle James; for it is compared to a man beholding his natural face in a glass.][1]
>   (2:163 [5.1.3.2]; trans. Burke 2:580)

By implication, a perfected self would be informed by such a sense. Still, to the extent that he allows for earthly perfectibility at all, Bacon might be seen as shifting the ground of the Pauline argument and anticipating Renaissance claims for the transcendental power of human reason.

My immediate point, however, is merely there are plenty of abstract Medieval precedents for the actual mirror – the 'glas of Reson' (2) – that effects the protagonist's reform in *Wit and Science*, John Redford's moral interlude dating from the second quarter of the sixteenth century. Yet the precedents do not extend to the surviving drama – not even the morality plays, from which Redford's allegorical method derives and which continually enact the struggle to keep the human will out of passion's clutches. The Medieval theatre never endows reason with a mirroring function; rather, reason is invariably a reflection of the universal divine discourse. *Wit and Science* takes a particularly significant step by effectively substituting Reason for God as the *father* of a romantic-comic plot structure, which figures Wit's salvation as his marriage to Reason's daughter.

Only in the conclusion does the perspective suddenly expand to subordinate the discourse of reason to that of God, whose 'gift' Science is now said to be, to be used 'Unto Godes honor and profit' (1055–6). Yet there is no question of reducing Science to the narrowly religious Knowlege of *Everyman*; the former's independent voice rings clear even as she echoes the latter text's moral eschatology: 'Th'end of our lives wold be in rememb'ring' (1089); 'Joy without end – that wish I to all' (1093). She remains a figure, not of one book, but of many. This is hardly to recuperate divinity as the *Nom du Père*; the latter function is here preempted from the start by

Reason, who, moreover, is identified with 'yes', in that he sponsors Wit's desire for Science – a desire characterized, in early Humanist fashion, as both natural and honourable. It is to this end that Reason bestows upon Wit the all-important mirror, with the assurance, 'While ye have that, ye have me, and shall' (8).

Still, this conditional wording calls attention to a potential for instability flowing from Reason's displacement of God as transcendental signifier. For on the level of allegory Reason remains an ongoing and fluid part of Wit, hence a product of fallen human discourse. The power of the mirror to show Wit to himself as he is proves subject, as the action demonstrates, to Wit's negligence. This in turn is related to his seduction, less by Idlenes herself (or itself), than by his own self-image. He misrecognizes himself as the proper young man whose picture is carried by Science ('Yea, marry, mine owne likenes this is' [767]), even after he has degenerated into a fool, unrecognizable by her. Despite the depersonalized dramatic technique, this process presumes the subversive intervention of the unconscious, which, moreover, asserts itself in specifically linguistic form. The dignified discourse derived from Reason gives way to vulgar speech matching impropriety of behaviour: 'I wil be bolde with my nowne darling. / Cum now, a bas, my nowne proper sparling!' (740–1). In fact, the extended farcical exchange between Idlenes and Ingnorance accompanying Wit's transformation as he lies asleep becomes a dream-like deconstruction of language, a chaotic detaching of sound from meaning so as to expose the fragility of signification itself.

In this context, when Wit is (literally) reformed as a result of viewing himself in the glass, Reason's reappearance and reassertion of discursive control carry the implication of the latter's production by Wit as superego, the *Nom du Père* now looming as sheer *non* – the embodiment of conscience, who, to the accompaniment of a scourging administered by Shame, reads out 'his fawtes . . . written' (843) in a book of reckoning. In the presence of such a psychologized Reason, the religious formulas of Wit's penitence and despair ('Oh, sir, I am not woorthy . . .' [865]), as he undergoes a purgation akin to Everyman's, can hardly help hinting at the contingent status of all transcendental signification. The 'truth' that appears in the mirror, when Wit finally turns to it, has become entangled with the subjectivity of the beholder.

I have outlined these discursive elements in some detail because the entrance of Reason and Shame enacts the resolution of a salient instance of self-speaking. Wit's first and only soliloquy, delivered at the pivotal moral moment and, at fifty pentameter lines, the longest single speech in the play, is sharply different in kind from those of the other characters. Their monologues all conform to the declarative mode standard in Medieval drama, even for cases of repentance: the nature of identity is never at issue, since identity is determined in relation to a fixed term, which the character either embodies or contradicts; a self-discovering sinner merely exchanges one transcendentally reflected role for another. Wit's soliloquy involves self-discovery only insofar as the 'self' is defined by its aphanisis, and his use of the mirror as a prop makes a metadramatic comment on the shift of perspective. These features anticipate Richard II's fall into soliloquized self-absence following confrontation with his mirror-image – a surprising intertextual presence to find in a text so much earlier and so frankly professing its characters' allegorical transparency.

Wit is defiant but defensive in taking up the mirror to test his self-image; the unconscious shows itself in his already 'fallen' language: 'Am I so fowle as those drabbes [Science and Experience] wold make me?' (798). He then resists the evidence of his foolish appearance with the ironically true claim, 'This glas, I se well, hath bene kept evill' (803). However, his subsequent test of the glass on the audience – the text's wry invitation to universal self-reflection – leads to an acute sense of isolation and self-loss: 'And I, by the mas, a foole alone' (811). This original 'fading' initiates a chain of more abstract reflections, each reacting to and building on the one before ('I trow? Nay verely, I knowe' [821]) in a compounding litany of failings and forfeits, punctuated by 'Alas' (825,828,830). By contrast with the N-Town Mary, this despair culminates in no sudden assurance of transcendental meaning. There is only the arrival of Reason and Shame, the latter – despite his shock ('Out upon thee, Shame! What doost thowe heere?' [840]) – virtually conjured by Wit's own words: 'I have woone Hatred, Begg'ry, and open Shame' (839).

Later Early Modern drama, especially that of Shakespeare, has been largely amenable to the modern critical project, which has assimilated to an essentialist 'psychological realism' precisely such a pattern of apparently unfolding thoughts. At the core, it is presumed, must be the character's 'true' self, on the principle that the ability to peel the layers of an onion proves the existence of something at the centre. The presumption has been so vigorously rejected as anachronistic by New Historicism and Cultural Materialism that the pattern itself may have been obscured. The example of *Wit and Science*, to which neither psychology nor realism can plausibly be attributed, at once throws the theatrical technique into relief and links it with Lacanian subjectivity, according to which the onion is all peel (and, I suppose, tear-provoking juice). Self-revisions within soliloquy may be taken as precisely that, hence as discursive enactments of aphanisis, infinitely recycling within the symbolic order the dynamic of promise and deception set in motion by the mirror-stage.

II

I have already noted that, as closure approaches in *Wit and Science*, the discourse of Reason is abruptly placed within the overarching context of the divine: Experience, Wit, and Science successively affirm the paramountcy of God's will and grace, as well as the ultimate hope of 'Joy without end' (1093). But while Reason seconds this hope, he also redirects his daughter's good wishes in a way that proclaims a more immediate allegiance. The transcendental note on which the play ends is not his self-subordination to the divine, as might be expected, but his preemptive wish for joy '[f]irst in this life . . . To our most noble king and quene in especiall', as well as '[t]o ther honourable cowncell' (1097–9). There may well have been a royal presence in the audience, given the play's probable association with the choirboys of St Paul's. In any case, such deference at once to secular contentment and to secular authority stands in sharp contrast to the Medieval drama, where figures of worldly power, status, and wealth are invariably negative (unless, like *Mary Magdalen*'s converted King of Marcyll, they put these advantages into the service of the church). In both dramatic and non-dramatic figurations, after all, it is death's regular function, as – spectacularly – in the N-Town *Death of Herod*, to bring home to the high and mighty the fact of their condition as Everyman.

Wit and Science, then, represents the instability of transcendental discourse not only in the ambiguous relation between Reason and Wit but also in the potentially competing claims to transcendence of divine and earthly authorities. Tudor political efforts to couple God and monarch constituted, of course, a major counterpoint to secularization throughout the sixteenth century. Those efforts, notoriously, were far from monolithic or uniformly successful: the doubleness of the King's Two Bodies tended to reproduce itself on the level of the subject's body and soul. And while the often bloody struggles over religious and temporal allegiance may be somewhat mitigated by invoking the New Historicist model, according to which the dominant ideology thrives by nurturing and consuming subversion, the dominance of any ideology was far from absolute.[2] Sites of contestation ranged from the very public (the pulpit, the circulation of published works) to the very private (the dungeon or torture chamber).

Midway between these, and sharing some qualities of both, lies the scaffold, from which condemned political and religious criminals might briefly speak before execution – if not in a coherent declaration, at least in resonant last words; and if not in fact, at least in fiction. In the paradigmatic speech from the scaffold, the subject looks into the mirror of death, which has summoned him to an accounting.[3] Yet the speaker in such a situation does not begin, at least, as Everyman: he is not an abstraction, and his circumstances are not self-evidently universal. His sentence of death is worldly discourse, even if it presumptively echoes the divine Word. These factors are anticipated within *Everyman* itself in the tension between the universal and the particular. The theatre of public execution problematically actualizes that tension in terms of subjectivity and authority.

It rather stretches the imagination to think of the scaffold as a 'ludic space' in the post-Bakhtinian sense, but contemporary accounts often make the analogy with the theatre explicit, especially by invoking the commonplace of the world-as-stage. Greenblatt, amongst others, has applied Foucault's concept of the theatricality of Early Modern punishment, focusing on the English examinations and executions for heresy as occasions for 'fashioning' the victim's 'self' in the eyes of both victim and tormentors.[4] The implications for self-speaking are worth developing, especially given the liminal state of the condemned person poised between life and death. Such a state is discursively figured in the traditonal attribution of prophetic or preternaturally truthful qualities to dying words, as if a transcendental presence suddenly informs fallen language – at the expense of subjectivity. Arguably, verbal self-representations at the point of (or even after) death, whether or not by execution, define a major genre of the sixteenth century: to take two prominent instances, acknowledged as important for the Elizabethan public theatre, this is the meeting ground of *The Mirror for Magistrates* and John Foxe's *Acts and Monuments*. Both of these monumental texts recurrently identify the doomed individual's sense of closure in the narrative of his life (or hers – there are women in both) with a transcendental perspective and a unitary voice to match. Both also, however, contain elements tending to destabilize that identification, while stopping well short of subversion. What is exposed, if hardly intentionally, is the fallen origins of language itself.

Their common ground helps to reveal these works' ideological projects as being poles apart. Following the Tudor party line, the *Mirror* maintains the congruence of secular power with the divine will, provided that such power is legitimate and virtuously exercised. (This proves a large escape clause, of course, although nothing is ever presented as justifying rebellion or treachery.) Acknowledgment of this congruence is part of the self-recognition the speaker achieves in death: whatever is, is divinely just. By contrast, the insistent moral of Foxe's biographies is the frequent variance between worldly authority (albeit garbed in religious robes) and the Protestant version of truth, grounded in the individual's reading of the Bible.[5] This moral is typically driven home by the dying martyr's affirmation of faith, which often uses the words of Scripture; thus the divine book, as in *Everyman*, supplies the mirror-image with which the soul destined for salvation – even more vividly summoned through the smoke of Smithfield as the 'excellente electe spouse' (*Everyman* 894) of Jesus – discursively aligns itself.

In contrast with *Everyman*, however, Foxe does not discredit the secular realm as such; it retains the potential to reject false religion and ally itself with true, in which case disobedience would hardly deserve glory, but rather the ignominy it uniformly receives in the *Mirror*. Hence, for instance, the 'false dissimulation' of the nun Elizabeth Barton, who, acting 'as though she had been inspired of God', incited the people to 'idolatry' and against Henry's divorce of Katherine, earns its just deserts at the hands of church and state united:

> which her naughtiness being espied out by the great labour and diligence of the archbishop of Canterbury, the lord Cromwel, and Master Hugh Latimer, she was condemned and put to death, with certain of her affinity and counsel.
>
> (Townsend, ed. 5:62)

The real contest, then, is between two discourses with a claim to transcendence, and, without a readership as partisan as Foxe's intended one, the brilliant spiritual colours with which he paints his martyrs pale into fallen rhetorical ones. The very possibility of (indeed, responsibility for) choosing between mirror-images of the self, as documented by proliferating conversions and recantations, implies the mirror's capacity for deception, the image's propensity for fading. Precisely because the light of truth shines directly from God, it can shadow forth the 'opacity' of subjectivity – at least, in the overdetermining voice of the chronicler, who projects his self-speakers at the moment of death beyond language into the Word.

By contrast, the monologic project of the *Mirror* is undermined by its multiplicity of voices, especially when it is considered as a collection – a remarkably fluid one, at that, evolving over a succession of editions from 1559 to 1610. It is this structure, moreover, which gives the work its more direct bearing on dramatic strategies of self-representation. Historians of the drama are too often content to acknowledge the *Mirror* as ideological background to Elizabethan political tragedy. Arguably, it exerted as much influence on theatrical practice by way of its mode(s) of self-speaking – self-speaking, if not actually from the scaffold, at least from the perspective of inglorious death, and always as in a mirror. The 'magistrates' of the title are called to witness more than cautionary crime and punishment; the testimonials also document the tenuous discursive relation of the human subject to royalty-as-godhead. And where the speaker was himself a misgoverning king (the list includes Richard II, Richard III, and James I of Scotland), the instability of the latter compound is also highlighted.

All the doomed figures take on the role of Everyman, inasmuch as they deliver essentially the same speech acknowledging the providential justice of their falls, as well as the vanity of worldly power and wealth. They do so, however, from the perspective of widely differing lives and deaths, while, in keeping with their liminality, their destinations in the afterlife are not at issue. Moreover, as befits the compilers' motives for supplementing Lydgate's *Fall of Princes* (and indirectly Boccaccio), the narratives and the issues they raise have a pressing immediacy, as in Shakespeare's Tetralogies. Fortune's operations appear far less abstract when filtered through mechanisms of power – ranging from pitched battles to legal proceedings – that continue to resonate within recent national memory. Death, in functioning as the great leveller, must now traverse the tangled terrain of individual identities and secular authority. To write this world off as the realm of the arbitrary becomes a political act, case by case.

It is tempting to suggest that, in giving primacy to self-speaking, the *Mirror* may itself owe something to drama. First-person complaints are common, of course, in Medieval and Early Modern non-dramatic texts, but (as in *The Testament of Cresseid*) they are usually firmly embedded within a narrative framework – at least before the late-Elizabethan period, when the influence of dramatic forms might almost be taken for granted.[6] Prior to the *Mirror*, the major English collection of 'tragedies' – apart from Chaucer's *The Monk's Tale*, where the first-person is effaced altogether – was *The Fall of Princes*, and Lydgate displays an even stronger tendency than Boccaccio to minimize direct relation on the part of the figures appearing within the dream-vision framework. Third-person narration, moralizing commentary, and dialogue have the effect of truncating and forestalling self-representation by the exemplary speakers. The additional narrative layer in Lydgate, moreover, distances Boccaccio's own 'I' behind a second author-dreamer, who even more strikingly exemplifies Zumthor's observation that such Medieval figures function as rhetorical guarantors of objectivity, rather than as sites of subjectivity: 'Si l'auteur . . . a fait d'un *je* le sujet de l'énoncé, ce *je* fonctionne comme une forme virtuelle, dont l'actualisation varie selon les circonstances [If the author . . . has made the subject of speech from an *I*, that *I* functions as a virtual form, whose actualization varies according to circumstances]' (*Langue* 168).[7] The successive editor-compilers of the *Mirror*, who in varying ways imitate Boccaccio and Lydgate in interpolating narrative machinery and moral lessons,[8] nevertheless agree that their main business is to give the stage to fortune's victims, and the effect is unprecedented except *by* the stage. For the late morality plays and their offshoots furnish abundant instances of unmediated self-commentary by figures fallen from worldly prosperity.

John Skelton's *Magnificence* (circa 1520) affords a particularly resonant example, given that Cardinal Wolsey, its veiled satirical target,[9] becomes a prolific commentator on his own fall in subsequent texts, including the *Mirror* and Shakespeare's (and Fletcher's?[10]) *Henry VIII*. Skelton, writing during Wolsey's heyday, could hardly name names. Both the situation (the coming of Adversity) and the language in which *Magnificence* bemoans it remain safely abstract, in close conformity with *Everyman*: 'Where now is all my kin, my friends, and my noble blood? / Where is now all my pleasure and my worldly good?' (2061–2). Yet a similar abstraction prevails in the moralizing of Wolsey in the *Mirror* (composed by Thomas Churchyard, his is the final tragedy in the edition of 1587):

> Yet some will say, when they haue heapes of golde,
> With flocks of friends, and seruaunts at theyr call,
> They liue like Gods, in pleasure treble folde,
> And haue no cause, to finde no fault at all.
> O blinde conceite, these gloryes are but small,
> And as for friends, they change their mindes so mych,
> They stay not long, with neither poore nor rich.
>
> ('Cardinal Wolsey' 428–34)

Nothing in either speech subverts the character's recognition of himself as the tragic *exemplum* of a universal principle. But the political specifics of the case remain powerfully present – close behind the scenes in Skelton, richly detailed in the *Mirror*. The resulting interplay of identities establishes the ludic quality of these scaffold-speech equivalents – a perspective, it should be emphasized, proper to the audience rather than the character.

III

To align a non-dramatic text – a conservative one, at that – with the sixteenth-century evolution of theatrical discourse, including the latter's capacity to problematize authority, infringes a near article-of-faith amongst Cultural Materialist commentators. The latter generally endorse Robert Weimann's identification of radicalism, in *Shakespeare and the Popular Tradition in the Theatre*, with a virtual 'people's theatre' (the original German title speaks of a '*Volkstheater*'). Shepherd, for instance, approaches the Elizabethan 'politics of rhetoric' through the unique potential of the theatre to subvert 'Elizabethan assumptions about language use, particularly with regard to ideas of social order':

Drama was specifically capable of thus challenging dominant ideas, given the nature of its pre-written oral medium, for a mass audience, produced by those who were equated with vagabonds.

(3)

Yet this description defines – rather loosely at that, given the vagueness of 'pre-written' – only one form of dramatic practice in the period; most notably excluded are the school plays and Inns of Court entertainments. Shepherd's immediate focus is the emergent public theatre of the 1580s, and he goes on to allow for the contrary tendency of the professional players 'to inflect gentry values' (3). Still, he appears to be imposing restrictions on theatrical subversiveness that weaken ties with what Weimann himself considers to be its Medieval dramatic roots. I propose to recuperate and broaden Weimann's fundamental concept, which is after all indebted to Bakhtin's broad theory of carnival, by focusing on the destabilizing potential of self-speaking, whether actually staged or not.

To leave the question of performance to one side for the moment and sight instead along the axis of self-speaking, a particularly striking contrast emerges between Thomas Sackville's contributions to the *Mirror* and to the political tragedy *Gorboduc*, which he wrote (in collaboration with Thomas Norton) for the Christmas revels of the Inner Temple in 1561–2 and which was staged before the queen early in the new year. In its relentless sermonizing against the standard political sins of both monarchs and subjects, as defined by Tudor orthodoxy, the latter text considerably outmirrors the *Mirror*. In authentic Medieval fashion, its many lengthy soliloquies and monologues reflect their speakers to the audience as conforming or opposed to an omnipresent transcendental discourse – a discourse that univocally unites political wisdom with personal morality and religious truth. Even such self-speaking is controlled by the quasi-classical bookending of each act between dumb-show and moralizing Chorus, as if to contain any possible divagations of direct speech.

Indeed, the monologue of Queen Videna after her elder son (Ferrex) is murdered by his younger brother (Porrex) – eighty-one lines comprising the whole of Act 4, Scene 1 – effectively links the subjectifying potential of self-speaking with a deviant female violation of the natural order. In her frenzied grief at this perversion of nature and religion ('The gods on thee in hell shall wreak their wrath' [4.1.33]), Videna is allowed to proclaim self-absence by defining herself in terms of living death. Still, the seamless formal rhetoric of her expression, guaranteeing language-as-presence, reinforces the picture of her identity as merely pivoting, not fading. The inner void is instantly supplied by an even more unnatural passion for revenge against her remaining child. Her deviance appears more starkly against the traditional rhetorical models of maternal mourning, as she regressively collapses the Mary of the *planctus*, who likewise wishes she were dead, into the mothers of the Slaughter of the Innocents, who call on God for vengeance. In vowing, then performing, the murder of Porrex, however, she carries their grief-stricken fury a significant step further. This is not only to usurp the retributive prerogative of the Christian Father but to complete the undoing of fatherhood itself – and in the father's *name*: 'Ferrex yet sweet life mought have enjoyed, / And to his agèd father comfort brought' (58–9). From this moment, the fate of Gorboduc and of his kingdom is sealed. Perhaps all the more because of its rigorous containment of the potential for subjective slippage, Videna's soliloquy makes a deceptively complex anticipation of the numerous discursive transitions from self-loss to self-recovery effected by (mostly male) revengers in the later public theatre.

Gorboduc's final moral, by contrast, may be safely entrusted to the hundred-line monologue of Eubulus ('well-counselling'), whose nominal individuality dispels itself centrifugally in depersonalized lament ('O Britain Land!' [5.2.203]), political sermonizing, and, especially, prophecy – to the point where, apparently, a final chorus becomes unnecessary. The core of the speech is an apocalyptic vision of the disaster – the terrible wrath of God, administered by his messenger, death – that now looms because discord amongst both rulers and ruled has left the throne without a recognized heir. Lest any taint be attached to Elizabeth in the course of delivering this moral lesson, the prophetic mode is pointedly extended at the conclusion to God's eventual restoration of the legitimate line. Given the touchiness of portraying, however remotely, not merely civil strife in Britain but mayhem within the royal family, every effort has been made to render this theatrical discourse anti-ludic, and the effect specifically depends on expunging the enunciating 'I'.

In the narrative context of the *Mirror*, on the other hand, Sackville actively exploits self-speaking as an instrument of subjectivity. Moreover, although there is nothing to flout the compilation's moralistic purpose, 'The complaynt of Henrye duke of Buckingham', long praised as more poetically adroit than the other contributions, also carries farther than any other the tendency to problematize the alignment of the human subject with transcendental authority. It does so not merely through the uneasy yoking of terrestrial and divine power but also by the more theatrical means of collapsing the speaker's transcendental perspective.

In 'The Induction' to Buckingham's complaint, Sackville uses a naïve authorial persona to generate a quasi-Medieval framing narrative, which purports to fill – but effectively enlarges – the eschatological vacuum standard in the *Mirror*'s histories. The narrator's guided tour through a pseudo-classical underworld, where finally he encounters the shade of Buckingham, functions, like the pagan framework in Kyd's *The Spanish Tragedy* – even, arguably, like *Hamlet*'s elusively otherworldly Ghost – to suspend judgement of events in standard moral and religious terms. Providence is placed at a distant remove, as is secular authority with its discourses of law and justice. Only the fickleness of fortune remains as a conventional moral, but while Buckingham regularly reverts to articulating it, and to regretting his complicity with Richard of Gloucester, his image of himself is notably variable. Other objects of blame move into place – Richard himself, 'commontie' ('The complaynt' 421 ff.), and especially 'Banastair' (Banister), the trusted protégé who finally betrayed him to his death. For, in contrast with those of his fellow *exempla*, Buckingham's monologue – indeed his capacity to speak – is grounded in an individual identity defined through ongoing, not past, suffering, which periodically overwhelms him:

> Thryse he began to tell his doleful tale,
> And thrise the sighes did swalowe vp his voyce,
> · · · · · · · · · · · · · ·
> Tyll at the last recovering his voyce,
> Supping the teares that all his brest beraynde
> On cruel Fortune weping thus he playnde.
>   ('Induction' 548–53)

The relation between poet-persona and protagonist is not dissimilar to that in *The Testament of Cresseid*.[11] Sackville's persona, whose guide is Sorowe, interposes a variable subjectivity of his own, which enables Buckingham's sufferings to be pitied despite his evident guilt: 'And I the while with spirites wel nye bereft / Beheld the plyght and panges that dyd him strayne' ('The complaynt' 603–4).

Given his egregious betrayals of trust and loyalty on Richard's behalf, the fact that roughly one-third of Buckingham's speech (two hundred lines or so) dwells with vituperative intensity on Banastair's similar act points, with subjectifying effect, to a mechanism of substitution. Concomitantly, his memory of the event triggers a striking aphanisis, as Buckingham's mental image of himself as more-or-less deserving victim of fortune dissolves in self-pity. The process

begins with a vivid recreation of his abandonment by the common
soldiers: 'And beyng thus alone, and all forsake, / Amyd the thycke,
forwandred in despayer, / As one dismayed ne wyst what waye to
take' (512–14). His sense of lost self next becomes attached to
Banastair's treachery, but, given the latter's status as 'one whom
earst I had vpbrought / Euen from his youth, and loved and lyked
best' (519–20), there are potent overtones of self-betrayal. This obsessive memory carries Buckingham to the point where speech fails
him; the ghost's entrapment between life and death is suddenly
crystallized, by way of the narrator's empathy, in the form of living
non-entity:

> Depe groanes he fet, as he that would awaye.
> But loe in vayne he dyd the death assay:
> Although I thinke was never man that knewe,
> Such deadly paynes where death dyd not ensewe.
>
> (718–21)

At this point, the sufferer 'Came to him selfe' (727), but only to
find that self vanished; memory gives way to amnesia: 'Ah where
am I, what thing, or whence is this? / Who reft my wyts? or howe
do I thus lye?' (729–30). From this state he eventually recovers a
'selfe' and, with it, speech: '. . . by and by / Vpraysde he stoode,
and wyth a sygh hath stayed, / When to him selfe retourned, thus
he sayed' (733–5). However, this recovery depends on turning from
inwardness, figured as the heart, to a view of himself again in the
mirror of transcendental discourse:

> Suffiseth nowe this playnt and this regrete,
> Whereof my hart his bottome hath vnfraught:
> And of my death let pieres and princes wete
> The worldes vntrust, that they thereby be taught.
>
> (736–9)

Thus, inevitably, the conclusion reverts to the moralizing pattern of
the *Mirror* and the received significance of its title. As with Cresseid's
actual 'Testament', however, the final exemplary situating of the
protagonist within a unitary discourse has been made contingent
on (literal) self-aversion, the turning away from an inward mirror
whose evanescent images, the messengers of (self-)betrayal, reflect

not the fall of a sinner but a fall into language – that is, into its failure.

IV

The *Mirror*'s use of dramatic monologue is explicitly and insistently linked with the commonplace figuration of the world as a stage. This element, too, may be seen as feeding into the development of the soliloquy. Of course, the image is pervasive in Renaissance dramatic and non-dramatic contexts. It supplied the metaphorical foundation (if not the actual motto[12]) of Shakespeare's Globe and arguably constitutes the epistemological key to the broad self-referentiality of the plays staged there. With regard to the Middle Ages, however, a 'history of ideas' approach draws a virtual blank,[13] and at the cost of obscuring significant discursive factors. It is remarkable, for example, that a conceit eminently suited to expressing the vanity of this transitory world as against the eternal verity of the next does not appear to figure in the Medieval *de casibus* tradition. Nor, to my knowledge, does it occur in the Medieval drama,[14] whose very *raison d'être* is the staging of the two worlds' competing claims to allegiance.

In these terms, perhaps, the latter absence explains itself. The drama of the Middle Ages may be considered inherently meta-dramatic, for it actively exploits the audience's consciousness that contemporary Englishmen are miming figurations – whether 'historical' or allegorical – of universal spiritual truths. The affinity of this world with the artifice of the stage, including the provisional nature of all human identities, is built into the exercise, even where it is not reinforced by a Mankind figure's assumption of successive roles or by staging that displays the supernatural framework. The surfacing of such a deep-seated premise in imagistic form would seem to depend on serious competition from a worldly perspective. Such a mechanism may actually be glimpsed in Chaucer's *Troilus*, which, having previously emphasized the love 'tragedye' (5.1786), supports the sudden transcendental perspective of Troilus' ascended spirit with the following injunction to youth:

> Repeyreth hom fro worldly vanyte,
> And of youre herte up casteth the visage

> To thilke God that after his ymage
> Yow made, and thynketh al nys but a faire,
> This world that passeth soone as floures faire.
>
> (1837–41)

In Early Modern tragedy, at least (I will be focusing on comedy in a subsequent chapter), the world-as-stage conceit is often associated with self-speaking at points of existential crisis, usually when the protagonist is approaching death. This phenomenon epitomizes the Shakespearean tragic experience in famous instances ranging from Richard II ('Thus play I in one person many people, / And none contented' [5.5.31–2]) to Macbeth ('Life's but a walking shadow, a poor player' [5.5.24]). Shakespeare, however, has both precursors and successors involving 'shallower' characters: on the one hand, Hieronimo in *The Spanish Tragedy* ('now behold Hieronimo, / Author and actor in this tragedy' [4.4.146–7]); on the other, Webster's Bosola: 'Such a mistake as I have often seen / In a play' (*Duchess* 5.5.95–6). Related, too, are cases where a sense of insubstantiality is experienced, if not formulated, metadramatically, as in Antony's view of himself as one of those seeming realities that 'mock our eyes with air' (*Ant.* 4.14.7): 'Here I am Antony, / Yet cannot hold this visible shape' (13–14). The insistent visual element in such speeches delineates a process of fading, as if the speaker's mirror-image recedes into unreality, non-being, or non-humanity: 'Othello's occupation's gone' (*Oth.* 3.3.357); 'Is man no more than this?' (*Lr* 3.4.102–3). The instance of Macbeth is especially to the point, given the double meaning of 'shadow', as well as his earlier aphanitic image, 'my way of life / Is fall'n into the sear, the yellow leaf' (5.3.22–3) – an ironic contrast, it turns out, with the supernaturally vibrant foliage about to come against him.

The same imagistic dynamic marks those variations on the world-as-stage theme delivered by Jacques and Prospero. As befits set-pieces coded as tragic, in that they propose no alternative stage to 'the great globe itself' (*Tmp.* 4.1.153), yet situated in non-tragic contexts, both speeches remain relatively abstract and impersonal. They thereby maintain their speakers' distance from tragic subjectivity – at least, until Prospero falls from 'we' into 'I' and an accompanying 'infirmity' (160). The world-as-stage portion of his speech, like Jacques' rendition of the Seven Ages of Man, is less a soliloquy than a lecture-meditation, spoken *around* the self. Jacques constructs fading in merely physical terms:

> Last scene of all,
> That ends this strange eventful history,
> Is second childishness, and mere oblivion,
> Sans teeth, sans eyes, sans taste, sans every thing.
>
> (*AYL* 2.7.163–6)

Prospero approaches the same conclusion by a contrary stress on the incorporeality of humankind ('We are such stuff / As dreams are made on' [*Tmp.* 4.1.156–7]) and its works, which time will dissolve 'like this insubstantial pageant faded' (155).

In chapters to follow, I will focus on the evolving discourse of aphanisis within Renaissance tragedy. My immediate point is the precedent for such a discourse in the adaptation made by Sackville's Buckingham of the world-as-stage motif, the *Mirror*'s common currency:

> Like on a stage, so stept I in strayt waye,
> Enioying there but wofully god wot,
> As he that had a slender part to playe:
> To teache therby, in earth no state may stay,
> But as our partes abridge or length our age
> So passe we all while others fyll the stage.
>
> ('Henry, Duke of Buckingham' 44–9)

The last line of this passage expands and refocuses the conventional metaphor by contracting the field of vision: the mirror of divine truth, showing the individual's true as well as his false place, yields to a glass reflecting a continual emptying and refilling of roles – a process that leaves the speaker infinitely far behind. This insight ironically harks back to Buckingham's introduction of himself as deriving identity from his father and especially his grandfather, the previous bearer of his title ('In place of whom, as it befel my lot . . .' [43]). In similarly falling into the political machinery they sought to operate, those figures turn out to have foreshadowed – in the full sense of the word – Buckingham's fall into subjectivity.

In thus anticipating the mode of self-speaking most closely identified with tragic characterization in Elizabethan drama, Sackville is perhaps best seen not as radically pioneering (either intellectually or technically) but rather as at once realizing and defusing some of the discursive implications of the *Mirror*'s standard figurations of fortune's power. His contribution arguably offers, in the shapely form of the secular tragic subject, despairing of a 'real' alternative to this unreal world, an artificial resolution of the unruly and inchoate tensions that lurk in the larger text's insistence on the world as a stage, when that stage is so often a version of the scaffold. Gracefully sidestepped in Sackville's formulation is the question of the production and control of discourse itself – a question entailing consideration of subjectivity as a political (and more broadly social) function.

V

This question is regularly addressed in the later drama, however, and not only by works set in a *Mirror*-like realm of fickle fortune. A substantial cluster of Shakespearean plays, including several comedies, either depict the outright (re)production of identity through manipulation or suggestively place self-speaking within frameworks of overlooking and overhearing. From this point of view, Berowne and the Sir Toby Belch gang share a bond with more potent manipulators – Henry V, Vincentio, and Prospero. The latter have often been considered metadramatically and are increasingly approached in terms of subjectivity and discursivity. What occurs in their respective texts may be read as the progressive subjection of the play-world's inhabitants to a single hegemonic will, not only through control of events, but also through the conspicuous, though limited, subjectifying of key supporting players.[15] Figures ranging from *Henry V*'s English traitors and Princess Katherine, to Angelo and Isabella in *Measure for Measure*, and to Prospero's friends and foes alike are brought to internalize versions of a transcendental discourse that originates with the dominant character.

The other side of this coin is the de-subjectification of the manipulators themselves, their virtual renunciation of interiority, which is thrown into relief by both the paucity and the centrifugal style of their soliloquies. The few soliloquies of Vincentio hardly qualify as self-speaking in any sense; they consist mainly of moralizing commentary, couched in trochaic tetrameter couplets. Prospero's only formal soliloquy (in the strictest sense), which accompanies his abjuration of magic, is formal indeed – of a piece with his arm's-length presentation of himself to others, including his daughter. Only his quasi-tragic monologue, cited earlier, leads to a glimpse of absence behind such abundant discursive presence. As for the unique soliloquy of Henry V, delivered on the eve of the battle of Agincourt, it conspicuously fails to discharge the debt of authentic disclosure that has been accumulating since Prince Hal's problematic declaration early in Part 1 of *Henry IV.* 'I know you all . . .' (*1H4* 1.2.195 ff.). The puzzle of Henry's 'true nature' is renewed as the cornerstone of the final play in the Tetralogy by the opening discussion between the wondering churchmen. Yet the much-deferred moment of unmediated self-speaking merely reflects the previous (and ensuing) double discourse: the vulnerable personhood of a monarch without 'ceremony' is spoken of impersonally, if sentimentally. And when, after an interruption that recalls him to 'himself', he is left alone again, God is with him, by whose discursive help responsibility for the death of Richard II is simultaneously assumed and sloughed off onto the '[f]ive hundred poor' (4.1.298) hired to pray for pardon. Finally, this is less self-disclosure – that is, self-production – than a rhetorical realignment with transcendental authority. Indeed, all three of Shakespeare's prominent metadramatic manipulators effectively withdraw, under cover of copious diffusion of 'self' in words and action, towards the still centre, the mystical union of source and reflection that is reserved for divinity in the Medieval drama.

Logically enough, then, the most extreme Shakespearean portrayal of the metadramatic construction of identity through the imposition of a transcendental discourse entirely eliminates self-speaking on the part of the metadramatist and enshrouds him within the silence of a quasi-divine mystery. Even the world-as-stage metaphor – the sign, after all, of anxiety about position within the discursive system – becomes distinctly attenuated, as I will show. Yet *Henry VIII* is also the play that otherwise engages most actively, from an intertextual perspective, with both the matter and the manner of the *Mirror*. The fact that critics have been bothered precisely by the discrepancy between the laconic Henry and the lengthy declamations of the characters who successively fall is the strongest possible testimony to Henry's discursive power.

The *Mirror* is not the only pertinent intertext. Apart from the pervasive influence of Holinshed's *Chronicles*, the principal source for most of the plot, the indebtedness of the Cranmer sequence to Foxe's fulsome biography (Townsend, ed. 8:3–90) has long been recognized.[16] In the play, as in Foxe, the king is the archbishop's champion, wondering at his humble integrity – 'Now, by my holidame, / What manner of man are you?' (5.1.116–17) derives from Foxe's 'O Lord, what manner of man be you!' (Townsend, ed. 8:25) – and sending him to face his enemies on the Council armed, like a chivalric romance hero, with the quasi-magical royal ring. This ring exerts its power on the level of discourse, instantly stilling the hostile voices and causing the case to be referred immediately to the king, who, of course, has been secretly observing.

In Foxe's account, however, this incident figures merely as one of Cranmer's earlier tribulations, and Henry is not the focus; he serves largely as an anticipatory foil to Queen Mary, whose enmity undermines and eventually destroys the archbishop. Obviously, the play is far less anti-Catholic – indeed, only Katherine has any claim to martyrdom – while Cranmer's concluding triumph, especially in contrast with Wolsey's fall, shows religion in dutiful service to royalty, rather than the other way round. This king's concerns are notably less spiritual than political, and when the play-text follows Foxe in having Henry proclaim his obligation to Cranmer 'if a prince / May be beholding to a subject' (5.2.190–1), the key deferential expression of Foxe's king, 'by the faith I owe to God' (Townsend, ed. 8:26), is stripped away.

Accordingly, the seamless sequel to Cranmer's vindication in the dramatic version is his christening of the Princess Elizabeth – the occasion for a speech-act without precedent in Holinshed or Foxe and even beyond the one Henry had requested: 'I long / To have this young one made a Christian' (5.2.212–13). Cranmer's prophetic vision enfolds Henry's words into the divine Word, whose creative power ironically justifies the false report of the Old Lady, who had sought to ingratiate herself with Henry by representing the girl-child as a boy (5.1.164 ff.). Queen Elizabeth will, in fact, be gloriously transfigured beyond her sex, indeed beyond mortality. When Henry piously exclaims, 'when I am in heaven I shall desire / To see what this child does, and praise my Maker' (5.4.67–8), he speaks as if from heaven's vantage point already, thanks to the 'oracle of comfort' (66) delivered by a man instrumental in effecting his divorce – a role emphasized by Foxe (Townsend, ed. 8:5–11) – and recently confirmed as his creature: 'Do you think, my lords, / The King will suffer but the little finger / Of this man to be vex'd?' (5.2.140–2). Here, in contrast to *Gorboduc*, the ultimate authority of prophecy is harnessed to a single character's hegemonic project – a contrast all the clearer because that project purports to fulfil, now explicitly through Elizabeth, the earlier play's promise of divinely ordained succession: 'Yet must God in fine restore / This noble crown unto the lawful heir' (Sackville and Norton 5.2.276–7). All in all, Cranmer's righteous Protestantism falls into place as the least *self*-reflective of the inward selves that Henry's key subjects are successively called upon to display.

Various further narratives by Foxe might have functioned inter-textually for a contemporary audience to problematize the relation between royal authority and divine will in the play. Not long before he became the defender of the Protestant faithful, Henry was lending his power to their Catholic persecutors, who at times included Cranmer himself. This was the case when John Lambert's questioning of transubstantiation came to public notice. He was summoned to dispute the matter with Cranmer, '[f]or the archbishop had not yet favoured the doctrine of the sacrament, whereof afterwards he was an earnest professor' (Townsend, ed. 5:228). He then appealed to the king, and Foxe's account of the subsequent public trial drives home the point that Henry tyrannically usurps divine authority, even while pretending to defer to it. Also remarkable is the exposure of visual spectacle – a more neutral feature of the chronicle accounts of Henry and, of course, a distinctive element of the play – as actively abetting that usurpation:

> At last the king himself did come as judge of that great controversy, with a great guard, clothed all in white, as covering, by that colour and dissembling, severity of all bloody judgment. On his right hand sat the bishops, and behind them the famous lawyers, clothed all in purple, according to the manner. On the left hand sat the peers of the realm, justices, and other nobles in their order; behind whom sat the gentlemen of the king's privy chamber. And this was the manner and form of the judgment, which, albeit it was terrible enough of itself to abash any innocent, yet the king's look, his cruel countenance, and his brows bent unto severity, did not a little augment this terror; plainly declaring a mind full of indignation far unworthy such a prince, especially in such a matter, and against so humble and obedient a subject.
>
> (Townsend, ed. 5:229)

After angrily rejecting Lambert's effusive (and sadly misplaced) thanksgiving for the king's interest in religious controversies, Henry questioned him directly, then set Cranmer and others to dispute with him again on the spot. Finally, impatient, he demanded that Lambert choose between life and death, and when the latter proffered his submission, the king demurred, Pilate-like, 'Commit thyself unto the hands of God, and not unto mine' (Townsend, ed. 5:234). When Lambert then commended his soul to God but yielded his body to Henry's will, the latter condemned him. To match the grievous state of his soul, Lambert was subjected to greater bodily torments than any other of the Smithfield martyrs.

In at least one case, a substantial change in the (posthumous) 1596 edition of the *Acts* serves to bring Henry out from behind the scenes, as, finally, does the play itself. In earlier versions, Robert Barnes is persecuted by the Machiavellian Stephen Gardiner, Bishop of Winchester, while the king seeks 'the means of his safety' (Townsend, ed. 5:420) in examining him and otherwise remains a detached and hidden arbiter. But while the treachery is Gardiner's, the ultimate power of the king swirls as a mysterious and sinister vortex; after displeasing the Bishop in Easter sermons they were forced to preach, Barnes (and two like-minded divines)

> were sent for to Hampton Court; who from thence were carried to the Tower, by sir John Gostwike. From thence they never came out till they came to their death.
>
> (Townsend, ed. 5:420)

In the account of 1596, not only is the king's responsibility fore-grounded, but the examination is made to echo that of Lambert, with the king similarly exploiting the deferential position of 'de-fender of the faith'. Precisely by claiming to be, not the 'authour of truth', but merely its custodian, Henry makes truth the instrument of authority:

> when Barnes had submitted himselfe: Nay said the King, yeeld thee not to mee, I am a mortall man, and therewith rising vp, and turning to the sacrament, and putting off his Bonnet, saide: yon-der is the maister of vs all, authour of truth, yeeld in truth to him, and that trueth will I defend, and otherwise yeeld thee not vnto me.
>
> (2:1093)[17]

In this intertextual light, the progressive arrogation of discursive hegemony by the play's Henry emerges more clearly as the princi-pal thread connecting the successive falls of Buckingham (in Act 2), Wolsey (in Act 3), and Katherine (in Act 4), as well as Cranmer's fifth-act near-fall and ascension. Once all of these events are seen, not as contrived in a narrow Machiavellian sense, but as *de facto* speech-acts of the royal will, the long lamenting monologues of Buckingham and Wolsey – frank adaptations of the *Mirror*'s (historically grounded) model of self-speaking as if from the scaffold – take on new significance. Buckingham veritably grafts his Act 2 speeches, as he is led off to execution, onto the complaint of his father as imagined by Sackville. Not only does the later duke write himself into the family history sketched by his predecessor, but he draws a parallel between his own betrayal by his surveyor and that suffered by his father at the hands of Banister – the obsessive focus of the monologue in the *Mirror*. The fickleness of friends generally, the slippery slope of high office – these staples of *de casibus* moralizing are predictably present. Anticipating the severing of his body from his soul, he hopes the latter may rise to heaven on the prayers of well-wishers. Yet his forbear's view of this world as a stage, populated by insubstantial images pursuing false values, is absent; this would, after all, call the metadramatist's bluff.

On the contrary, the very worldly potentate who 'life, honor, name, and all / That made me happy, at one stroke has taken / For ever from the world' (2.1.116–18) is elevated morally and spiritually:

> Commend me to his Grace;
> And if he speak of Buckingham, pray tell him
> You met him half in heaven. My vows and prayers
> Yet are the King's; and, till my soul forsake,
> Shall cry for blessings on him. May he live
> Longer than I have time to tell his years;
> Ever belov'd and loving may his rule be;
> And when old Time shall lead him to his end,
> Goodness and he fill up one monument!
>   (2.1.86–94)

This is extravagantly to play up the scaffold convention (to which the historical Buckingham evidently conformed[18]) of having good words for the king regardless of the injustice; the excess in the play-text is set off by the terse comment recorded by Holinshed (following Hall), with its tinge of suppressed hope: 'I shall neuer sue to the king for life, howbeit he is a gratious prince, and more grace may come from him than I desire' (Boswell-Stone, ed. 450 [3.865/1/68]). Henry firmly holds the mirror in which the play's Buckingham sees himself; indeed, the king has already gone some distance towards harnessing the discourse of prophecy.

The play's Wolsey, as befits that figure's traditional repentance for betraying his religious profession, comes duly to detest the '[v]ain pomp and glory of this world' (3.2.365) and to acknowledge the ephemeral nature of human greatness. However, he too stops short of dismissing all things terrestrial as quasi-theatrical illusions. Rather, he implies an ideal of balance between royal and divine authority, which momentarily intersect, moreover, in the grammatically equivocal 'he':

> Had I but serv'd my God with half the zeal
> I serv'd my king, He would not in mine age
> Have left me naked to mine enemies.
>
> (455-7)

Rhetorically obscured in this speech, which derives (complete with ambiguous syntax) from the chronicles of Holinshed (Boswell-Stone, ed. 482 [3.917/1/45]) and Stow, are two points clearly focused by the *Mirror*'s treatment – namely, that Wolsey has always served himself above all and that the king has *unequivocally* become his enemy. Wolsey's narrative in the *Mirror* (crudely anti-Papist and couched in Churchyard's exceptionally banal verse) depicts the king as actively plotting against him: 'The King deuisde, a secrete vnder shade, / Howe Cardnall shoulde, bee reste and brought away' ('Cardinal Wolsey' 311–12). As usual in the *Mirror*, moreover, this earthly instrument fulfils the divine will: 'Who knowes the time, and howre when God will strike?' (383). In the play, the very heart of Wolsey's new-found interiority overflows with praises and blessings for the king: 'That sun, I pray, may never set!' (3.2.415). This king too has done God's own work – not, however, by imposing retribution, but by effecting transformation. When Wolsey looks within, he sees no fading human subject but the stable image of himself in a mirror that is at once God's and the king's:

> I know myself now, and I feel within me
> A peace above all earthly dignities,
> A still and quiet conscience. The King has cur'd me,
> I humbly thank his Grace; and from these shoulders,
> These ruin'd pillars, out of pity taken
> A load would sink a navy – too much honor.
>
> (378–83)

The internalizing response of Buckingham and Wolsey is con-- spicuously varied by Katherine. Her persecution – clearly presented as such, in contrast with the chronicles[19] – involves a veritable projection of royal subjectivity, with her downfall set up as the visible emblem of Henry's conscience. Hence, her unfailing resistance threatens to reflect light into his darkest recesses. In resorting to the impersonal discourse of law, including a public trial, Henry exposes his project of altering reality through the manipulation of language, as he purports to undo the speech-act of marriage in the name of the *true* word of God as he now possesses it (and Cranmer seconds it). His closest dramatic precursor is Leontes, who enlists legal ritual against the former repository of his 'heart' to sanction a new-found plenitude as a (poisonous) antidote to self-absence: 'While she lives / My heart will be a burthen to me' (*WT* 2.3.205–6).

As has often been noted, the sympathetic treatment of Katherine makes a strange counterpoint to the text's otherwise firmly (if not militantly) Protestant stance. Even more strangely, the discrepancy extends to a rough equivalent, in Katherine's final message to the king, of Cranmer's apocalyptic rhetoric on behalf of Elizabeth:

> . . . I have commended to his goodness
> The model of our chaste loves, his young daughter –
> The dews of heaven fall thick in blessings on her! –
> Beseeching him to give her virtuous breeding –
> She is young, and of a noble modest nature,
> I hope she will deserve well – and a little
> To love her for her mother's sake that lov'd him
> Heaven knows how dearly.
>
> (4.2.131–8)

Here the dramatic text elaborates a dry observation in Holinshed, where Katherine is merely described as 'commending to him hir daughter and his, beseeching him to stand good father vnto hir' (Boswell-Stone, ed. 489 [3.939/2/13]). What must have seemed, to an English audience of 1613, the grotesque failure of Queen Mary to fulfil the hopes of the play's Katherine thus becomes, however indefinitely, Henry's responsibility.

As this suggests, the most distinctive feature of Katherine's final monologues is her refusal to take on the burden of the king's actions, even to the extent of invoking the arbitrariness of fortune. And while her references to Henry are as charitable as those of Buckingham and Wolsey, they are lacking in sacred overtones and tinged with irony, as when she backhandedly acknowledges the king's imposition of linguistic power: 'So may he ever . . . flourish, / When I shall dwell with worms, and my poor name / Banish'd the kingdom!' (125–7). Her response to Henry's message of comfort, as delivered by Lord Capuchius, rejects the transformative power of the royal discourse by insisting on the contradiction between the king's words and his deeds. This is precisely to crystallize the issue blurred in the standard speech from the scaffold, as in the discourses of Buckingham and Wolsey:

> O my good lord, that comfort comes too late,
> 'Tis like a pardon after execution.
> That gentle physic given in time had cur'd me;
> But now I am past all comforts here but prayers.
>
> (120–3)

In fact, in thus repudiating the false assurances offered by a secular authority on religious grounds, while commending herself wholly to heaven, Katherine is treading the path of Foxe's martyrs. And the text supports her with a visual alternative to Henry's vicarious self-sacralizing. The '[s]pirits of peace' (4.2.83) – in contrast with the Cardinal's new-found conscience – not only figure her discursive escape from the king's (equivocally termed) Grace but mirror an inner state beyond (or before) language, a subjectivity not subject even to the inevitably deceptive impulse to fix signification: the spirits are silent, and although Katherine makes a cursory attempt at exposition, they remain suspended within the ambiguity of dream. Nor does Katherine fall again into self-speaking. It is, perhaps, above all in her self-exemption from discursive self-display that she proves more of a match for Henry than he can live with.

VI

For the final few pages of this chapter, I would like to turn from heaven to hell so as to pick up another thread of the Tudor fabric of self-speaking. Popular Medieval treatments of hell stress the dimension of bodily torment – that is, objective rather than subjective suffering. Such a view matches an epistemological system that firmly contains mental anguish in this world – even that of the mothers whose Innocents are slaughtered – within the framework of the divine will. A condition of the drama's development of tragic subjectivity is the valorization of human anguish in itself. This entails, at least for the character in question, resituating that anguish in a problematic relation to the transcendental discourse that makes spiritual sense of it; hence, for instance, Hamlet's response, which, however scornful, cannot be outright rejection, to the orthodox consolation offered by his mother for his father's death: 'Ay, madam, it is common' (*Ham.* 1.2.74). In those rare tragic texts (comedy needs to be considered on its own terms) where human suffering readily defers to its higher meaning, both tragedy and subjectivity are necessarily circumscribed, and there is a palpable throwback to the Medieval model. Such is the case, for instance, with Thomas Heywood's *A Woman Killed with Kindness*, whose spiritual rarification of the torment incurred through adultery contrasts with the emotional rawness of works ranging (on the scale of 'sophistication') from *Arden of Faversham* to *Othello*.

Still, even in *Woman Killed*, adultery is made the linchpin of a complex human situation, and this reflects a substantial change from Medieval literary practice, which by and large confined the topic to farcical laughter (as in the fabliaux) or solemn abomination – two sides of the same coin, equally reflective of a transcendental discourse. Of course, the post-Elizabethan drama in all genres makes adultery its stock-in-trade, and in subsequent chapters I will explore some manifestations of this virtual obsession in terms of self-imaging and self-speaking. Here I will focus on the transitional qualities of *A Mery Play Betwene Johan Johan the Husbande, Tib His Wife, and Sir Johan the Preest*, which was probably written by John Heywood in the 1520s or early 1530s. 'Mery' as this text undoubtedly is, and ridiculous as its cuckolded husband still appears to most modern critics, a countervailing pathos anticipates later tragedies.

This element is developed largely through soliloquy, supported by aside, and the complex result marks an innovation in English dramatic technique. While Heywood, for the most part, follows his French original, *La farce du pasté*,[20] quite faithfully – often word-for-word – his departures consistently support the tragic countercurrent. The effect begins with the extraordinary opening monologue, 110 lines of flowing and flexible five-stress couplets (as opposed to the more rigid octosyallabics of the French), calculated to create the impression of Johan Johan as baring his soul (such as it is) to the audience, which he actively engages in his dilemma.[21] Indeed, both the actual audience and an imagined audience of neighbours confront Johan Johan with a wavering self-image, as his boisterous fantasies of beating his unfaithful wife and thereby *doing* something about the intolerable situation – albeit something so egregiously futile that it might have revolted even a sixteenth-century audience – repeatedly yield to pusillanimous evasions.

To use as a mirror for self-speaking, not a transcendental spiritual or moral discourse, but the projected idea of what others will think of him, ensures fading, hence subjectification. This process is enacted, as in the pivotal monologue of *Wit and Science* – the only contemporary parallel of which I am aware – by a pattern of successive reactions to prior thoughts: 'Yes, by Cokkes blood, that shall I do!' (30); 'But abide a while – yet let me se!' (98). At one point, in a development of the French, he actually places himself at a third-person distance: 'Battre, mais quoy?' (*Pasté* 28) becomes 'Beten, quod a? Yea, but . . .' (19). In contrast to *Wit and Science*, however, the fluctuation, hence the contours of inwardness, are circumscribed by the two constant poles of assertion and passivity. There is a vivid picture of entrapment, not only within the triangular situation, but within a psychological dynamic of impotence and victimization. Johan Johan might as well be engaged already in the task his wife and her lover consign him to through most of the action: as they eat the pie together, he must hunch over the fire, hungry and smoke-bothered, vainly chafing wax with which to mend his wife's pail.

In short, Johan Johan's soliloquy establishes him within the psychological hell that the subsequent action unfolds in more concrete yet symbolic form – to the point where he threatens to fling hot coals at the woman he perceives as diabolical. This threat is an addition to the original, as are several other infernal allusions: 'deça la' (*Pasté* 26) becomes 'betwene heven and hell' (17); Johan Johan calls his state a 'purgatory' (486), rather than a 'martire' (*Pasté* 521), and complains that 'the smoke put out my eyes two, / I burned my face, and ray'de my clothes also' (637–8). I have written elsewhere about the embodiment of the character's impotence within language itself.[22] This begins, perhaps, with the priest's 'topping' of his name with the honorific 'sir',[23] but it chiefly involves the formulaic repetitiveness and evasiveness of the dialogue, which highlight Johan Johan's inability to express his resentment, except in asides. The subjection of Johan Johan to proverbial discourse in literalized form extends this effect. The motif of chafing the wax evidently derives its point in the original from the expression 'chauffer la cire' in the sense of 'wait'.[24] This had no currency in English, however, and Heywood seems also to be engaging the common proverb, 'He that worst may shall (must) hold the candle'.[25] Even when Johan Johan does speak, his own words turn against him, as when he agrees to invite Sir Johan and immediately, in another addition to the original, regrets his self-betrayal in an aside: 'By Kokkes soule, I was a-curst / Whan that I graunted to that worde furst! / But sinse I have said it, I dare not say nay' (206–8).

It further matches the surprising subjectivity of its protagonist that Heywood's version ends, not with the wife and the priest chasing the husband out of his house, as in *La farce du pasté*, but with Johan Johan's temporary illusion of victory, which crumbles in a short concluding soliloquy. In these final lines, Johan Johan makes it clear, by his abrupt reversion to timorous anxiety – an addition to the source – that his recent physical outburst has settled nothing. The cycle will merely continue in another venue before, potentially, another audience: 'Therfore, by God, I will hie me thider / To se if they do me any vilany. / And thus, fare well this noble company' (676–8). A masochistic truth lurks in his earlier sarcastic dig (added by Heywood): 'I love thee well, though thou love not me' (196).

One way in which *Johan Johan* announces the dramatic advent of hell on earth is by casting the third member of the play's triangle, the veritable father of Johan Johan's tragic subjectivity, as a priest. Such casting is common enough in French farce. However, Sir Johan taunts his victim with *double entendre*, largely absent in the French, that establishes his sexual prowess as the closest thing in this text to a transcendental discourse. Thus, in order to ascertain Tyb's spiritual state, he 'lie[s] uppon her many a time and oft / To prove her' (350–1); he tells of a man returning from a voyage to find that his wife has miraculously had seven children in the interval: 'Yet had she not had so many by thre / If she had not had the help of me' (547–8).

While such anti-clerical satire is thematically jejune – except as an indication that a secularized English drama could now follow the French lead (*La farce du pasté* probably dates from the late fifteenth century) – there are notable implications for the dramatic construction of subjectivity. If Johan Johan is a victim of language itself, not least in using it to deceive himself, Sir Johan is language's past master, deploying its duplicity as a weapon even when Johan Johan finally succeeds in calling a spade a spade:

Johan   Nay, get thee out of my house, thou prestes whore!
Sir Johan Thou liest, whorson kokold, evyn to thy face!

                                                              (656–7)

As Johan's accusation rebounds upon him (a further twist added by
Heywood), the mirror of public contempt in which he earlier saw
himself is transcendentally validated. The identity he feared is no
longer merely his own imagining, subject to fading, but is now
fixed as truth by the ultimate authority of the one who is a position
to know. All he can do is impotently diabolize his enemy ('And
thou liest, pil'd preest, with an evill grace!' [658]) and drive him
away – with his wife. Moreover, he is bound to follow – a reversal
of the pursuit in the original – as if the struggle over something like
his soul has been lost; the inward hell of tragic subjectivity has
found an 'objective correlative'.

                             VII

At the very intersection between Renaissance and Medieval modes
of thought, according to standard literary history, stands a rather
better known play, in which the literal existence of hell is explicitly
an issue and the protagonist's mind vies with the eschatological
plane itself for legitimacy as a site of struggle. These thematic and
dramatic contours of Marlowe's *Doctor Faustus* are staked out between prominent and distinctive instances of self-speaking: the
protagonist's opening meditative soliloquy and the terrible final
one, in which he confronts his imminent damnation. At the outset,
he chronicles a series of fading images of himself as philosopher,
physician, lawyer, and theologian – Humanist ideals of what a man
may make himself, but to Faustus, gripped by the conceit of the
world as a stage unredeemed by transcendental meaning, mere roles
that are ultimately futile.[26] In Shakespearean tragedy, the perception of universal futility is typically a forerunner of closure, marking the most intense state of tragic subjectivity; here the process is
short-circuited, its conclusion deferred for a fixed period, by the
delusory promise that natural existence may be supernaturally
validated. In effect, literal magic takes the place of the magical thinking by which several of Shakespeare's protagonists, in effect, vainly
seek to 'get a deity' (*Faustus* 1.1.64) before they fall into despair.
Here, however, one transcendental discourse deserves another; they

are, it turns out, two sides of the same spiritual coin, as the Medieval drama also shows in squeezing subjectivity between multiple versions of the good and evil angels.

As in *Johan Johan*, then, though on a cosmic scale, limits are set to the vanishing of the self: hell becomes more than a personal narrative of self-absence, a 'fable' (2.1.128); a fluid subjectivity hardens to a 'soul' that cannot be 'dissolv'd in elements' (5.2.103) or 'be changed into little water drops' (110). Yet Faustus's final act of self-speaking reenacts the imposition of a transcendental discourse upon the human subject by maintaining a double vision. This is focused, and problematized, in his despair. It is not that Faustus can see himself only in the mirror of God's judgement, for that judgement, in Faustus's confident knowledge, abounds with mercy: 'See, see where Christ's blood streams in the firmament: / One drop would save my soul, half a drop!' (5.2.71–2). There is, then, a crucial distinction between his attitude and archetypal despair, such as mediates divine condemnation under the Old Law for the Wakefield Cain:

> Syn I haue done so mekill syn,
> that I may not thi mercy wyn,
> And thou thus dos me from thi grace,
> I shall hyde me fro thi face. . . .
> In hell I wote mon be my stall.
> It is no boyte mercy to craue,
> ffor if I do I mon none haue.
>   (England and Pollard, eds,
>   *The Killing of Abel* 358–77)

Cain's lineal successor in this role, of course, is Judas, to whom, affirms Christ in the Wakefield *Resurrection*, 'I was redy to shew mercy, / Aske none he wold' (England and Pollard, eds 308–9). Thus, when Faustus denies himself access to mercy, yielding (as he has done on previous occasions) to a mysterious counterweight that 'pulls me down' (70), he registers the persistent and compelling claim of the alternative mirror of aphanitic subjectivity – his first allegiance. To this extent, Mephastophilis emblematizes the tyranny of the unconscious made conscience. Not only can Faustus's thought not abolish hell, but hell, however ferocious its physical manifestations, more profoundly fulfils itself by subsuming thought – a version, after all, of Mephastophilis' self-proclaimed state: 'Why this is hell, nor am I out of it' (1.3.76). Deprivation of the beatific vision enacts entrapment in the mirror-stage and constitutes the wrathful Father as superego, the judgemental Word that at once mandates and blocks the flight of Faustus into the fluidity of the symbolic order. And so Faustus verbally tears himself asunder, not just in 'contradictory fantasies' (Frieden 124) but soul from body – a metaphysical struggle of which the final sparagmos in the 1616 version makes a pallid physical echo.

Indeed, to approach *Faustus* through conflicting discourses of subjectivity sheds further light on the general tendency of the so-called 'B' text, probably under the censor's hand, to defuse the stark effects of the shorter version of 1604 (the 'A' text). Michael Keefer has provocatively argued (lx–lxix) that those effects include an unremittingly Calvinistic view of Faustus as irrevocably damned, true-sighted rather than blinded in his despair, while the later text strives to portray mercy as always available to the sinner. In doing so, it would be reinstating the fundamentally consolatory hegemony of the Medieval discursive system. Yet the question remains of whether an audience would be as ready as Keefer supposes to reduce (or elevate) the inward force that 'pulls' Faustus 'down' to a function of election, as opposed to psychological self-subversion. A Calvinist perspective, in effectively collapsing Faustus into Cain ('Ordand ther is my stall, / with sathanas the feynd' [England and Pollard, eds, *The Killing of Abel* 466–7]), may daringly impart a tragic bias to the divine dispensation, but it threatens to pull the play's punches in its own way – by disallowing the disjunctive overlay of divinity itself upon an emergent discourse of tragic subjectivity. In any case, the pattern of revision suggests considerable discomfort with a Faustus whose image of himself in the traditional mirror of sin and redemption is what actually slips away in self-speaking, as if in 'little water drops'.

When Faustus seeks refuge from his reflections on – and of – himself as, on the one hand, humanly evanescent and, on the other, theologically overdetermined, he effectively interposes between the mirrors of aphanitic subjectivity and of divine discourse the traditional magic glass of 'hidden knowledge' (Grabes 125), which purports to confer a 'deity' by transforming reflection into clairvoyance. This metaphorical subtext is energized by the intertextual intersection between Marlowe's tragedy and Robert Greene's roughly contemporary romantic drama, *Friar Bacon and Friar Bungay*, which turns on Bacon's use of such a glass. Moreover, Greene's source, *The Famous History of Fryer Bacon*,[27] although fantastic as biography, actually incorporates some of the historical Bacon's extensive writings about optical science,[28] which combined the latter's belief that thereby 'one might gain insight into the very nature of God' (Edgerton, *Perspective* 75) with proposals for the extraordinary manipulation of physical sight. More broadly, the career of that famous thirteenth-century scholar, a daring combination of religious philosopher and multi-faceted scientist, whose speculations (including those touching on magic) led to persecution by the church, clearly grounds his fictional role as patriotic hero:[29] in both the legend and the play he humiliates the foreign magician Vandermast and plans magically to encircle England with a protective wall of brass. Such status, in turn, contributes quasi-tragic overtones to his conscience-stricken renunciation of supernatural powers.

Although the chronological relation between the plays of Marlowe and Greene remains uncertain, it has long been recognized that one is indebted to the other for the representation of magic and, to a lesser extent, of the magician. There is a particular parallel as regards self-speaking. Bacon delivers a monologue of renunciation and repentance roughly analogous to that of Faustus, but with telling differences. Whereas Faustus desperately vows, 'I'll burn my books' (5.2.115), as Mephastophilis enters, Bacon explains to Bungay why he has already broken his magic glass and embraces the mercy offered in the blood of Christ:[30]

> Yet, Bacon, cheer thee: drown not in despair.
> Sins have their salves. Repentance can do much.
> Think Mercy sits where Justice holds her seat,
> And from those wounds those bloody Jews did pierce,
> Which by thy magic oft did bleed afresh,
> From thence for thee the dew of mercy drops
> To wash the wrath of high Jehovah's ire,
> And make thee as a new-born babe from sin.
> (13.98–105)

The fact that Bacon, while he admits to 'using devils to countervail his God' (97), has made no bargain for his soul figures the absence of double vision in his case.[31] No mechanism of aphanitic subjectivity undercuts his self-incorporation into the divine discourse, which is signalled by a further familiar step, absent from *The Famous History*. There the penitent Bacon becomes an anchorite; Greene's Friar likewise vows to 'spend the remnant of my life / In pure devotion, praying to my God' (106–7). But at the play's conclusion, he virtually takes the place of the prophetic brazen head, the emblem of his magic's presumptuous failure: in an anticipation of Cranmer's apocalyptic rhetoric, Bacon prophesies the future glory of England as deriving, no longer from impregnable isolation, but from fertile intercourse within the match just celebrated between Prince Edward and a Spanish princess. Thus, as in *Henry VIII*, but without the agency of an internal dramatist, a divinely authorized comic trajectory deflects tragic tendencies.

Those tendencies are emblematized by the operations of Bacon's magic glass, which, by promising earthly perfection and the bypassing of aphanisis, fosters perilously false self-images. This is the essence of the devil's work – precisely the sort of misappropriation of knowledge warned against in *Wit and Science*. The scholars who see their fathers fighting to the death promptly make themselves their fathers' mirror-images, turning fatally on each other; for Bacon, this is the final straw. A similar disaster threatened earlier when the glass revealed that Lord Lacy was (honourably) courting Margaret of Fressingfield for himself, rather than furthering the Prince's design of seduction. His sight distorted by lustful jealousy, the Prince views himself as a victim of treachery and hastens to confront Lacy. However, the willingness of each of the lovers to die for the other confronts him with an image of noble self-sacrifice, and this he proceeds to internalize, re-adapting himself to his publicly attested princely identity:

> Edward, art thou that famous Prince of Wales
> Who at Damasco beat the Saracens
> And brought'st home triumph on thy lance's point,
> And shall thy plumes be pulled by Venus down?
> Is it princely to dissever lovers' leagues,
> To part such friends as glory in their loves?
> Leave, Ned, and make a virtue of this fault,
> And further Peg and Lacy in their loves.
> So in subduing fancy's passion,
> Conquering thyself, thou get'st the richest spoil.
> (8.112–21)

This speech is remarkable, hardly for its commonplace sentiments, but for the dynamic of transcendental mirror-speaking, which contrasts with the self-destructiveness engendered by Bacon's magic glass. Next, it is up to Bacon himself to follow the prince's lead by heeding his own higher calling, which is more directly divine. Such forthright re-speaking of a straying self amounts to a nostalgic, romantic-comic reversion to a Medieval ideal. For Faustus, by contrast, the tortuous negotiation of tragic subjectivity within a Medieval eschatology comes to no resolution: it is curtailed at midnight as time runs out. Indeed, Faustus's final moments tend to expose such negotiation as a cruel sham – a matter, like Smithfield itself, of self-consuming smoke and mirrors.

Notes to Chapter 3

1. See *Jas.* 1:23–4: 'For if anie heare the worde, and do it not, he is like vnto a man, that beholdeth his natural face in a glasse. For when he hathe considered him self, he goeth his way, and forgetteth immediately what maner of one he was'.
2. Cf., in terms of the relation between language and power, Shepherd 16–18, who cites Elizabeth's management of language to 'create a sense of the presence of God behind her speech, more real than that speech' (17) but also notes that the 'discourse of the essential unitary truth was not confined to the monarch and her officers but was spoken, in opposition to them, by puritans who followed their consciences in expressing the truth of God's word, the word that precedes all other speech' (18).
3. Lacey Baldwin Smith was a forerunner in discussing the 'prescribed formula for scaffold addresses' (481). Despite some indications of the subversive potential of such speeches, his emphasis on the tendency of those condemned for treason, whether guilty or not, to proclaim their submission to both human law and divine will still seems largely justified. See also Foucault, *Surveiller* 68–70 (*Discipline* 65–6); Molly Smith, esp. 217–22; and Spierenburg 59 ff.
4. For Foucault, see esp. *Surveiller* 9–72 (*Discipline* 3–69); for Greenblatt, see *Self-Fashioning* 74–114, esp. 77–81. Greenblatt's discussion turns on 'the critical role taken, at the height of the drama of abjuration and relapse, by the printed book' (76). To my knowledge, the most concise and valuable account of the 'ludic space' is by Zumthor ('Carrefour' 318), who, like all theoreticians concerned with this concept, is indebted to Bakhtin's early work on the carnivalesque; see also my discussion in *Intertextuality* 13–14. On the aesthetic and ritual aspects of Renaissance executions, see Edgerton, '*Maniera*'; on public execution as drama, see also Spierenburg 43–80.
5. Foxe's *Acts* is an important text for Maus's exploration of Early Modern inwardness and its representation (esp. 12 ff., 41–3, 87).

6. A spate of autobiographical quasi-dramatic monologues (most with sexual themes) appear towards the turn of the century, including *The Complaint of Rosamond*, by Samuel Daniel (*Poems*), and Michael Drayton's *Piers Gaveston* and *Matilda* (*Works*, Vol. 1). The speakers amply display their feelings (extending to strong homoeroticism in Gaveston's case), which are firmly contained, however, within their consciousness of themselves as moral exemplars. Thus Rosamond deflects an experience of self-loss into an allusion to the Fall:

    > Into my selfe my waking thought retires:
    > My nakednes had prou'd my sences liers.
    >   Now opned were mine eyes to looke therein,
    >   For first we taste the fruite, then see our sin.
    >
    >   Now did I find my selfe vnparadis'd . . .
    >   (445–9)

    Given the prominence of Lucrece as self-speaker, Shakespeare's *Luc.* also fits the category.
        This strain of the complaint tradition runs parallel rhetorically with another Elizabethan phenomenon: the popular ballad narrated by a repentant malefactor either executed, about to be executed, or otherwise doomed. The latter tradition, in turn, sometimes closely parallels the theatre, as in the much-reprinted ballad of the damned Faustus (Chappell and Epsworth, eds 6:702–5).

7. In discussing 'Le *je* du poète [The *I* of the poet]', Zumthor observes that very few Medieval narrators are self-historicizing in the manner of Augustine in the *Confessions* (*Langue* 166).

8. See Wright 22–7.

9. See Neuss 31–42.

10. The question of authorship is immaterial to my approach.

11. In fact, it is hard to avoid seeing Henryson's poem behind Buckingham's strange curse upon Banastair: 'Thou shalt still lyve, that thou thy selfe mayst sée / Thy deare doughter stroken with leprosye' (704–5).

12. See Knowles and Mattern, eds, *AYL* n. to 1118 and p. 373.

13. See Curtius 138–44, who nevertheless considers that the twelfth-century *Policraticus* of John of Salisbury gave rise to the wide circulation of the concept in sixteenth-century Europe.

14. Curtius (142) cites Calderón for the first use of the concept in religious drama.

15. I have explored these plays elsewhere in such terms and in relation to commentary by others: for *MM*, see esp. *Problem Plays*; for *H5*, esp. *Intertextuality*; for *Tmp.*, esp. *Subversions*. A recent addition to the debate is by Maus (157–81), for whom *MM*'s Duke emerges as 'Shakespeare's rather desperate contrivance to mediate between the characters' secret, subjective worlds, and the external domain of publicly administered law' (178).

16. The more obvious parallels with Foxe are included in Boswell-Stone, ed. 494 ff., inevitably at the expense of context.

17. I cite the 1597 variant of vol. 2, available on microfilm.
18. See Lacey Baldwin Smith 477.
19. Holinshed, again following Hall, stresses her stubbornness ('persisted still in hir former opinion') and her failure to appear at her final hearing, where she was divorced *'by the assent of all* the *learned men* there present' (Boswell-Stone, ed. 483–4 [3.929/2/58]). Presiding was Archbishop Cranmer, whom the play seems concerned to keep as far from Katherine as possible.
20. Heywood's interlude was long treated (e.g., by Lee 373 and Maxwell 56–69) as a far looser adaptation of the *Farce . . . de Pernet qui va au vin*, which contains some of the same elements but no substantial monologues.
21. The interactive element ('But, masters, for Goddes sake, do not entrete / For her whan that she shal be bete!' [65–6]) is developed well beyond the original, although addressing the audience is common in 'foreign adaptations in early English drama' (Arnold 104) and monologue is very much part of Medieval French farce tradition (Maxwell 20–1).
22. See *Intertextuality* 94–7.
23. In *Pasté*, there is no such play on the names; 'le curé' is named Guillaume. On 'Jehan' as the name of a simpleton or cuckold, see Maxwell 68–9.
24. The expression and its literalization in action also figure in *Pernet*, though not with reference to mending a pail.
25. See *Intertextuality* 96.
26. It is tempting to see behind this soliloquy the English Faustbook's comment on Faustus's attraction to magic: 'for the old proverb saith, Who can hold that will away?' – although this is glossed as 'who can hold Faustus from the devil' (excerpted in *Faustus*, ed. Keefer 152). On Faustus's monologues as negotiations with divinity, cf. Frieden 119–24.
27. The earliest extant edition (1627) of this Elizabethan work survives in a single defective copy; see Assarsson-Rizzi 24–5. I cite the edition of 1640(?), available on microfilm.
28. This material is taken from an English translation entitled *An excellent discourse of the admirable force and efficacie of Art and Nature*, whose first known printing was in 1597, together with *The Mirror of Alchimy* (*STC* 1182); prior existence in print or MS must therefore be assumed, as with *The Famous History* itself (Sandys 365; Assarsson-Rizzi 25–6).
29. Bacon was silenced and imprisoned, probably for fourteen years (Bridges xxxi–xxxiii; Little 26–7). On his circumspect interest in magic, see Little 25; his status as proto-Protestant hero is evident from the 1659 translation of his treatise on natural and magical powers with a preface asserting, "Twas the *Popes* smoak which made the eyes of that Age so sore, as they could not discern any open hearted and clear headed *soul* from an *heretical Phantasme*' (cited Tenney L. Davis 53).
30. Greene consolidates two monologues from *The Famous History*, where Bacon delivers a soliloquy before he smashes his glass and another

highly public speech before he burns his books (sig. G2^r–G3^r). There, however, the assertion that 'Magicke makes a Man a Devill' (sig. G2^v) is as close as Bacon comes to expressing spiritual transgression; mainly, he regrets the time he has wasted on vain knowledge, as opposed to divine studies. There is little sense of a transcendental spiritual discourse.

31.   Indeed, in *The Famous History* (sig. B2^r ff.) Bacon performs some fancy legal footwork to undo a Gentleman's bargain with the devil.

4

The Subject of Revenge/
The Revenge of the Subject
in Elizabethan Drama

My discussion of aphanitic subjectivity as a representational effect associated with self-speaking will by now have made clear, I hope, both why *Hamlet* occupies the centre of this book and why I resist endorsing that text as an epistemological watershed, in keeping with New Historicist/Cultural Materialist narratives of subjectivity. On the one hand, I share the widespread fascination with the play's sustained exploration, conducted largely through soliloquy, of a fictive interiority consisting in self-absence. On the other hand, precisely from this perspective I see as many continuities as disjunctions – among them, the foregrounding of the mirror and the book. In fact, as I will argue, the physical staging of the latter symbol offers a salient opportunity of interrogating current critical stances concerning authors, authority, and identity. Such a concretizing of a conventional abstraction is profoundly self-reflexive, and the same might be said of *Hamlet*'s unprecedented preoccupation with the individual as subject. Here, perhaps, lies the key to its mixture of discursive innovation and intellectual continuity, given the possibility of reading Lacan's concept of the unconscious, with Beaujour, 'comme une contribution à la théorie métapsychologique, qui dès lors apparaît à son tour comme le repli sur le sujet individuel des procédures mises en oeuvre à la Renaissance pour décrypter le secret perdu de l'antique [as a contribution to metapsychological theory, which from then on appears in turn as a folding in upon the individual of the procedures employed in the Renaissance for decoding the lost secret of antiquity]' (209).

Certainly, it is thanks to the combination of self-reflexivity and elusiveness in the matter of genre that *Hamlet* – at once a revenge drama without a revenger and *vice versa* – has so much to reveal about the changing contours of subjectivity on stage within the total theatrical picture. This suggests more broadly that the turn-of-the-century revival of the older tragic form, with its ambivalent presentation of a central figure defined successively through self-loss (in suffering) and self-recovery (in revenge), may have given impetus to an active, rather than a passive, discourse of aphanisis by suiting to action the words of Lacan: 'interne à ce qu'on appelle l'acte, c'est qu'il se méconnaît lui-même [in the interior of what we call the act lies its own failure to recognize itself]' (Response 104). In the absence of the putative *Ur-Hamlet*, there is no more accurate record of this discursive evolution than the anonymous Additions provided for the most consistently popular of such plays, *The Spanish Tragedy*, and published in the edition of 1602. These passages, in my reading, serve largely to flesh out the skeletal subjectivity indicated in the original text, especially in its soliloquies. Hence, they suggest how, in returning to the well-known earlier blood-tragedy of *Hamlet* to initiate his sequence of virtual subject-studies in the 'Great Tragedies', Shakespeare was taking up the gauntlet of adaptation (and taking off, as it were, old-fashioned Kyd gloves). But I will also consider this process against the background of Shakespeare's *oeuvre*, including earlier work tending to confirm that a change in the mode of representation, rather than in underlying assumptions about the nature of the self, is at issue.

I

Let me begin by suggesting that, with respect to Shakespeare at least, it is in *Richard II* that the 'new' discourse of subjectivity is paradigmatically engendered. In my introductory chapter, I noted Fineman's passing remark linking the smashing of the looking-glass in Act 4 of that play with a transition in the *Sonnets* from an 'ideally specular' to a 'corruptingly linguistic' concept of language.[1] In effect, Richard is catching up on the linguistic level, as on others, with the Fall, from whose effects he had imaginatively exempted himself. Where Richard's language falls is, specifically, into soliloquy, and on a grand scale: in notable contrast to the analogous sequence in Marlowe's *Edward II*, the prison scene (5.5) where Richard makes his next (and final) appearance opens with sixty-six lines of solitary monologue – his first in the play, despite his earlier verbosity. But then that verbosity has been inextricable from the public staging of his now-defunct royal self, which depended on viewing itself in the submissive 'favors' (4.1.168) of his subject lords.

When the world around him ceases to reflect his power, the buried metaphor rises to the surface to be abjected.

A single broken mirror, however, actually becomes many – a fact that Richard himself makes hard to miss: 'For there it is, crack'd in an hundred shivers' (4.1.289). Similarly, as they interpose on every side between Richard and his former realm, the opaque prison walls reflect to him his new condition, comprised of multiple and fragmentary identities, in violent contrast with his former presumption of unitary selfhood: 'Thus play I in one person many people, / And none contented' (5.5.31–2). Shortly thereafter, as with Hamlet, whose self-division is most evident just before the fencing match, the imminence of death precipitates a renewal of 'wholeness' effected through aggressive action: 'Villain, thy own hand yields thy death's instrument, / Go thou and fill another room in hell' (106–7). Indeed, the king's defiance of his opponent's henchmen remarkably anticipates the prince's moment of revenge:

> The point envenom'd too!
> Then, venom, to thy work. . . .
> Here, thou incestious, murd'rous, damned Dane,
> Drink off this potion! . . .
> Follow my mother!
>
> (*Ham.* 5.2.321–7)

Richard II itself is scarcely a revenge play, but subsequent events – as Carlisle's prophecy foretells and the physical introduction of Richard's coffin begins to demonstrate – trace a trajectory of vengeance across the tetralogy.

Richard's fifth-act articulation of self as, in effect, the absence of stable identity entails an acute experience of subjection to time – a distinct reversal of the previous balance of power: 'I wasted time, and now doth time waste me; / For now hath time made me his numb'ring clock' (5.5.50). This perception – the fulfilment of York's warning against appropriating Bullingbrook's inheritance – usefully differentiates the discourse of interiority here from the scene-opening soliloquy of the despairing King in 3 *Henry VI*, whose entrapment in 'the equal poise of this fell war' (2.5.13) anticipates his own imprisonment and death shortly after. In announcing, 'on this molehill will I sit me down' (14), and exclaiming, 'Would I were dead, if God's good will were so' (19), Henry comes close to Richard's bleak invitation earlier in the play: 'For God's sake let us sit upon the ground / And tell sad stories of the death of kings' (*R2* 3.2.155–6). For Richard, however, this is yet another public occasion, and he is calling upon his on-stage audience to model his grief for him. When he is finally brought to speak alone, both the appeal to divinity and the anticipation of death give way to entrapment in the temporally driven processes of life:

> So sighs, and tears, and groans
> Show minutes, times, and hours; but my time
> Runs posting on in Bullingbrook's proud joy,
> While I stand fooling here, his Jack of the clock.
> (*R2* 5.5.57–60)

By contrast, Henry vents his sorrow in a fantasy of pastoral content: 'O God! methinks it were a happy life / To be no better than a homely swain' (*3H6* 2.5.21–2). Whereas Richard's physical substance is grotesquely dissolved into a fluidity suggestive of time itself, with even his tear-wiping finger turned back upon him in self-accusation 'like a dial's point' (*R2* 5.5.53), Henry's imagination projects the power to

> . . . carve out dials quaintly, point by point,
> Thereby to see the minutes how they run . . .
> When this is known, then to divide the times:
> So many hours must I tend my flock,
> So many hours must I take my rest . . .
> (*3H6* 2.5.24–32)

Time passed thus peacefully, in harmony with that medium, '[w]ould bring white hairs unto a quiet grave' (40). The speech posits a stable 'I' – however miserable – viewing itself in the transcendental mirror of the divine creation. Only the sequel of the scene, in which his realm's reality is mirrored emblematically by the mutual butchering of a father and son, dissolves this vision and puts a stop to soliloquy. Even then, what Henry sees converts to static self-reflection, involving Richard II-like 'care' and self-portrayal in the pose of living death: 'Sad-hearted men, much overgone with care, / Here sits a king more woeful than you are' (*3H6* 2.5.123–4).

This king's escapist reverie is the first in a series of analogous monologues delivered by Shakespearean Henries, all of whom shelter their 'self-fashioning' beneath the presumption that a divine hand holds the mirror. Next (in order of composition) come Henry IV's troubled effusions on the easy sleep of his poorest subjects (*2H4* 3.1.4 ff.) – the lead-in to a dialogue with Warwick, whose would-be comfort, based on a quasi-Machiavellian reading of history, only drives the despondent Henry deeper into a sense of current trials as 'necessities' (93).[2] Here, paradoxically, he finds comfort, which turns out to lie in the idea of order underlying the fear of doom: 'Then let us meet them like necessities' (94); for Warwick's would-be consolation actually threatens the entire structure on which the royal self depends.

The value of pastoral fantasy in preserving a royal self-image becomes even clearer when Henry V depreciates 'ceremony' in his only soliloquy (*H5* 4.1.230 ff.). On the eve of Agincourt, the audience appears to be in store for a long-delayed self-disclosure on Henry's part – the 'true' identity that has proved tantalizingly elusive ever since the winsome Hal, at the conclusion of the second scene of *1 Henry IV*, abruptly turned to outlining his programme for self-fashioning. In a similar swerving at the verge of proffered intimacy, Henry, still in his borrowed cloak, now cloaks himself in an idyllic vision of peasants in harmony with nature – a vision that sours even as it is spoken, however eloquently, and whose wispy traces will be dispelled by Burgundy's powerful (if discretely indirect) portrayal of Henry as the spoiler of pastoral in the next act (5.2.24 ff.). And given that Henry's incessant piety smooths over (or, in the play's own imagery, buries) the contradictions in his father's attitudes towards Richard's murder and the expiatory crusade, it is not surprising that his subsequent prayer, in the midst of humility, drives a bargain with God in a parodic anticipation of the 'Non Nobis': 'Not to-day, O Lord, / O, not to-day, think not upon the fault / My father made in compassing the crown!' (4.1.292–4). The discourse of subjectivity opened up as a theatrical possibility by Richard II, precisely when he loses control of theatricality, is the stuff, not of successful royalty, but of tragedy.

II

Recent editors of *The Spanish Tragedy* welcome the suggestion that when Hieronimo, in soliloquy, anticipates the success of his multilingual revenge plot – 'Now shall I see the fall of Babylon, / Wrought

by the heavens in this confusion' (4.1.195–6) – he alludes not only
to the sinful city doomed by God in *Isaiah, Jeremiah, Daniel*, and
Revelation, but also to the Tower of Babel (*Gen.* 11:1–9), given that
the Old Testament of the Geneva Bible usually employs the form
Babel, glossed as 'confusion', in referring to both locales.[3] Some
thirty years ago, S. F. Johnson developed this point with reference
to a variety of Biblical texts and commentaries, which, he argued,
would have associated these two instances of divine retribution
with the just vengeance of Hieronimo, the thwarted magistrate,
besides reinforcing the anti-Catholic overtones of his blow against
'the whole succeeding hope' (4.4.203) of Spain. The prophetic factor, with the same militant Protestant baggage, has recently been
reapplied to the play by way of *Daniel*.[4] Indeed, the play's intertextual
relations with the prophetic books may be considerably developed
– with the sidelong encouragement of the protagonist's name (especially in its alternative early spellings, such as 'Jeronimo'); for at
least as much to the point as St Jerome[5] is Jeremiah – a figure so
closely associated with the mode of aggrieved lamentation that his
name later became a byword for it.

Prophecy itself, of course, entails questions about the signifying
mechanisms and the efficacy of language. Both Isaiah and Jeremiah
deplore the fact that their warnings – the divine Word itself – are
ignored as if spoken in an unintelligible tongue (*Isa.* 28:11–13; *Jer.*
5:14); in the latter case, moreover, retribution will entail the triumph over Judah of 'a nacion whose language thou knowest not'
(*Jer.* 5:15) – namely, Babylon. Both books, like that of Daniel, look
forward to the apocalyptic dispensing of absolute justice by the
Messiah. In *Revelation*, the redeemer who 'judgeth and fighteth right-
eously' (19:11) after the fall of Babylon is 'clothed with a garment
dipte in blood' (19:13), thereby fulfilling Isaiah's prophecy of the
blood-stained righteous avenger (63:1–8). Even if (depending on
stage practice) Hieronimo does not bloody himself until he bites
out his tongue, his sudden display over his parodically resurrected
son is richly informed by this intertext:

> And here behold this bloody handkercher,
> Which at Horatio's death I weeping dipped
> Within the river of his bleeding wounds:
> It as propitious, see I have reserved,
> And never hath it left my bloody heart.
>
> (4.4.122–6)

The redeemer of *Revelation* is a figure at once of mystery ('he had a name written, that no man knewe but him self' [19:12]), as is Hieronimo to his victims and onlookers, and of the vengeful truth at last made plain: 'and his name is called, The Worde of God' (19:13). Indeed, in a way that echoes the destructive abuses of language excoriated by Jeremiah ('they bend their tongues *like* their bowes' [9:3]; 'Their tongue *is* as an arrowe shot out' [8]), his tongue becomes his weapon: 'And out of his mouth went out a sharpe sworde, that with it he shulde smite the heathen' (*Rev.* 19:15). So, finally, does Hieronimo's in expounding his spectacle, taunting his foes, and then silencing himself. (It is worth noting that even in the story of Zeno of Elea, on which Hieronimo's last moments seem to have been most immediately modelled, that defiant Stoic first bites his enemy.[6])

The particular affinity between Hieronimo and Jeremiah extends to the prophet's self-spoken struggles with his feelings. At the scornful reception of his prophecy that God will deliver 'all Judah into the hand of the King of Babel' (*Jer.* 20:4), Jeremiah falls into a wavering state of impotent frustration and angry fantasy strongly reminiscent of Kyd's protagonist:

> I am in derision daiely: euerie one mocketh me.
>
> For since I spake, I cryed out of wrong, and proclaimed desolation: therefore the worde of the Lord was made a reproche vnto me, and in derision daiely.
>
> Then I said, I wil not make mencion of him, nor speake any more in his Name. But *his worde* was in mine heart as a burning fyre shut vp in my bones, and I was wearie with forbearing, & I colde not *stay....*
>
> But the Lord is with me like a mightie gyant: therefore my persecuters shalbe ouerthrowen, and shal not preuaile, & shal be greatly confounded: for they haue done vnwisely, *and their* euerlasting shame shal neuer be forgotten.
>
> But, o Lord of hostes, that tryest the righteous, & seest the reines & the heart, let me se thy vengeance on them: for vnto thee haue I opened my cause.
>
> (20:7–12)

When this outburst gives way to despair, Jeremiah curses 'the day wherein I was borne' (20:14), as well as his father's joy at the birth of a son. In the event, of course, his vindictive feelings are amply gratified, and in terms that constitute a concise outline for Hieronimo's revenge: 'Then the King of Babel slewe the sonnes of Zedekiah in Riblah before his eyes: also the King of Babel slewe all the nobles of Iudah' (39:6).

Finally, the lamenting lines of Hieronimo that came notoriously to epitomize Kyd's rhetorical approach to character bear a strong family resemblance to those attributed to Jeremiah (in the book of *Lamentations*) over the fall of Jerusalem:

> O eyes, no eyes, but fountains fraught with tears;
> O life, no life, but lively form of death;
> O world, no world, but mass of public wrongs,
> Confused and filled with murder and misdeeds!
> (3.2.1–4)

> Mine eyes do faile with teares: my bowels swell: my lieuer is powred vpon the earth, for the destruction of the daughter of my people, because the children and sucklings swoune in the stretes of the citie.
> (*Lam.* 2:11)

The loss bewailed is even closer to Hieronimo's at one point – 'those that I have nourished & broght vp, hathe mine enemie consumed' (2:22) – while the ensuing prayer anticipates the dimensions of his revenge, at once precisely fitting and grotesquely excessive:

> Give them a recompence, o Lord, according to the worke of their hands.
> Give them sorowe of heart, *euen* thy cursse to them.
> Persecute with wrath and destroie them from vnder the heauen, o Lord.
> (3:64–6)

In extending the range of prophetic intertexts for *The Spanish Tragedy*, I seek by no means to support but rather to problematize the position of Hieronimo as righteous avenger that has commonly been bolstered by such evidence. My point is that his status as divine instrument is not merely Biblically defined but Biblically overdetermined: it is one thing to serve as a conduit for divine words of warning, quite another, decidedly transgressing the prophetical, to enact the physical triumph of the Word itself or even to appoint oneself the King of Babel, the scourge destined to be scourged. The crucial distinction is clear to Hieronimo himself as late as Act 3, Scene 13, when he soliloquizes a conflict between seductive Senecan role-models and the Biblical text that reserves – as the Pauline gloss on the Old Testament lines reinforces[7] – retribution to the Lord:

> *Vindicta mihi!*
> Ay, heaven will be revenged of every ill,
> Nor will they suffer murder unrepaid:
> Then stay, Hieronimo, attend their will,
> For mortal men may not appoint their time.
> (3.13.1–5)

Yet by the time of the first scene of the next and final act, Hieronimo's anticipation of 'confusion' documents an imaginative slippage towards the role, not of prophet, but of God himself. On the one hand, Hieronimo positions himself as the passive witness of a divine intervention ('Now shall I see . . .'); on the other hand, with the support of the performative overtones accruing to 'see'[8] in this context, he proclaims his role as prime mover of the event. This dual perspective embraces both Babylonian symbologies. Insofar as the Spanish court is the sinful city, Hieronimo is the originator, as well as the destined final victim, of a scheme for retributive annihilation. With respect to the play 'in sundry languages' (4.4.10 S.D.), which recalls the Tower of *Genesis*, Hieronimo is, as he triumphantly reveals at the end, both 'author' and (in a double sense) 'actor' (147). Such double signifying helps to unfold a more fundamental split in Hieronimo's discourse – to the point where, to adapt Shoshana Felman's application of speech-act theory, the gap between the *sujet de l'énonciation* and the *sujet de l'énoncé* widens into the *'breach in knowledge* (the break in the constative)' from which 'the act takes its performative *power*' (96). According to Lacan's theory of speech in psychosis (that is, psychosis in speech), as summarized by Ragland-Sullivan, 'A delusional psychotic discourse implicitly alludes to the Other(A) as a mechanical god of power and destruction' because 'the existential subject of synchronic relations (*je*) disappears. The primordial ideal ego has substituted itself for *je* and the ego ideal has taken the Other's place' (199). Thus Hieronimo's 'I' becomes 'the heavens'.

To lay claim to godhead is not only a traditional but a Lacanian

measure of a psychotic state: 'The ideal ego, heretofore unsymbol-
ized, emerges as the 'miraculous infant', looming forth with a new
name, such as Christ, God, Napoleon' (Ragland-Sullivan 199).[9] And
for commentators to diminish the madness of Hieronimo, which
after all goes with the generic territory, by making infinite allowance for the role of heaven's 'scourge and minister' (*Ham.* 3.4.175)
entails the same interpretative limitation as does the contrary (and
at least equally common) critical extreme, whereby his losing touch
with the 'real world' marks him as damnably, if pitiably, evil.[10]
Either judgemental reading denies full access to the mingled identification, titillation, and horror that must originally have been part
of the theatrical impact, as with the early revenge plays generally.
More to my purpose, such perspectives distract from the construction of the character through the discourse(s) of subjectivity.

It is this process that I wish to address here as, in effect, a conflicted collaboration between Kyd and the author of the five Additions of 1602 (whom, by the way, I am quite content to leave
unknown). This model is frankly artificial, especially given that the
text of 1592 may incorporate indeterminate revisions of the original
(Edwards xl) and that there is ambiguity regarding the theatrical
function of the Additions, which may well have served as replace-
ments beyond what can be deduced (Mulryne xxxiii–xxxiv). However, the central fact remains that the Additions consistently elaborate
the mental processes of the protagonist by giving him more language, as well as language of a more personal kind, including the
most fully realized expressions of both his pain and his madness.
Such an approach opens up the very concept of 'character', which
Clemen needs to keep closed in order to sustain his hierarchical
judgement, based largely on the 'sense of isolation in Hieronimo's
mind' (*English Tragedy* 111), that Kyd was the 'first playwright in
the history of English drama who ... succeeded in creating a con-
vincing character by means of soliloquy' (108).[11] Especially because
they intervene in a text already preoccupied with the functioning of
language itself, as has been widely recognized, the Additions bear
productively on the discursivity of subject-formation. In reconstituting Hieronimo stylistically to the mimetic standard that prevailed
a decade or so after the play was composed, they effectively stipulate that before the 'existential subject of synchronic relations ...
disappears', it must be made visible.

It seems clear enough, in both the 'original' and the supplemented
texts, that Hieronimo's revenge entails a symbolic assumption of

power over language, which has failed him as a route to justice because of its corruption and suppression by villainy.[12] The duplicity of the play-world contaminates language itself as early as Balthazar's riddling when the King straightforwardly asks, 'to whether didst thou yield?' (1.2.160): 'He wan my love, this other conquered me: / And truth to say I yield myself to both' (164–5). Hieronimo's response, however deferential to the King as 'just and wise' (166), involves his first venturing of his 'tongue', which 'should plead for young Horatio's right' (169). The subsequent breakdown in the system of values and social relations amounts, for Hieronimo, to a fracturing of the connection between sign and signified: 'my thoughts no tongue can tell' (3.2.67). Finally, Babylon blurs into Babel, one sense of 'confusion' into another, as he acts to restore unitary signification – by way, paradoxically, of double meanings imposed upon unwitting and impotent spectators. A fitting pivot is provided by Balthazar, ironically punning at his own expense when Hieronimo reveals that the performance will be multilingual: 'But this will be a mere confusion, / And hardly shall we all be understood' (4.1.180–1). Hieronimo turns the tables by confronting his adversaries with the fragmentation and incoherence of speech, then suddenly resolving that confusion, on the model of *Revelation*, into the Word incarnate. He reenacts the fall of Babel complete with Augustine's commentary, which, however, cuts both ways: 'Quoniam dominatio imperantis in lingua est, ibi est damnata superbia, ut non intellegeretur iubens homini, qui noluit intellegere ut oboediret Deo iubenti. [As the tongue is the instrument of domination, in it pride was punished; so that man, who would not understand God when He issued His commands, should be misunderstood when he himself gave orders]' (*De Civitate Dei* 48:505 [Bk. 16, Ch. 4]); *City of God* 313).

The Additions make the reversal more explicitly a matter of language, as Hieronimo counters the threat of torture with his newfound verbal power – 'Do, do, do, and meantime I'll torture you' (5th Add. 30) – and the Viceroy duly responds, 'Be deaf my senses, I can hear no more' (43). In both texts, the ultimate emblems of triumph are the dumb speech of Horatio's corpse, which recalls Felman's understanding of action as 'an enigmatic and problematic production of the *speaking body*' that 'breaks down the opposition between . . . matter and language' (94), and Hieronimo's own withdrawal into unbreakable silence: 'thus I end my play: / Urge no more words: I have no more to say' (4.4.151–2). Again, however, the Fifth

Addition accentuates the linguistic dimension. In it, Hieronimo's last two lines – 'Pleased with their deaths, and eased with their revenge, / First take my tongue, and afterwards my heart' (4.4.190–1) – are recast into closing couplet form and refocused by a new initial verse that vividly and ironically suits words to the action: 'Now to express the rupture of my part' (5th Add. 47). What is being expressed – besides, physically, the organ of speech – is his rupture of the confines of signification, the unattainability of any but a physical 'heart', which is no longer the richly symbolic core of self-lack. As Maus puts it, 'A creature that seems wholly realized through forms of theatrical and rhetorical display finally declares the insufficiency of these forms' (70) – but triumphantly, as if not just 'protecting his hard-won privacy' (Maus 70) but transcending creatureliness itself.[13]

Hieronimo's triumphant silence begins with abundant speech even in the original text, from which his torturing taunts (5th Add. 19 ff.) are absent. Yet his highly detailed confession, an extensive parade of facts and motives announced with the claim that his 'tongue is tuned to tell his latest tale' (4.4.85), strangely appears incomplete to his horrified royal audience: superficially, at least, 'Hieronimo, do but inform the king of these events . . .' (157) is an incongruous response, and it is seconded by desperate 'why'-questions posed in successive lines by the King, the Viceroy, and Castile (165–7). The proposal that in their 'grief-stricken bewilderment . . . they have not taken in what Hieronimo has said' (Mulryne, ed. n. to 4.4.165–7 and 179–82) gains force from Hieronimo's acquisition, through his production of apocalypse, of a quasi-Messianic mystery. It is as 'the heavens' themselves that he finally refuses to speak and, instead of sharpening his pen, uses the knife to write into the script his final exit. What the spectators want from him, as if from God, is an answer that would performatively restore the signifying system on which their identities have equally depended. Their question is not merely 'why', but rather the more pointed and less deferential one that Hieronimo, too, began by asking and could only answer by becoming God himself:

> O sacred heavens! if this unhallowed deed,
> If this inhuman and barbarous attempt,
> If this incomparable murder thus
> Of mine, but now no more my son,
> Shall unrevealed and unrevengéd pass,

> How should we term your dealings to be just,
> If you unjustly deal with those that in your justice trust?
>
> (3.2.5–11)

Hieronimo's final discursive stance intertextually engages two Shakespearean revengers – one equivocally noble, the other unequivocally villainous. Horatio's final account of the action of *Hamlet*, especially given his pretence of fulfilling Hamlet's request to 'tell my story' (*Ham.* 5.2.334), is ironically undercut. Obviously, such plot summary cannot '[t]ruly deliver' (386) the Prince's 'heart's core' (3.2.73) – that indeterminate locale where Horatio is supposed to reside but whose 'mystery' (366), overdetermined in Hamlet's prolific self-interrogations, fades along with the 'rest' that 'is silence' (5.2.358). Yet Hamlet's projection of his 'dying voice' (356) upon the heroic Fortinbras tends to confirm that Horatio is doing the job as intended, indeed that Fortinbras' funeral plans, which will confine Hamlet's identity to that of 'soldier' (396) – when even Ophelia saw two other sides to him – consummate a devout wish for unitary signification, the ultimate translation of the self from 'Words, words, words' (2.2.192) into the 'speaking body' of action. The moral obverse of the coin is Iago, another copious soliloquizer, whose heart's mystery notoriously deepens over the course of the play in proportion as it appears impervious to his own words. Finally, that mystery, too, acquires a supernatural incarnation sealed by the privilege of silence:

> Othello Will you, I pray, demand that demi-devil
> Why he hath thus ensnar'd my soul and body?
> Iago Demand me nothing; what you know, you know:
> From this time forth I never will speak word.
>
> (5.2.301–4)

These analogues make it easier to see that, contrary to facile assumptions about self-speaking as implying presence, to enrich and individualize Hieronimo's language, as the Additions do, is hardly empowering. The point is, on one level, an obvious one, at least if discourse is granted primacy over 'character': the fuller the expression of pain, the greater the pain. But the more 'realistic' style of the supplementary language, its enhanced pretensions to trace the contours of inwardness, also extends the register of self-referentiality.

The new semiotics of his subjectivity encompass the character's existence as both a mortal and a social creature. These self-mapping coordinates join with the discourse of personalized grief at once to define and to fail to fill an interior space, making the core of the self by making it indeterminate.

This is the space finally occupied (or covered over) by Hieronimo's success, according to the Fifth Addition: 'Methinks since I grew inward with revenge, / I cannot look with scorn enough on death' (27–8). As I observed some years ago ('Meaning and Mortality'), such a sentiment figures in revenge and villain drama from the inception of the genres; it is implicit even in Videna's vengefulness in *Gorboduc*, which arises out of the conceit of her 'living breast' as her son's 'ruthful tomb / Wherein my heart, yelden to death, is graved' (4.1.19–20). Hence Francis Bacon, in derogating death's power, feels no need to elaborate his almost matter-of-fact declaration that '[r]evenge triumphs over death' ('Of Death' 380). In *The Spanish Tragedy*, Maus notes, there is a distinctly political dimension: 'for Kyd, the connection between a challenge to authority and a highly developed sense of personal inwardness is not accidental but abolutely intrinsic' (70). But the point is not articulated in the unsupplemented text; nor, despite his instantaneous intuition that 'in revenge my heart would find relief' (2.5.41), is the mechanism by which Hieronimo's loss engenders an existential vacuum. This gap is addressed in the Third Addition: 'He was my comfort, and his mother's joy, / The very arm that did hold up our house: / Our hopes were stored up in him' (31–3). The groundwork is laid here for Hieronimo's triumph as 'the paranoid psychotic [who] has foreclosed the signifier for death and separation and retained that psychic sense of wholeness which is on the side of immortality' (Ragland-Sullivan 199).

At the same time, this picture of Horatio reinforces the nexus of subjectivity and social identity. The element of class tension, introduced in the original mainly through Lorenzo's contemptuous resentment of Horatio, is engaged from Hieronimo's point of view even in the First Addition, as his mind slips away from the horrible discovery into thoughts of his son's hobnobbing with the great ('[he] said he would go visit Balthazar / At the duke's palace' [3–4]) and advancement at court: 'His majesty the other day did grace him / With waiting on his cup' (11–12). Yet the ultimate articulation of Hieronimo's transcendental 'hopes' in the Third Addition issues from his fullest imaginative realization of his son as a human creature. The 'what's a son?' monologue develops its remarkable affective power negatively, projecting love through the denial of reasons for love:

> What is there yet in a son
> To make a father dote, rave or run mad?
> Being born, it pouts, cries, and breeds teeth.
> What is there yet in a son? He must be fed,
> Be taught to go, and speak. . . .
>
> (3rd Add. 9–13)

Thus the plenitude of subjectivity – that of both the father and the child, who progresses within the speech from 'it' to '[h]e' – is made contingent on, and coterminous with, the (self-)image's 'signification mortifère'.

By contrast with the Additions, those points in the earlier text where Hieronimo's loss shakes his attachment to existence represent death, not as negation, deprivation, and absence, but as a substantial entity, a competing presence, much as the Bible and Seneca compete for the character's moral allegiance – and in so doing circumscribe the competition. Such representation is highly emblematic and heavily rhetoricized, as in the famous passage that, by the time of the Additions, had come to epitomize the absurdity of pre-mimetic lamentation: 'O life, no life, but lively form of death'. The phenomenon actually begins, however, with the fourteen-line soliloquy in Latin verse ending the discovery scene. This extraordinary '*pastiche*',[14] intertextually overdetermined and iconographically framed by the placement of 'his breast unto his sword' (2.5.67 S.D.), marks Hieronimo's interpellation as neo-Senecan victim-revenger. It also sets up the climactic inversion, when Hieromimo will cast others in his own multilingual tragedy. But only in the last two lines does he (abruptly) turn to revenge, already associated with his son's body ('Here he throws [his sword] from him and bears the body away' [81 S.D.]); the rest are devoted to the pain of his newly bereft existence, and they culminate in the impulse, expressed with the help of the *Aeneid*, to join his son in the other world: '*Emoriar tecum: sic, sic juvat ire sub umbras*' (78). The language of grief available to Hieronimo is not 'his own' – that is, the Other's.

When Hieronimo next contemplates suicide in the opening soliloquy of Act 3, Scene 12, his language may be English, but his inability to plead his cause is his starting point ('Why, is not this a strange and seld-seen thing, / That standers-by with toys should strike me mute?' [3.12.3–4]), and again his props – here the dagger and halter emblematic of despair – highlight the artificiality of his discourse, hence the dependence of his ideas of death and revenge on derivative models. Even the 'outrage' and 'fury' (79, 80) ensuing when he fails to make himself heard denote his madness according to a standard semiotic code, applied by the King. When, digging with his dagger, Hieronimo seeks to bring Horatio back from the afterlife to 'show his deadly wounds' (73), he enacts the wish, as expressed in the opening soliloquies of both this scene and Act 3, Scene 6, to believe that justice is supernaturally guaranteed, even though the heavens appear to 'Resist my woes, and give my words no way' (3.7.18).

The disclosure immediately after this last line of Pedringano's letter opening the door to revenge – a reprise of Bel-imperia's wind-blown answer to Hieronimo's prayer in Act 3, Scene 2 – sustains the ambiguously ironic relation between Hieronimo's initiatives and the framing plot involving Don Andrea's ghost and Revenge. Nothing prepares us, however, for the extreme turn this irony takes in the play's final lines, where Revenge promises 'endless tragedy' (4.5.48) for the enemies of Hieronimo and Andrea. Not only has retribution been realized within the play-world, but eternity itself has been bent to the shape of quintessential vindictive fantasy, as articulated by Andrea (4.5.29 ff.). It is as if Hieronimo has displaced not only God but the playwright. The existential and social barriers he had vainly attempted to penetrate with prayer, private and public complaint, symbolic action – in short, the very 'opposition between . . . matter and language' – suddenly collapse, and with them the containment walls of the inner text. First to collapse, however, are the confines of the alternative fictive world he finally fashions to match his vision – a world in which his victims speak his languages rather than their own and fail to read his silence. The basis of this creation is a bounded space within his control, in contrast with the open air, the site of impotent knowledge: 'Let me entreat your grace / That, when the train are passed into the gallery, / You would vouchsafe to throw me down the key' (4.3.11–13). This is the space of subjectivity, and its explosion marks Felman's shift from constative stasis to performative power – with a vengeance.

In the original text, such subjectivity largely remains a missing link, visible only in elusive glimpses. In general, intertextual overdetermination and rhetorical inflation make Hieronimo's speech conspicuously the discourse of others, not of the Other, while his social alienation puts public questions of justice and power in the way of the private – unspeakable – 'matter of a son, or so'. Even Isabella's pathetic suicide soliloquy, 'histrionic and theatrically effective' as Clemen finds it to be (*English Tragedy* 111), is a rhetorical set-piece accompanying rather than generating action: 'with this weapon will I wound the breast, / The hapless breast that gave Horatio suck' (4.3.37–8).[15] The only striking anticipation of the Additions occurs in Hieronimo's third-act encounter with another father of a murdered son. The highly emblematic configuration of this scene is initially supported by the usual linguistic and mythological formulas declaring justice 'exiled from the earth' (3.13.140) and invoking supernatural vengeance. But when Hieronimo is finally induced to acknowledge Bazulto as neither his son's ghost nor a Fury but merely a 'grieved man' (159), he finds a 'lively image of my grief' (162) that breaks his monopoly, pluralizing sympathy and paradoxically freeing language to function as a spontaneous and associative – even playful – index of the personal:[16]

> Come in old man, thou shalt to Isabel;
> Lean on my arm: I thee, thou me shalt stay,
> And thou, and I, and she, will sing a song,
> Three parts in one, but all of discords framed –
> Talk not of cords, but let us now be gone,
> For with a cord Horatio was slain.
>
> (170–5)

These lines, far from being fodder for parody, anticipate the distracted but chastened Lear in his various reachings-out towards the Fool, Poor Tom, Gloucester, and Cordelia.

More immediately, they lay the groundwork for the more fully developed psychological interaction with the Painter that comprises the Fourth Addition. The latter episode, though actually inserted earlier in the text, builds on the existing model of self-production through the self-mirroring of grief and points this process towards Hieronimo's eventual revenge in fictive form. Hieronimo is here given his most authentic 'mad speech' of all, mostly in prose, and the issue of language is again foregrounded:[17] that the Painter's art finally cannot '[m]ake me curse, make me rave, make me cry . . .' (4th Add. 154–5) restates the barrier Hieronimo is about to cross, converting his unceasing nightmare ('there is no end: the end is death and madness!' [159]) into his victims' 'endless tragedy'. Meanwhile, he has cast off the presence of the self, which is *not* himself, in favour of the absence of the self, which *is* – as when the Athenian painter covered the face of Iphigenia's father.[18]

Such a principle of subjectivity remains latent in the original text, a gap to be further defined, if not filled. It is built into the allusiveness of Babel, insofar as Hieronimo thereby gestures towards the burden of unutterability. Similarly suggestive through its instability as a signifier is Hieronimo's office of Knight Marshall. It makes obvious sense to stress the judicial dimension: the Knight Marshal in England was responsible for administering justice within a twelve-mile radius of the court. But the ceremonial side of marshalship figures from the start in the perception of Hieronimo by both the court and the audience, and, as the revenge plot takes shape, this aspect comes to displace the other vitiated function of his office in his own imagination: thus he will 'here surrender up my marshalship: / For I'll go marshal up the fiends in hell' (3.12.76–7). The way out of the speechless impotence he suffers as victimized magistrate lies through the dumb-shows of conquest with which he regaled the court in Act 1 and which similarly depended, for their meaning, on the supplement of his explication. Then, too, the King was eager for that supplement – 'Hieronimo, this masque contents mine eye, / Although I sound not well the mystery' (1.4.138–9) – while Hieronimo's social and personal stability issued in full disclosure.

But if the Additions pick up and expand a concept of subjectivity latent in the original, their treatment of that element hardly makes for a neat aesthetic fit. A reading in terms of interiority developing by smooth stages – an organic growing 'inward with revenge' – is thwarted by the placement of the Painter Scene: it comes just before the '*Vindicta mihi*' soliloquy, which shows Hieronimo's identity constituted by a very different mirroring process – bracketed, one might say, between moral bookends that show him conflicting images of himself. Moreover, whatever the form of the revised theatrical script, the revisor's fabrication of a discursive subjectivity for the protagonist fundamentally conflicts with the functioning of language in the original. There the stability of the linguistic medium grounds the capacity to formulate, focus, and articulate grievance. In the supplemented text, the extreme gap between the veritable deafness of the exterior world and Hieronimo's more personal effusions problematizes communication itself. Even as his self-speaking richly extends the range of language, it builds higher the wall of linguistic isolation that surrounds him.

As a consequence, Hieronimo's keen sense of verbally turning the tables in the Fifth Addition – 'meantime I'll torture you' – takes on a metadramatic tinge, as if ultimately directed against the revisor who has forced him into such abject utterance. There is a hint of resemblance to the protest of Caliban against his self-styled benefactors: 'You taught me language, and my profit on't / Is, I know how to curse' (*Tmp.* 1.2.363–4). And it is worth noting that even as Miranda, in provoking this outburst, boasts of liberating Caliban's imprisoned self, rather as Prospero liberated Ariel from the pine-tree – 'I endow'd thy purposes / With words that made them known' (357–8) – she reveals the epistemological contingency of the signified on the signifier: 'When thou didst not, savage, / Know thine own meaning, but wouldst gabble like / A thing most brutish...' (355–6). At stake in Hieronimo's case, too, is the question of whether stable signifiers, hence the self for which speaking is a privilege, exist at all. Caliban's attempted solution is to find a new god; Hieronimo's is to take God's place and to resurrect his son, the Word re-made flesh, to preside over apocalypse.

Hieronimo's self-speaking, in both the original texts and the Additions, issues from a sense of lost paradise: 'Our hopes were stored up in him'. From this perspective, the Additions document a supplementary fall into the inadequacy of signification. This is a distinct step beyond the original conception of Hieronimo as plunged into an acute sense of his mortality, then torn between the mirror-images offered by his human and divine texts, which confront him with support and chastisement, respectively. His self-speaking remains, in effect, ventriloquized by these exterior discourses of authority, according to the dyadic structure of Lacan's imaginary register. The Additions, by contrast, involve the formation of the unconscious through speech that is Hieronimo's 'own' – that is, speech of the Other – as initiation into the symbolic order. To adapt the metaphor of the mirror to this second condition, Hieronimo now sees, not an illusion of plenitude, at once magically seductive and alienating, but Bazulto, the 'lively image of my grief', figuring the evanescent self with whom he can and cannot communicate. At the same time, the intensified intertwining of social inferiority and personal impotence in the Additions foregrounds the dependence of identity on symbolic exchange relations.

Of course, the double process of the production of subjectivity, as Lacan conceives it, is an ordinary – indeed, the quintessentially ordinary – drama, rather than the melodrama of 'death and madness'.

To account for the subsequent breakdown of subjectivity in *The Spanish Tragedy*, we may return to Lacan's attribution of psychotic discourse to the insufficient imprinting of 'the unconscious signifier linking the infant to difference – the Father's Name functioning to break up identificatory fusion with the Other' (Ragland-Sullivan 199). Actual '[p]sychotic episodes occur when the intrinsic lack of this key phallic signifier – the Name-of-the-Father – is challenged within the Symbolic order' (198) and '[m]ind ... unravels into the fragmented parts which previously functioned as a unity as long as anchored by the sense of a cohesive self' (199). Such a sense depends on the ability to 'imitate normative father/son or father/daughter Imaginary models' (198) in relations with others. In fact, the Additions, in carrying the psychological drama of Hieronimo from the imaginary register into the symbolic order, substantially develop Horatio as the key to a fragile structure of exchange relations for his father. The paradox that the son here occupies the phallic position of the *Nom du Père* suggests the instability of that structure in terms conventional for the period. A similar inversion is the precondition of Lear's madness: 'thou mad'st thy daughters thy mothers' (*Lr* 1.4.172–3).

It is, however, the insistent intertext of *Hamlet*, where the *Nom du Père* remains conspicuously tied to its presumptive origin, that points to the broader pattern. The drama of the turn of the century – with revenge tragedy provocatively in the lead – begins to portray the field of human relations as a symbolic order in which subjectivity is continually negotiated, rather than as an allegorical testing ground for humankind's moral standing *vis-à-vis* the collective superego. And as part of this shift, on the evidence of the Additions, God is effectively transformed from the straightforwardly punishing Father of the Fall, who is also the destroyer of sinful Babylon in the prophetic books, to the self-effacing and mysterious – not to say mean-spirited – catalyst of human self-alienation adumbrated in *Genesis* 11:

Also they said, Go to, let vs buylde vs a citie and a tower, whose toppe *may reach* vnto the heauen, that we may get vs a name, lest we be scatred vpon the whole earth. . . . And the Lord said, Beholde, the people *is* one, & thei all haue one language, & this thei beginne to do, nether can thei now be stopped from whatsoeuer thei haue imagined to do. Come on, let vs go downe, and there confounde their language.

(*Gen.* 11:4–7)

The very cognizance of divine intervention here, as with the super-natural framework of *The Spanish Tragedy*, is a function of dramatic irony, dependent on a cosmic perspective. And it is telling that the human offence against godhead amounts to an attempted circum-vention of the first Fall through, in effect, a 'psychic sense of whole-ness which is on the side of immortality', the getting of a 'name' *not* 'of the Father'. Thus, Derrida takes God to be 'clamant son nom, le nom propre de "confusion" qui sera sa marque et son sceau [pro-claiming his name, the fitting name / proper noun of "confusion", which will be his mark and his seal]' in order to punish the build-ers, not for simple aspiration to a heavenly height, but

> d'avoir voulu ainsi *se faire un nom*, se donner à eux-mêmes le nom, se construire eux-mêmes leur propre nom, s'y rassembler ('que nous ne soyons plus dispersés') comme dans l'unité d'un lieu qui est à la fois une langue et une tour, l'une comme l'autre. Il les punit d'avoir ainsi voulu s'assurer, d'eux-mêmes, une généalogie unique et universelle.
> [for having wanted thus *to make a name for themselves*, to give themselves the name, to construct for and by themselves their own name, to gather themselves there ('that we be no longer scattered'), as in the unity of a place which is at once a tongue and a tower, the one as (well as) the other. He punishes them for having thus wanted to assure themselves, of themselves, a unique and universal genealogy.]
>   ('Des Tours de Babel' 213; trans. Graham 169)[19]

Ultimately, Hieronimo's double usurpation of the role of God enacts the double role of God himself, which appears more clearly in light of the Additions' construction of Horatio as the repository of Hieronimo's prelapsarian 'hopes'. That such 'hopes' are as provi-dentially doomed as the efforts of the tower-builders of Babel sug-gests the ambivalence necessarily lurking in this relation ('what's a son?') – an ambivalence more evident and pressing, of course, in the father-son dynamic of *Hamlet*. Both Hamlet and Horatio are bound to let their fathers down.

The chain of signification linking the human and the divine in these terms is succinctly delineated in Lacan's revisionist analysis of the Oedipus complex, which I earlier applied to the representa-tion of the divine Father (and his enemies) in Medieval drama. It is worth citing a slightly larger extract here, so as to bring out Lacan's distinction between the real father and

le père imaginaire, le père qui l'a, lui le gosse, si mal foutu. . . . Ce
père imaginaire, c'est lui, et non pas le père réel, qui est le
fondement de l'image providentielle de Dieu. Et la fonction du
surmoi à son dernier terme, dans sa perspective dernière, est
haine de Dieu, reproche à Dieu d'avoir si mal fait les choses.
[the imaginary father, the father who has fucked the kid up. . . . It
is this imaginary father and not the real one which is the basis of
the providential image of God. And the function of the superego
in the end, from its final point of view, is hatred for God, the
reproach that God has handled things so badly.]

(*Séminaire 7* 355; trans. Porter 308)

It is when the *surmoi* collapses that God becomes maddeningly
present-absent as the presiding deity of the second fall, impossible
to hate because impossible to find – the signified that is merely
another signifier, the means of eternally deferring meaning: 'there
is no end: the end is death and madness'. The most profound contribution of the 1602 Additions to *The Spanish Tragedy* is to constitute the God that Hieronimo is driven to replace as less of a 'prick',
more of a phallus.

III

A 1988 New Historicist study by Leah S. Marcus makes room for
its proposed 'local reading' of Shakespeare by toppling the statue
of Ben Jonson's Bard 'for all time' ('To the Memory of My Beloved,
the Author Mr. William Shakespeare: and What He Hath Left Us'
43). Some version of this exercise is standard these days, but Marcus
opens up particularly useful issues by focusing her deconstructive
procedures, not on the institutionalization of Shakespeare, but on
the foundation of the institution – the First Folio of 1623, that famous
book which has authorized so many others (including, of course,
her own). Marcus exposes with fine dexterity the 'rhetorical tur-
bulence' (25) of that volume's prefatory matter, showing that the
supposedly direct route from this to the playtexts themselves – a
route signposted by Jonson's commendatory sonnet as leading to
the authorial identity behind the frontispiece 'face' ('To the Reader'
7) – is in fact a primrose path to a sort of hermeneutic hell, paved
with the intentions of generations of readers; the latter, more than

willing to 'looke / Not on his Picture but his Booke' (9–10), have superimposed mere images of themselves.

Even by thus redirecting our gaze, Marcus points out, Jonson's poem disrupts the 'mirroring or continuity between the facing pages' (18) and helps to pre-inscribe the authorial self as unstable. The point is easier to see, perhaps, when one recognizes the redeployment of the dynamic of epitaph, which conventionally deflects attention from the present-absence of the buried corpse to the absent-presence of the deceased's immortal part. Here the book is imaged as the transcendent embodiment of its author's higher being, effecting the translation into timeless Art of what might have been considered theatrical ephemera. Yet between the quasi-epitaph and the image of the dead poet, the volume's very title intervenes, as Marcus notes (19–20), in a disjunctive way. Not only does it anticipate the Table of Contents in partitioning the departed playwright's *corpus* generically ('Mr. William Shakespeares Comedies, Histories, & Tragedies'), but it also undermines its own textual authority with the oxymoronic overprotestation, 'Published according to the True Originall Copies' (19). All in all, states Marcus, 'Shakespeare . . . is an author who is simultaneously not an author in the proprietary sense that contemporaries were beginning to claim for themselves' (21).

This statement articulates a familiar New Historicist / Cultural Materialist position, founded theoretically on Foucault's historicization of authorship (especially as formulated in his influential lecture, 'Qu'est-ce qu'un auteur? [What is an Author?]'[20]) and built more or less empirically on the evident difference between the attitudes of Shakespeare and Jonson toward their dramatic writings, as well as on the problematic contemporary status of plays, players, and playing. Yet there has been a tendency to build beyond the evidence – by not merely tracing the evolution of such categories as dramatic literature, literature itself, and authorship, but actually denying their currency. To state such a case absolutely is to invite an absolutist response: Levin, the arch-sceptic when it comes to contemporary historical criticism, has had no difficulty in finding polemical ammunition here.[21] And even those more receptive to the thesis might reasonably expect its advocates to engage the complex question – productively focused by Cave, A. J. Minnis, and Thomas M. Greene,[22] amongst others – of the place of the classics (not to mention the Bible) in Medieval and Early Modern theories of imitation and communication.

More fundamentally and more problematically at stake, of course, is the issue of historical subjectivity. For these same critical schools, the valorizing of an author's book as, in effect, the index of an authentic self and repository of stable significance manifests the ideologically mandated construction of human subjectivity itself as continuous, autonomous, and centred. There are varying views of this process,[23] but they share a perception of Shakespearean characterization as transitional, featuring imperfect figurations of this 'modern' self. Still, Shakespeare is commonly held to be more or less complicit with ideology. Marcus refers to 'places where we encounter a Shakespeare every bit as captivated by the humanist enterprise as contemporaries like Ben Jonson' (40). Steven Mullaney zeroes in on the choric Gower in *Pericles* as 'an emerging figure of the author that would eventually eclipse the popular stage' and, paradoxically, 'Shakespearean dramaturgy' itself – a figure that 'occupies the place of both author and authority and seeks to legitimize the play in the way a father or a monarch legitimizes a genealogy, by authorizing it in a rather full sense of the term' (148–9).

I will defer my response to this reading of Shakespeare's Gower, in whom I have a longstanding critical interest,[24] but it is opportune to note here that, given the fourteenth-century poet behind (hence within) that invention, Mullaney has hit on particularly cogent evidence that, even with regard to English authors, authorship was not an early seventeenth-century addition to the cultural register. Chaucer's commendation of his *Troilus and Criseyde* to 'moral Gower' (5.1856) unequivocally amalgamates the man and his *oeuvre*, thereby constructing the former in terms of the latter but also indirectly confirming, perhaps, the judgement of Minnis that 'whereas Gower was interested in presenting himself as a "modern author", Chaucer was not' (209).[25] Yet Chaucer himself, incidentally, thereby takes responsibility, and asserts propriety, of an authorial kind, even while practising the deference to *auctoritas* ubiquitous in Medieval literature.[26] (For the latter rhetorical technique, of course, need not be simply deferential – even where the appeal is to the divine word itself, as the Wife of Bath illustrates.) To return to Gower, we should not forget that the *Confessio Amantis* not only foregrounds the process of authorship, as do dream-visions generally, but depicts the very production of an authorial self ('John Gower') out of the ruined identity of a failed lover ('Amans') – a point reinforced by the Latin commentary on the poem in numerous manuscripts (Minnis 188–90).

Gower demonstrably came to Shakespeare authorized 'in a rather full sense' by the edition of the *Confessio Amantis* first published in 1532 by T. Berthelette, whose dedication to King Henry VIII lays claim to exalted status for the book, its author, and, implicitly, its editor. The volume is a conscious contribution to a burgeoning English literary tradition, and Berthelette holds up Gower as a stylistic model for current authors, advising them similarly to cultivate a native, as opposed to a foreign, vocabulary:

> The whiche if any man wante, let hym resorte to this worthy olde writer *Iohn Gower*, that shal as a lanterne giue him lighte to write cunningly.
>
> (sig. *iiv)

Jonson, then, is hardly implementing an epistemic revolution when his Pallas invokes Gower (with Chaucer, Lydgate, and Spenser) as a patron of artistic revival in *The Golden Age Restored* (1615).

If an idea of authorship broadly consistent with the 'humanist enterprise' substantially predates the First Folio, what does this mean for the much more elusive question of subjectivity? I propose that a range of Shakespeare's plays, virtually spanning his career, deploy the products and, to a lesser extent, the processes, of authorship in ways that implicate subjectivity in a nexus of slippery signification, betokening instability. This pattern might be grist to the New Historicist / Cultural Materialist mill, except that the theatrical effects communicating such instability patently depend on the subversion of the contrary assumption. And on the level of characterization, this implies the pre-existence of 'centred' selves – however 'self-fashioned' – to be decentred. But then Greenblatt's formulation carries no implication that Early Modern individuals failed to invest the identities they constructed – for which, as he himself shows (and as Maus has emphasized), they sometimes died in fact as well as fiction – with a sense of interiority. Indeed, the tendency of characters to gain an inward dimension when self-fashioning is foregrounded – Othello, in Greenblatt's own treatment of him (*Self-Fashioning* 232–52), makes a signal instance – suggests an intimate alliance between interiority and the very role-playing that can obscure it.

In the following survey of what might be termed 'authorial occasions' in Shakespeare, I seek to demonstrate that the plays themselves, in their capacity to disrupt forms of textual authority, including the authority of the self as text, anticipate Marcus's approach to their first collected edition, as well as the broader poststructuralist challenge to the traditional privileging of speech – as represented by spoken dialogue – over writing. In the process, moreover, these texts deploy modes of reflection far less stable than is suggested by the phrase, 'mirroring or continuity'. Finally, because the effects I have identified depend very much on staging, the result may be to recuperate more of the 'Shakespearean dramaturgy' associated with the 'popular stage', to return to Mullaney's formulation, than is accessible to a criticism whose primary concern is, after all, with the demolition of a monument.

IV

Before turning to authorship destabilized, I should stipulate that the literary work as fixed signifier and source of trustworthy revelation is available even within early Shakespearean texts – and in forms that take the concept for granted. In documenting the cultural momentum of the classical tradition of 'The Book as Symbol', Curtius (332–40) assembles a number of instances, including several combining the motif of the mirror. The most graphic – literally – representation invokes the 'king of rhetoric' (Curtius 334): in *Titus Andronicus*, Lavinia's writing in the sand glosses Ovid's account of Tereus and Philomel to explicate her own pitiable metamorphosis.[27] Equally telling is a metaphorical strand prominent in *Romeo and Juliet*. In asking her daughter to '[r]ead o'er the volume of young Paris' face' (1.3.81), then concluding, 'This precious book of love, this unbound lover, / To beautify him, only lacks a cover' (87–8), Lady Capulet fuses the mediating role of wife with the notion of the book as radiating virtuous influence. Recognizing that commonplace is necessary to appreciating her hollow use of it: insofar as he is a book, Paris is envisaged less as a profound treatise than as something to adorn the Capulet coffee table. Thence the metaphor enters into the play's broad movement from *auctoritas* to *experientia*. A transitional moment is Juliet's comment when Romeo usurps Paris's place on the shelf: 'You kiss by th' book' (1.5.110). But the future direction has already been indicated by the Capulet Servant's naturally witty riposte to Romeo's witticism:

Servant . . . I pray, sir, can you read?
Romeo   Ay, mine own fortune in my misery.
Servant Perhaps you have learn'd it without book.

                                        (1.2.57–9)

Finally, it is worth adding that Warwick's attempt to comfort Henry IV, cited earlier in this chapter, opposes history as continuously (re)written to the king's transcendentally authoritative 'book of fate' (*2H4* 3.1.45). The absence looming through the latter sign of presence is precisely the point.

Ironically, author-centred critical practices have muted the repercussions of the two Shakespearean moments at which authorship is most strikingly highlighted as an issue – by being withheld. In the virtually contemporaneous *Hamlet* and *Troilus and Cressida*, a central character's on-stage reading of a book precipitates an encounter involving duplicity, double-talk, and a disappearing author. In Act 2, Scene 2, Hamlet responds to Polonius' query about his book's 'matter' (193) with mystifying and insulting '[w]ords, words, words' (192); in Act 3, Scene 3, of *Troilus and Cressida*, Ulysses baits Achilles into asking the same question, then expounds his unnamed 'author' (113) so as to expose the precarious transience of reputation and introduce his feigning praise of Ajax. Generations of scholars have risen to the same bait, effectively pressing the questions of Polonius and Achilles by proposing candidates for authorship. Given the inconclusive results, criticism has now largely stopped trying to read the titles on the props. Still, these scenes – and, for *Hamlet*, the 1603 Quarto's indication that the protagonist again enters reading before the Act 3, Scene 1, soliloquy – plausibly authorize *some* book as at least a shaping intellectual influence. The work most persistently so identified in both cases over many years is the *Essais* of Montaigne, especially in Florio's 1603 translation.[28]

In the absence of a theory of intertextuality, such approaches have had to follow the rules of evidence for the study of source and influence. These rules equally compelled John M. Robertson, speaking in 1909 of the idea Ulysses terms 'familiar' (3.3.113), to 'admit that Shakespeare may well have met with it elsewhere than in Montaigne' (102) and Robert Ellrodt, in a 1975 article focusing on innovative self-consciousness in Montaigne and Shakespeare, to rebut Hardin Craig's case (of forty-one years earlier) that 'Cardan's *De Consolatione*, not Montaigne's *Essays*, was Hamlet's book' (Ellrodt 40).[29] From a contemporary theoretical perspective, the very discourse centred on Montaigne's influence may be taken as producing significant intertextual (co-)presence, which in turn throws into relief the indeterminacy – obstinately in conflict with the physical object on stage – that is archly signalled by Hamlet and Ulysses themselves: the former identifies his author only as a 'satirical rogue' (2.2.196), the latter as a 'strange fellow' (3.3.95). These impositions of anonymity intervene between the cited texts and their authority – manipulatively, for the on-stage interlocutors; 'ungrammatically', for the audience.[30] Analogous sites of intertextuality thus redefine the common ground occupied by Hamlet and Ulysses as manipulators of language, meaning, and identity.

Both plays deploy multiple figurations of textuality in foregrounding the issue of control over words in relation to action and inaction. The books carried by Hamlet and Ulysses are emblematic of secret scripts those characters are attempting to impose on their playworlds, hence of their engagement with competing scenarios. The 'method' in Hamlet's 'madness' (2.2.205–6) directly flows from his inscription of the Ghost's directive '[w]ithin the book and volume of my brain' (1.5.103) and of his uncle's smiling villainy in his 'tables' (107). Ulysses is implementing the scheme previously hatched with Nestor for shaming Achilles into action. More openly applied in both cases is the traditional function of the book – accurately termed 'satirical' by Hamlet – of mirroring defective 'truth' beneath a deceptive appearance.[31] On this level, the contemptuous image of an old man with which Hamlet twits Polonius matches Ulysses' portrayal of human beings as dependent upon 'reflection' (3.3.99) for self-knowledge, with the insinuation that Achilles is no longer what he thinks he is.[32] The two manipulators use their texts, then, as Hamlet urges the Players to act theirs – that is, so as to 'hold as 'twere the mirror up to nature: to show virtue her feature, scorn her own image . . .' (3.2.22–3).

As Grabes has pointed out, beyond the mirror's function in Medieval and Renaissance symbology as a stable didactic signifier, projecting an ideal or minatory image, lies the destabilizing menace of the 'lack of fixed identity in the reflection as compared with the object mirrored' (109). Holding a mirror up to others implies a power to reveal and expose while keeping the self inviolate; self-fashioning, however, requires turning the mirror round, and when one does, signification is at once intensely focused and loosed into free-play by the image-shattering 'fact that the mirror has no image of its own' (111). This is potentially to step beyond the looking-glass of the first Lacanian fall – beyond, that is, what Goldin figures as Narcissus' painful discovery of an interior *moi* (31). On the contrary, what the mirror, in its brittle and varying two-dimensionality, threatens to reflect is the self-beholder's evanescence, Lacan's aphanitic subjectivity. Hamlet's struggle to control textual signification is the struggle to keep the mirror turned outward – 'up to nature' – because what he actually sees in the mirror, like the book he keeps *to himself*, is indeterminate, the image of an image and thus of an absence.[33] On this point, Freedman, tracing psychoanalytic ramifications of 'the gaze' and cognizant that 'Shakespeare constructs self-conscious characters by having them refer to an unseen space within' (29), reveals what she herself would call a 'blind spot': when she credits Hamlet with 'awareness that [his] lack merely serves as a trap for others' (75), she occludes her own Lacanian premise: '"Man . . . is an other for himself"' (53).

The Mousetrap seems even more aptly named when it is recognized as imaging the conflicted nature of textual mirroring for Hamlet. His indeterminate re-authorizing of *The Murther of Gonzago* is no straight reflection of the Ghost-written text he purports to reproduce – evidence against Goldberg's conclusion from this and the play's other 'scriptive gestures' (311) that 'there is no notion of human character save as a locus of inscription' (316). Claudius may see his crime truly portrayed, but the reading of the other courtiers is inaccessible, while for Hamlet to 'know' his 'course' (2.2.598) reinscribes his difficulty in following it. Hence, his subsequent confrontation with Gertrude takes an ironic and inconclusive turn, from his proposal to 'set you up a glass / Where you may see the inmost part of you' (3.4.19–20) – and in his view, the images of the two kings drive home his point – to his apparent 'ecstasy' (138), which shows him to her in a frighteningly ambiguous light. She, not only he, is now seeing double.

By this point, Act 3, Scene 1, has already suggested, in moving from the 'To be, or not to be' (55) soliloquy to the 'nunnery' encounter, that Hamlet is less in alignment with his own script than is Ophelia with the prayer-book thrust into her hands for deceptive purposes; by the end she is praying in earnest: 'O, help him, you sweet heavens' (3.1.133); 'Heavenly powers, restore him!' (141). When Hamlet first attempts to interpolate himself, as 'fallen' intertext, into Ophelia's presumptive translinguistic communion with God ('Nymph, in thy orisons / Be all my sins remmb'red' [3.1.88–9]), he collides with 'remembrances' that she has 'longed long to redeliver' (92–3) – the mirror-image of a now unacceptable self. His counterattack is in kind, turning the mirror back on her with an image of herself as all women, presuming to re-write the book of created nature: 'God hath given you one face, and you make yourselves another' (143–4). But then even Yorick's skull is uneasily under Hamlet's control as such a mirror: 'let [my lady] paint an inch thick, to this favor she must come' (5.1.193–4). It first shows him an image of the futility of desire: 'Here hung those lips that I have kiss'd I know not how oft' (5.1.188–9).

Among the much-discussed mechanisms by which the character of Hamlet is endowed with its illusion of interiority, Burns has recently included Hamlet's (Act 2) book, observing that '[r]eading is one way of presenting interiority, or at least contemplation, on stage' (146).[34] What seems to have escaped notice is that the indeterminacy of that book, coupled with Hamlet's would-be use of it as a satirical mirror, entails self-production through self-evasion. This point emerges more clearly in contrast with a notable antecedent of Shakespeare's scene, mentioned earlier – the soliloquized deliberations over revenge of Hieronimo, who enters 'with a book in his hand' (Kyd 3.13.1 s.d.) – and with one in his head as well. The pre-inscribed Biblical prohibition, '*Vindicta mihi!*' (3.13.1), is countered by Seneca's tragedies.[35] Such 'contemplation' is far from being 'interiority' on the order of Shakespeare's figure. The double-binding of Hieronimo book*ends* the self between potent presences, rendering it doubly present.

The absence figured by Hamlet's book is one that, anticipating liberal-humanist critics, the character himself strives to fill over the course of the play – and with no greater success. The pattern is introduced in Hamlet's initial exchange with the Queen, when he opposes *being* – 'that within which passes show' (1.2.85) – to *seeming*: the 'forms, moods, shapes of grief' that cannot 'denote me truly' (82–3); thereafter 'that within' remains an excessive emptiness. Continually, in both dialogue and soliloquy, he works at 'self-fashioning', most obviously when he measures himself against Horatio, Fortinbras, and especially Laertes: 'by the image of my cause / I see the portraiture of his' (5.2.77–8) – wishful thinking, given that 'to make true diction' of Laertes, 'his semblable is his mirror, and who else would trace him, his umbrage, nothing more' (118–20). This last statement of Hamlet is picked up by Lacan, who, however, skews its most distinctive feature: it is not strictly true that 'Laertes is for Hamlet his double' ('Desire' 31), but rather that

Hamlet wants him to be, and that he projects upon Laertes a fantasy of perfect self-reflection within seamless – hence sutured – signification, *making* him 'true diction' (albeit at the safe distance of parody).[36] Yet for Hamlet, even to constitute himself as inadequate by comparison is to *remember* the Ghost together with his own fragmented identity: 'I am very sorry, good Horatio, / That to Laertes I forgot myself' (5.2.75–6). Non-comparative messages of deficiency are safer, even to be embraced: 'Do you not come your tardy son to chide . . . ?' (3.4.106 ff.); mere deficiency implies presence, the potential for coherence through the supplementarity that is the function of the Ghost-as-sign – until it fades into the signified of revenge.

Such an enfolding of deferral within avowed deficiency is also the business of the 'antic disposition', which simultaneously projects non-deficiency from behind the satirical reflection of a 'time . . . out of joint' (1.5.188). Yet this posture also opens up a space within which the self drops out of its own sight, where action is not deferred but made impossible. Hamlet's '[w]ords, words, words' ultimately announce less his mediation of the text that is his prop than the failure of texts to escape from mediation – a failure of which he is the most immediate victim. In Felman's reading, 'the tragedy stems from the *act of swearing* to which the ghost commits Hamlet' (95–6); hence, the very discourse that projects (and defers) the act of revenge would be 'always already'[37] inscribed within the collapse of the 'opposition between . . . matter and language' (94). Finally, Hamlet *cannot* answer Polonius' question about 'the matter that you read' (2.2.195), for, to adapt Beaujour, 'le Livre qui le contient (et qu'il contient en puissance) n'est plus à son tour qu'un livre parmi les autres livres [the Book that contains him (and that he potentially contains) is no more in its turn than one book amongst others]' (286). If '*Il n'y a pas de hors-texte* [*There is nothing that is not part of the text*]',[38] as Derrida famously affirms / denies (*De la grammatologie* 227), it is equally true that 'Il n'y a pas de *Livre* [There is no *Book*]' (Beaujour 286).[39]

To apply more specifically Lacan's theory of subject formation, Hamlet's successive mirror-images remain within the field of the Other, inevitably contained within the sphere of Meaning (Hamlet would say 'seeming') and enforcing the aphanisis of Being.[40] And, as Paul Smith observes, 'Exactly *between* the field of the "subject" and the field of the Other, and imbricated into both, is the unconscious' (71). The limitation of traditional – including traditional psychoanalytic – criticism has been to look for Hamlet's unconscious in his being – that is, to look for it at all. Yet much New Historicism / Cultural Materialism denies that the character possesses subjectivity because he never gets beyond seeming, failing to reach a 'promised essence', as Francis Barker puts it, that 'remains beyond the scope of the text's signification' because it is the property of 'a historical order whose outline has so far only been sketched out' (37). And from a rhetorical angle, even as the perception of a 'crisis in language, a divorce of "is" and "seems"' conjures the spirit of Lacan, Burns comes to the similar conclusion that 'Hamlet has no . . . innerness to, in a romantic sense, "write out of"' (8). One may surely deplore, with Belsey (*Tragedy* 48–9), the tendency of 'humanist critics' to occlude Lacanian gaps between Hamlet's two 'I's' (of the speaking subject and the subject of speech), while recognizing that the very existence of such a gap – of which Hamlet is intensely if intermittently aware – implicates Lacan's definition of 'modern' subjectivity.[41]

This brings us back to the dominant intertext bearing on Hamlet's self-consciousness and self-questioning. It is highly pertinent that Montaigne figured prominently in intellectual circles at the time as a revolutionary kind of author, whose constant subject was his own inconstant subjectivity and whose method was an innovative form of self-speaking. Yet even Dollimore's approach to the *Essais* as subverting essential selfhood (*Radical Tragedy* 173–4) effectively reauthorizes the familiar Hamlet trapped between conflicting images of man: the 'beauty of the world' *versus* the 'quintessence of dust' (2.2.307–8).[42] Closer to the contours of the play's de-authorizing procedures are recent psychoanalytically informed readings of Montaigne, especially Philippe Desan's re-application of Cave, by way of Lacan, to argue that 'the Self lies not with Montaigne but instead in the interaction *between* Montaigne and the Other' (226) – that is, in an ongoing dynamic of exchange.[43] Key to Desan's analysis is the mirror-image, which figures throughout the *Essais* as a means of expressing, not self-fashioning, which implies a fixed model, but self-(re)production through interactive imagining.[44] Apparently developing Cave's perception that 'the circling movement of the subject back towards itself as object is refracted by the endless variety of topics . . . to which it can be attached' (274), Desan proposes 'an infinite play (*je-u*) between mirrors placed around Montaigne, a succession of doublings always modified and deformed by other mirrors' that 'gives the illusion of movement' (227). And it especially matches *Hamlet* that Desan singles out the book as one important form of mirror. Montaigne himself saw the proliferating texts of his day as imaging each other, deferring signification: 'Il y a plus affaire à interpreter les interpretations qu'à interpreter les choses, et plus de livres sur les livres que sur autre subject: nous ne faisons que nous entregloser [There's more adoe to enterpret interpretations, than to interpret things: and more bookes upon bookes, then upon any other subject. We doe but enter-glose our selves]'. This passage is followed, moreover, by a distinction that highlights the fading (hence the pre-existence) of authorship itself: 'Tout fourmille de commentaires; d'auteurs, il en est grand cherté [All swarmeth with commentaries: Of Authors their is great penury]' (3:316; trans. Florio 3:327).

Yet to recognize such intersections between Hamlet and Montaigne is also to run up against a fundamental disjunction. The self-writing practised by Montaigne is liberating in its infinite self-productivity. That the process in the 'prison' (2.2.242) of Denmark has an antithetical ambiance (coded as 'melancholy') and trajectory (coded as 'tragedy') focuses Hamlet's lack of freedom to re-create himself. He remains, if not the mere 'echoing' letter (Goldberg 313), certainly the creature, of his father's text, which, since he lacks Claudius' compartmentalizing capacity to 'think on him / Together with *remembrance* of ourselves' (1.2.6–7), he is bound to reinscribe upon those representations of the Other in which he seeks himself. I mean 'creature' here in its Medieval sense, including an obligation to regard the self in the natural mirror furnished by the divine Father. Because Hamlet cannot allow his book to be indeterminate, its insistent indeterminacy transforms the field of Meaning into a nightmare landscape of the meaningless.

By comparison, Ulysses appears eminently in control of the indeterminate text he incorporates into his script. He may seem more like *Hamlet*'s Ghost, having the power to precipitate others into self-doubt while remaining aloof. Yet the undercutting of Ulysses' authority begins with his famous sermon on order in the play's third scene. The traditional enlistment of the so-called 'degree' speech (1.3.75 ff.) on behalf of 'The Elizabethan World Picture' at least distorted its emphasis: of sixty-three lines, only ten (85–94) depict the functioning of 'degree'; the rest pursue – and are pursued by – the ramifications of its absence.[45] Ulysses' image of the chaos precariously kept at bay ('Take but degree away . . .' [109]) inscribes the futility of a belief in order, so powerfully does it envisage 'being' as contingent. Again, the emblematic mirror held up to nature turns on its (be)holder with an image of dissolving identity and meaning:

> Force should be right, or rather, right and wrong
> (Between whose endless jar justice resides)
> Should lose their names, and so should justice too!
> Then every thing include itself in power,
> Power into will, will into appetite,
> And appetite, an universal wolf
> (So doubly seconded with will and power),
> Must make perforce an universal prey,
> And last eat up himself.
>
> (116–24)

That Ulysses is effectively proposing to reverse the identities of Achilles and Ajax confirms that, whatever his intended final version of the world, such a vision represents his working copy. Already, he joins the other instruments by which the play extends its deconstructive satire to the ideals of honour and love – the soul and heart of the idea of universal harmony.

Ulysses' exploitation of the authority of the 'strange fellow''s book ultimately negates all authority. The process of getting Achilles to question not just his self-image but the substance behind it begins with the commonplace that a person '[c]annot make boast to have that which he hath, / Nor feels not what he owes, but by reflection' (3.3.98–9). The formulation is provocative and slippery, touching on the problematic nature of selfhood but allowing the implication to be deflected. This Achilles does by refocusing the remark on the physical principle that 'speculation turns not to itself, / Till it hath travell'd and is mirror'd there / Where it may see itself' (109–11). He presumes an originating essence, with mirror-imaging its reliable guarantor. Ulysses is thereby cued to expound his 'author's drift' (113) by developing subjectivity as actually contingent on the *forming* power of reflection:

> . . . no man is the lord of any thing,
> Though in and of him there be much consisting,
> Till he communicate his parts to others;
> Nor doth he of himself know them for aught,
> Till he behold them formed in th' applause
> Where th' are extended.
>
> (115–20)

It remains only to destabilize the reflective process itself with the picture of 'these Grecian lords' who 'clap the lubber Ajax on the shoulder, / As if his foot were on brave Hector's breast' (138–40), and the bleak relativism of the 'degree' speech virtually recreates itself. Even the imagery of unruly appetite reappears, first cannibal-istically – 'How one man eats into another's pride' (136) – then in the famous lines extending the *tempus edax* motif to self-production:

> Time hath, my lord, a wallet at his back,
> Wherein he puts alms for oblivion,
> A great-siz'd monster of ingratitudes.
> These scraps are good deeds past, which are devour'd
> As fast as they are made, forgot as soon
> As done.
>
> (145–50)

This is far from Humanist ideas of enduring glory, farther yet from the Medieval schema whereby Good Deeds goes into the grave with Everyman. The satirical mirror-book held up to Achilles dis-gorges intimations of the futility of all projects, including Ulysses' own. To perceive this undercurrent is to make better sense of his failure.[46] After all, only the death of Patroclus will make Achilles take the field, and when he does, his hunger for vengeance will mark him, not as regathered into the sheep-fold of order, but as the 'universal wolf' incarnate.

Achilles' slaughter of Hector will in turn engender a retributive counter-force, as Troilus converts his despair at losing Cressida into '[h]ope of revenge' (5.10.31). This process redounds again, though less directly, upon Ulysses' imperfect mediation of his indeter-minate book. It highlights Troilus' superior control of texts – chiefly the text of his own tragic love-story. When he receives Cressida's letter, Troilus withholds the contents from both Pandarus and the audience, reprising Hamlet's exchange with Polonius: 'Words, words, mere words, no matter from the heart' (5.3.108). He thereby finishes stripping Cressida's subjectivity and consolidates his self-fashioning as love's faithful martyr. I have explored elsewhere the process whereby the passive Troilus acquires power metadramat-ically[47] – to the point of deferring his death at Achilles' hands, which is part of the story. Ulysses is effectively coopted in that project: it is he who transmits Aeneas' encomium of Troilus as Troy's 'second hope' (4.5.109), who interprets the 'language' (55) of Cressida's body as duplicitous, and who guides Troilus in the night scene (5.2) where Troilus so readily confirms that reading. In a textual milieu where 'every thing include[s] itself in power', Ulysses plays second fiddle, even if he finally gets to play it while Troy burns. Ulysses, like Hamlet, is condemned to succeed despite himself – that is, despite self-lack.

V

Given that *Hamlet* and *Troilus and Cressida* notoriously mark a relativistic turn in the depiction of character (and much else) in Shakespearean drama – in keeping with the dramatist's 'discovery' of Montaigne, according to a venerable strain of speculation – it is easy to neglect prior associations of indeterminate reading or writing with the destabilizing of identity. The slightly earlier *Julius Caesar* and the much earlier *Richard III* (usually dated 1592–3) offer further instances, which, though somewhat more transient and oblique, similarly depend on theatrical business to subvert a presumption of authorship as at once disclosing, containing, and validating meaning. They also, however, throw into relief, as a distinctive element uniting Hamlet and Ulysses, the latter characters' would-be manipulation of the authorial function – and effective hoisting with their own textual petards.

Julius Caesar presents identity-formation in particularly clear terms of authority *versus* experience. The intellectual allegiances of both Brutus and Cassius enter into a shifting and problematic relation to the action. And while in this respect as in others Cassius is simplistic, he is so in a way that calls into question, if not Brutus's sophistication, at least its practical and ethical value. The crude ironies framing Cassius' premature suicide (based as it is on a false reading of events) begin with his abandonment of a materialist mentor in the face of adversity: 'You know that I held Epicurus strong, / And his opinion; now I change my mind, / And partly credit things that do presage' (5.1.76–8). An Elizabethan audience would presumably have discerned the clouds of providential punishment gathering over Cassius' rather weak head. He was bound to be let down by his Epicureanism, a self-serving and dangerously atheistical stance. Yet in the event, ironically, he would have been better off sticking to his sceptical guns.

Plutarch, in his *Life* of Brutus, actually makes Cassius 'somewhat comfort and quiet Brutus' (117) with Epicurean scepticism after the latter encounters the ghost. Shakespeare takes pains to maintain the contrast with the more respectable Stoicism of Brutus. In the same conversation, the latter outlook, doubly demonstrated over Portia's death in the previous scene, is reaffirmed in a fulsome repudiation of suicide:

> Even by the rule of that philosophy
> By which I did blame Cato for the death
> Which he did give himself – I know not how,
> But I do find it cowardly and vile,
> For fear of what might fall, so to prevent
> The time of life – arming myself with patience
> To stay the providence of some high powers
> That govern us below.
>
> (100–7)

Yet it takes a mere reminder of the possible alternative to drive Brutus into pompous evasion – 'Think not, thou noble Roman, / That ever Brutus will go bound to Rome; / He bears too great a mind' (110–12) – and, finally, it is precisely Cato's course and rationale that he limply falls back on: 'I shall have glory by this losing day / More than Octavius and Mark Antony / By this vile conquest shall attain unto' (5.5.36–8). Thus the Epicurean and the Stoic, having joined in the same doubtful enterprise, come to analogously self-deceptive ends – the more conspicuously because of Antony's posthumous distinction between them. And they do so in almost the same terms: Cassius' superstition and despair, which vitiate his philosophy as they warp his vision, culminate in the apostrophe, 'Caesar, thou art reveng'd, / Even with the sword that kill'd thee' (5.2.45–6); Brutus cites the appearances of Caesar's ghost, over Volumnius' objections, as evidence that his 'hour has come' (5.5.20).

Supernatural manifestations are, of course, a standard code for the operations of conscience. Yet on this basis, one can redistinguish between Cassius and Brutus. The latter's encounters with the spectre, which Cassius never actually sees, problematize the logic of self-vindictiveness. The ghost's very identity is enfolded into Brutus's subjectivity when it names itself (as in Plutarch [116]) 'Thy evil spirit' (4.3.282), thereby engaging the Lacanian principle that doubt 'renvoie au "malin génie", à l'Autre trompeur [refers to the "evil genius", to the deceitful Other]' (Cottet 20).[48] Moreover, Brutus's confrontation with this figure is associated with an unidentified book – a contrast with the text's explicitness about authors elsewhere.

Shakespeare foregrounds, with mingled specificity and indeterminacy, the background remark of Plutarch that Brutus often read 'some booke' (116) at night when in the field.[49] This element is evocatively combined with the 'sleepy tune' (4.3.267) of Lucius and the flickering taper (Plutarch's 'litle light' [116]), yet it is also made more than merely atmospheric. Brutus had impatiently missed a particular book, which he finds unexpectedly:

> Look, Lucius, here's the book I sought for so;
> I put it in the pocket of my gown.
> *Lucius* I was sure your lordship did not give it me.
> *Brutus* Bear with me, good boy, I am much forgetful.
> (252–5)

To remember, as in *Hamlet*, is to have one's text again, to re-collect oneself. But what text (and therefore what self) is it? Brutus turns to the volume with eager expectancy: 'Let me see, let me see; is not the leaf turn'd down / Where I left reading? Here it is, I think' (273–4). In a double sense, he appears anxious to find his *place*. But what he finds, or what finds him, is not the reassuring authority of a ideal image, or even its counterpart – outright accusation – but rather a destabilizing image of himself in the field of the Other, the mirror turned round upon him. And the medium is the message; the spectre merely comes '[t]o tell thee thou shalt see me at Philippi' (283).

This is the indeterminate text that will come between Brutus and his philosophy, as befits the long-standing entanglement of his subjectivity with his 'reading' of Caesar. Brutus's initial image of himself as cleanly divided along ethical lines – 'with himself at war' (1.2.46) – is cunningly destabilized by Cassius in an anticipation of Ulysses:

> Tell me, good Brutus, can you see your face?
> *Brutus* No, Cassius; for the eye sees not itself
> But by reflection, by some other things.
> *Cassius* 'Tis just,
> And it is very much lamented, Brutus,
> That you have no such mirrors as will turn
> Your hidden worthiness into your eye,
> That you might see your shadow.
> (51–8)

The result is a potent intimation of aphanitic subjectivity: 'Into what dangers would you lead me, Cassius, / That you would have me seek into myself / For that which is not in me?' (63–5). The act of assassination seductively promises to restore the ethical perspective, to re-project Caesar outside the self, where he belongs, then to seal this determinate text with the ultimate closure: 'As Caesar lov'd me, I weep for him; as he was fortunate, I rejoice at it; as he was valiant, I honor him; but, as he was ambitious, I slew him' (3.2.24–7). We may usefully reinvoke Felman, especially her observation that 'it is precisely from the *breach in knowledge* (the break in the constative) that the act takes its performative *power*: it is the very *knowledge that cannot know itself*' – Lacan's definition of the unconscious – 'that, in man, *acts*' (96). For Brutus, then, the ghost means not merely self-division, as with Cassius, caught squarely between materialist tenets and a conscience projected as Caesar's wrath, but self-fragmentation, the evanescence of meaning, identity, and authority. From this perspective, Brutus's suicide ironically anticipates Shakespeare's later portrayal of that of Antony, driven to render himself invisible because he is unable to 'hold this visible shape' (*Ant.* 4.14.14) – the ultimate fulfilment of the Soothsayer's perception that in the presence of Octavius Caesar, 'thy angel / Becomes a fear' (2.3.22–3).

д ?

Thus to open up Brutus's conscience into his unconscious is to recognize the ghost, who in effect emerges from the unknown book, as producing subjectivity by the same mirroring processes experienced by Richard II at Pomfret and deployed by Montaigne. But as in *Hamlet* and *Troilus and Cressida*, and in contrast with the unkinged Richard, the pull of the overdetermined countertext – Brutus's self-fashioned (if self-contradictory) identity as philosopher-cum-man-of-action – is strong, and it pulls away from continued self-production. Once Brutus has 'taken heart' (4.3.287), the spirit vanishes, according to standard ghostly procedure: parallels include Banquo at Macbeth's feast, Hamlet's father in the closet scene. Yet the protagonists in these latter cases know very well what is being conveyed to them, and the sooner the spirit leaves, the better they like it. Brutus alone wishes to pursue the matter – but abstractly and ambivalently: 'Ill spirit, I would hold more talk with thee' (288). It is thus, perhaps, that transference impels the subject of psychoanalysis, especially if one considers, with Lacan, that, paradoxically, '[l]e transfert est le moyen par où s'interrompt la communication de l'inconscient, par où l'inconscient se referme [transference is the means whereby the communication of the unconscious is inter-rupted, whereby the unconscious closes up again]' (*Séminaire 11* 119; *Concepts* 130). Brutus's wish is, necessarily, a function of only part of himself, and to pursue it would mean precisely recognizing the self in parts. In short, the condition of engagement would be to *lose* heart, the self-centre that slips through Hamlet's verbal fingers even as he invokes it: 'my heart's core . . . my heart of heart' (*Ham.* 3.2.73).

The brief remainder of the scene displays in swift steps Brutus's reversion from indeterminate subjectivity into action – action not externally imposed upon him, as in Richard II's case. (Hamlet's final recourse to action falls between these two precedents – at once externally and self-imposed). As he earlier projected his misplacing of the book, Brutus projects his own disturbing vision upon Lucius – 'Didst thou dream, Lucius, that thou so criedst out?' (294–5) – then throws himself into preparations for the fateful battle. Perhaps most significantly, he fails to soliloquize. Verbal mirrors too, he has now learnt *by experience*, may produce disturbing reflections.

A focus on subjectivity somewhat mitigates the irony that the supernatural experience of the most idealistic political usurper in Shakespeare is modelled on that of the most cynical. A striking precursor of Brutus's concern to find and read his unidentified book is Richard III's reiterated call for writing materials as he retires on the night before Bosworth field – a detail unprecedented in the sources and analogues. As in Brutus's case, there are two pointed interventions of the motif – 'Give me some ink and paper' (5.3.49) and 'Is ink and paper ready?' (75) – separated by signals of pro-found unease.[50] Still, that unease so far remains nebulous – a liminal state never experienced by the conscience-stricken King in *The True Tragedy of Richard III*, straightforwardly haunted by purely imagin-ary ghosts (1872 ff.). Shakespeare's as-yet-unshaken villain seems more likely to be preparing orders for his troops than about to pen his part in *The Mirror for Magistrates*. The point, however, is that no explanation is provided. His writing is as indeterminate as Brutus's reading, and it leads (with the help of a bowl of wine) into a simi-larly animated sleep.

The motif of the mirror is insistently present in the play, both intertextually – through elements shared with the *Mirror* itself[51] – and explicitly, in helping to mark Richard's political project as a project also of self-construction.[52] The irony of his opening declara-tion that he is 'not shap'd for sportive tricks / Nor made to court an amorous looking-glass' (1.1.14–15), so that he has no pastime 'Unless to see my shadow in the sun / And descant on mine own deformity' (26–7), is developed in his gloating gloss on the wooing of Anne:

> I do mistake my person all this while!
> Upon my life, she finds (although I cannot)
> Myself to be a marv'llous proper man.
> I'll be at charges for a looking-glass,
> And entertain a score or two of tailors
> To study fashions to adorn my body
> . . . .
> Shine out, fair sun, till I have bought a glass,
> That I may see my shadow as I pass.
> (1.2.252–63)

Richard mocks Anne for reflecting an image of him that he knows to be false, but the mockery equally serves to keep at bay the false-ness of any definite image. After all, his murder of Henry VI was most immediately triggered by that king's scornful portrayal of Richard's birth as a dentally precocious 'indigested and deformed lump' (*3H6* 5.6.51); in striking Henry down, he smashes a mirror as surely as does Richard II, although for him self-fashioning is just beginning, not at an end. He also, with a blow of the knife, converts dialogue into soliloquy, and his villainous identity, with its assertion of self-sufficiency, now first emerges in explicit terms of not-likeness:

> I have no brother, I am like no brother;
> And this word 'love', which greybeards call divine,
> Be resident in men like one another,
> And not in me: I am myself alone.
> (80–3)

The sense of Richard's self-conscious wickedness as a flight from subjectivity's middle-ground, of his vaunted shape-changing ('I can add colors to the chameleon, / Change shapes with Proteus for advantages' [*3H6* 3.2.191–2]) as an attempt to preempt the mirror's fracturing power – to outrun his shadow – lays the groundwork for the tormented soliloquy produced by his encounter with the ghosts. As recently as his pleading with Queen Elizabeth for her daughter's hand in Act 4, Scene 4, he has dared to swear 'by myself', while the angry rejoinder that cuts him off in mid-line, 'Thyself is self-misus'd' (374), has, in a familiar way, proved grist to his self-imaging mill;[53] despite the gathering clouds that herald the fulfilment of curses, he has even risked one upon himself in affirming his love: 'Myself myself confound!' (399). This time, however, he conspicuously deludes himself in supposing that the 'villain' has successfully counterfeited the 'lover', according to the true-false binary that his opening soliloquy put in place, with the audience's tacit complicity, as the containment structure of identity (1.1.28–31).

This delusion helps to open the inner space in which the discourse of the loveless 'self alone' is finally brought, as it were, face to face with its consequences. Richard's self-*un*speaking follows the exhaustion of possible objects for his subjectivity-preempting rhetoric, as well as the virtual defection of the play's audience as co-conspirators on the level of theatrical engagement:

> What do I fear? Myself? There's none else by.
> Richard loves Richard, that is, I am I.
> Is there a murtherer here? No. Yes, I am.
> Then fly. What, from myself? Great reason why –
> Lest I revenge. What, myself upon myself?
> Alack, I love myself. Wherefore? For any good
> That I myself have done unto myself?
> O no! Alas, I rather hate myself
> For hateful deeds committed by myself.
>
> (5.3.182–90)

There is plenty of precedent, including the precursor soliloquy in *The True Tragedy*, for self-interrogation as a rhetorical technique, and even Wolfgang G. Müller, for whom this speech marks a thorough internalizing of inner conflict, hence a development beyond the quasi-allegorical method of the morality plays, perceives only dialectic: 'Das Ich ("myself") erscheint als Subjekt und Objekt, Verursacher und Opfer seiner Not [The I ("myself") appears as subject and object, originator and victim of its distress]' (322).[54] I suggest that there are more than two sides to the question here – that, in fact, the question keeps shifting its ground, so that the standard pattern of conscientious self-division is transformed into a intensely solipsistic circularity, a search for self premised on, and productive of, self-absence.

This effect is supported by the representation of the ghosts – paradoxically, since, in contrast with Caesar's appearance to Brutus, they proclaim their identities and unambiguously impart their unanimous message, 'Despair and die' (135,140,143, etc.). On the other hand, they come closer to the experience of Brutus than to that of Cassius, or of the King in *The True Tragedy*, by refusing to remain within consciousness and so suggesting the operation of the unconscious. Moreover, although 'every tongue brings in a several tale' and 'every tale condemns me for a villain' (194–5), their tales come at Richard from very different angles and therefore show him to himself in a variety of forms. The bonds he has violated run the gamut of modes of self-definition: family, erotic love, friendship, political trust. It is not just that Richard is again shown himself as the monster he is; indeed, his reasoning with himself indicates an effort to contain the experience on this level. Rather, he hears himself spoken in the aural equivalent of Richard II's shivered mirror: 'My conscience hath a thousand several tongues' (193).

When Richard picks up the ghosts' keynote, he broadens its resonance by, for the first time, breaking out of the dialectic between self-loving and self-loathing to view himself through the eyes of others – horseless, in effect, on the (battle)field of the Other – and what he discerns is a void: 'I shall despair; there is no creature loves me, / And if I die no soul will pity me' (200–1). This proves as true a prophecy as any in the play; after the battle Richmond will dismiss him anonymously and succinctly: 'the bloody dog is dead' (5.5.2). In anticipation of Hamlet, who writes it in his tables that 'one may smile, and smile, and be a villain' (*Ham.* 1.5.108), Richard is confronted by more than his failure to filfil the unitary word he adopts as his creed, discovering that finally he cannot 'smile, and murther whiles I smile' (*3H6* 3.2.182). He faces the dissolution of that creed itself into '[w]ords, words, words'. His indefinite impulsion to write first announces, by the indeterminate space it opens within the text, the collapse not only of a fashioned self, or selves, but of Richard as the author of himself and others.

VI

I will conclude this tour of the author-function in Shakespeare's plays by briefly leaping forward to the four final romances, which will figure more fully, from the perspective of genre, in Chapter 6. In associating written texts with processes of identity-(re)formation, these plays, too, constitute textuality as a site where authorized significance – again, the presumption is that texts have authors, who may or may not be 'strange fellow[s]' – is suddenly and dislocatingly rendered contingent upon mediation. This is most obviously the case in *The Winter's Tale* and *Cymbeline*, where divinely authored texts, ultimately validated by the outcomes of the plays, are subjected, like the Bible itself, to subjectifying reading – a process modelled on mirror-imaging. Leontes begins by resisting but must later acknowledge the image of himself as a 'jealous tyrant' (*WT* 3.2.133–4) presented by Apollo's Oracle (whose precept, of course, was 'know thyself'); the resulting self-absence proves the condition of fulfilling that text's promise of recovered presence. (These are romances, after all.) Likewise, the richly bound book found by Posthumus, awakening from symbolic death, actually fulfils the fatuous promise of Lady Capulet: 'That book in many's eyes doth share the glory, / That in gold clasps locks in the golden story' (*Rom.* 1.3.91–2). This fulfilment, however, is inextricable from an unwillingness to judge books by their covers: 'Be not, as is our fangled world, a garment / Nobler than that it covers' (*Cym.* 5.4.134–5).

That Posthumus' scepticism is the 'healthy' variety is confirmed when he refrains from interpreting the enigmatic contents, even as he discerns his own blurred outline:

> 'Tis still a dream, or else such stuff as madmen
> Tongue and brain not; either both or nothing,
> Or senseless speaking, or a speaking such
> As sense cannot untie. Be what it is,
> The action of my life is like it, which
> I'll keep, if but for sympathy.
>
> (145–50)

In the romance context, to accept the unresolved image is to gain access, legitimately, to the magic glass that Friar Bacon's attempted manipulations render damnable. Posthumus, like Leontes, steps through the looking-glass. And when the mystery has been realized, the seal is set on the comic vanity of human mediation by the retrospective *explication de texte* offered by the Soothsayer, whose reading, though it can hardly now go wrong, also earns no higher praise than the acknowledgement of limited likeness: 'This hath some seeming' (5.5.452).[55]

Let me now return to Mullaney's claim that Gower in *Pericles* functions as a 'not yet available figure, that of the author' by 'introduc[ing] *Pericles* as a tale of universal significance, ancient but unaging, forever timely and uncontaminated by historical and cultural contexts' (147–8). Strangely, Mullaney finds in Jonson's dismissal of the play as a 'mouldy Tale' ('Ode to Himselfe' 21) evidence that he was 'one of Shakespeare's contemporaries not taken in by Gower's claims to an ageless authority' (149). In the first place, Jonson's contempt itself needs to be placed in historical context, as a response to the failure of *The New Inn* in 1629, twenty years after *Pericles*. Moreover, he was hardly reacting to the supposed exaltation of the 'purely aesthetic' (Mullaney 147) at the expense of the historical and theatrically populist, but, on the contrary, to the popular appeal *Pericles* still enjoyed by virtue of its affinity with the crudely dramatized romances of earlier (arguably more populist) theatrical practice. And the key to this quality is the quaint representation of Gower, who makes as unlikely a stand-in for Shakespeare as, arguably, does Prospero.

Certainly, there are aspirations to 'universal significance'. But that significance, far from being 'purely aesthetic', functions on the elusive and indefinite level of quasi-religious mystery, and Gower is pointedly no deity. He presents himself, not as the originator and controller of his numinous text, but as its imperfect interpreter, mediating between a sophisticated modern audience ('born in those latter times, / When wit's more ripe' [1.Cho.11–12]) and the 'lame feet' of his 'rhyme' (4.Cho.48). Given his authorial status and stature, his frank embodiment of the play's main source,[56] Gower steps onto the Shakespearean stage with imposing authority, but he at once proceeds to disclaim it, deferring meaning, in plausibly Medieval terms, into the indefinite antiquity of romance: 'I tell you what mine authors say' (1.Cho.20). Finally, having spent his borrowed time 'like taper-light' (16) – a reminiscence of the 'lanterne'-like Gower of Berthelette, however Mullaney may consider 'his role . . . far from an illuminating one' (148) – he writes himself into silence and dependency: 'More a little, and then dumb. / This, my last boon, give me, / For such kindness must relieve me' (5.2.2–4). The result is an even more radical deconstruction of presumed textual authority than in the previous examples. The audience is called upon, not merely to observe a process of uncertain self-mirroring but to enter an interpretative space beyond the reach of mediation: the textual mirror becomes a magic glass, but Gower disjunctively stands aside from it. As with Knowlege in *Everyman*, his role as guide stops at the threshold of immortality. Gower's earth-bound authority is figured precisely in the delicate balance between the sacred and the banal that makes the play's aesthetic *impure* – and genuinely innovative.

It is more than conventional here to give the last word to *The Tempest*, pointedly uniting as that play does the functions of deity and textual interpreter in a magician whose power depends on his much referred-to (but unspecified) books. The traditional view that the text validates Prospero's transcendental authority has been challenged in recent years from various angles. It is worth adding to these the vexed relation between the book and the self, which Prospero presents as one of essential identity, but which is subjected to sceptical scrutiny. Caliban urges his new-found allies, 'Remember / First to possess his books; for without them / He's but a sot, as I am' (3.2.91–3). To take him more or less at his word, encouraged by his disarming self-awareness and the motif of the sorcerer's apprentice (à la Wagner in *Faustus*), is to recognize that texts and identities here are intertwined and up for grabs. Conflicts of interpretation notoriously abound – witness the paradigmatic dispute between two pairs of courtiers (Gonzalo and Adrian *versus* Antonio and Sebastian) over the image nature seems to hold up to them. The issues raised by Caliban include the value of language itself: 'You taught me language, and my profit on't / Is, I know how to curse' (1.2.363–4). The core at once of Prospero's power and his moral authority, the centre of the self he displays to others – including the audience – is not only indeterminate but contingent, as his dependence on Gonzalo's charity confirms: 'Knowing I lov'd my books, he furnish'd me / From mine own library with volumes that / I prize above my dukedom' (166–8).

From this perspective, Prospero's project, which blatantly contradicts the preference for books over dukedom affirmed here, takes on an evasive and defensive cast matching his touchiness of temperament. His magical power is perhaps not an unequivocal source of presence but carries the menace of absence, a dissolution of the self such as is associated with numinous experiences in *Cymbeline* and *Pericles*. Prospero's eventual abandonment of his magic thus does more than set the seal on his recovery of temporal authority; it enacts a victory – however pyrrhic, given his 'despair' (*Epi.* 15)

– over indeterminacy itself. Hence, his performative discourse of renunciation ('this rough magic / I here abjure' [5.1.50–1]) comes in the only speech of his that is unequivocally a soliloquy and suddenly allows into the open, by way of the account of Medea in the *Metamorphoses*, the hitherto suppressed darker and unruly aspects of that 'so potent art' (50). Hence, the prized volumes can be imaginatively consolidated into one and banished beyond the bounds of human knowledge – that is, not only beyond the reach of Caliban but beyond consciousness itself: 'deeper than did ever plummet sound / I'll drown my book' (56–7).

As is conveyed by his uneasy relation with Ariel, Prospero has struggled to maintain control of his magic glass, keeping it turned toward the objects of his manipulations, though Sebastian and Antonio, at least, confirm the infinite human capacity for seeing what they want to see. Only when nature itself is properly redeployed to reflect an image of himself '[a]s I was sometime Milan' (86) does Prospero prompt Ariel to mirror to him that identity, the merely human rendered transcendental. As it happens, *The Tempest* unquestionably draws (in Gonzalo's vision of the ideal commonwealth) on Florio's Montaigne – on that section of it, moreover, where Montaigne holds up the cannibals of the New World to mirror nature at the satirical expense of corrupt European civilization (1:230–45; trans. Florio 1:215–29). Yet Montaigne's text, too, whose subversive implications rise close to the surface by way of Caliban, is ultimately defused to become grist to Prospero's mill, thanks to Gonzalo's unwitting interpretative support. It is Gonzalo, finally, who obligingly figures the dénouement as the miraculous and definitive discovery of true self-images: 'and all of us, ourselves, when no man was his own' (212–13). But then the chief text Prospero relies on to supplant his mysterious books – a work of which he is the author (if her mother is to be trusted) and which will continue to reflect his re-fashioned self in a successful version of Lear's attempt to 'set' his 'rest' (*Lr* 1.1.123) on Cordelia, Othello's to fix his self-image in Desdemona – serves him as a veritable magic glass, with the support of her etymological genealogy. Miranda's name would have prepared a contemporary audience to accept her as simultaneously 'to be wondered at' (from *mirari*) and 'to be looked at' (from late Latin *mirare*, the root of 'mirror' [see OED]), in keeping with Ferdinand's train of thought on learning it (his first sight of her, of course, had already struck him with 'wonder' [1.2.427]):

> Admir'd Miranda,
> Indeed the top of admiration! worth
> What's dearest to the world! Full many a lady
> I have eye'd with best regard . . .
>
> . . . .
>
> But you, O you,
> So perfect and so peerless, are created
> Of every creature's best!
>
> (3.1.37–48)

VII

In the light of the subversive power that accrues to authorial evanescence in the texts I have considered, Jonson's promotion of
transcendental authorship in the First Folio appears primarily backward-looking, part of his much-recognized 'nostalgia', which Don
E. Wayne, for one, accuses traditional criticism of sharing (27). (Hence
the soft glow of *The Light in Troy*: '[Jonson] justifies in himself the
goals of the humanist enterprise, and if he is often presented in his
genetic role as a father, he can also be understood as a culmination'
[Greene 274].) Wayne is persuasive in demonstrating that 'Jonson
looked ahead as much as he did backward in time' (29), and he is
more flexible than many New Historicists in acknowledging intimations of the 'independent and important role' (6) of authors as
early as Chaucer. But his own model of Jonson as fundamentally
conflicted, uneasily positioned between old and new moral and
social values, might serve to re-energize, rather than to efface, the
standard notion of Jonson's construction of a conservative 'bulwark'
(29). At least, that notion emerges all the more strongly with respect
to authorship. Instead of positing either a defence specifically against
topical interpretation (Marcus 29) or an ideal of 'enlightened historicism' (Greene 292), I prefer to give full weight to the literally
reactionary quality of Jonson's exaltation of the classics (into which
canon he wishes to incorporate Shakespeare) and his various pro-
clamations of contempt for the 'loathsome Age' ('Ode to Himselfe'
2). He conceived of himself as – and in – reinstating, not inventing,
his ideal of 'artistic transcendence' (Marcus 30) in response to the
proliferating degradation of authorship. The Book is elevated, like
an icon, to ward off too many books.

We may usefully turn to the reception of Florio's Montaigne by

Samuel Daniel, whose own prefatory verse-supplement to *that* volume (1:12–14) records a sense similar to Donne's in 'The First Anniversarie' of a decadent world proliferating opinions and fragmenting former certainties. Here, following Montaigne, the focus is books, which *'So stuffe the world . . . as they confound / The apetite of skill with idle store'*. Daniel specifically connects this 'Babel' of minor authors with failed attempts at defining human nature: *'[t]he likliest images frailtie can finde'* to please the restless *'soule'* rolling *'[a]bout this doubtful* center of the right'. It is this presumed 'center' that *'this great Potentate, / This Prince* Montaigne' undertakes to *'discover'*.

Daniel's encomiastic mechanism is akin to Shakespeare's production as a transcendental author / authority at the hands of Jonson. And the image that Daniel purports to erect is self-subverting in a way that corresponds to Shakespeare's dramatic fracturings of the direct bond between textuality and identity. The self-portrait of this author becomes a mirror for the very *'manifold incertaintie'* Daniel would like him to cure. Montaigne is unequivocal about incorporating his own self-production through self-fragmentation into the world's Babel of voices: 'Et quand seray-je à bout de representer une continuelle agitation et mutation de mes pensées, en quelque matiere qu'elles tombent . . .? Que doit produire le babil,[57] puisque le begaiement et desnouement de la langue estouffa le monde d'une si horrible charge de volumes? Tant de paroles pour les paroles seules! [And when shall I come unto an end of representing a continuall agitation or uncessant alteration of my thoughts, what subject soever they happen upon . . .? What is idle babling like to produce, since the faltring and liberty of the tongue hath stuft the world with so horrible a multitude of volumes? So many words onely for words]' (3:177–8; trans. Florio 3:183).

As is clear from Montaigne's effective extension of distrust from *parole* to *langue* (the double meaning of the latter term regrettably vanishes in translation), his interrogations do not stop with scepticism. The 'center' becomes more *'doubtful'* to the point of vanishing. As Lacan puts it, 'Montaigne est vraiment celui que s'est centré, non pas autour d'un scepticisme, mais autour du moment vivant de l'*aphanisis* du sujet [Montaigne is truly the one who has centred himself, not around scepticism but around the living moment of the *aphanisis* of the subject]' (*Séminaire 11* 203; *Concepts* 223). Yet even as Lacan situates Montaigne historically at the birth of modern subjectivity, positing a phylogeny to recapitulate his posited ontogeny, he gestures transhistorically as unmistakably as does Gusdorf (29–33), when the latter constructs his essentialist history of subjectivity, again with Montaigne as watershed, under the rubric of *La découverte du soi*. For a Lacanian subject susceptible to aphanisis has, by virtual definition, 'always already' undergone that operation. We come back to the 'cadre' provided by the symbolic order for the mirror-stage – a point firmly nailed down by Jacques-Alain Miller: 'If a child can learn language, it is on the precondition that he is already in language' (33). Lacan himself was in the audience when Foucault so resonantly addressed the question, 'Qu'est-ce qu'un auteur?', and his strong response to the lecture and the ensuing discussion is revealing:

> je voudrais faire remarquer que, structuralisme ou pas, il me semble qu'il n'est nulle part question, dans le champ vaguement déterminé par cette étiquette, de la négation du sujet. Il s'agit de la dépendance du sujet, ce qui est extrêmement différent; de la dépendance du sujet . . . par rapport à quelque chose de vraiment élémentaire, et que nous avons tenté d'isoler sous le terme de 'signifiant'.
>
> [I would like to point out that, whether this is structuralism or not, it seems to me that there is no question, anywhere in the field vaguely defined by that label, of the denial of the subject. The issue is the dependence of the subject, something far different . . . the dependence of the subject with respect to something truly basic, which I have tried to isolate under the term 'signifier'.]
>
> (Response 104)

No surprise, then, that Lacan also grants Montaigne the status of an author dealing in universal human truths: 'il est guide éternel, qui dépasse tout ce qu'il a pu représenter du moment à définir d'un tournant historique [he is an eternal guide, who goes beyond everything that he was able to represent of the moment to be defined as an historical turning-point]' (*Séminaire 11* 203).[58] Seemingly, Montaigne has *discovered* that the nature of the subject consists in its perpetual fading, and the result is to expose history as the product of such subjects, hence an unstable construction of shifting discourses – infinitely '*à définir*'. When the centre vanishes, there is not nothing left: the evanescent residue is subjectivity itself. Ultimately, Daniel admits, the authority of Montaigne consists in doubtfully coherent fragments, '*most rich pieces and extracts of man; / Though in a troubled frame confus'dly set'* (14). Just so do Jonson and the First Folio editors 'confus'dly' frame 'Mr. William Shakespeares Comedies, Histories, & Tragedies' – 'rich pieces and extracts' indeed.

Notes to Chapter 4

1. Cf. Soellner's discussion (105–111) in terms of character development and self-awareness.
2. With Warwick's lecture on predicting the future on the basis of past behaviour (3.1.80 ff.) cf. Machiavelli:

> E' si conosce facilmente, per chi considera le cose presenti e le antiche, come in tutte le città ed in tutti i popoli sono quegli medesimi desiderii e quelli medesimi omori, e come vi furono sempre. In modo che gli è facil cosa, a chi esamina con diligenza le cose passate, prevedere in ogni republica le future e farvi quegli rimedi che dagli antichi sono stati usati; o, non ne trovando degli usati, pensarne de' nuovi per la similitudine degli accidenti. Ma perché queste considerazioni sone neglette o non intese da chi legge o, se le sono intese, non sono conosciute da chi governa, ne séguita che sempre sono i medesimi scandoli in ogni tempo.
> [If the present be compared with the remote past, it is easily seen that in all cities and in all peoples there are the same desires and the same passions as there always were. So that, if one examines with diligence the past, it is easy to foresee the future of any commonwealth, and to apply those remedies which were used of old; or, if one does not find that remedies were used, to devise new ones owing to the similarity between events. But, since such studies are neglected and what is read is not understood, or, if it be understood, is not applied in practice by those who rule, the consequence is that similar scandals occur at all times].
> (*Discorsi* 196–7 [Bk. 1, Ch. 39]; *Discourses* 1:302)

> Not surprisingly, the conclusion of this statement does not figure in Warwick's attempt to reassure the king.

3. Both the identification and the gloss are traditional, having been sanctioned by Augustine's commentary on *Genesis*, which, incidentally, contains a sentence ironically embedding the problematic of post-Babel signification: 'Babylon quippe interpretatur confusio [For Babylon is interpreted as meaning confusion]' (*De Civitate Dei* 48: 504 [Bk. 16, Ch. 4]).
4. See Ardolino, ' "Now Shall I See the Fall of Babylon" '; cf. Goodstein.
5. See Ardolino, 'Hieronimo as St. Jerome'.
6. See Johnson 34, who raises the possibility of taking the tongue-biting as 'a symbolic refusal to participate in the confusion of the world after Babel'.

7. 'Dearly beloued, auenge not your selues, but giue place vnto wrath: for it is written, Vengeance is mine: I wil repaye, saith the Lord' (*Rom.* 12:19).

8. The *OED* dates from Middle English the following meaning: 'To ensure by supervision or vigilance that something shall be done or not done' (6b).

9. That Hieronimo's madness refracts a subjectivity now widely presumed to be post-Cartesian may be gathered from Foucault's distinction: 'Pour le XIXe siècle le modèle initial de la folie sera de se croire Dieu, alors que pour les siècles précédents il était de refuser Dieu [For the nineteenth century, the initial model of madness would be to believe oneself to be God, while for the preceding centuries it had been to deny God]' (*Folie* 275; *Madness* 264). Indeed, Hieronimo's isolation from social discourse and condemnation to soliloquized self-imaging recall practices of the nineteenth-century asylum that Foucault finds epistemologically distinctive. Cf., e.g., his account of the inmate given physical liberty but subjected to silence:

    > à la contrainte physique est substituée une liberté qui rencontre à chaque instant les limites de la solitude; au dialogue du délire et de l'offense, le monologue d'un langage qui s'épuise dans le silence des autres; à toute la parade de la présomption et de l'outrage, l'indifférence.
    > [for physical constraint yielded to a liberty that constantly touched the limits of solitude; the dialogue of delirium and insult gave way to a monologue in a language which exhausted itself in the silence of others; the entire show of presumption and outrage was replaced by indifference.
    >
    > (*Folie* 271; *Madness* 261)

    Note, too, the therapeutic use of mirror-imaging techniques, by which a patient's 'solide souveraineté de sujet s'effondre [solid sovereignty as a subject dissolves]. . . . Et dans le silence de ceux qui représentent la raison, et n'ont fait que tendre le miroir périlleux, il se reconnaît comme objectivement fou [And in the silence of those who represent reason, and who have done nothing but hold up the perilous mirror, he recognizes himself as objectively mad]' (*Folie* 274; *Madness* 264); madness now 's'emprisonne dans son regard indéfiniment renvoyé à elle-même; elle est enchaînée finalement à l'humiliation d'être objet pour soi [imprisoned itself in an infinitely self-referring observation; it was finally chained to the humiliation of being its own object]'. It is from such imprisonment, one might say, that Hieronimo escapes through action, recovering for his madness 'l'essentiel de sa liberté, qui est celle de l'exaltation solitaire [the essence of its liberty, which was solitary exaltation]' (*Folie* 275; *Madness* 265).

10. See Empson, Aggeler, and esp. Hallett and Hallett 160.

11. Cf. Arnold's judgement that the play's soliloquies 'reveal thoughts and emotions with the ring of sincerity' (11).

12. For generally compatible perspectives on this process, see McMillin, Sacks, and Faber and Skinner.

13. In general, Maus's treatment (55–71) of *The Spanish Tragedy*, though very different in emphasis, dovetails with mine.
14. See Mulryne, ed. n. to 2.5.67–80, citing Boas.
15. These lines seem to have lent themselves to parodic recycling in *MND* 5.1.296–9: 'Out, sword, and wound / The pap of Pyramus; / Ay, that left pap, / Where heart doth hop'.
16. Cf. McMillin 39–40 on Hieronimo's perception of the Old Man as an image first of Horatio, then of himself.
17. Cf. Sacks 584.
18. A well-known instance in the Renaissance; see Montaigne 1:8 (trans. Florio 1:22) and 684n17 (Rat, ed.).
19. Cf. Bost 224 on the destruction of the tower as symbolic castration; his emphasis, however, is on the necessity of this event for the formation of the subject: 'alors que le Sujet, pour être sujet de Désir et verbaliser ce qu'il est, doit accepter la nomination préalable du Père, les hommes tentent ici de *s'auto-nommer* [while the Subject, in order to be the subject of Desire and to articulate what he is, must accept the prior naming of the Father, men attempt here to *name themselves*' (223).
20. I am less concerned here with Foucault's own position than with certain rigid applications of his model. I am happy to accept his poststructuralist problematization of the author-function across the board, as well as his parallel between Medieval authentication of texts and modern construction of authorship (86–7), given that 'on peut retrouver à travers le temps un certain invariant dans les régles de construction de l'auteur [one can recover across the ages a certain constant principle in the rules for constructing the author]' (86).
21. See 'Unthinkable Thoughts' 441.
22. See esp. Greene's stimulating remarks on authority (12).
23. See the deft, if tendentious, survey of Levin, 'Unthinkable Thoughts' 436–7.
24. See *Intertextuality* 106–23, where I put to different use some of the material on Gower included here.
25. For a detailed discussion of Gower's position in the context of Medieval authorship / *auctoritas*, see Minnis 168–90.
26. Foucault ('Qu'est-ce qu'un auteur?' 84–5) at least oversimplifies in claiming that only 'les textes que nous dirions maintenant scientifiques [the texts that we would now term scientific]' required such authorial 'indices [indicators]' in the Middle Ages; nor is his distinction between 'les formules d'un argument d'autorité [formulas of an argument on the basis of authority]' and 'les indices dont étaient marqués des discours destinés à être reçus comme prouvés [indicators marking certain discourses which were to be taken as proven]' self-evidently functional once 'la fonction-auteur [the author-function]' is recognized as invariably a discursive construction.
27. From his Cultural Materialist perspective, Shepherd finds that in this episode 'the ideological status of books and poetry is shifted, in the exploration of a newer expressivity' – an argument that depends on finding in earlier drama 'an exploration of the political operations of language' (39).

28.   Hamlet was identified with Montaigne as early as 1838 (Ellrodt 40n4), and the association is still current; see Jenkins, ed. 108–10.

29.   Craig, who accepted Montaigne as a major influence ('Hamlet's Book' 36–7), used the First Quarto's version of 3.3 as his starting point, then argued for an identification that would hold 'irrespective of whether or not Shakespeare presented his hero as reading this particular book before his soliloquy' (18). Neither he nor Ellrodt mentions the book introduced at 2.2.168, whose identity is explicitly at issue. The latter has most often been attributed to Juvenal, who is similarly hard on old age in the tenth *Satire* (see Jenkins, ed. 467, Longer Note to 2.2.196). Nevertheless, Hamlet's optimistic-pessimistic picture of mankind in 2.2.295 ff. is of long-standing importance as evidence for Montaigne's influence (Robertson 53–4; Ellrodt 40).

30.   On this concept in intertextual theory, see Riffaterre, esp. 627; also my *Intertextuality* 2–3,17,23 *et passim*.

31.   See Grabes 99–103.

32.   My reading of the Ulysses-Achilles dynamic overlaps with that of Girard (141–51), who also stresses the contingency of Achilles' self-conception and whose theory of 'mimetic desire' (applied with a broad brush across Shakespeare's *oeuvre*) extends to the operations of 'specularity'.

33.   This is not part of Lacan's own reading of *Hamlet* as a 'tragedy of desire' ('Desire'), although the function of the Other in that dynamic makes for a certain overlap.

34.   On *Hamlet*'s contribution to the evolving literary depiction of subjectivity, see also Ferry 2–3.

35.   We are free to wonder whether the *Ur-Hamlet*, putatively by Kyd, brought its protagonist on stage with a clearly identified book, as is also the case in Marston's *Antonio's Revenge* 2.3.42 ff., where the prospective revenger finds Senecan philosophy insufficiently consoling. On the latter play's problematic relation to the other three texts, see Gair, Introd., *Antonio's Revenge* 12–19.

36.   When Lacan says, further, that '[t]he image of the other, as you see, is presented here as completely absorbing the beholder' ('Desire' 31), he appears to miss the fact that Hamlet implicitly positions himself outside the exchange of true images as mere 'umbrage', radically alienated.

37.   'Toujours *déjà*'; on this phrase's origin (in Heidigger) and usage (by Derrida, Lacan, *et al.*), see Fuss 122n13.

38.   Both of Spivak's translations, 'There is nothing outside of the text' and 'there is no outside-text' (*Of Grammatology* 158) (although the former is fine for *Derrida's* alternative, 'il n'y a rien hors du texte' [*De la grammatologie* 233; *Of Grammatology* 163]) have the effect of excluding the dictionary sense of '*hors-texte*' – namely, illustrative matter separately printed and inserted into a book as unnumbered pages. On '*hors-texte*' as a theoretical term in its own right, see Angenot 127–8.

39.   Beaujour offers a fascinating analysis of the soliloquizing Hamlet, 'comme Montaigne arpentant sa tour [like Montaigne pacing in his tower]', effectively suspended

entre l'*affirmation élocutoire*, inhérente à la rhétorique (mais qui produit un sujet vide, incapable de résoudre par lui-même la question d'être ou de n'être pas, puisqu'il n'existe que de poser cette question sur tous les tons et à tout bout de champ) et la *disparition élocutoire*, qui, elle aussi, est inhérente au choix rhétorique, puisque celui-ci implique que le sujet (qui se demande s'il est ou n'est pas) n'est pas un 'sujet plein', un Signe *pour lui-même*.

[between *elocutionary affirmation*, which is inherent in rhetoric (but which produces an empty subject, incapable of resolving by himself the question of whether to be or not to be, since there is only the posing of that question in every tone and at every moment) and *elocutionary disappearance*, which is also inherent in the rhetorical choice, since it implies that the subject (who asks himself whether he is or is not) is not a 'full subject', a Sign *for himself*.]

(286)

40. See Lacan, *Séminaire 11* 188–9,192,199 (*Concepts* 206–8,211,218); also Paul Smith 70–82 and Silverman 196–7.

41. On this point, see Silverman 196–7.

42. Dollimore further ascribes to Montaigne a 'quest for his essential substantial autonomous self' (173). This is to neglect even Ellrodt's attempt ('the essence here is in the passage' [44]) to reconcile the apparent contradiction (less pronounced in the original than in Florio's translation) between two statements of Montaigne: 'Ce ne sont mes gestes que j'escris, c'est moy, c'est mon essence [I write not my gests, but my selfe and my essence]' (2:52; trans. Florio 2:60); 'Je ne peints pas l'estre. Je peints le passage [I describe not the essence, but the passage]' (3:18; trans. Florio 3:23).

43. See also Regosin 170–97; Rigolot, *Les métamorphoses* 150–93; and Rider 96.

44. Herein may lie a distortion in Greenblatt's treatment of the *Essais* as the 'last brilliant flowering' of a non-representational discourse premised on the '*presence* in the written word of identity' – a phenomenon that, following the common critical path, he links with Hamlet's soliloquies as 'claim[ing] not access to the inner life but existence as the inner life' (*Self-Fashioning* 87). Goldberg similarly denies a gap between the inscribed and inscribing self but, thanks perhaps to the influence of Derrida, allows for inscription itself as a dynamic, disjunctive, and deferring process.

45. In an opposite but equal reaction, Mullaney reclaims the speech for Cultural Materialism as subversively parodic (52).

46. Cf. Girard's conclusion that Ulysses is 'so fascinated with the politics of desire, the very disease he is fighting, that his maneuvring ultimately backfires' (149).

47. *Intertextuality* 58–81; *Problem Plays* 17–53.

48. The common Shakespearean practice of dramatizing the inward through the outward suggests that the Cartesian connection need not limit the 'malin génie' historically, *pace* Foucault: 'Il n'a pas fallu moins que le Malin Génie de Descartes pour mettre un terme à ce

grand péril des Identités où la pensée du XVIe siècle n'avait pas cessé de se "subtiliser" [It took nothing less than the Evil Genius of Descartes to put an end to that great peril of Identities in which the thought of the sixteenth century had not ceased to complicate itself]' ('Prose' 445).

49.   The characteristic foreshortening in the dramatic treatment tends to assimilate the night of the ghost's appearance into the eve of Philippi, when, according to Plutarch, Brutus and Cassius argued about whether to give battle the next day, much as Shakespeare's characters do about 'marching to Philippi presently' (4.3.197); once the decision was made, Plutarch reports, 'Brutus all supper tyme looked with a cherefull countenaunce, like a man that had good hope, and talked very wisely of Philosophie, and after supper went to bed' (119). Intriguingly, the indeterminate nature of this talk is focused by an intertext of Montaigne, especially as translated by Florio, who makes *a* battle into *the* battle:

> j'ayme bien autant voir Brutus chez Plutarque que chez luy mesme. Je choisiroy plutost de sçavoir au vray les devis qu'il tenoit en sa tente à quelqu'un de ses privez amis, la veille d'une battaille, que les propos qu'il tint le lendemain à son armée.
> [I love as much to see *Brutus* in *Plutarke*, as in himselfe: I would rather make choice to know certainly, what talke he had in his Tent with some of his familiar friends, the night foregoing the battel, than the speech he made the morrow after to his Armie.]
> (2:92; trans. Florio 2:101)

50.   To Capell, the first mention appeared so incongruous as to indicate textual corruption (see Furness, ed. n. to 5.3.59).

51.   See Bullough 3:229–33.

52.   With respect to Richard, Maus's account (47–54) of inwardness and Machiavellianism again complements my approach.

53.   By contrast, the menace of self-absence lurking within the tautology of self-swearing comes to the fore in Juliet's inability to sustain her reckless figuration of Romeo as 'the god of my idolatry' (*Rom.* 2.2.114). When, in response to her invitation to 'swear by thy gracious self' (113), he begins, 'If my heart's dear love –' (115), she abruptly shrinks back – 'Well, do not swear' (116) – as if the proffered display of the self's core affords instead a glimpse of the abyss.

54.   On *disputatio* in Richard's speech, with emphasis on the syntax as an index of self-division, see also Dahl 33–4.

55.   For Goldberg, the Soothsayer's gloss inscribes royal authority on the divine text that had seemed to reveal Posthumus' 'interiority', so that 'the historicity of the unconscious is staged' (316). This reading ignores the Soothsayer's self-discrediting pedantry, which is couched in a familiar Shakespearean comic style and highlighted by the context.

56.   Mullaney argues as if the Apollonius of Tyre legend had a fixed original form, with Lawrence Twine's prose romance 'a relatively faithful version' (138), from which the playwright expunged materialist and 'theatrical' elements. This is to ignore the primary influence on

the plot of the very different redaction in the *Confessio Amantis* (see Hoeniger xiv–xvi).

57.   'Babil', recorded as a substantive from the fifteenth century, is etymologically unrelated to 'Babel' but, as in English (see *OED*), became associated with it (Demonet 42).

58.   Here I offer my own translation, as that of Sheridan (*Concepts* 223–4) seems to me to be (most exceptionally) in error.

5

Some Unspeakably Tragic Subjects

In sketching an epistemology of self-speaking on the Elizabethan stage, my discussion to this point has elicited substantial continuities with earlier dramatic tradition. These appear more clearly when the staged 'unconscious' is approached, not as a cultural marker of changing subjectivity, but as a stylistic effect, which, while accessible to dramatists from the earliest period of English drama, becomes aggressively and variously deployed within new generic and thematic frameworks. Continuity is worth stressing again at the start of the present chapter, which will focus on late- and post-Elizabethan plays, mainly tragedies, including some (*The Duchess of Malfi*, *The Changeling*) that are commonly thought of as combining new heights of 'psychological realism' – hence, an anticipation of the modern humanist subject – with new moral and affective depths.

From my perspective, this disjunctive combination points beyond individual characters as autonomous vessels of subjectivity and towards a recognition of the ensemble of textual elements as engaged in a dynamic negotiation among subjectivities of different kinds and degrees. This effect arguably applies in some measure to any drama concerned with representing the subject, including the texts I have been discussing, and it may be approached, as Freedman's work demonstrates, from the perspective of the audience. I prefer to approach it here by way of theatrical technique, as a grafting of the stage-semiotics of individual subjectivity onto the mechanisms (never far below the surface in Elizabethan drama) of morality-play psychomachia. Increasingly in the post-1600 drama, the operations of the unconscious, comprising a sort of virtual Humanum Genus, are 'writ large' across a shifting tableau comprising both characters and actions. If the latter categories, moreover, are then roughly translated into the speech-act terms of 'constative' and 'performative' respectively, Felman's formulation, part of which I earlier applied to Hieronimo and Hamlet, becomes suggestively applicable to the play-text as a whole, and as a process:

The 'unconscious' is the discovery, not only of the radical divorce or breach between act and knowledge, between constative and performative, but also . . . of their undecidability and their constant interference . . . subjectivity is henceforth a cognitive (constative) struggle to overcome a series of performative 'infelicities'.

(96)

With the help of Hamlet's dying words, the 'felicity' that looms as the prize in this struggle posits the ultimate refuge from the unconscious as unconscious*ness*. In this context, to project subjectifying knowledge upon others through transcendentalizing action – the practice, I have suggested, of figures as diverse as Hieronimo and Henry VIII – serves to display 'self-fashioning', for both sides of the transaction, as a function of the Other, inevitably carrying the message of self-absence.

This is substantially to complicate, and partly to undercut, the individualizing argument of Greenblatt in *Renaissance Self-Fashioning*, notably as applied to Othello's relation with Iago (222–54). But it is also to confirm the latter relation, complete with its widely recognized Medieval dramatic heritage, as a paradigm for the treatment of subjectivity in numerous villain-plays of the Stuart period. Greenblatt's account of the superficial dynamic remains compelling: Iago, with a brilliant talent for narrative improvisation, undermines the heroic self fashioned in Othello's mythologizing language and effectively entrusted by him to Desdemona's safekeeping. Nevertheless, in situating Othello's vulnerability in a specifically sexual insecurity fostered by contemporary religious discourse, Greenblatt veers at once away from the text (given the paucity of internal evidence that 'Christianity is the alienating yet constitutive force in Othello's identity' [245]) and towards essentialist analysis of a traditional psychologizing sort. He swells, in fact, the crowded ranks of those who have plumbed the character's 'hidden depths' for the missing piece of the puzzle (and some of whom have similarly configured those depths in sexual terms). Greenblatt's claim that Othello's weak spot originates in Venetian cultural discourse, rather than, say, Oedipal forces or even an innately 'savage nature', amounts to a minor variation on a major critical theme.

To follow to its end the thread of (self-)subversion in Shakespeare's play is to recognize that, on a deeper level, Iago does not undermine subjectivity in Othello; on the contrary, he produces it – subjectivity, that is, in the aphanitic sense. He does this by exposing as illusory, not merely a fashioned self, but the very principle of self-fashioning. He forces the improvisatory mode – that of indefinite 'becoming' – upon his victim by opening the gap between the constative and the performative, between seeming and being, that constitutes the unconscious. To read the process in this way is to accommodate Iago as a full participant in it. The unconscious that Iago begets in Othello commensurately takes the place of his own, placing him in his turn beyond improvisation. Iago's notorious 'motive-hunting' – he gets ten soliloquies, by the way, to Othello's seven – comprises perhaps the most fully developed pattern in Early Modern drama of self-speaking that attempts to fix a fading mirror-image, to supplant the Other through verbal 'takes' on the self in relation to others: 'Now I do love her too, / Not out of absolute lust (though peradventure / I stand accomptant for as great a sin) . . .' (2.1.291–3). Iago appears to be introducing self-images mechanically into an absolute void. (As with the shadow-fixated Richard III, one is reminded that vampires, the drainers of life-blood, are supposed to have neither shadows nor mirror-images.)

Iago's cold-blooded and prosaic style encodes a rationality that, however spurious, makes the most effective possible weapon for puncturing Othello's poetical fantasies, which, in the guise of self-inflation, are ultimately self-evasive, eloquently enacting a transcendental silence. As Iago pursues his machinations, the activity of futile motive-hunting takes possession of his adversary's self-speaking ('Haply, for I am black . . .' [3.3.263]). Finally, Iago is wholly freed from the burden of such speech in becoming the 'speaking body', the manifest answer that refuses to provide one, while Othello is reduced to posing questions about his own 'soul and body' (5.2.302). The apocalytpic manifestation of Iago-as-devil reflects Othello's earthly damnation, the hell of raw subjectivity: 'Whip me, ye devils . . .' (277). The 'turban'd Turk' (353) that Othello imaginatively liquidates in killing himself has often been identified with the unacceptable image of himself that Iago has inculcated. From the perspective of self-speaking, what stands out in Othello's suicidal monologue is his direct assault on the unconscious itself, as he forcibly subsumes the constative into the transcendentally performative, gathering up and expunging all the deceptions of language in its fallen state. The act reprises Richard II's mirror-shattering but leaves no room for re-opening, as does Bullingbrook, the gap between image and reality: 'The shadow of your sorrow hath destroy'd / The shadow of your face' (*R2* 4.1.292–3).

It is suggestive for more than moral and thematic reasons that Iago reflects the unconscious of his victim in diabolic form. Even in Medieval dramatic allegories, the hidden inward operations of the devil are implied, and sometimes they are ingeniously foregrounded, as in Titivillus' deceptions of the title character in *Mankind*. I earlier proposed that the significance of Mephastophilis in *Faustus* specifically extends to the unconscious that 'pulls . . . down' Marlowe's protagonist into tragic subjectivity, ensuring that he sees himself, in the mirror of his own discourse, as at once more and less than God's sinful creature. Later Renaissance tragedy, especially where (as often) it problematizes the notion of a transcendental discursive framework, makes abundant use of diabolic imagery in figuring subjectivity as 'a cognitive (constative) struggle to overcome a series of performative "infelicities" '.

This metaphorical function of the diabolic receives perhaps its clearest illustration and most succinct commentary in Webster's *The Devil's Law-Case* – a tragicomedy redeemed from tragedy by the skin of its characters' teeth (and despite their best efforts). The generic implications of this fact properly belong in the next chapter. It is worth citing here, however, the concluding moralization offered by the Capuchin, who defines the self-subversive mechanism all the more effectively by enfolding it within the rhetoric of sin and providential punishment:

> wretches turn
> The tide of their good fortune, and being drenched
> In some presumptuous and hidden sins,
> While they aspire to do themselves most right,
> The devil that rules i'th' air, hangs in their light.
>
> (5.5.17–21)

In the Jacobean theatre, it seems, to 'give the devil his due' may mean confronting the inevitably shaky foundations of discursive self-constructions. And if the devil in such anxiously humorous aphorisms suggests a tame version of the 'malin génie', this makes the point that the unconscious becomes less threatening in proportion as its operations are accommodated. It is the thoroughly repressed unconscious that produces Iago and gives teeth to Hermione's mock-fear, as expressed to Polixenes: 'Of this make no conclusion, lest you say / Your queen and I are devils' (*WT* 1.2.81–2).

I

Before looking further at subjectivity as a site of discursive contestation, I hasten to acknowledge the continuing presence, even the dominance, in post-Elizabethan tragedy of the standard Medieval dramatic procedure, whereby self-speaking is contained within a transcendental discourse of unchallenged validity. Certainly, as *A Woman Killed with Kindness* (cited in Chapter 3) would suggest, this mode prevails in those highly moralistic dramas that were aimed primarily at a popular audience and that distinguish themselves, from a mimetic point of view, for having 'characters describe themselves self-consciously' and 'stand outside their own emotions' (Leggatt 82–3).[1] Such works probably included Tourneur's *The Atheist's Tragedy* (of uncertain date and theatrical affiliation), which, in keeping with its title, provides perhaps the most straightforward instance of a tragic protagonist defining himself strictly in (oppositional) relation to conventional religious discourse, which thereby retains him within its moral binarism – its *vice*-grips.

He does so at first, like *Lear*'s Edmund, by setting up Nature in the place of God, but whereas Edmund plunges headlong into soliloquy (*Lr* 1.2.1 ff.), constructing a self to fill a void on the model of Richard III, D'Amville declares his exclusive belief in himself by using his henchman Borachio as a sounding-board for a series of monologues. It is as if, despite his ostentatious temerity, D'Amville fears to look discursively into the mirror, which must inevitably show him as a self-deluding sinner. The mirror is always there and always reflective of divine authority, as when thunder frightens Borachio with its 'fearful noise' (2.4.151), dismissed by the atheist as 'a mere effect of Nature' (142). When D'Amville finally begins to soliloquize, the divinely empowered superego clearly looms as the Other(A): 'Now to myself I am ridiculous. / Nature, thou art a traitor to my soul. / Thou hast abus'd my trust. . . .' (5.1.115–17).

This is preparation for D'Amville's bizarre self-braining with the axe aimed at his innocent enemies – a (literally) striking instance of a failure to put others in the place of the Other. The contrast with the dénouement of *Othello* is telling: conscience stands in the place of the unconscious; God supplants the 'demi-devil'. A closer parallel would appear to be with the dying Edmund, gathered up into the transcendental discourse he had denied: 'The wheel is come full circle, I am here' (*Lr* 5.3.175). A provocative difference, however, lies in the fact that, in the agnostic (if not atheistic) universe of *Lear*, where thunder appears to mean only as it is humanly construed, that discourse is contingent on the manipulations of Edgar, just as is Gloucester's illusion of divine solicitude.

While the question of intended audience is often hard to settle, the moralistic strain in the drama of the period certainly crosses any putative boundaries between the naïve and the sophisticated, and in Chapman and Jonson it finds exponents whom it would be hard to exceed in the domains of the recondite and the Latinate, respectively. In their hands, morality and religion, while no less insisted upon, become less cut-and-dried than is the bourgeois Puritanism of *Woman Killed* or the providential absolutism of *The Atheist's Tragedy.* Chapman's neo-Stoic exemplars of *virtù* include an adulterer (Bussy D'Ambois) abetted into apotheosis by a pious Friar. The code by which the Romans of *Cataline* and *Sejanus His Fall* are deemed virtuous or vicious is more conventional yet stands in a more subtly problematic relation to the supernatural, which displays a distinctly pagan character: Cataline is inspired by Sylla's Senecan ghost; the corrective intervention of the gods in *Sejanus* is coloured by superstition, notably when the image of Fortune (the only power beyond himself that Sejanus acknowledges) averts her face. And while the divine intervention in the latter case dovetails morally with Christian providential historiography, as indicated in Jonson's preface, the concluding focus on hubris remains resoundingly neo-classical:

> Let this example move th'insolent man
> Not to grow proud, and careless of the gods.
> It is an odious wisdom to blaspheme,
> Much more to slighten or deny their powers.
> (5.908–11)

In this context, the insistent foregrounding of Sejanus as an atheist produces a tinge of heterodox excess reminiscent of the endings of *Every Man in His Humour* and *Volpone,* where justice, emanating from a higher (albeit a human) power, is at once celebrated and skewed. The effect is akin to that of the opposite ideological extreme – Chapman's attachment of divine resonances to the heroic human will – and it similarly suggests an impulse to contextualize subjectivity within *some* transcendental discourse. Given the overwhelmingly secular orientation of the contemporary drama, mechanisms imposing such a discourse and thereby, in effect, short-circuiting the process of aphanisis no longer simply inhere in the discursive system. Rather, they carry the sense of being grafted onto it as an anxious supplement, revealing the lack in the signified: on the model of *Faustus*, hell must be, in a sense, reinvented as more than a metaphor. Thus Sejanus' defiant soliloquy against fear, in taking a predictably impious turn, collides with piety in a surreptitious recognition of himself as a mere creature, no longer self-created: 'By you, that fools call gods, / Hang all the sky with your prodigious signs . . .' (5.390–1).

The equivalent 'ventriloquizing' effect in Chapman is the rhetorical inflation by which his protagonists are subsumed into a transcendental order. That order is most clearly defined in the dance of spirits witnessed by Clermont D'Ambois before his death in *The Revenge of Bussy D'Ambois* (1610). This anticipation (by roughly three years) of Katherine's vision in *Henry VIII* differs from it suggestively. Rather than indefinite heavenly forms, these figures are re-inductees of Chapman's heroic pantheon, who transcend their earthly differences on the spiritual plane. They summon Clermont, not to a peaceful yielding of his ghost, but to suicide. More immediately, it is the news that Guise, who 'alone gaue meanes of life to me' (5.5.150), has been murdered at the king's instigation that inspires Clermont's baroque exercise in self-reflection, laden with metaphor, with its concluding affirmation of the self as derivative and wholly dependent: 'I come, my Lord, Clermont thy creature comes' (193). These performative words of self-recuperation through self-undoing are coded as feminine, thanks to a tradition stretching back at least to Marlowe, with Zabina's suicide soliloquy in *Tamburlaine, Part 1* (to be discussed in Chapter 7), and passing through the swooning Maria in *Antonio's Revenge*, by John Marston ('Andrugio, my lord, I come, I come' [1.5.16]). For a contemporary audience, the most immediate intertext would have been furnished by Shakespeare's Cleopatra ('Husband, I come! / Now to that name my courage prove my title!' [*Ant.* 5.2.287–8]) – an echo that points up the contrasting absence in Chapman of an ironic sense of self-creating imagination at work, of transcendence as a function of subjectivity. Instead, Clermont is simply giving voice once again, though now as a prelude to the sacrifice of his body, to a set of abstract beliefs embedded in the text.

In contrast, too, with Cleopatra's wry satisfaction at triumphing over Caesar ('ass / Unpolicied' [*Ant.* 5.2.307–8]), Clermont muffles his grievance in a gesture of submission: 'There's no disputing with the acts of Kings, / Revenge is impious on their sacred persons' (5.5.151–2). In the context, this is less to deify terrestrial authority than to confirm the derivation of his spiritual code from another world entirely. Thus does the dying Bussy, *en route* to (literal) stardom, forgive his murderers (including the Guise) at the behest of the Friar's ghost (*Bussy* 5.3.159). Thus does Byron observe from the scaffold that 'kings' suspicions need no balances' (*Tragedy of Byron*, 5.4.229), even while enjoining his brothers '[t]o keep their faiths that bind them to the King' (234). His lecture to arrogant 'statists . . . ere ye fall' (254), which concludes this last monologue, intertextually engages both *The Mirror for Magistrates* and Foxe's *Acts and Monuments*. Worldly authority is acknowledged yet destabilized, given that it cannot impinge on the transcendentally authorized self:

> Vitry My lord, you make too much of this your body,
>   Which is no more your own.
> Byron   Nor is it yours!
>   I'll take my death with all the horrid rites
>   And representments of the dread it merits.
>   (191–4)

In language suggesting a Faustus who redeems hell itself through heroic defiance, Byron's faith in his 'commanding soul' (260) is set off against his faithlessness to his king, which justifies his body's tormentors: 'Hell take me, but I'll strangle half that's here, / And force the rest to kill me. I'll leap down / If but once more they tempt me to despair' (200–2).

In the tragedies of Jonson and Chapman, then, as in numerous less intellectual post-1600 specimens of the genre, the spoken self is pre-formed rather than performed, discursively posed against the contours of an ideal image that supplies reinforcement or correction. The language of self-speaking remains nostalgically 'unfallen'. The *double entendre* of the card-game in *Woman Killed*, the deceptions of Sejanus, the misinterpreted message of *Bussy D'Ambois* – these and other instances of linguistic duplicity represent deviations from a trustworthy norm, which is eventually reinstated and revalidated all the more strongly because of such lapses. The extent to which this discursive dynamic was at once entrenched and precarious is suggested by the virtual commentary on it supplied by three plays of Marston, dating from just before and after 1600.

In each of the abundant instances of soliloquy and monologue in the two Antonio plays and *The Malcontent*, self-speech is in service to a transcendental moral discourse, ventriloquized so as to reflect unambiguous identities. These identities, however, are subject to abrupt change, while the governing moral perspective is relentlessly inconsistent, especially with regard to the revengers. On the one hand, Antonio's fulsome speeches display noble principles and deep sentiments; on the other, they grotesquely wallow in neo-Senecan bloodlust. The virtuous Altofront in *The Malcontent* actually has two faces, while the fact that the role of Malevole allows him '[f]ree speech' (1.3.163) helps to blur the distinction between true and false. Malevole's scurrilousness and self-serving manipulation of moral lessons (as when he instantly converts the egregious Pietro) infiltrate the voice of Altofront from the latter's first soliloquy, which follows his disclosure to Pietro of Aurelia's infidelity:

> Lean thoughtfulness, a sallow meditation,
> Suck thy veins dry, distemperance rob thy sleep!
> *The heart's disquiet is revenge most deep:*
> *He that gets blood, the life of flesh but spills,*
> *But he that breaks heart's peace, the dear soul kills.*
> (156–60)

The killing of a 'soul', identified with a peaceful 'heart', by means of a vampiristic draining of emotional 'blood' – such imagery establishes aphanitic subjectivity as an index of powerlessness. This perspective depends on the radically unstable nature of post-Babel language; indeed, the indignant cry, 'Are ye building Babylon there?' (1.1.3), provoked at the opening by Malevole's discordant music, issues from a collective discursive state so thoroughly 'fallen' that the lack of contrast becomes the point. In deploying, Iago-like, the slipperiness of signification as his instrument of policy, Altofront-Malevole taps into the policy of the text itself, whereby language, like the characters constructed by it, continually undercuts and undoes itself – an effect epitomized by Piero's astonishing palindrome: 'Fly, call, run, row, ride, cry, shout, hurry, haste, / Haste, hurry, shout, cry, ride, row, run, call, fly' (*Antonio and Mellida* 3.2.271–2).

But while Marston's work thus puts one foot into the category of plays to be considered next, the resemblances are passing ones, and for suggestive reasons. Marston's comprehensive satire takes aim, not only at claims to metaphysical presence – the stock-in-trade of orthodox moralists – but also at the agonies of absence. The fading of the subject through discourse is taken for granted, not made an occasion for tragic self-consciousness, much less for existential enquiry. The vacuum at the 'heart' of the human condition is so violently abhorred – not, it seems, by the dramatist, but by his caricatures of self-delusion – that it is endlessly filled and refilled with stock roles, attitudes, and postures.

Even on the single occasion when one of his self-speakers flirts with an experience of aphanisis, Marston deflects the discourse of self-seeking into parody, here of Petrarchism. The love-stricken Antonio runs on stage, not only addressing but literally chasing himself: 'Stop, stop Antonio! Stay Antonio! / Vain breath, vain breath, Antonio's lost. / He cannot find himself, not seize himself' (*Antonio and Mellida* 4.1.1–3). Then, instead of following this discursive thread into an inner labyrinth, the hero expounds his divided state in direct address to the audience – a dislocating throwback to the in-joking technique of *Wit and Science* and *Johan Johan*:

> Alas, this that you see is not Antonio.
> His spirit hovers in Piero's court,
> Hurling about his agile faculties
> To apprehend the sight of Mellida.
>
> (4–7)

Indeed, Antonio goes so far as to respond, like Johan Johan, to imaginary objections: ''Tis so. Ill give you instance that 'tis so. / Conceit you me . . .' (12–13).

From this point, Antonio's language grows increasingly elaborate along Petrarchan lines, absurdly giving the lie to the absence of 'discursive powers' (18) of which he complains, as he appears suddenly to realize: 'what was't I said? / O, this is naught but speckling melancholy' (23–4). Next, as if recalling that he is supposed to be a mere empty 'trunk' (16), devoid of 'soul' (20), he collapses to the resounding accompaniment of hollow cliché: 'Clod upon clod thus fall. / Hell is beneath, yet Heaven is over all' (28–9). Thus a discourse of transcendental authority is at once restored and discredited – exposed as artificial and arbitrary, yet also as the necessary substance of the otherwise vacant world-as-stage, where '[n]ever more woe in lesser plot was found' (*Antonio's Revenge* 5.3.176).

However Antonio (especially in the second play) came to be Hamlet's *Doppelgänger* – G. K. Hunter suggests independent derivation from the *Ur-Hamlet* (xx) – the figure developed by Shakespeare as the epitome of the tragically aphanitic subject emerges here as a caricatured emblem of the psychological processes by which self-subversion may itself be subverted, or short-circuited. The impasse thereby delineated lies at the core of Marston's dramatic parody-satires and extends to their genre; for however much 'woe' provokes and attends Antonio's revenge – and regardless of the tragicomic label mandated by Altofront's refusal to shed physical blood – all three works effectively reconfigure tragedy, substituting for the invariable (though spiritually varying) fall of the tragic subject a pathetically ingenious resistance to gravity (in both senses of the word). The problematic relation between character and content, key to the notoriously puzzling tone of these works – how serious are they, and how are they serious?[2] – is focused by their complex engagement with current models of dramatic self-speaking.

II

The seriousness of Webster's *The White Devil* and *The Duchess of Malfi* (probably written in 1612 and 1614, respectively) is unchallenged; so is their concern with the problematic position of the individual subject in relation to larger forces – social, cultural, supernatural. To refocus the question on subjectivity itself is to acknowledge those forces as failing to supply characters, at least unequivocally, with a transcendental source and measure of identity. It is also to recognize the texts as unusually rife with self-speaking, as well as with motifs, embodied in both speech and action, of the self reflected (or deflected or refracted) in what it chooses (or is made) to see. Broadly speaking, both plays, which are largely studies in obsessive persecution, adapt the dynamic of subjectivity set out in *Othello*. There such persecution enacts an outrunning of the unconscious and a transfer of its aphanitic burden to a figure emblematic of discursive self-sufficiency, of presence. For the relative black and white of Shakespeare's antagonist and protagonist, however, Webster substitutes – and proliferates – shades of grey, which, far from standing out against the backdrop of the play-world, blend indistinctly into it.

This process begins with the female characters at the centre of the main intrigues. Far from staking a claim to presence through narrative self-fashioning, the women who give Webster's plays their titles incur the imputation of presence, hence of menace, by negative, passive, and *silent* mechanisms. The White Devil herself delivers no soliloquies, unless we count (and they certainly do count in their way) her aphoristic reflections as death approaches. The single brief soliloquy of the Duchess of Malfi is the exception that proves the rule of silence, effectively interposing the shield of a 'masculine' persona before the 'feminine' self with which her brothers are so obsessed:

> . . . as men in some great battles,
> By apprehending danger, have achiev'd
> Almost impossible actions – I have heard soldiers say so –
> So I, through frights, and threat'nings, will assay
> This dangerous venture.
>
> (1.1.344–8)

The deeper 'wilderness' (359) she is exploring, the mysterious and intuitive stuff from which 'old wives' are to weave their tale of how she 'wink'd and chose a husband' (348–9), will remain inaccessible. Thus, too, the relatively few self-speaking monologues of the Duchess, as well as Vittoria, are mostly in the mode of resistance, as they defy the efforts of their persecutors to make them at once reveal and unsay themselves. They are subjected to – but never by – a barrage of harsh judgements, cynical opinions, and outright assaults. These include formal confrontations with symbolic images intended to manifest a transcendental authority, but which recoil upon their originators. It is significant that one such confrontation – Ferdinand's doubly insinuating gift of the dagger he had shown the Duchess in the opening scene ('This was my father's poniard' [*Duchess* 1.1.331]) – comes when she has inadvertently found herself speaking alone ('have you lost your tongue?' [3.2.68]), thanks to the trick played on her by Antonio. What her brother overhears – 'I enter'd you into my heart / Before you would vouchsafe to call for the keys' (61–2) – at once gives him superficial power over her and confirms her inner mystery in such daunting terms that he begs her to keep it hidden.

The moral contrast between the two central women makes the similarity in their resistance all the more striking. The Duchess is patently victimized by Bosola's ghoulish disguises, the show of madmen, the waxen figures representing Antonio and the children as dead. Vittoria largely deserves the image that Montalto seeks to fix upon her at her trial. Yet the latter's 'brave spirit' (*White Devil* 3.2.140) discursively produces a similar core of untouchability in terms that anticipate the Duchess's situation – and that gain further intertextual support from Shakespeare's slandered Hermione, who had appeared on stage a couple of years before:[3]

> For know that all your strict-combined heads,
> Which strike against this mine of diamonds,
> Shall prove but glassen hammers, they shall break, –
> These are but feigned shadows of my evils.
> Terrify babes, my lord, with painted devils,
> I am past such needless palsy, – for your names
> Of whore and murd'ress they proceed from you,
> As if a man should spit against the wind,
> The filth returns in's face.
>
> (143–51)

In thus repudiating the diabolic (and energizing the paradox in the play's title), Vittoria effectively links the devil with the unconscious motives of her persecutors – a point reinforced later by the revengers' Moorish disguises. Such a link is more evident in the Duchess's case, thanks to her hellish tormenting. But then even the Duchess's chosen husband, when she woos him with her ring, senses anxiously that 'a saucy and ambitious devil / Is dancing in this circle' (*Duchess* 1.1.412–13). The imagery helps to develop the extraordinary disjunction between the performative and the constative in Webster's tragedies, whereby characters tend to act first and explain themselves later, and often lamely, in a sort of retrospective self-fashioning, as if to illustrate the principle that 'it is the very *knowledge that cannot know itself*, that, in man, *acts*' (Felman 96).

The association between rejection of an alien discourse and possession of a solid core of identity, Vittoria's 'mine of diamonds', also underlies Bosola's account to Ferdinand of the Duchess's endurance: 'her silence, / Methinks, expresseth more than if she spake' (4.1.9–10). Still, it is important to pick up the signal in 'methinks' (a virtual indicator of the obtruding unconscious in soliloquies of the period[4]) that this remains a *reading*, hence a projection – precisely the one that drives Ferdinand, first to greater extremities aimed at dividing the Duchess from herself, then to mad self-division of his own, when he finally realizes, in effect, that his utmost intimacy with the Duchess must still be no more than to 'study in the book / Of another's heart' (16–17). It is in the thwarted ears of their would-be auditors that the women's actions speak, if not louder, at least more deeply and truly, than their words, which remain frustratingly *ad hoc* and tangential, as if they merely assume a 'fallen' language to conceal their prelapsarian one.

Even when the Duchess enjoins her murderers, 'Pull, and pull strongly, for your able strength / Must pull down heaven upon me' (4.2.230–1), then, as she kneels, opposes 'heaven-gates' (232) to 'princes' palaces' (233), she appears less to yield to conventional religious discourse than to appropriate it, martyr-like, at her enemies' expense: 'Go tell my brothers, when I am laid out, / They then may feed in quiet' (236–7). So, from a contrary moral position, Vittoria seems to do when she turns violently on her lover: 'I had a limb corrupted to an ulcer, / But I have cut it off: and now I'll go / Weeping to heaven on crutches' (*White Devil* 4.2.121–3). On the point of death, however, Vittoria finally gives way, mingling with her courage a succinct concession to a transcendental discourse: 'O my greatest sin lay in my blood. / Now my blood pays for't' (5.6.240–1). Tellingly, this is what it takes to make Flamineo, also mortally wounded, exclaim, 'Th'art a noble sister – / I love thee now' (241–2). She then joins him – 'My soul, like to a ship in a black storm, / Is driven I know not whither' (248–9) – in the characteristic final posture of Webster's aphanitic subjects: 'O I am in a mist' (260). The imminence of an end to discourse itself – 'I have lost my voice / Most irrecoverably' (271–2) – imposes on Flamineo the ultimate futility of seeking the self in a transcendental mirror: on the one hand, 'There's nothing of so infinite vexation / As a man's own thoughts' (205–6); on the other, 'While we look up to heaven we confound / Knowledge with knowledge' (259–60).

It goes without saying, at least by the female protagonists themselves, that the mainspring of their actions is sexual desire. Their threatening presence is a reflection of attempts, especially on the part of their brothers, to circumscribe their sexuality. The egregious physical obsession of Ferdinand with his (twin) sister points to analogous repression and displacement in *The White Devil*. As becomes clearer when he loses his influence after Bracciano's death, Flamineo, too, aims to control his sister sexually, though by the inverse expedient of pandering her. Francisco is like Ferdinand (and likewise backed, though to a more limited extent, by a Cardinal-brother) insofar as he seeks to avenge his sister's sexual humiliation, hence his own. In both plays, the overtones of incest help to delineate the dynamic of subjectivity with regard to the male characters generally – including those who, as it were, take the brothers' places: the women are crucial to the way in which the men see (or fail to see) themselves, the projection of presence amounting to an index of self-absence. There is little distance between Bracciano's conventionally Petrarchan but resonant declaration, which opens the main plot of *The White Devil* – 'Quite lost Flamineo' (1.2.3) – and Ferdinand's raving to the Cardinal about the Duchess's sexual behaviour: 'I could kill her now, / In you, or in myself, for I do think / It is some sin in us, heaven doth revenge / By her' (*Duchess* 2.5.63–6).

When the female objects of male projection are removed, the mechanisms of self-reflection swarm to the textual surface. This effect is most conspicuous in *The Duchess of Malfi*, where the corpse of his murdered sister suddenly images, for her twin, the ultimate absence: 'mine eyes dazzle: she died young' (4.2.264); 'should I die this instant, I had liv'd / Her time to a minute' (268–9). Subsequently, Ferdinand's lycanthropy enacts the revenge of his projected unconscious, re-possessing him through monstrous thoughts and psychotic speech, causing him to dismember rather than remember. In the play's other villains, the reflective mechanisms of the unconscious-made-conscience remain contained within frameworks of self-speaking. Bosola seems ('methinks' [5.2.345]) to be haunted by the Duchess's ghost but concludes, ''Tis nothing but my melancholy' (347). The Cardinal cannot escape a diabolical mirror-image, but his commentary keeps it at a distance:

> – how tedious is a guilty conscience!
> When I look into the fish-ponds, in my garden,
> Methinks I see a thing, arm'd with a rake
> That seems to strike at me.
>
> (5.5.4–7)

In both cases, 'methinks' encodes the entire mechanism of self-regarding subjectivity.

When the Cardinal tricks Julia into kissing the poisoned book (Webster seems chary about identifying it as a Bible) on the pretext of sealing an oath of silence, he symbolically manipulates transcendental discourse in the cause of discursive hegemony, although, in fact, his confession has reached the ears of Bosola. The Cardinal has just made Julia, at her insistence, the repository of his secret; now he sacrifices her, scapegoat-like, as if ironically accepting her offer to 'remove / This lead from off your bosom' (5.2.232–3) by making the lead a wrapping for her corpse. The terms of the offer are suggestive in themselves. Julia proposes to become the mirror-image of his conscience, the reflection of a merely divided self, and so to stop the slippage in signification entailed in keeping the secret to himself:

> Tell your echo this,
> Or flatterers that like echoes still report
> What they hear though most imperfect, and not me:
> For, if that you be true unto yourself,
> I'll know.

>   (243–7)

A key phrase here is the apparently innocuous 'though most imperfect'. The Satanic subtlety of Julia's attempted seduction ('You shall see me wind my tongue about his heart, / Like a skein of silk' [222–3]) consists in her surreptitious promise to substitute the 'truth' of unitary signification for the aphanitic speaking of the 'self alone' – a discourse for which the imperfect 'echo', whose very essence lies is its fading, serves as an apt image.

It is an image taken up in action shortly afterwards. The ambiguous relation throughout the play between inward and outward, natural and supernatural, self and Other, is focused in Antonio's echo-punctuated monologue in Act 5, Scene 3. The sequence culminates in an equally ambiguous vision, dismissed by Delio as '[y]our fancy, merely' (5.3.46), when the echo apparently answers Antonio's question, 'O heaven, / Shall I never see her more?' (41–2), by repeating his last four words: 'I mark'd not one repetition of the echo / But that: and on the sudden, a clear light / Presented me a face folded in sorrow' (43–5). Until this moment, the echo, despite evoking 'my wife's voice' (26), has seemed as much 'a dead thing' (39) as Antonio's spirit: it is dismissable as a mere carbon copy, mechanically tracing the contours of the self while having nothing to do with it. But to answer a question is suddenly to come to life and seize an epistemological middle-ground, breaking the illusory chain of perfect self-communication. Antonio's words now come back to him as the self made Other, a mirror-image as dazzling in its way as that which confronted Ferdinand and as fully charged with the message of self-absence. Antonio flees from aphanisis into the discourse of the absolute, desperately resolving to achieve either 'true' absence or 'true' presence:

> Come: I'll be out of this ague;
> For to live thus is not indeed to live:
> It is a mockery, and abuse of life –
> I will not henceforth save myself by halves;
> Lose all, or nothing.
>
> (47–51)

The climactic multiple revenge in *The White Devil* is also riddled with imagery confirming that self-images are at stake. The pattern begins, however, with Bracciano's murder of Isabella by means of his poisoned portrait, which she reverently kisses, and with the staging of this scene as a vision produced by the Conjurer's glass. As in *Friar Bacon*, this technique at once confers and problematizes a god's-eye-view, such as Bracciano also exercises over the trial of Vittoria. The 'lost' Bracciano evidently supposes that he has found himself; later, the very helmet that at once protects and conceals his face will turn on him. The project of Francisco, seconded by Lodovico, counters in kind the manipulators of deceptive appearances and ultimately imposes non-(id)entity upon them. I have already mentioned the realizations of self-absence marking the deaths of Vittoria and Flamineo; Bracciano will 'be forgotten / Before thy funeral sermon' (5.3.166–7) – or so he is assured by Lodovico, whose murderous fantasies earlier ran to poisoning those instruments of self-reflection, 'his prayer book' and 'his looking-glass' (5.1.69–70). The broad dynamic is standard, of course, for stage retribution from the time of *The Spanish Tragedy*, and it includes the revengers' own transcendental self-definition through bloody action – a feature highlighted here through their self-speaking.

Lodovico's identity as a villain emerges as a given, authorized by Montalto's 'black book', but he seems at first to be drifting in the currents of a generalized vindictive impulse. He is about to give up the project when Francisco tricks him into believing in the Pope's sanction. But he has already begun to fasten his idea of himself, his 'soul', to the righting of Isabella's wrong, to judge from his strange 'confession' to Montalto, which recalls Iago:

> Sir I did love Bracciano's duchess dearly;
> Or rather I pursued her with hot lust,
> Though she ne'er knew on't. She was poison'd;
> Upon my soul she was: for which I have sworn
> T'avenge her murder.
>
> (4.3.111–15)

By the end of the play, he has so deeply imbued his identity in the cause that he not only echoes Iago's triumphant vow to meet torture with silence but arrogates Bracciano's transcendental mastery of a visual discourse that 'truly' reflects him:

> I do glory yet,
> That I can call this act mine own: – for my part,
> The rack, the gallows, and the torturing wheel
> Shall be but sound sleeps to me, – here's my rest –
> I limb'd this night-piece and it was my best.
>
> (5.6.293–7)

Lodovico's progression from constative to performative self-imaging summarily traces the process undergone by the prime conspirator, which is self-documented in the play's most extensive soliloquy (over sixty lines) in Act 4, Scene 1. Francisco's initial response to his sister's death is limited to the agony of self-absence, precipitated by the sight of her son:

> O, all of my poor sister that remains!
> Take him away for God's sake. . . .
> Believe me I am nothing but her grave,
> And I shall keep her blessed memory
> Longer than thousand epitaphs.
>
> (3.2.339–43)

The conception of his revenge in and through soliloquy is explicitly an act of self-fashioning, a discursive conjuration:

> To fashion my revenge more seriously,
> Let me remember my dead sister's face:
> Call for her picture: no; I'll close mine eyes,
> And in a melancholic thought I'll frame
> Her figure 'fore me.
>
> (4.1.98–102)

The image Francisco conjures, however, is supposed to remain part of himself, under control. When Isabella's ghost actually appears, the subversive impact resembles that of the objectified echo in *The Duchess of Malfi*. Self-fashioning, which presumes a prelapsarian discourse with no gap between the constative and the performative, is abruptly destabilized. The closed system of self-reflection, the symmetrical filling of absence with presence, is disrupted by the threatening image of the self as Other, the source and object of interrogation. Yet again 'methinks' signals the process, as a unitary and seemingly self-sufficient discourse dissolves into fragments whose inadequacy (hence 'authenticity') discloses the unconscious:

> Now I ha't – how strong
> Imagination works! how she can frame
> Things which are not! methinks she stands afore me . . .
> . . . 'Tis my melancholy, –
> How cam'st thou by thy death? – how idle am I
> To question mine own idleness? – did ever
> Man dream awake till now? . . .
>
> (102–12)

Now that it carries the message of difference, Isabella's image must be expunged – that is, reabsorbed – before the role of revenger can be transcendentalized in an exchange of presence for absence, life for death:

> . . . remove this object –
> Out of my brain with't: what have I to do
> With tombs, or death-beds, funerals, or tears,
> That have to meditate upon revenge?
>
> (112–15)

The performative element thus engendered takes on a metadramatic dimension, including a reappropriation of 'idleness': 'My tragedy must have some idle mirth in't, / Else it will never pass' (119–20). Francisco's final condition is that of the self-flatterer – 'being alone I now flatter myself' (125) – whose solipsism obviates the imperfection in flattery, the slippage of which Julia in *The Duchess of Malfi* cunningly (but not wisely) reminds the Cardinal. And when the revenge is finally realized, for Francisco, too, there is a god-like transcendence at once of morality and mortality in the thrill of self-creation:

> Tush for justice.
> What harms it justice? we now, like the partridge

> Purge the disease with laurel: for the fame
> Shall crown the enterprize and quit the shame.
>   (5.3.267–70)

With regard to dramatic practices in Stuart tragedy, Webster stands at the opposite end of the stylistic spectrum from Chapman and Jonson, taking to an extreme the subjectifying tendencies found in Shakespeare. The discursive transcendentalism that in Chapman and Jonson pervades self-speaking here flashes intermittently through the 'mist' of aphanitic subjectivity, an *ignis fatuus* signifying nothing but characters' erratic attempts to find their way out. Given the absence of any ultimately controlling script – even one produced by an internal dramatist, as in certain Shakespearean cases – the insistent imagery of the world-as-theatre points to multiple scenarios, competing on a nearly equal basis. Instead of holding the transcendental mirror up to an hypostatized nature – a conceptual counterweight, at least, throughout Shakespeare's tragedies – Webster's theatre shows human nature infinitely (de)constructing itself through discursive self-mirroring, whose ultimate effect is to expose discourse itself as an instrument for repressing what 'no subject can bear' – namely, 'the reduction of its being to no more than its flesh and blood reality' (Safouan 85). Such a perspective provides a theoretical link between the 'psychological depth' with which Webster's characters are traditionally credited and the critical commonplace that his tragedies are deficient not merely in eschatological confidence but also, more unsettlingly, in moral focus.

III

To situate Middleton and Ford within this framework is to draw back from extremes and find the relation between transcendentalism and aphanitic subjectivity made once again, as generally in Shakespeare, a matter of variable negotiation. In contrast with Shakespearean practice, however, the nature of the transcendental is clearly defined in the work of both playwrights – as clearly as in Chapman and Jonson. Indeed, Middleton, like Jonson, sets his characters against a conventional moral and religious background, while Ford, whose quasi-heroic rebels bang their heads against a wall of neo-pagan destiny (with predictably fatal results), performs ironic renovations on Chapman's dynamic of *virtù*. Still, Middleton and Ford differ radically from these predecessors in creating figures who are *discursively* 'free to fall' – to fall, that is, into the gap between the constative and the performative defining the unconscious. Such falls are typically chronicled in self-speaking and supported by the imagery of self-reflection.

From this point of view, the main plots of Middleton's two tragedies, *The Changeling* (a collaboration, of course, with William Rowley) and *Women Beware Women*, tell essentially the same story. In both cases, there is an initial fall, easily read in terms of Medieval moral theology; that fall, however, comprises two stages – discursively encoded, as I hope to show – in keeping with the two-part induction into subjectivity formulated by Lacan. First, the members of the key couples (Alsemero and Beatrice-Joanna, Leantio and Bianca) lose sight of the religious and social precepts by which they ought to measure themselves. Spiritual and moral authority is henceforth suspended – except in the audience's view and in passing repentant glimpses – until the catastrophe, at which point those characters still in speaking condition refigure themselves by gazing, with astonishment and horror proportionate to their guilt or negligence, in that forgotten mirror. Before this, however, there is a second fall into aphanitic subjectivity, the 'nothing' that is unbearably something. Hippolito's summary pins the blame not only on sexual appetite but also, effectively, on the unconscious: 'Lust and forgetfulness has been amongst us, / And we are brought to nothing' (*Women* 5.2.146–7).

The initiating unions in both plays involve various forms of theft and deception. However, the couples initially escape the implications of their actions by viewing themselves in the delusive mirror of sensuality, whose function, in characteristic Medieval fashion, is at once idolatrous and narcissistic. The lovers' first condition is thus akin to Lacan's mirror-stage, with its simultaneous illusion of plenitude and surreptitious reminder of defect. The latter element is shadowed by the defensiveness and rationalization that pervade the self-speaking of all four characters.

The Changeling opens with Alsemero's effort, in soliloquy, to justify the diversion of his devotions from God to Beatrice-Joanna, whom he configures as an alternative means of reversing the Fall:

> The place is holy, so is my intent:
> I love her beauties to the holy purpose,
> And that, methinks, admits comparison

With man's first creation, the place blest,
And is his right home back, if he achieve it.
                                                    (1.1.5–9)

The linguistic indicators of slippage here ('intent', 'methinks') join his dismissal of his misgiving as 'imaginary' (3) to manifest unconscious stirrings. No less (if less concisely) defensive is Leantio's attitude in his two early soliloquies. To accord Bianca the transcendental status of 'jewel' and 'treasure' (*Women* 1.1.160 ff.) is at once to confirm her as his possession and to render her vulnerable to (re)stealing; after all, the essence of property is its transferability. Two scenes later, in a narcissistic, even masturbatory, monologue, reeking of obsession, he sets up sensuality as a alternative 'religion'; this is to go Alsemero a step farther, with the result of precipitating the unconscious as conscience: 'Oh fie, what a religion have I leaped into! / Get out again, for shame' (1.3.21–2).

Despite his pervasive *double entendre* and rampant imagination, Leantio clings to unitary meanings and moral commonplaces, as in his lecture to Bianca a few lines later: 'As fitting is a government in love / As in a kingdom . . .' (43–4). The contradiction is encapsulated in his soliloquy in Act 3, Scene 2, just before the axe falls. Here, as he returns home, his transcendental 'Bower of Bliss' rhetoric ('How near am I now to a happiness / That earth exceeds not . . .' [3.2.1–2]) modulates into extended self-congratulation – infiltrated, however, by 'methinks' – for his ability to resist prostitutes:

                              . . . I do liken straight
        Her beautified body to a goodly temple
        That's built on vaults where carcasses lie rotting;
        And so by little and little I shrink back again,
        And quench desire with a cool meditation;
        And I'm as well methinks. Now for a welcome
        Able to draw men's envies upon man . . .
                                                    (16–22)

The motif of prostitution proves pivotal, for when Bianca's changed behaviour subverts his self-congratulation – and even before he knows the worst – he turns to envying men who obtain sex without engaging anything more than the body; such a person keeps his identity whole, self-sufficient: 'And if he find her dead at his return,

/ His pity is soon done – he breaks a sigh / In many parts, and gives her but a piece on 't!' (209–11).

Bianca's mere 'alteration' (197) entails Leantio's immeasurable 'loss' (204): 'The distractions, / The fears and doubts it brings are numberless' (197–8). Next, knowledge of the facts brings the unconscious home to roost, causing emptiness to overflow, although, as is characteristic of Middleton, self-loss is mitigated by a tinge of transcendentally authorized self-discovery in the form of an accusing conscience: 'I'm rightly now oppressed; / All her friends' heavy hearts lie in my breast' (3.3.95–6). Still, that the void of self-absence will swallow up Leantio is evident in his soliloquy later in the third scene, where he figures his life as a set of impossible conditions, a labyrinth of symbolic exchange relations (in contrast with his previous splendid isolation), from which he can hope to take flight only through a down-to-earth version of the traditional revenger's counter-identity:

> Then my safest course,
> For health of mind and body, is to turn
> My heart, and hate her, most extremely hate her;
> I have no other way.
>
> (337–40)

He mimics not Daedalus but Icarus, however, when, by making Livia the instrument of his hatred in the guise of loving her – an oblique realization of his prostitution fantasy – he flies too near the 'court sun' (4.2.21).

The untenable commitment of Alsemero to signs supposedly at once objective and within his control is figured literally in the letter-marked vials described in ' "The Book of Experiment, / Call'd Secrets in Nature" ' (*Changeling* 4.1.24–5) – clearly a poor substitute for his Bible. Beatrice-Joanna's successful deception, when Alsemero tests her virginity, enacts the reality of significatory slippage, to which, however, Alsemero remains blind until his friend supplies (conspicuously unlike Iago) 'ocular proof' (*Oth.* 3.3.360) of the liaison with De Flores.[5] Still, Alsemero is given only a brief aside evocative of self-loss before the entrance of Beatrice-Joanna begins the dénouement: 'Did my fate wait for this unhappy stroke / At my first sight of woman? – She's here' (5.3.12–13). After all, his textual destiny is to survive as the mouthpiece of the restored transcendental discourse: 'justice hath so right / The guilty hit, that innocence is quit / By proclamation, and may joy again' (185–7). It suits this role that he affirms the validity of signs while backhandedly admitting his failure to interpret his wife correctly ('You read me well enough, I am not well' [16]) and that, with her confession of complicity in Piracquo's murder, his previously ill-defined misgivings flow into the prepared channel of conscience:

> Oh, the place itself e'er since
> Has crying been for vengeance, the temple
> Where blood and beauty first unlawfully
> Fir'd their devotion, and quench'd the right one;
> 'Twas in my fears at first, 'twill have it now:
> Oh, thou art all deform'd!
>
> (72–7)

Nevertheless, Beatrice-Joanna's new image in Alsemero's eyes at first reflects the ugliness of his own unconscious complicity, and her assertion that she has been 'true unto your bed' (82) subverts the value of such truth, until now an absolute signifier for him. An overwhelming perception of mortality – a standard index of self-loss – obtrudes on his conscience's clear directives: 'The bed itself's a charnel, the sheets shrouds / For murdered carcasses; it must ask pause / What I must do in this' (83–5). But again he gets only a moment alone on stage, once he has locked up Beatrice-Joanna, before a way out of the aphanitic labyrinth is offered, this time by De Flores in an ironic reprise of the latter's timely appearances earlier: 'Oh, in what part / Of this sad story shall I first begin? – Ha! / This same fellow has put me in – De Flores!' (87–9).

The phrase 'put me in', although it carries the secondary sense of 'got me embroiled' and so highlights Alsemero's fall into a nightmarish parody of exchange relations, more immediately means 'given me my cue', thereby alluding metadramatically to the opportune answering of Alsemero's question. This is, moreover, an answer in a broader sense, since with De Flores comes the revelation of Beatrice-Joanna's adultery. Once she can be labelled as 'whore' (107), her sexual fallenness resumes primacy of place in Alsemero's imagination; the semiotic logic of his value-system is restored, and with it his impeccable position, to judge from the undertone of relief: 'It could not choose but follow; oh cunning devils!' (108). Sin should flow from sin, not from such virtue as he had read into Beatrice-Joanna's love. Alsemero authoritatively summarizes (197 ff.)

the labyrinthine changes to the doomed household so as at once to reclaim his original status as innocent outsider – any sexual transgression on his part having been 'paid before' (201) by the death of Diaphanta – and to centre himself confidently (and advantageously) within the purged family: 'Sir, you have yet a son's duty living, / Please you, accept it' (216–17). The 'deform'd' Beatrice-Joanna now clearly reflects De Flores – and *vice versa* – not himself. How far, then, has he progressed beyond the love-sick 'fool' of the subplot, Antonio, who assures Isabella, 'Look you but cheerfully, and in your eyes / I shall behold mine own deformity, / And dress myself up fairer' (3.3.185–7), and who can still claim at the conclusion that 'my innocence always excuses me' (5.3.206–7)?

As in Webster's tragedies, the moral and imaginative centre of *The Changeling* and *Women Beware Women* is female sexuality, constituted as a source and emblem of moral failure. And if these texts contrast with Webster's in appearing broadly to validate rather than to subvert that view, the difference flows at least partly from its broader diffusion into relatively 'normal' social conditions: Beatrice-Joanna, Bianca, and both Isabellas are all conspicuously trapped within a repressive patriarchal web. With respect to subjectivity and self-speaking, moreover, a basic pattern recurs across the gender boundary, except that the women destined for fallen status are initially positioned at a greater remove from the subversive unconscious. By comparison with Alsemero and Leantio, respectively, Beatrice-Joanna and Bianca appear more 'wholeheartedly' committed to present gratification. In contrast with Alsemero's soliloquized evasiveness about an 'omen' (*Changeling* 1.1.2) in conflict with desire, Beatrice-Joanna, in brief asides, handily aligns destiny with fancy – 'Sure, mine eyes were mistaken, / This was the man was meant me' (1.1.84–5) – and recycles Alsemero's language as if parodically: 'I shall change my saint, I fear me' (155).

Bianca has neither soliloquy nor aside until Act 4, as suits a subjectivity allowed into play only in male-serving (if female-facilitated) games, in which she initially figures as a pawn. (Witness the chess match framing her encounter with the Duke [*Women* 2.2.294 ff.].) Her conflicted internalization of the rules is established when she makes a belated transition from object to subject of speech 125 lines into the first scene, at once purporting to transcend exchange relations through a prelapsarian discursive power and revealing a profound self-abnegation:

I have forsook friends, fortunes, and my country,
And hourly I rejoice in't. . . .

· · · · · · · · · · · · · · ·

I'll call this the place of my birth now,
And rightly too: for here my love was born,
And that's the birth-day of a woman's joys.

(1.1.131–41)

This double message, suggestive of regression to the mirror-stage, graphically undercuts Bianca's claim to be fulfilled in 'all' her 'desires' (1.1.126). So does the bourgeois materialism of Leantio, with which his own mirror-stage fantasizing remains uneasily in tension.

Their self-divided (initial) male partners, then, help to expose both Beatrice-Joanna and Bianca as more profoundly naïve and self-deluded, not just playing tricks with conscience but placing the unconscious itself beyond its capacity to destabilize identity. Isabella (in *Women Beware Women*) is in the same category, so desperately driven by incestuous love for Hippolito – a mirror-stage obsession – that she rushes to believe Livia's lies about her parentage. Her conscience remains intact: she never has to stop 'knowing better' in the moral sense. Consequently, according to the psycho-logic epitomized in *Othello*, the unconscious confronts these women in the Iago-like form of the projected 'malin génie'. This comparison particularly fits De Flores, who effectively transfers to Beatrice-Joanna – 'I'm in pain, / And must be eas'd of you' (*Changeling*, 3.4.98–9) – the burden of his own self-subverting and incommunicable desire, a burden initially registered in a succession of tortured soliloquies and asides. Both he and *Women Beware Women*'s Duke resemble Iago, too, in plunging their victims into self-absence, then immediately offering a new role to supply that absence: the progressive engagement of Beatrice-Joanna and Bianca in their roles as whores and secret murderers signifies, not merely an escalation of sinful depravity, but also a form of self-(re)fashioning, such as Othello, like numerous other male tragic protagonists, is 'free' to implement more actively (if no less self-destructively). Again, Isabella (in *Women Beware Women*) belongs in this group; her speech in Act 4, Scene 2, after she learns of her incest, typically moves from total self-loss – 'Was ever maid so cruelly beguiled / To the confusion of life, soul, and honour' (4.2.129–30) – to the plenitude of vengeful anticipation:

> If the least means but favour my revenge,
> That I may practise the like cruel cunning
> Upon her life, as she has on mine honour,
> I'll act it without pity.
>
> (147–50)

De Flores' failure, in refusing her money, to fulfil Beatrice-Joanna's image of him shatters her secure semiotic system: his ugliness and subservience had confirmed her beauty and power – an illusion of self-sufficiency proper to the mirror-stage. Communication is revealed as having been illusory, speech itself unreliable: they have been building the tower of Babel all along. She had fixed on him as an instrument for circumventing the *Nom/non* of her father. Now De Flores serves up an absolute but dislocatingly mysterious negation, backhandedly reimposing the phallic prohibition and so precipitating the exchange relations of the symbolic order, in which signification is up for grabs and infinitely slippery. The self fades out of its own view: 'I'm in a labyrinth' (3.4.71). Next, in arguing that he already possesses her morally and so might as well sexually, De Flores elevates the *Nom du Père* to the status of superego, inviting Beatrice-Joanna to discover her 'true' identity by using him as a mirror. To her denial of resemblance on the grounds of 'the distance that creation / Set 'twixt thy blood and mine' (130–1), he responds with an extraordinary rebuttal, using the emblems of both the mirror and the book:

> Look but into your conscience, read me there,
> 'Tis a true book, you'll find me there your equal:
> Push, fly not to your birth, but settle you
> In what the act has made you, y'are no more now;
> You must forget your parentage to me:
> Y'are the deed's creature; by that name
> You lost your first condition, and I challenge you,
> As peace and innocency has turn'd you out,
> And made you one with me.
>
> (132–40)

Thus, even while he threatens exposure, on another level De Flores offers refuge from the abyss of the unconscious through the sting of conscience, personified in himself. The dead feel nothing – witness the severing of Piracquo's finger; to cut oneself is to prove the presence of life, hence the life of presence. Beatrice-Joanna can escape self-fragmentation by (literally) embracing self-division, recuperating sin as reliably the mirror-image of virtue. This is to recover a prelapsarian discursive state at the core of a fallen 'condition'. The gap – now become an all-swallowing gulf – between the constative and the performative ('the act', 'the deed') is closed and foreclosed. A fixed link between signifier and signified is forged (the word works in both its senses) as surely as by any revenger's 'speaking body'.

'I could not get the ring without the finger' (28), De Flores explains, triumphing in the token that, in a parody of romantic heroism, he has fetched from the labyrinth of the castle. Neither, of course, can Beatrice-Joanna: murder and sexuality notoriously unite as signifieds here. But ultimately there is comfort in this union. De Flores' offer of shelter as he leads her off to bed – 'Come, rise, and shroud your blushes in my bosom' (167) – is as substantial as it is grotesque, while her subsequent transfer of mirror-stage idealization from Alsemero to De Flores does not simply reflect a deformed spirit newly in love with sin: 'How heartily he serves me! His face loathes one, / But look upon his care, who would not love him? / The east is not more beauteous than his service' (5.1.70–2). For both of them now, and until the final restoration of transcendental authority, whatever interrupts the mechanism of self-confirming self-reflection, threatening to separate the constative and performative modes – 'Ha! What art thou that tak'st away the light / 'Twixt that star and me?' (58–9) – can be dismissed as 'but a mist of conscience' (60) and dispelled in action.

Bianca's discursive fall and restitution begin with an even more abrupt and no less visual encounter with the *Nom du Père*, grotesquely incarnate. Besides her idealized union with her husband, the Duke fractures her previous unitary language, enmeshing her – the interweaving of pentameter lines is significant – within the duplicitous discourse of exchange relations:

> Bianca   Oh my extremity!
>   My lord, what seek you?
> Duke   Love.
> Bianca   'Tis gone already,
>   I have a husband.
> Duke   That's a single comfort;
>   Take a friend to him.

Bianca	That's a double mischief,
Or else there's no religion.	
Duke	Do not tremble
At fears of thine own making.	

(Women 2.2.345–50)

The last lines, beneath their 'atheism', gesture with Satanic subtlety towards aphanitic subjectivity.

Bianca's silent exit with the Duke shortly after (387) has traditionally been read as signalling a culpable susceptibility to his mingled erotic and material blandishments. Recently, Anthony B. Dawson has focused on this mingling to argue that the context of 'sexual blackmail, social institutions, and political power' (318) marks the encounter as a *de facto* rape, since Bianca, by her silence, is 'cut off from subjectivity, desire, and action' (305). This view, however, like the psychological analysis Dawson uses to support it, presumes a 'self' prior to and beyond discourse. If, on the contrary, the self is a function of discourse, Bianca emerges as more profoundly victimized, the Duke's voluble appeal as more profoundly diabolical: he at once cuts her adrift from her feeble discursive moorings and offers her, in effect, silence-as-power. When he promises, in return for her virtue, to 'give better in exchange: wealth, honour' (369), he effectively proposes to re-confine exchange relations within a closed system of signification. His subsequent argument that her mother would praise her prudence in accepting him and thereby undoing the consequences of her rash elopement ('Do not I know y'have cast away your life / Upon necessities, means merely doubtful / To keep you in indifferent health and fashion' [375–7]), is not strictly material; it precisely taps into the issue of family disapproval earlier established as a point of vulnerability. Finally, in place of the 'fears' he himself has just consigned her to on the principle of Marston's Malevole (*'he that breaks heart's peace, the dear soul kills'*), he hints at transcendence of time ('provide for ever' [382]) and – absurdly, on the surface – inner wholeness: 'Put trust in our love for the managing / Of all to thy heart's peace' (385–6). Given his power, however, the absurdity is less extreme than in the analogous appeal of De Flores, who similarly appears to impose silence but actually proffers it as an escape from discourse: 'Silence is one of pleasure's best receipts: / Thy peace is wrought for ever in this yielding' (*Changeling* 3.4.168–9). Certainly, the Duke's promise of protection is greater in both scope and credence: 'Let storms come when they list, they find thee sheltered' (*Women* 2.2.383). In short, he makes plain that the authority with which he first threatens her (334 ff.) is grounded in the phallic transcendental signifier – a 'Monument' (451) indeed.

No law of depravity's momentum, then, is needed to account for Bianca's declared commitment to sin when she reappears. Her new language is no more 'authentic' than that of her idealistic monologue in the first scene. It is just that an avowedly lost soul, fostered by the Duke, is better than none at all. The Duke's Satanic parody of divine creation, as he ushers his new creature into the public eye, extends to his sponsorship of women's souls:

> Come, Bianca,
> Of purpose sent into the world to show
> Perfection once in woman; I'll believe
> Henceforward they have ev'ry one a soul too
> 'Gainst all the uncourteous opinions
> That man's uncivil rudeness ever held of 'em.
>
> (3.3.22–7)

Yet from the height of her new position – that is, from the depths of her new 'soul' – Bianca has sufficient perspective to formulate in soliloquy, if only obliquely, the repressive mechanism that rendered her vulnerable to self-subversion:

> 'tis not good, in sadness,
> To keep a maid so strict in her young days;
> Restraint breeds wand'ring thoughts, as many fasting days
> A great desire to see flesh stirring again.
>
> (4.1.30–3)

The sexual focus, worldly-wise tone, and fatalistic resignation all reinforce her new self-image, which, however, blurs into a fantasy of vicarious liberation: 'I'll ne'er use any girl of mine so strictly: / Howe'er they're kept, their fortunes find 'em out; / I see't in me' (34–6). Bianca is thereby marked as still on the run from intimations of emptiness.

Hence, her resolution to remove the Cardinal as a threat to her relation with the Duke, as well as her collapse into acute self-absence when – precisely as if thwarted by the 'malin génie' – she misdirects the poison to the sun of her new universe:

> Oh the curse of wretchedness!
> My deadly hand is fallen upon my lord.
> Destruction take me to thee; give me way;
> The pains and plagues of a lost soul upon him
> That hinders me a moment!
>
> (5.2.184–8)

Bianca herself, of course, is the chief 'lost soul', but the allusion is far from narrowly religious, thanks to her history of recurrent self-subversion. Similarly, the masquers' mutually destructive efforts at transcendental self-fashioning make it difficult to reduce the catastrophe to a brusque gesture of the hand of Providence. The cumulative result is that even Bianca's dying vision of herself in the transcendental discourse of divine judgement – 'Leantio, now I feel the breach of marriage / At my heart-breaking' (208–9) – appears to fade aphanitically.

IV

Nobody would accuse Ford's tragic characters of falling prey to 'forgetfulness' – least of all those characters themselves. This points to a major divergence from Middleton when it comes to the relation between subjectivity, as developed through self-speaking, and the transcendental discourse posited by the text at large. In Ford's plays, that discourse inscribes fatality, which looms as a more or less constant presence in the consciousness of his principal figures, thanks to the inexorably contrary circumstances of their existence. The latter chiefly take the form of obstacles to the legitimate fulfilment of sexual love: marriage to another, friendship, rank, consanguinity; and it is that love, indelibly stamped as impossible (the very nature of desire, after all) which encodes the condition of aphanitic subjectivity. Broadly speaking, the 'heart' in Ford's drama supersedes the 'soul' in Middleton's – from *The Broken Heart* to the heart of Annabella, brandished on her brother's sword in *'Tis Pity She's a Whore*, to the vow of Fernando in *Love's Sacrifice*, which Bianca will later (2.4 [54][6]) echo to him, substituting her name for his:

> If, when I am dead, you rip
> The coffin of my heart, there shall you read

With constant eyes, what now my tongue defines,
Bianca's name carv'd out in bloody lines.

(2.3 [49])

In Ford's inwardly focused development of Petrarchan convention, the unattainable love object does not simply enter into a dyadic
structure of plenitude and privation – the poles of 'hot' and 'cold'
between which the traditional lover's desire endlessly circulates.
This is to operate as if the mirror-stage were detached from the
'cadre' of 'l'Autre(A)' or, on the discursive level, as if the very
inadequacy of words made them 'enhanced with a halo of Presence, a dimension of Source they cannot quite capture' (Regan 38).
For Ford's desperate lovers, alienation from the beloved object takes
full account of radical alienation from language itself; the impossibility of their situations resonates in the discursive structure of each
text. And, paradoxically, what highlights at once their dependence
on language and its inadequacy is an element foreign to Petrarchism
– the reciprocity of desire.

Love's Sacrifice pivots on a particularly vivid transformation of the
Petrarchan mechanism. As long as Fernando supposes himself dis-
dained by the Duchess, he remains within the role of the longing
lover, soliloquizing (and writing) in highly conventional terms: 'if
I must not speak, I'll write' (2.2 [36]); 'she is all icy to my fires, /
Yet even that ice inflames in me desires' (2.1 [35]). His disclosure
of his 'heart' to her promises to be as futile as Mauraccio's absurd
plan to give his beloved a picture of himself that will open to reveal
'a clear and most transparent crystal in the form of a heart', so that
the lady will 'behold the excellence of her excellency's beauty in the
prospective and mirror, as it were, in my heart' (2.1 [31–2]). Given
Mauraccio's grotesque ineligibility – he would be seen through
figuratively as well as literally – his proposition neatly emblematizes
the Petrarchan solipsism whereby a mirror masquerades as a picture, a self-image as a gift of self.

When the Duchess, like an adored statue coming to life, confronts
Fernando at once with her equal desire and with a discourse –
'bridal vows' (2.4 [53]) – having prior claims, the Petrarchan strain
abruptly ceases. There is no further impulse to speak the self, since
language reveals only Otherness, by contrast with the silent presence of their united hearts. Yet that presence remains conditioned
by a discursive imposition of absence. Speech cannot be escaped,
and it proves both fragmented and fragmenting: 'This kiss, – best

life, good rest!' (2.4 [54]). Thus, when Bianca verbally mirrors
Fernando's extravagant vow that his heart will be hers in death, she
renders that assertion at once richly meaningful and more profoundly futile – the double effect, in fact, of the final double sacrifices and arguably the key to all Ford's tragedies of subjectivity.

As is clear from the recurrence of scenes showing speech as forbidden, Ford specializes in lovers who would speak to each other
but cannot, or not without the *inter*diction of the *Nom du Père*, enforcing the three linguistic conditions – arbitrary signification, symbolic exchange, and self-alienation – that are concisely foregrounded
by Giovanni in *'Tis Pity*:

> Shall a peevish sound,
> A customary form, from man to man,
> Of brother and of sister, be a bar
> 'Twixt my perpetual happiness and me?
> (1.1.24–7)

'Love' in Ford emerges as the most slippery signifier of all, modu-
lating into adultery, incest, jealousy, chastity, lust, murder, and death
– but never into satisfaction. These lovers all become, like the starved
Penthea, shadows possessed by others. Again and again in these
plays, the ideal of mutual desire is figured as impossible by the
impossibility of discursive fulfilment. And, ultimately, '[t]hey are
the silent griefs which cut the heart-strings' (*Broken Heart* 5.3.75)
because silence is imposed by, hence reflects, the nature of speech
itself.

If the leitmotif of *The Broken Heart* furnishes the very emblem of
love as aphanitic subjectivity, the central situation in *'Tis Pity* crys-
tallizes the typical discursive dynamic. Brother and sister are both
self and inescapably Other; their mutual desire manifests same-
ness only to activate subversive difference. Annabella's heart can *be*
Giovanni's only at arm's- (indeed dagger's-) length. These two plays
offer nothing so positive as the accommodation – unstable and
destructive as it proves – of chaste lovers in *Love's Sacrifice*. Orgilus
and Giovanni mimic the traditional revenger in violently closing an
intolerable gap between the performative and the constative, transcending the dictate that, while Penthea and Annabella may be
their wives in deed, they never can be in name. Thus, when the
desperately tempted Penthea forbids him to talk of love – 'If ever
henceforth thou appear in language, / Message, or letter to betray

my frailty . . .' (*Broken Heart* 2.3.113–14) – Orgilus resolves, 'Action, not words, shall show me' (126).

Annabella's fifth-act soliloquy, which records her conscience's message that she is 'lost' (*'Tis Pity* 5.1.11), signals the reappearance of her image in the mirror of divine discourse. It is the first self-speaking on either side since the lovers' physical union, and it documents the separation – Annabella's re-emergence as Other – that threatens to plunge Giovanni back into his initial state of aphanitic self-loss: 'Lost, I am lost; my fates have doomed my death; / The more I strive, I love, the more I love, / The less I hope' (1.2.144–6). His recourse is to stake a cosmic claim for their spiritual union, figured as the 'heart', at the expense of the physical: 'Fair Annabella, / How over-glorious art thou in thy wounds, / Triumphing over infamy and hate!' (5.5.102–4). In this final soliloquy before his self-consuming, and self-subsuming, performance, he enlists in the service of the heart the stock metaphor of the world-as-stage, as if turning the tables on the transcendental discourse that normally controls it: 'stand up, my heart, / And boldly act my last and greater part!' (105–6).

The problematic relation between 'true' identity and a transcendental discourse also lies at the core of *The Chronicle History of Perkin Warbeck* and is there figured in similar terms, although love is now a secondary issue. In his final confrontation with King Henry, the condemned imposter insists on the untouchability of his 'heart', which

> Will mount till every drop of blood be frozen
> By death's perpetual winter. If the sun
> Of majesty be darkened, let the sun
> Of life be hid from me in an eclipse
> Lasting and universal.
>
> (5.2.54–8)

As Warbeck embeds himself within the discourse of providentially managed royal history, Henry refuses Daubeney's request to 'check his tongue' but merely realigns that discourse with his own silence: 'The player's on the stage still, 'tis his part; / A'does but act' (68–9). Henry has no need of words to fashion a royal identity; he is the thing itself.

At least for the audience, however, matters are not so clear-cut, especially given the intertextual presence of the deposition scene in *Richard II* (4.1), where the laconic Bullingbrook indulges the voluble performance of the rightful king. Not that Ford encourages doubt about the historical and genealogical facts. But those facts carry the status of fatal necessity – the equivalent of consanguinity or marriage to another – and are set off against Warbeck's verbal production of royal presence. According to King James of Scotland, 'He must be more than subject who can utter / The language of a king, and such is thine' (2.1.103–4). Moreover, Warbeck's discursive presence is pointedly made a dramatic absolute, divorced from origins. By contrast, Giovanni and Orgilus are seen to react against the condition of being 'constituted as a subject by language', as the mere 'effect of discourse' (Grosz 97). And while, in their cases, the transcendental idiom depends on the very action in which it culminates (the 'speaking body') and remains essentially private, Warbeck's words *are* his actions – witness their power to stir others.

We see Warbeck, as others do, only from the outside, and the view is daunting; it palpably becomes so, as Warbeck matches 'truth' for 'truth', even for Henry: 'Sirrah, shift / Your antic pageantry, and now appear in your own nature' (5.2.87–9). The play departs radically from convention in not giving its protagonist a single soliloquy or aside. This is a necessity, if the question of his sincerity is ultimately to remain, not just unanswerable, but unaskable.[7] Another result, however, is to portray the plenitude of Warbeck's speaking self as a singularly successful escape from the self that is spoken – a revenge, in effect, upon subjectivity itself. The whole notion of a 'nature' that is Warbeck's 'own' is problematized. Yet he alone of Ford's transcendental aspirants never appears demented, even in Henry's view. On the contrary, he repeatedly inspires others to refigure themselves in the mirror of his discourse, as when, their fortunes collapsing, his wife renews the absolute gift of her 'poor heart' (3.2.168): 'You have a noble language, sir; your right / In me is without question' (163–4).

V

I conclude this eclectic survey of self-speaking in post-1600 tragedy by allowing *The Revenger's Tragedy* to furnish a brief afterword. This entails some chronological backtracking (to 1606 or so), but the complex method of this text appears most clearly in the light of the preceding instances – a reminder that I am not proposing any technical evolution over the period but merely chronicling a variety of roughly contemporary practices. Nor, incidentally, can my perspective clarify the question of authorship by supporting or rebutting the perennially popular case for Middleton as against Tourneur. For in its near-seamless synthesis of a self-fashioning hero-villain with a transcendental religio-moral discourse, *The Revenger's Tragedy* may be seen as taking to a quasi-parodic extreme either the method of *The Changeling* and *Women Beware Women* or that of *The Atheist's Tragedy*.

Perhaps surprisingly, however, the relatively mild-mannered *Perkin Warbeck* makes a closer analogue, insofar as it depicts a transcendental self-fashioning so thoroughgoing and sustained as to obviate tragic subjectivity. Vindice, in contrast with Ford's 'imposter', has frequent soliloquies, but they conspicuously fail to reflect any mirror-image at all. (He is otherwise vampire-like, too – one of the walking dead: 'My life's unnatural to me, e'en compell'd / As if I liv'd now when I should be dead' [1.1.120–1].) His self-speaking neither shows him his place within a universal scheme nor produces the aphanitic self in a gap between constative and performative. Rather, he constitutes himself as a sort of moral magic glass, rendering visible the incarnations of sin around him: 'Duke; royal lecher; go, grey-hair'd adultery' (1.1.1.).

The embedded stage direction and posture of commentary here announce a metadramatic dimension. Yet while Vindice's perspective, as is usual for would-be reshapers of their play-worlds, remains intensely personal and private, the text at large seconds and abets him in this project. The corrupt courtiers are 'objectively' displayed, beginning with their names, as precisely the caricatures he sketches. In abundant soliloquies they openly image their depravity – like morality play vices, but so as to work their own destruction and in conformity with an affect-driven authority felt to stem from Vindice himself. Hence, in the next scene, his vengeful hatred of the Duke is echoed by the equally sinful Duchess ('I'll kill him in his forehead' [1.2.108]) and Spurio ('Duke, thou didst do me wrong, and by thy act / Adultery is my nature' [1.2.178–9]). Occasions drop into Vindice's hands – even when it comes to morally testing his mother and sister. Finally, he is handily provided with a brother-accomplice, who not only lubricates the plot machinery but helps to stage Vindice's transcendental isolation: 'I'm lost again, you cannot find me yet; / I'm in a throng of happy apprehensions' (3.5.29–30). This is a rhetoric of self-loss like no other; Vindice is merely absent to his brother, overflowingly present to himself

('You flow well, brother [2.2.146]). Yet in this very excess, as in the satirical discourse of Marston's Malevole, there is a touch of self-subversion, the trace of the Other. And if Malevole finally reverts to Altofront, Vindice goes to his death invoking the memory of Piato, as if that fabricated persona were real, even real beyond the human.

Vindice's soliloquizing voice comes close to that of the offended deity in the cycle plays, as suits his apparent endorsement by the 'blazing star' (5.3.15) and by the thunder, which he smoothly incorporates into his revenge-masque script: 'Dost know thy cue, thou big-voic'd crier?' (43). The subjectified godhead then openly coincides with the de-subjectified human revenger, who, after all, like God in *Everyman*, begins by despatching Death as his messenger: 'Advance thee, O thou terror to fat folks' (1.1.45). The 'speaking body' achieved by the typical revenger only after traversing self-absence is here deployed from the outset, just as Vindice is the character's 'true' name. His improvisations teem effortlessly from a seemingly unshakeable identity. Yet, as with other metadramatic masters of the quick-change, such as Richard III and Iago, those very improvisations also point, as do his ecstasies, to something he is in flight from. To co-opt the mechanism of self-fragmentation suggests an effort to deflect it.

That there proves to be, after all, a signifying gap in the thunder's message, hence a transcendental discourse separate from and above Vindice's own, emerges forcefully in the final twist of plot, as he and his brother – surprised, for once – are condemned by their own confession. The readiness to die that is the revenger's stock-in-trade, the seal of his transcendence, must itself suddenly be improvised. And in the self-speaking monologue through which he adroitly performs this necessary act, Vindice momentarily resurrects and reburies his *alter ego*:

> Now I remember too, here was Piato brought forth a knavish sentence once: no doubt, said he, but time will make the murderer bring forth himself. 'Tis well he died, he was a witch.
>
> (5.3.115–18)

It is as if this sudden mirror-reflection of self-betrayal and intuition – this figure of the unconscious, whom he has aligned by *name* with a higher truth than his own – now looms as the mysterious father of discourse ('brought forth a knavish sentence') and must be put to rest with a stake through the heart if Vindice's transcendentally fashioned self is to remain intact. Thus revenge is effected upon tragic subjectivity itself, as in *Perkin Warbeck*, but also, as suits the ambiguity of the title, on its behalf: Vindice, in the quickest change of all, becomes the victim of Piato.

Notes to Chapter 5

1. In sketching the dramatic heritage and affiliations of this effect, Braunmuller stresses the influence of 'the binary bias' in '[h]umanist rhetorical education' (70).
2. Cf., e.g., Gair, Introd., *Antonio and Mellida* 24–39.
3. The connection made by Maus (104–27) between tragic subjectivity and judicial proceedings may be relevant here.
4. Hence, it is significant that, etymologically, 'methinks' means not 'I think' but rather 'it seems to me'. But cf. the N-Town Virgin's 'I suppoce', as discussed in Chapter 2, 48.
5. The ironic reminiscence of *Oth.* is unmistakable in the confrontations between the husbands and their wives (*Changeling* 5.3.14 ff.; *Oth.* 4.2.31 ff.).
6. Given the absence of line numbers in the edition of Gifford and Dyce, I supply page numbers in internal brackets.
7. According to Ure, it was Ford's 'real stroke of genius' that, contrary to the sources, 'Warbeck never does anything in the play to suggest either that he is playing a part and knows it, or – and this is the vital point – that he is . . . playing a part and no longer knows it' (xlii). The character is thereby placed even beyond the familiar model of self-fashioning.

6
Some Comic and Tragicomic Subjects

This chapter seeks to define the generic issue implicit in my concentration thus far on tragedies and explicit in the emergence of aphanitic subjectivity as tragically coded. I also want to caution against turning a discursive effect into a marker of 'psychological complexity' or 'realism'. A shift of generic perspective may usefully refocus the discourses of subjectivity as such, paradoxically by siting them at the crossroads of two basic formalist precepts regarding plot and characterization. These are the principles (to put them reductively) that tragedy kills off its main characters, while comedy does not, and that comedy, unlike tragedy, subordinates character-psychology to social pattern, the individual to the group.

In discussing (in Chapter 2) the Medieval and Renaissance commonplace that death offers a mirror-image of the instability of identity, I invoked the Lacanian postulate of an intimate bond between the mechanism of aphanisis and the subject's cognizance of mortality, given that 'à considérer son image, il en lit la signification mortifère, puisqu'elle lui est foncièrement "ravie" [in considering his image, he reads its death-bearing signification, since it is fundamentally "ravished" from him]' (Léger 42). To work backwards from this 'signification', the more-than-formal obsession of much Renaissance tragedy with death, often anchored in the existential predicament of a revenger-figure, broadly correlates with the subject's propensity to slip imaginatively out of its own sight. The instances cited in the preceding chapters may be concisely recapitulated by way of a mirror-talking monologue delivered by the central character in Marlowe's *The Jew of Malta*. This speech from the early days of the Elizabethan public theatre, when characterization was relatively 'crude', helps to define the pattern of self-fashioning through revenge as a response to the perceived negation of self – a negation imposed, in this case, by the seizure of Barabas' wealth:[1]

What, will you thus oppose me, luckless stars,
To make me desperate in my poverty?
And knowing me impatient in distress,
Think me so mad as I will hang myself,
That I may vanish o'er the earth in air,
And leave no memory that e'er I was?
No, I will live: nor loathe I this my life;
And since you leave me in the ocean thus
To sink or swim, and put me to my shifts,
I'll rouse my senses, and awake myself.

(1.2.260–9)

The pivotal image of self-fading ('vanish o'er the earth in air') here controls a nexus of common contemporary figurations of mortality: despairing suicide by hanging (Barabas specifically scorns the example of Judas); fame (including notoriety) as a surrogate for immortality; death as sleep (and *vice versa*).

Criticism has increasingly recognized that at least some comedy of the period – Shakespearean comedy, in particular, and not just the late romances – is far from unconcerned with death but, on the contrary, makes it the effective target of transformative processes. Where the menace of death or the fact of mortality does not actually form part of the framework for the comic action – as it does, with one or two arguable exceptions, in all of Shakespeare's plays in the genre – a metonymic relation often exists (supported by Petrarchan convention) between death and the separation of lovers, so that their eventual union signifies not merely the surmounting of tangible obstacles but a metaphysical transcendence. Such a dimension has routinely been recognized in 'festive' conclusions since the work of C. L. Barber and Northrop Frye,[2] and the principle proves its commonplace status by breaking the surface parodically in Beaumont's *The Knight of the Burning Pestle* and Middleton's *A Chaste Maid in Cheapside*, both of which (like *Wit and Science*) adapt the folk-play motif of resurrection to show 'dead' lovers popping out of their coffins.

I propose that it is not only death, and lovers' death-in-life, but also aphanitic subjectivity that the structural strategies of comedy work to counteract, beginning with the primacy of social patterning over individual identity. In order to foreground the issue of self-envisaging, with its implications for self-speaking, let me return to Freedman's psychoanalytic extrapolation of Nicholas of Cusa, cited in Chapter 3 in connection with the secularization of Tudor drama: 'As Renaissance games with the gaze become more complex and more internalized, God as the all-seeing other is displaced by the community as other, which in turn is displaced by an internalized other – whether soul, social conscience, or unconscious – as that point with which we can never merge' (20). Broadly speaking, such a shift also marks the depiction of subjectivity in, respectively, comedy ('the community as other') and tragedy ('an internalized other'), although, as I have stressed, numerous tragedies throughout the period persist in figuring the Other as divinity or community (or both – witness *A Woman Killed with Kindness*). Moreover, the very generic implications of Freedman's formulation undermine its application to literary history: comedy and tragedy maintain their currency side by side on the Renaissance stage. They also – with increasing self-consciousness, no doubt, but also from the start – mingle within individual texts. The results of such mingling will be considered later in this chapter.

When looking across as well as within genres, therefore, I prefer to approach the subject's relation to the Other as unstable and variable – 'always already' encoded with displacement, as, after all, befits 'games with the gaze'. The fullness of presence presupposes the subjectivity consisting in self-absence; however firmly fixed the mirrors supplied by God or the 'community' may be, the physical presence of the actor carries the reflection of the 'internalized other'. There are necessarily, then, in the character-drawing practices of comedy, as of tragedy that denies aphanitic subjectivity, an artificiality and defensiveness that may be only roughly correlated with a lack of psychological 'realism'. From this point of view, denial constitutes an essential aspect of comic affirmation, surreptitiously proffering the assurance that human beings are in discursive control, even as their dependency on deceptive signification is paraded.

Indeed, in the Early Modern theatre, such control precisely masquerades as abdication. A transcendental discourse can claim authenticity only by locating authority elsewhere. Whether the signifying system is grounded in God or the community, the objective is to restore language itself to its pre-Babel condition, the unitary (but self-negating) promise of the mirror-stage. In this cause (with which the effect of laughter is eminently compatible), many comedies proliferate ostentatiously 'fallen' speech, varieties of linguistic fragmentation and mis-communication, only to show such deviance finally contained by 'true' meaning. The process often entails visual 'games' involving identity and based, implicitly if not explicitly, on mirror-imaging. Thus the transcendental signifier is effectively constituted in an audience possessing superior knowledge and understanding, vision and insight, which need not undercut themselves by speaking.

In Thomas Heywood's verse preface to *An Apology for Actors*, as Burns points out, the 'intimation of nothingness' lurking in orthodox uses of the world-as-stage metaphor is eclipsed as the image is adapted 'to confer a god-like role on the human audience', including 'practices of judgement' (Burns 127–8). This is to at once to define all drama as tragic and to gather it into the Divine Comedy. Yet the discursive focus of most formal tragedy remains the individual's struggle to achieve meaning within the duplicity of signification. In instances of self-speaking, therefore – especially soliloquy – the audience is led to identify with tragic figures: to speak the 'self alone' is necessarily to speak with and for the audience, insofar as speech is revealed as belonging to the Other. There is a level beyond the moral, therefore, on which tragedy may implicate the audience in rebellion against God and its consequences. In comedy, by contrast, the audience effectively takes the place of God, being endowed with something of the same ironic capacity for overhearing, overseeing, and even enjoying human discomfiture that is displayed by him (and, for that matter, shared with the reader) in *Genesis* 11. Not only is the impact of Babel on stage thereby defused, but, in keeping with the patristic treatment of Pentecost, the very multiplicity of tongues becomes consolation for the linguistic fall by manifesting the presence of the Holy Spirit. Such a model more firmly places Augustine's profound sense of language as fallen, Pentecost notwithstanding, in the realm of the tragic – the realm elided, hence defined, by the cycle plays in staging Pentecost but not Babel.

In drawing the teeth of those modes of verbal and visual self-regarding that, in tragedy, at once conduce to and betoken self-privation, comedy's foremost expedient is to isolate self-delusion within a secure ironic framework. The more recognizably 'false' a character's self-image, the more assurance is communicated of an underlying 'true' identity – namely, that of 'fool', in one form or another. This technique is ubiquitous in the kind of satirical comedy – for instance, Middleton's and, especially, Jonson's – that specializes in the manipulation of character-types, pitting 'gulls' against 'gullers' so as to debunk supposedly universal affectations and vanities. Perhaps the most extreme instance – one with broad destabilizing potential, given the character's moral position – entails Justice Overdo in *Bartholomew Fair*, whose foolish disguise is a constant visual reminder of the fact behind his personal fiction (the project of exposing iniquity) and who verbally exposes himself in regular protracted soliloquies. Overdo's practice of addressing himself in the third person effectively collapses the *sujet de l'énonciation* and the *sujet de l'énoncé*, as if to enact the short-circuiting of self-knowledge in his self-fashioning: 'defy all the world, Adam Overdo, for a disguise, and all story; for thou hast fitted thyself, I swear' (2.1.2–3).

Such overweening on the part of a guller destined to be gulled recalls *Volpone*'s Mosca at the moment when that hitherto unswattable – and non-self-speaking – fly begins to acquire vulnerability, a sense of identity that palpably weighs him down, even as he celebrates his lightness:

> I fear I shall begin to grow in love
> With my dear self and my most prosp'rous parts,
> They do so spring and burgeon; I can feel
> A whimsy i' my blood: I know not how,
> Success hath made me wanton. I could skip
> Out of my skin, now, like a subtle snake,
> I am so limber. O! your parasite
> Is a most precious thing, dropped from above.
>
> (3.1.1–8)

As with Volpone himself from the start, such aggressive self-imaging betrays the pressure of a counter-discourse, destined eventually to impose 'true' identity along with justice in a fashion at once spectacular and discursive: 'This is called mortifying of a fox' (5.12.125).

By contrast, Overdo's folly is bound up with the failure of such a discourse to materialize. His humiliations merely render him more deeply 'resolv'd' (3.3.36) in the image of himself as transcendental signifier *in potentia*:

> ... come what come can ... I will not discover who I am till my due time; and yet still all shall be, as I said ever, in Justice' name, and the King's, and for the Commonwealth!
>
> (36–41)

At this point, Winwife breaks the convention of soliloquy by commenting, 'What does he talk to himself, and act so seriously? Poor fool!' (42–3). In thus representing the Justice's self-speaking as mere folly, the text prepares for the gentler collapse of this would-be Second Adam, chock-full of Doomsday sentences, into the first: 'remember you are but Adam, flesh and blood! You have your frailty, forget your other name of Overdo, and invite us all to supper' (5.6.100–2).

Such a sustained satirical treatment of the play's embodiment of moral authority makes for an especially smooth integration of the qualification that Jonson's comedies invariably attach, with varying degrees of bitter and sweet, to the purported triumph of truth. The daunting whimsicality of Justice Clement (in *Every Man in His Humour*), the impetuosity and venality of *Volpone*'s Avocatori, the complicity of Lovewit with Face (in *The Alchemist*) – these are all concessions to 'flesh and blood', which an audience is invited to laugh *with* (because it recognizes itself) but also *at* (because it knows better). Even *Epicoene*'s concluding joke at the audience's expense, when a boy-actor's off-stage gender is abruptly theatricalized, simultaneously pays the compliment of an in-joke, offering, in effect, a visit to the tiring-house, where the ultimate truth of any production resides (as opposed to the mundane discoveries made in the College of the ladies). In all cases, the exposure of self-fashioning practices becomes a matter of reassuring privilege, rather than menace; the aphanitic implications are neatly skirted. Thus Jonson plays a double game with the discursive mirror – one akin to that played with the idea of the book in *The Knight of the Burning Pestle*. On one level, Beaumont's play takes aim at the book as emblem of authority and guarantor of identity through interventions originating with the audience; on another, it offers the 'true' audience the luxury of laughter directed at its stand-ins, the Grocer and his wife.

I

In a significant number of comedies, including several by Shakespeare, the spectre of the aphanitic subject is more fully conjured, as if to be exorcized.[3] Two Shakespearean cases involve the scapegoating (in plays roughly contemporary with *Hamlet*) of figures associated with melancholy. I touched in Chapter 3 on the restrictions built into the monologue where Jacques figures human identity as fading in the face of death. The containment of that character extends, of course, to his structural isolation and the stigmatization of his melancholy as unnatural and hypocritical – factors that culminate in a final self-severing from festivity: 'I am for other than for dancing measures' (*AYL* 5.4.193). To accord such resistance a positive value runs counter to the celebratory bias of the romantic plot, yet there is a tinge of courageous self-exemption from the triumphant discourse of transcendental authority, with its glib promise to make comfortable courtiers out of exiles by dispensing 'the good of our returned fortune, / According to the measure of their states' (174–5). Rather than view himself in the new-old Duke's mirror, Jacques declares allegiance to self-loss, as emblematized by Duke Frederick's conversion 'from the world' (162) upon glimpsing himself as a sinner: 'Out of these convertites / There is much matter to be heard and learn'd' (184–5).

If Jacques is almost wholly discredited, Malvolio is 'notoriously abus'd (*TN* 5.1.379) by having madness, the sign *par excellence* of self-fragmentation, thrust upon him.[4] The fallenness of language is made part of this process: Feste as Sir Topas first spews the 'vain bibble babble' (4.2.96–7) of which he accuses his victim; likewise, Feste purports to 'read madness' (5.1.294) in (mis)delivering Malvolio's pathetic plea that Olivia acknowledge 'your own letter' (306) – a harking back, in turn, to the bizarre misconstructions of that letter (and its letters) in Act 2, Scene 5. The cumulative effect is to insist upon the conspiracy, to which Olivia's 'corrupter of words' (3.1.36) is instrumental, as destabilizing the system of signification itself – but only for Malvolio. The initial dislocation involves an (inevitably) false reflection, inducing him to 'make that resemble something in me! . . . M.O.A.I' (2.5.119–20) and parodically making him yet another Narcissus who has 'discovered the *moi*' (Goldin 31). Sir Toby might well suppose that they have 'put him in such a dream, that when the image of it leaves him he must run mad' (2.5.193–4), his reason tumbling into the gulf between sign and signified, the '*je*' subsumed by the 'primordial ideal ego' (Ragland-Sullivan 199). But while the 'image' indeed gives way with Olivia's reflection of his new-fashioned self as absurdly out of fashion, Malvolio's '*je*' proves resilient, re-emerging in the standard tragic antidote to aphanisis: 'I'll be reveng'd on the whole pack of you' (5.1.378).

To this extent, the joke is on the jokers, but in landing solidly on his discursive feet, Malvolio himself conspires with their larger point about language. Built into the 'overlooking' structure of the scene where the trap is sprung is the claim that, as corruptible as signifiers may be, they remain under control. No matter '[h]ow quickly the wrong side may be turn'd outward' (3.1.12–13), there exist, even for the play's proponents of moral topsy-turvydom, the comfort and stability of a right side. Such an assurance is equally conveyed by the sorting out of identities in the romantic plot. When Sebastian and Viola finally appear together, the 'glass' is indeed found to be 'true' (5.1.265) and Petrarchan love-relations are re-validated at the narcissistic level of the mirror stage. Thanks to the interposition of Viola / Cesario between Orsino and his desire for Olivia, as well as the elusiveness of Cesario as Olivia's love-object, those relations had become embroiled in the mechanisms of symbolic exchange and, accordingly, had taken on the threat of aphanisis – what Burns terms 'the loss of fixed subjecthood, which the play presents as the experience of love' (168). Hence, the Duke suddenly turns on Cesario with a violence that surprises modern spectators but that fills an inward vacuum in a manner familiar to Early Modern audiences of revenge plays: 'I'll sacrifice the lamb that I do love, / To spite a raven's heart within a dove' (130–1). The concluding revelation also dispels the intimations of self-absence in Viola's disguise, fulfilling her early wish that she 'might not be delivered to the world / Till I had made mine own occasion mellow / What my estate is!' (1.2.42–4).

In its implications for subjectivity and self-speaking, the mirroring pattern in *Twelfth Night* recalls earlier Shakespearean comedies. Various commentators, including Freedman (78–113), have approached *The Comedy of Errors* through the problem of two becoming one – of difference in relation to identity, absence in relation to presence. Elsewhere, I have applied that play's pattern to *A Midsummer Night's Dream* (*Subversions* 65–76).[5] Now I wish to refocus the issue on the containment of aphanitic tendencies within the mirror-stage dynamic of plenitude and negation – a control transferred to the audience through its capacity to solve the text's riddles. By means of a series of dislocatingly *erroneous* mirror-images, the central characters are plunged into exchange relations and self-fragmentation, but only so as to ground more firmly their recovery of 'an union in partition' (*MND* 3.2.210), a state transcending discourse (and extending to Bottom – 'Man is but an ass, if he go about t'expound this dream' [4.1.206–7]), yet purporting to inscribe the Other: 'And I have found Demetrius like a jewel, / Mine own, and not mine own' (191–2). The result is a specialized form of the effect sketched by Freedman for Shakespearean comedy generally: 'Shakespeare's characters derive place and position by referring to an unseen and inaccessible place within' (20).

In *A Midsummer Night's Dream*, it is the audience's privileged access to the fairy manipulations that reassuringly – comically – mediates the mirroring process whereby Hermia and Helena are compelled to see themselves, in effect, as each other: Hermia takes Helena's place as doubly rejected; Helena becomes doubly adored. Under this pressure, their naïve assumptions about love and childhood friendship dissolve. So, for each of them – in contrast with the self-asserting yet undifferentiated men – does the sense of identity. A limit is artificially set to this process, however, by the imposition of sleep, which paradoxically rescues them from the destabilizing dream-world. In a brief soliloquized prelude to unconsciousness, each of the 'poor females' Puck claims to have made 'mad' (3.2.441) effectively opposes her current self-alienation to daylight-as-presence:

> Shine, comforts, from the east,
> That I may back to Athens by daylight,
> From these that my poor company detest.
> And sleep, that sometimes shuts up sorrow's eye,
> Steal me a while from mine own company.
>
> (431–6)

> Never so weary, never so in woe,
> Bedabbled with the dew and torn with briers,
> I can no further crawl, no further go;
> My legs can keep no pace with my desires.
> Here will I rest me till the break of day.
>
> (442–6)

Yet that sleep should offer a respite from dream, the realm of the unconscious, points up the fact that, as the audience well knows, the apparently chaotic discursive system in the forest remains quite coherent. The play finally aims, as Puck's Epilogue confirms, at drawing the teeth of dream itself, defusing the very capacity of 'shadows' to 'have offended' (5.1.423).

The insistent daylight world of *The Comedy of Errors* is more reliant on self-speaking to register both its assaults on identity and its assurances. In his initial soliloquy, Antipholus of Syracuse announces his search for his mother and brother in terms of self-loss:

> He that commends me to mine own content,
> Commends me to the thing I cannot get:
> I to the world am like a drop of water,
> That in the ocean seeks another drop,
> Who, falling there to find his fellow forth
> (Unseen, inquisitive), confounds himself.
> So I, to find a mother and a brother,
> In quest of them (unhappy), ah, lose myself.
> (1.2.33–40)

This sense of defect, however, depends upon and implies perfection – the binary dynamic of Petrarchan longing and of the mirror-stage. The signifying system within which the self is constituted is not in question. By contrast, when Adriana reflects Antipholus to himself as her husband, she triggers a self-fading, and indeed dialogue fades into monologue, leaving behind the other characters on stage:

> Am I in earth, in heaven, or in hell?
> Sleeping or waking, mad or well-advis'd?
> Known unto these, and to myself disguis'd?
> I'll say as they say, and persever so,
> And in this mist at all adventures go.
> (2.2.212–16)

Still, the fact – known to us – that 'true' identities are lying in wait soon reasserts itself by way of his attraction for Luciana rather than Adriana, which restores the Petrarchan paradox of self-definition through self-abandonment:

> Are you a god? Would you create me new?
> Transform me then, and to your pow'r I'll yield.
> But if that I am I, then well I know
> Your weeping sister is no wife of mine,
>   . . . .
> Sing, siren, for thyself, and I will dote.
> (3.2.39–47)

Luciana may call him 'mad' (53), but the diagnosis and therapy later inflicted upon Antipholus of Ephesus will confirm that madness here, as in *Twelfth Night*, is a textually fabricated occasion for exorcism through laughter. So, therefore, is the discursive anarchy for which it stands.

The fact remains that the treatment of Malvolio is elaborated into a strong thematic and tonal counterpoint that does not merely reinforce a comic resolution or even, as with Jacques, introduce an alternative reading, but discordantly clashes with the discursive project of comedy itself. His persecutors' 'malice' appears less and less 'sportful' (*TN* 5.1.365) as the focus shifts from delusive self-fashioning to subject-(de)formation. Meanwhile, the main plot works against their implicit claim for the festive spirit's regenerative power – the very premise of transformative comedy – by splitting them off from the romantic resolution. That resolution, in turn, forfeits its underpinnings of festivity, together with any claim to produce universal self-discovery through self-loss, and reveals itself as a fragile structure of mutual narcissistic mirroring. Thus the distinctive contrary voice, far from being isolated, actually articulates an ongoing challenge to the transcendental discourse – figured as the 'whirligig of time' (5.1.376) – to which, from the first, self-speech has ostentatiously deferred, renouncing affirmation in the face of the *Nom/non* of this traditional Father: 'O time, thou must untangle this, not I, / It is too hard a knot for me t'untie' (2.2.40–1). That Malvolio's tragedy obtrudes upon the play's comic identity precisely by being 'personal' in the fullest sense appears more clearly in the quintessentially tragic light of *The Duchess of Malfi*, where Ferdinand supplies mirrors of madness and horror in an effort to drive a menacingly unitary identity into the aphanitic void. Given the standard coding of revenge as antidote to aphanisis, Malvolio's parting shot, 'I'll be reveng'd on the whole pack of you' (5.1.378), bears company, however improbably, with, 'I am Duchess of Malfi still' (4.2.141).

If *As You Like It* (1599) and *Twelfth Night* (1601–2) arguably interrogate comedy's project of containing aphanitic subjectivity, this interrogation is pressed further, with more radically destabilizing results, in the Problem Plays that follow. In *Troilus and Cressida*, *All's Well That Ends Well*, and *Measure for Measure*, a single meta-dramatic manipulator succeeds in re-fabricating the play-world, incorporating dissenting elements within a coherent, transcendentally authoritative structure, which, however, the audience (as opposed to the fictional participants) is free to take or leave. Consistently, this process and its result are represented on the level of discourse and in terms of subjectivity: a concluding hegemony of voice entails multiple silencings, which deprive opposing characters, not just of self-expression, but of self. I have explored this phenomenon in detail elsewhere,[6] and there is no point in re-covering that extensive ground merely to establish aphanitic subjectivity as a fundamental site of contestation, together with verbal and visual self-reflection as key indicators of that dynamic. Such an argument may readily be extrapolated from Chapter 3's reference to Vincentio, the most overtly hegemonic of the three manipulators, as undergoing a virtual de-subjectification. His soliloquies may now be recognized as functional in their very superfluity; by diverting the discursive potential for aphanisis into verbal rituals of self-transcendence, they produce a seamless and unitary identity in contrast to the exposed 'true nature' of Angelo:

> He who the sword of heaven would bear
> Should be as holy as severe;
> Pattern in himself to know,
> Grace to stand, and virtue go;
> . . . .
> O, what may man within him hide,
> Though angel on the outward side!
> (*MM* 3.2.261–72)

It is worth adding here that this angel's fall into aphanitic subjectivity is made correspondingly extreme on the discursive level. In the Lacanian terms cited at the outset of this study, his 'fall' at the sight of Isabella strikingly recapitulates the subject's entry into the symbolic order:

> . . . le sujet apparaît d'abord dans l'Autre, en tant que le premier signifiant, le signifiant unaire, surgit au champ de l'Autre, et qu'il représente le sujet, pour un autre signifiant, lequel autre signifiant a pour effet l'*aphanisis* du sujet. D'où, division du sujet – lorsque le sujet apparaît quelque part comme sens, ailleurs il se manifeste comme *fading*, comme disparition.
> [. . . the subject appears first in the Other, in so far as the first signifier, the unary signifier, emerges in the field of the Other and represents the subject for another signifier, which other signifier has as its effect the *aphanisis* of the subject. Hence the division of

the subject – when the subject appears somewhere as meaning, he is manifested elsewhere as 'fading', as disappearance.]

(*Séminaire 11* 199; *Concepts* 218)

Against this background, there is less mystery to the reaction – arguably on the parts of both Angelo and Isabella – of mingled attraction and hostility. Each can restore a narcissistic self-image only by re-establishing and mastering the other person as Other. Angelo's defeat in this psychological contest – a defeat that drives him, revenger-like, to outward aggression – is closely recorded in his soliloquies. His tragically coded 'fading' in these linguistic mirrors ('What dost thou? or what art thou, Angelo?' [2.2.172]) precipitates him into duplicitous dialogue with Isabella – duplicity that ironically vitiates his claim to authority, if not his tyrannical exercise of it. Thus there are intimations of triumph, despite her precarious situation (and her own unconscious *double entendre* previously), in the latter's protest, 'I have no tongue but one; gentle my lord, / Let me entreat you speak the former language' (2.4.139–40).

II

Rather than trace this pattern throughout the Problem Plays, I prefer at this point to pursue a distinctive phenomenon in the more out-of-the-way case of Chapman's *The Widow's Tears*, whose main plot adapts (with a significant twist) the tale of the Ephesian widow from the *Satyricon* of Petronius. Despite the uniform valorization of a transcendental discourse in the same author's tragedies (as discussed in the preceding chapter), this is the only contemporary comic instance, to my knowledge, where those suggestions of self-loss that comedy often appears to accommodate, then banishes, are frankly pursued to their aphanitic conclusion. If comic form is taken to the limit in the Problem Plays, here it is pushed over the edge, thanks largely to a manipulator who combines the cynical ambition of *King Lear*'s Edmund (likewise a younger brother) with the heroic *virtù* of Bussy D'Ambois. (All three plays are roughly contemporary.)

Tharsalio also resembles his counterparts in the Problem Plays, insofar as he pulls the rug from under the self-images of others while setting up one of his own. Yet, far from claiming transcendental authority, he insists on the untenability of any such idea. Cynicism is so sure an article of faith with him that, in contrast with

Edmund, he never mistakes his fashioned self for something essential. Thus, although a type of Machiavellian ambition, he avoids the standard downfall of overreaching. In this he has structural help. On a hint from the *Satyricon*, where the tale provokes one indignant auditor to object that the woman herself should have been crucified '[i]f the governor of the province had been a just man' (cited Yamada, ed., *Widow's Tears* 143), Chapman invests the play-world's ultimate power in an emblem of arbitrary vacuity, the epitome of nothing at the centre. The Governor appears only at the conclusion – a sort of dunce *ex machina* – and, far from sorting out the confusion of plot (like Vincentio) or ratifying the manipulator's dénouement (like the King in *All's Well That Ends Well*), he finally throws up his hands: 'For my part, I am at a non-plus' (5.5.313). The resemblance to Jonson's self-undermining figures of authority points up a major difference: here the audience has no secure grasp on a higher, more stable truth.

On the surface, Chapman's treatment of Petronius might seem merely to redirect the satire from the fragility of widows' vows of chaste fidelity – a somewhat outmoded target, perhaps, given that Hamlet's obsession is not shared by his fellow-characters – to female carnality itself, a pervasive Jacobean theme. This shift is reinforced by the interwoven subplot, in which Tharsalio incredibly gains the hand of the former governor's widow, whose servant he once was, by a pretence of hormonal excess (including a bawd's purchased testimony regarding his sexual prowess). The deeper tendency, however, is to render sexuality a vehicle less for a critique of social mores than for an exploration of subjectivity, discursively understood. Hence, arguably, the frequency and centrality of soliloquies in this text, together with the sustained symbolism of the mirror and of death and resurrection.

The soliloquies fall, roughly speaking, into the two types recurrent in tragic negotiations of subjectivity; to put this in a way that captures the subject's variable relation to language, verbalized enactments of self-fashioning are counterpointed by verbalizing experiences of aphanisis. The pattern begins with Tharsalio's dedication of himself to Confidence over Fortune – a speech delivered 'with a glass in his hand' (1.1.0 S.D.), as he is dressing for the day. The intertextual relation to Edmund's soliloquy addressing Nature is insistent, and it highlights a divergence from the essentialism of Shakespeare's character. The latter considers that 'my dimensions are as well compact, / My mind as generous, and my shape as true,

/ As honest madam's issue' (*Lr* 1.2.7–9) – an element again soliloquized later in the same scene: 'I should have been that I am, had
the maidenl'est star in the firmament twinkled on my bastardizing'
(131–3). Self-fashioning thus functions in support of Edmund's sense
of himself as he truly is – a linkage bound to result, paradoxically,
in a reversion to the world's reading of him: 'Some good I mean to
do, / Despite of mine own nature (5.3.244–5). By contrast, Tharsalio
makes no bones about 'true' identity and 'false' appearances: the
entire object of his reflection(s) is subjectively up for grabs.

This view pointedly contrasts (much along the lines of Edmund
and Edgar) with the naïve security of the elder brother, Lysander,
who enters at the end of the opening soliloquy, also 'with a glass
in his hand' (14 S.D.). Lysander's self-image is ostentatiously complete: he chides Tharsalio for not being ready; it is also vulnerable,
precisely because he takes it for reality. That vulnerability is most
immediately sexual; his brother retorts by crudely positing his inadequacy: 'I dare say, your wife is many times ready, and you not
up' (16–17). But this is also to figure the gap between desire and
performance that defines the aphanitic subject. Sustained though it
may be by his prosperity and social position, Lysander's sense of
self remains grounded in a fantasy – overconfident, to say the least
– of his wife's exclusive desire for him, which he invests with
transcendentalizing power, as if he will derive a form of immortality from its 'undying' quality. That quality, from which, moreover,
Cynthia has derived her own self-image, can logically be tested
only by confronting her with death – at once his and her own, for
she will prove herself by starving in his tomb.

In fetishizing not just his wife's present but her future loyalty,
Lysander goes a step beyond Othello, and Tharsalio's calculated
insinuations are free to echo Iago in a lower key. The resemblance
between the two texts is strongest in Lysander's tormented reactions.[7] He is conspicuously more the object than the subject of the
gnawing he refers to, tangled in a chain of self-interrogations, as
answers slip ever further away:

> All the Furies in hell attend thee! 'Has given me a bone to tire
> on with a pestilence. 'Slight, know?
> What can he know? What can his eye observe
> More than mine own, or the most piercing sight
> That ever viewed her?
>
> (2.1.37–41)

Tharsalio's bait has already been taken when his success with Eudora – 'So great and vowed a pattern of our sex' (3.1.121), in Cynthia's view – offers both husband and wife a potently destabilizing tableau: 'if you see me in my chair of honour, and my Countess in mine arms, you will then believe, I hope, I am lord of the palace' (130–3). In this context, Lysander's feigned death actualizes his condition as 'one absent from himself' (237).

Tharsalio may be prompt to exploit his adversary's construction of female sexual appetite as an index of threatening Otherness and to magnify his own sexuality as a metonymy for presence in Eudora's eyes (and ears). His career depends, however, on the demystifying stance of the text at large, which promotes sexuality as linked with appetite generally and appetite as the essence of material humanity, the sole condition of being that cannot be fashioned or unfashioned. Eating and drinking are foregrounded in the tomb scenes, which refocus upon Cynthia Petronius' point about the soldier ('you know which temptation generally assails a man on a full stomach' [cited Yamada, ed., *Widow's Tears* 142]) and so make sexual desire equally a matter of survival.

The appetitive condition similarly asserts itself in Eudora – naturally, for otherwise it would be 'as if Nature had made her all in vain' (1.1.128) – when the bawd depicts Tharsalio as a paragon of potency. That false image reflects something true, which, however unspeakable, now speaks the self in soliloquy:

> What might a wise widow resolve upon this point, now? Contentment is the end of all worldly beings. Beshrew her, would she had spared her news!
>
> (2.2.126–9)

There is a pointed contrast with the fourth-act sequence in which the maid's vow to the disguised Lysander that she will make Cynthia 'turn to flesh and blood, / And learn to live as other mortals do' (4.2.176–7) begets his soliloquized address to a Cynthia whose absence is the premise of his self-presence:

> O Cynthia, heir of her bright purity,
> Whose name thou dost inherit, thou disdain'st
> (Severed from all concretion) to feed
> Upon the base food of gross elements.
> Thou art all soul; all immortality.
>
> (181–5)

It is amply clear both that such projections of immortality are death-serving and that to choose life over death, as Cynthia does in choosing to shame her husband's body for the sake of her new-found lover, can be no betrayal – of the self least of all.

Nevertheless, Tharsalio's happy expedient of tipping off the 'fallen' Cynthia as to the soldier's identity, so that she may expose Lysander to himself as a 'transformèd monster' (5.5.81) while keeping his image of her intact, links a version of tragedy with indulgence of the need for self-deception. Her claim to have recognized Lysander from the start deflates the new role of misogynistic revenger with which he had hauled himself out of the aphanitic pit after discovering (or rather constructing) her wife's 'infidelity'. He had made his borrowed shape, purportedly a means of exposing falseness, the key to a renewed assertion of transcendental truth:

> Thou that in truest shape hast let me see
> That which my truer self hath hid from me,
> Help me to take revenge on a disguise
> Ten times more false and counterfeit than thou.
>
> (5.5.3–6)

This, too, seems a variation on a theme from *Othello*: 'It is the cause, it is the cause, my soul'; 'Yet she must die, else she'll betray more men' (*Oth.* 5.2.1,6). In one way or another, a tragic protagonist typically fails to discover the truth in time; *The Widow's Tears* exposes comedy's penchant for the timely lie.

Left alone after Cynthia's improvised revelation, Lysander sinks back into inner emptiness, death-in-life: 'What have I done? / O, let me lie and grieve, and speak no more' (5.5.89–90). By the end of the scene, however, Tharsalio is able, in effect, to take him down from his spiritual cross and resurrect him under the aegis of his original illusion: 'think you have the only constant wife' (317). Meanwhile, Cynthia's whispered conversation with the Countess, unheard by the audience, lends her concluding silence a quality of female conspiracy and lends that conspiracy a suggestion of freedom from illusion, of self-absence as the only presence. In this light, Tharsalio's earlier condemnation of hypocritical widows moves even further from satirical convention and closer (though Tharsalio is not the type to be haunted) to Hamlet's situating of plenitude within lack – 'that within which passes show', as opposed to 'actions that a man might play' (*Ham.* 1.2.85,84):

These griefs that sound so loud prove always light,
True sorrow evermore keeps out of sight.
This strain of mourning wi' th' sepulchre, like an overdoing actor, affects grossly, and is indeed so far forced from the life, that
it bewrays itself to be altogether artificial. . . . Truth, the substance,
hunts not after the shadow of popular fame.

(4.1.103–10)

A thematic reading readily grasps that all of the action of *The Widow's Tears* is aimed squarely at the mistaking of shadow for 'truth,
the substance'. Only the aphanitic, discursively dependent nature
of such substance, however, explains how the text's triumphant
architect of his own identity can unhypocritically enlist his mirror
against self-fashioning:

While I am with it, it takes impression from my face; but can
I make it so mine, that it shall be of no use to any other? Will it
not do his office to you or you; and as well to my groom as to
myself?

(1.1.120–3)

III

It remains, in this genre-oriented chapter, to relate discursive subjectivity to the innovative amalgams of tragedy and comedy that
flourished from the second decade of the seventeenth century to the
closing of the theatres (and indeed beyond). With good reason,
literary historians increasingly approach the new form as having
English, not just Italian, roots, especially in the exuberant romantic
drama of the early Elizabethan period. (*Friar Bacon and Friar Bungay*,
discussed in Chapter 3, makes a convenient example.) Such drama
survived through revivals and off-shoots well beyond the turn of
the century – witness the perennially popular *Mucedorus*, staged for
King James in 1610. Some such plays, among them George Whet-
stone's *Promos and Cassandra* (principal antecedent of the arguably
tragicomic *Measure for Measure*), conform with precision to the pre-
scription for a tragicomedy with which John Fletcher introduced
the printed text of *The Faithful Shepherdess* (also *circa* 1610): 'it wants
deaths, which is inough to make it no tragedie, yet brings some
neere it, which is inough to make it no comedie' ('To the Reader'

497). Still, with regard to self-speaking, little in pre-1600 tragicomedy goes beyond the standard techniques established in Medieval
drama. It is chiefly due to the association of self-reflection with
tragic experience, beginning with Kyd and Marlowe, that Fletcher's
formula acquires implications for the representation of subjectivity.

Within the 'Beaumont and Fletcher canon'[8], at least, those implications are best considered a matter of style, rather than of genre,
since (to confuse matters) they extend to the formal tragedies of the
group, whose chief difference lies in welcoming into their plots the
sensational enormities (sexually driven murder is the norm) that
are miraculously averted elsewhere. Their characters, however, are
cast in the standard tragicomic mould, which produces an elusive
synthesis of 'psychological realism' and fairy-tale reductivism. The
result is, for some critics, a blameworthy lack of 'motivation', for
others (with whom I have more in common), a distinctive stylistic
effect. And when one turns (as I will shortly do) to Shakespeare's
late 'romances', particularly *The Winter's Tale* and *Cymbeline*, that
effect may again be coordinated with formal features.

I wish to begin, however, with Webster's only known tragicomedy, *The Devil's Law-Case*, in which the mixture of genres produces
no stylistic 'third term' and which, in its approach to characterization, does not materially differ from Webster's tragedies. Its model
seems to have been, not the late Shakespeare or 'Beaumont and
Fletcher', but works such as *Measure for Measure* and *The Malcontent*. (Webster had helped to prepare the latter play for performance
by the King's Men.[9]) My main argument – namely, that a comic plot
mechanism is here overlaid upon a tragically coded conception of
subjectivity – applies to the latter two texts as well, but in them the
mediation of the comic by a metadramatic manipulator complicates
the picture. Moreover, in Marston's case (as was suggested in the
previous chapter), the 'fallen' linguistic condition grounding the
effect of aphanisis is so thoroughly assumed that subjectivity as
such never becomes a site of contestation. It very much does, on the
other hand, in *The Devil's Law-Case*, as in *The White Devil* and *The
Duchess of Malfi*. At the same time, the absence of a dominant agent
of the comic throws into relief the pervasive operation of a transcendental discourse, which ensures that, to cite the character Ariosto,
its final mouthpiece, 'these passages, / Which threatened ruin, built
on rotten ground, / Are with success beyond our wishes crowned'
(5.6.91–3). In marked contrast with the unsignposted wildernesses
of the tragedies,[10] this play-world features timely interventions

calculated to frustrate ill-willing humanity and keep characters alive – at all costs to plausibility. Thus Romelio's treacherous stabbing of Contarino becomes, thanks to the 'hand of heaven', '[t]he very direct way to save his life' (3.2.152,154).

More (literally) spectacular is the exposure of Leonora's false claim regarding her son's paternity by means of the very portrait from which she had appeared to derive vindictive inspiration. Her inspirational soliloquy is either a reminiscence or an anticipation of Francisco's melancholic framing of his sister's image (at first, he actually calls for her picture) '[t]o fashion my revenge more seriously' (*White Devil*, 4.1.98):

> I was enjoined by the party ought that picture,
> Forty years since, ever when I was vexed,
> To look upon that: what was his meaning in't,
> I know not, but methinks upon the sudden
> It has furnished me with mischief, such a plot
> As never mother dreamt of. Here begins
> My part i'th' play....
>
> (*Devil's Law-Case* 3.3.345–51)

As elsewhere (including Francisco's soliloquy), 'methinks' calls attention to a gap in signification. And indeed, when produced in court, the picture proves to reflect, not her illicit lover, hence the adulterous identity Leonora has assumed, but her virtuous judge, Crispiano. Thus the transcendentally sanctioned significance of the picture, as established by Crispiano's fortuitous presence, overrides discursive self-fashioning – the construction of a villain's 'part' to supply self-absence.

With regard to the play's outright villain, Romelio, the same process is adumbrated in a manner familiar from those tragic malcontents, Bosola and, especially, Lodovico. That is, we are shown, not a linear progression, but a drift from amoral materialism and self-interest into active criminality. Even in Romelio's pursuit of such actions, there remains a quality of play-acting. Hence, his soliloquized delight (again, accompanied by the slippery 'methinks') in the disguise he adopts for the intended murder:

> Excellently well habited! Why, methinks
> That I could play with mine own shadow now,
> And be a rare Italianated Jew;

> To have as many several change of faces
> As I have seen carved upon one cherrystone.
>
> (3.2.1–5)

As the continuation of this speech confirms ('Betray a town to th'
Turk, or make a bonfire / O'th' Christian navy' [13–14]), and as
certainly has been recognized (Bliss 257), the theatrical allusiveness
is quite specific: this 'false' identity is the 'true' one of Marlowe's
stage-Jew Barabas, who, in an anticipatory mirror-image of Romelio,
playfully disguises himself as a French musician in one of his
murderous escapades (*Jew of Malta* 4.4). Such role-playing, however, blurs the distinction between true and false, and when Romelio
catches himself up for excessive enthusiasm – 'But stay, I lose myself'
(17) – he calls attention to that self's evanescence. Beneath his
villainous self-consciousness lurks the unconscious, relentlessly insisting on the gap between constative and performative that self-
speaking in Webster typically tries, and invariably fails, to close: 'I
am full of thoughts, strange ones, but they're no good ones' (2.3.162);
'Oh how this wicked world bewitches' (167); 'The devil has on the
sudden furnished me / With a rare charm' (3.3.87–8).

What is unparalleled in Webster's other plays – and what makes
for such radical discrepancy between tragic and comic forces in
this one – is the intensive depiction, in its complete trajectory, of
Leonora's self-struggle, whose culmination is the 'devil's law-case'
against her son. For once, in representing the subjectifying interaction between self and Other, Webster subordinates the brother-
sister dynamic to that of mother and son, developing an effect
adumbrated through Cornelia and Flamineo in *The White Devil*.
Like theatrical revenge generally, Leonora's desperate effort at self-
redemption is self-destructive – transparently so, to judge from
Crispiano, whose down-to-earth comments begin with surprise that
she should thus proclaim her own dishonour:

> ... 'tis most strange:
> Or why with such a poisoned violence
> Should she labour her son's undoing? We observe
> Obedience of creatures to the law of nature
> Is the stay of the whole world: here that law is broke.
>
> (4.2.238–42)

What Crispiano does not realize is that, like Lear and Gloucester,
whose reactions against their children are evoked here, Leonora

counts herself the victim of an injury enacting a child's equally unnatural wish for a parent's death.

The event that initiates Leonora's career as tragic subject conspicuously engages the mechanism of self-delusion by way of an image she presumes to be her own. When the courtly Contarino indicates his interest in her daughter by asking for the gift of Leonora's 'picture' (1.1.135), she re-images herself as beloved by him. As part of the process, she invests her mirror-image at once with the 'truth' of her mortal condition – 'My looking-glass is a true one, and as yet / It does not terrify me' (142–3) – but only so as to extrapolate a transcendental idealism:

> If ever I would have mine drawn to th'life,
> I would have a painter steal it, at such a time
> I were devoutly kneeling at my prayers;
> There is then a heavenly beauty in't, the soul
> Moves in the superficies.
>
> (159–63)

At the pivotal point between Leonora's two efforts at self-fashioning – through love and through revenge – comes her experience of aphanisis, documented in the second most extensive soliloquy in Webster's *oeuvre* (after that of Francisco, mentioned above). Forty-five lines track the dissolution of Leonora's sense of self in a mixture of despair and as-yet-impotent fury, as she reacts to the supposed death of Contarino at her son's hands. Frustrated desire would seem to be the real route ('oh I shall run mad!' [3.3.245]) to the 'fearful madness' (*Duchess* 1.1.506) with which Webster's other prominent widow is branded when she places desire before her public image (and her brothers' private reasons). The fraught stereotype of lustful widowhood – starkly polarized in the tragedy between images of healthy sexuality and Ferdinand's diseased contempt – here reveals an expanse of middle-ground, where the relation between desire and subjectivity is painfully negotiated.

Contarino's disappearance begets Leonora's self-absence, which she virtually diagnoses, with fair psychoanalytic precision, as a condition of desire, although she hardly intends the text's deft insinuation that all desire is 'impossible':

> Is he gone then?
> There is no plague i'th' world can be compared
> To impossible desire, for they are plagued

> In the desire itself: never, oh never
> Shall I behold him living, in whose life
> I lived far sweetlier than in mine own.
>
> (3.3.235–40)

She comes close to recognizing her desire, however, at least in its 'impossible' state, as preeminently metaphysical. A signifying supplement to aphanisis, it at once promises to fill and produces a void, which is figured, according to her circumstances, in terms of aging and death: ''tis indeed our latest harvest-home, / Last merriment 'fore winter' (250–1). Fulfilment, on the other hand, presents itself as transcendentally self-creative, mimicking the power of the artist whose love for a projected image – here a glancing Pygmalion allusion neatly encodes her narcissism – takes him out of time:

> . . . and we widows,
> As men report of our best picture-makers,
> We love the piece we are in hand with better
> Than all the excellent work we have done before.
> And my son has deprived me of all this.
>
> (251–5)

The remainder of Leonora's monologue, by a series of self-revisions, prismatically breaks down a familiar dynamic into distinct stages. First, in the realization of her hatred for her son, the unconscious is forced to the surface, effectively reformulated as answer instead of question. The precedent is thereby set for her shift later in the scene, in reaction to the picture, from 'what was his meaning in't, / I know not' to 'such a plot / As never mother dreamt of' – a movement, indeed, out of the mode of dream. The first suggestion of revenge, however, proves too terrible to acknowledge, and its repression reproduces subjectivity as discursive fragmentation:

> – Ha, ha, what say you?
> I do talk to somewhat, methinks; it may be
> My evil genius. Do not the bells ring?
> I have a strange noise in my head: oh, fly in pieces!
>
> (261–4)

This pattern is then repeated, beginning with a conscious effort at villainous self-fashioning ('let me have / One property more than the devil of hell' [266–7]), which consciousness itself, as she considers her state ('That have no good to hope for' [270]), turns back into despair. She recoils aphanitically in the manner of Webster's dying tragic villains – 'Let me sink / Where neither man, nor memory may ever find me' (275–6) – and completes that trajectory by falling, this time literally, into unconsciousness.

For an audience trained in the semiotics of subjectivity, such intense unspeaking and respeaking of the self would make an incongruous prelude, at least, to the play's final discursive assurance, as conveyed by the Capuchin's reading of Romelio: 'Some evil angel / Makes him deaf to his own safety' (5.5.3–4). The undermining of signification has, it seems, been the work of another, not the Other. Meaning remains a solid edifice, and if Leonora has lost herself amidst the supposed ruins of language, reduced to hopelessly 'building Babylon' (to invoke the preter-lapsarian perspective of *The Malcontent*), she has simply failed to recognize the restoration of significance achievable by building a monastery. This is, in fact, the moderate punishment imposed by the court, '[t]hat these so comical events be blasted / With no severity of sentence' (5.6.62–3). Still, the condition of 'impossible desire' remains suspended in the ending's failure to resolve her relation with Contarino, whom she has recently reidentified with identity itself. Ercole follows in the footsteps of his classical namesake, his heroic strength diffusing in apotheosis, when, in a (speech-)act of union with his former rival, he appropriates the Other in support of the transcendental discourse of eternal friendship: 'now I make you / Myself for ever' (23–4). At this moment, it is Leonora who enacts the principle of subversive intervention: 'Oh here's one between, / Claims to be nearer' (24–5). The ever-gallant Contarino may affirm, 'to you, dear lady, / I have entirely vowed my life' (25–6), but after her disguised daughter, evidently still cherishing her 'sweetheart' (5.1.28), reveals first her presence, then her purity, he falls into telling silence.

IV

By contrast with *The Devil's Law-Case* (and, for that matter, *Measure for Measure*), Shakespeare's last plays more fully integrate their pending comic resolutions into the representation of quasi-tragic experience. Such experience is often recorded through self-speaking, where it particularly becomes a matter of style. The integrative process is easiest to see in the *The Tempest*, but for the same reason that it is also problematized: the presence, again, of a dominant manipulator – one, moreover, whose own experience shades into tragic subjectivity, with unsettling generic consequences. The discursive synthesis in question appears more straightforwardly in *Pericles*, *The Winter's Tale*, and *Cymbeline*, and the closer balance in the latter two plays between situational extravagance and 'realism' in characterization makes it opportune to concentrate on them.

Key to the containment of tragic tendencies in these plays is the audience's sense that the comic trajectory of the plot depends, not merely on more-or-less arbitrary miracles – miracles that, indeed, verge on the perverse in *The Devil's Law-Case* – but on the frank fantasy that universal powers are promoting justice, even human happiness (when compatible with merit). A specific set of social and political relations is established initially as right, possible, and – especially – natural; this configuration, built into the text's insistent symbolism and so amounting to a transcendental discourse, always 'audible' in the background, has pervasive implications for characterization. 'True' identities are ever-present in suspension, waiting to be realized, and displacement or deviation from them carries a quality of alienation, which is reflected discursively. It is largely through such displacement that subjectivity is developed in these plays – a process all but confined to characters with positive destinies. Villainy becomes two-dimensional – with the exception, arguably, of Jachimo, who furnishes the only case of villainous self-speaking that is not mere inverted ventriloquy of the transcendental discourse, as in the Medieval drama.

When Jachimo begins the soliloquy accompanying his voyeuristic research in Imogen's bedchamber, an unconscious susceptibility to self-destabilization is signalled by his glimpse of himself in the role of Tarquin (*Cym.* 2.2.12–14) – a role transcendentally confirmed by his victim's bedtime reading, the tale of Tereus and Philomela. His attempt to rewrite her as adulteress runs up against a pre-recorded contrary message: 'No more: to what end? / Why should I write this down that's riveted, / Screw'd to my memory?' (42–4). The scene's parodic anticipation of the tablets to be divinely bestowed on the dreaming Posthumus – a token of restoration to 'true' identity – helps to develop Jachimo as an *alter ego* of the flawed hero. (Cloten, also often recognized as Posthumus' double, qualifies, on the other hand, as an *alterum id*.) It is, then, Jachimo who symbolically takes on Posthumus' burden of self-loss at the conclusion. That burden manifests itself in his desperation to escape it – ultimately, like Angelo, through death ('Take that life, beseech you, / Which I so often owe' [5.5.414–15]), but first by discursively assimilating himself to conscience: 'I am glad to be constrain'd to utter that / Which torments me to conceal' (141–2). The inverse echo of Iago, Jachimo's tragic forerunner, who defiantly vows silence in the face of torture, points up the futility of self-fashioning in a universe where individual autonomy is transcendentally superseded.[11]

That futility is more fully displayed in the case of Posthumus himself, even as he seeks refuge in the role of misogynistic revenger from what Philario terms the 'wrath / He hath against himself' (2.4.151–2). As with Othello, the collapse of an identity dependent on Imogen's quasi-divinity and, of course, on his possession of her, has left him self-less; the 'ocular proof' (*Oth.* 3.3.360) of the bracelet, once a vehicle of his investment in Imogen, now carries the menace of death: 'It is a basilisk unto mine eye, / Kills me to look on't' (2.4.107–8). A soliloquized diatribe against women occupies the whole of the next scene. In contrast with Othello's focused discourse of revenge, however, the anti-feminist rhetoric of Posthumus is depersonalized and diffused, excessive and empty. Even his bestial fantasy of the adulterous act, unlike the infestation of Othello's imagination by toads, goats, and monkeys, has a *self-conscious* comical absurdity: 'Perchance he spoke not, but / Like a full-acorn'd boar, a German one, / Cried "O!" and mounted' (2.5.15–17). In short, the voluble self-production of Posthumus is discursively filtered through the lens of better knowledge, so as to produce a built-in detachment. This quality connects, in turn, with the perfunctory 'introspection' (Desmet 75) accompanying his subsequent repentance, when his revenge fantasy is reflected in stark reality by the bloody cloth. The consequent renewal of self-loss, together with the impulse to seek death, is counterbalanced by a resolution, in the voice of the transcendental discourse, to 'begin / The fashion: less without and more within' (5.1.32–3).

Still more conspicuously, according to the standard code, Imogen is plunged into tragic subjectivity by Posthumus' more substantial infidelity to her. His letter to Pisanio, which effectively recants the love-discourse that lured her to Milford Haven ('The scriptures of the loyal Leonatus, / All turn'd to heresy' [3.4.81–2]), bereaves her of an Other-mirrored self. Yet the very intensity of the shock, as mediated by Pisanio, implicitly justifies an other-worldly detachment in her despair:

> Look
> I draw the sword myself, take it, and hit
> The innocent mansion of my love, my heart.
> Fear not, 'tis empty of all things but grief.
> Thy master is not there, who was indeed
> The riches of it.
>
> (3.4.66–71)

Moreover, her disguise, which begins as a temporizing expedient, quickly comes to supply death-in-life with a sort of *posthumous* existence: by the end of the scene she feels herself 'almost / A man already' (166–7). Like the cross-dressing comic heroines, she stands at a discursive remove from her previous self, and the distance is greater because she lacks their sense of 'true' identity: to 'see a man's life is a tedious one' (3.6.1) is a far cry from speaking oneself '[a]s I am woman' (*TN* 2.2.38).

Imogen's remark on 'a man's life' initiates her first soliloquy by appropriating a god's-eye-view, which extends to moral commentary ('falsehood / Is worse in kings than beggars' [13–14]) and a humorous perspective on her own impersonation: 'if mine enemy / But fear the sword like me, he'll scarcely look on't. / Such a foe, good heavens!' (25–7). Only when the theme of falseness recalls Posthumus is she brought down to earth – to find, ironically, the aching emptiness of the body displaced by its metaphysical counterpart: 'Now I think on thee, / My hunger's gone' (15–16). The same pattern takes more extreme form in Imogen's extraordinary soliloquized encounter, in the next act, with the decapitated body she supposes to be that of Posthumus. Again, a physical correlative of self-absence – the lingering effects of the sleeping potion – grounds her distracted perception, which is here intensified by the joke (part of her almost seems to share it) that she is so positively wrong in identifying those limbs that she at least verbally, and certainly with sexual feeling, caresses: 'I know the shape of's leg; this is his hand, / His foot Mercurial, his Martial thigh, / The brawns of Hercules' (4.2.309–11). As with Posthumus earlier, her emotionalism verges on the bathetic: 'O Posthumus, alas, / Where is thy head? Where's that? Ay me! where's that?' (320–1). In collapsing upon the body, she enacts yet another symbolic death, from which she will rise to realize an even wider split between the role of the boy-servant Fidele, shrewdly acting his way into the service of Lucius – a necessary means to the comic end – and the vanished identity of which she declares, 'I am nothing; or if not, / Nothing to be were better' (367–8).

Hermione's experience obviously overlaps with that of Imogen in several elements fraught with the symbolism of identity: the unaccountable irruption of sexual slander into a 'secure' emotional relation, the vindictive attempt on her life, her exile and supposed death. From this study's perspective, however, a comparison foregrounds *The Winter's Tale*'s reluctance to document that experience through self-speech. It makes a significant paradox that a character routinely endowed by criticism with so high a degree of subjectivity and possessing such a vivid dramatic presence, thanks to her abundant representation in dialogue, never speaks alone, either aside or in soliloquy. Even her suffering in prison is related indirectly, through description and reported speech (2.2). This fact may be approached by way of the double-edged idea of the silent woman, which I will be pursuing in the next chapter. Here I wish to suggest only that Hermione's eloquence at her trial, when she is forced '[t]o prate and talk for life and honor 'fore / Who please to come and hear' (3.2.41–2), extends the typically tragicomic division evident in Imogen between aphanitic subjectivity, functioning as a hallmark of mortal existence, and a transcendental perspective connected with the larger forces at work in the play-world. The latter perspective mediates Hermione's initial reaction even when disaster first strikes, almost magnetically drawing a potential aside into a public declaration: 'There's some ill planet reigns; / I must be patient, till the heavens look / With an aspect more favorable' (2.1.105–7). The same faith conditions her sixteen years of symbolic death:

> . . . thou shalt hear that I,
> Knowing by Paulina that the oracle
> Gave hope thou wast in being, have preserv'd
> Myself to see the issue.
>
> (5.3.125–8)

Whatever psycho-sexual mechanism the text may be read as attaching to Leontes, subjectivity is preeminently at stake in his scapegoating of Hermione, which entails, not just publicly remaking her according to a warped image, but projecting upon her an intolerable self-evanescence, whose outward sign is 'such a countenance / As he had lost some province and a region / Lov'd as he loves himself' (1.2.368–70). This standard objective of the revenger –

developed or not, it inheres in the compulsion to inflict mental suffering, knowledge as pain – is the focus of Leontes' soliloquized refashioning of himself: 'say that she were gone, / Given to the fire, a moi'ty of my rest / Might come to me again' (2.3.7–9). Against the background of Hermione's domestic fulfilment – vividly evoked at the opening of Act 2, as Leontes is about to obtrude his private hell – to snatch away first Mamillius, then her newborn daughter, is all the more clearly to cut away layers of her being in quasi-physical fashion. These are precisely the terms in which she recounts her progressive suffering – a spiritual dying, beginning with the loss of Leontes' love, that renders physical death superfluous:

> The crown and comfort of my life, your favor,
> I do give lost, for I do feel it gone,
> But know not how it went. My second joy
> And first-fruits of my body, from his presence
> I am barr'd, like one infectious. My third comfort
> (Starr'd most unluckily) is from my breast
> (The innocent milk in it most innocent mouth)
> Hal'd out to murther; myself on every post
> Proclaim'd a strumpet . . .
> . . . .
>   . . . Now my liege,
> Tell me what blessings I have here alive,
> That I should fear to die?

>   (3.2.94–108)

But this enforced self-speaking is not, after all, soliloquy, and no slippery linguistic self-reflection matches the aphanitic experience. Rather, that experience is contained – even, at a profound level, invested with acceptance – by means of Hermione's appeal to 'honor', as opposed to 'life'. The transcendental potency of that virtue, at once private and public, is deployed in aligning the vicarious survival of her 'true' self ('a derivative from me to mine' [44]) with a higher justice. In entrusting her honour to 'pow'rs divine' (28) at both the beginning and the end of her refutation, Hermione thus invokes a framework of unimpeachable signification – except in Leontes' climactic discursive act of folly, 'There is no truth at all i' th' oracle' (140) – to bracket the site where meaning slips out of her grasp. When Hermione seems to die along with Mamillius, she disappears, as it were, simultaneously into that inner void and into divinity itself. Hence her revival at first miraculously incarnates truth beyond expression, her breath hovering momentarily – and engaging Leontes – in a Kristevan realm prior to speech, as if to delay the inevitable lapse into mortal language:

Camillo   She hangs about his neck.
            If she pertain to life let her speak too.
Polixenes   Ay, and make it manifest where she has liv'd,
            Or how stol'n from the dead.
Paulina   That she is living,
            Were it but told you, should be hooted at
            Like an old tale; but it appears she lives,
            Though yet she speak not. Mark a little while.
                                                (5.3.112–18)

That there is no language for such a truth, so mingling joy and sorrow, would seem to be confirmed by contrast with Cordelia, whom the needy Lear manoeuvres into a verbal profession foretelling her more concrete sacrifice to come: 'No cause, no cause' (*Lr* 4.7.74). These words represent the ultimate fulfilment of Lear's injunction to '[m]end your speech a little' (1.1.94), while Hermione's silence recuperates the unfallen condition that Leontes forbade her: 'Tongue-tied our queen? Speak you' (*WT* 1.2.28). Yet the conclusion also makes amply clear that the symbolic order, including here, as before, the language of the body, is by *nature* an inescapable 'cadre' of exchange relations and gaps in signification: 'What? look upon my brother. Both your pardons, / That e'er I put between your holy looks / My ill suspicion' (147–9).

That Hermione's discourse during the trial-scene thus synthesizes aphanitic and transcendental voices helps to account for its rhetorical power. The impact is heightened by the linguistic self-subversion of Leontes. As with Posthumus, the hollowness of his accusations resounds through his bluster, menace, and sarcasm, thereby signalling his 'better knowledge'. When she accuses him, in effect, of talking to himself, his response actually undoes itself by a contrary double meaning:

Hermione   Sir,
           You speak a language that I understand not.
           My life stands in the level of your dreams,
           Which I'll lay down.
Leontes   Your actions are my dreams.
                                              (3.2.79–82)

In what Leontes takes to be the decisive jibe that follows – 'You had a bastard by Polixenes, / And I but dream'd it' (83–4) – the sarcastic tone instantly evaporates, leaving the factual residue.

The tendency of Leontes' word-play to play with him ('Go play, boy, play. Thy mother plays, and I / Play too, but so disgrac'd a part . . .' [1.2.186–7]) serves from the start to make his discourse 'realistically' self-delusive, but also to set limits to tragic subjectivity. In this respect, as in wilfully leaping to his conclusions unassisted, he makes a caricature of Othello. The profuse monologues in Act 1, Scene 2, are kept on the near side of soliloquy, as Leontes wavers between self-address and addressing Mamillius, so that his experience never becomes a fully 'private' matter. Moreover, the rules of the tragicomic game apply by way of the doomed Mamillius himself, whose part in Leontes' agonized self-mirroring pivots on his fidelity as a 'copy' (1.2.122), hence his fitness as both the image of a childhood self and a guarantor of immortality.

This doubtful self-imaging *vis-à-vis* his son is a parodic displacement of the mutual mirroring relation that had obtained between Leontes and Polixenes, and whose passing is associated with female sexuality. The latter point lends itself to analysis in Freudian terms: witness the deft account of Janet Adelman (222–3), who takes her cue from both kings' perception of the pregnant Hermione as an emblem of threatening female Otherness. A Lacanian reading might stress instead the inherent doubleness of any 'mirroring other who reassuringly gives back only himself' (Adelman 223), including Polixenes. The adult Polixenes, after all, is ineluctably not the child, and his initial 'no' to Leontes' request that he forego mature responsibilities and play out the childhood idyll re(in)states the *Nom du Père*, the gateway to subjectivity. For Leontes, the imagined union of Polixenes and Hermione at once mocks and recalls an Edenic perfection ('making practic'd smiles, / As in a looking-glass' [1.2.116–17]) from which he is now excluded. On the level of discourse, too, he is ambivalently nostalgic, proclaiming (and secretly denying) that Hermione's power to transform Polixenes' 'no' into 'yes' recapitulates her former (now duplicitized) speech-act: 'I am yours for ever' (105). Insofar as Leontes' interaction with Mamillius enacts such a regression to the mirror-stage, complete with alternating visions of plenitude and privation, his construction of Hermione as an emblem of self-loss takes a back seat to his constitution of aphanitic subjectivity itself as tragic. And this is absurdly to defy, in the standard tragicomic guise of 'the gods', the comic processes of time and nature.

V

To conclude this chapter, a brief word about one further tragicomic mode of self-speaking – brief because this technique, although a 'Beaumont and Fletcher' hallmark, amounts to an expansion of the 'Imogen-effect' already discussed. That is, an acute experience of self-loss fuses with an intense intuition of transcendental forces at work in the play-world. The result is less a conflict than a strange harmony, with each element at once intensifying and modifying the other. Musical analogies come naturally: with its predilection for emotional and situational extremes and reversals, the drama associated with Beaumont and Fletcher is notorious for privileging sensory appeal over intellectual engagement. The model of nineteenth-century melodrama is often invoked, and with good reason, especially considering its use of music to heighten dramatic sensation.[12] More immediately to the point, the Early Modern romantic drama made a remarkably smooth passage, not only onto the post-Restoration stage, but, by way of adaptation, into its musical theatre.

The affinity with opera thereby implied leads to a further musical comparison: self-speaking monologues in Beaumont and Fletcher – including, but by no means limited to, soliloquies – tend to function like (at least pre-Wagnerian) arias. That is, they constitute virtuoso displays of extravagant passion, which is contained within a seductive and reassuring melodic pattern. One hears, in effect, two voices in one – self-speaking as self-accompaniment. As in so much contemporary drama, moreover, a recurrent focus of passion is precisely the experience of self, whether as present or absent. Doubleness of voice, then, becomes doubleness of identity: one voice is implicated in the pressing dynamic of subjectivity; the other is transcendental.

Only one voice – the former – is heard when the dying Cardinal in *The Duchess of Malfi* consigns himself to oblivion: 'And now, I pray, let me / Be laid by, and never thought of' (5.5.89–90). In the fulsome expostulation of the condemned Philaster, Beaumont and Fletcher's misguided hero, the same sentiment is distanced, and its speaker effectively doubled, through rhetorical inflation and embellishment:

> I am a man
> False to a pair of the most trusty ones
> That ever earth bore. Can it bear us all?

> Forgive, and leave me. But the king hath sent
> To call me to my death; O show it me
> And then forget me.
>
> (*Philaster* 5.2.5–10)

Philaster's fall *ought* to extend to discourse itself: the signifying system on which he has staked selfhood ('false' *versus* 'true') collapses in a tangle of symbolic exchange-relations. His view of himself in the mirror of death reduces him, like Everyman, to reciting the inadequacy of his 'reckoning'. Yet even in so doing he hyperbolically invests language with plenitude, effectively reconstituting the mirror-stage and overriding the 'signification mortifère' of his own image:

> ... for thee, my boy,
> I shall deliver words will mollify
> The hearts of beasts to spare thy innocence.
>
> (10–12)

Words traditionally have such power, of course, when combined with music, as in the legend of Orpheus.

It helps that Philaster's aphanitic condition is not chronic, as with the Cardinal (and Webster's characters generally), but a passing phenomenon, triggered by the discovery that his previous image of himself as a betrayed lover has been based on false premises. This proves a 'fortunate fall' indeed. Even as they provoke his self-condemnation for lack of faith and attempted murder, the ever-loving Bellario and Arethusa show him what the audience has never doubted – that he is better than he thinks. The text, in effect, stands up for moral essentialism. In Beaumont and Fletcher's tragicomedy, self-evanescence is merely another test to which characters may be *subjected* (if they are important enough), only to be restored, inevitably, to 'true' identity by a magnetic force that infiltrates the very language of aphanisis. This is to bring them near to death-in-life but to keep them safe. And in a way that harks back to the Medieval drama, the link between the individual subject and the transcendental discourse is furnished by conscience.

Hence, for instance, the prolonged immersion of Arbaces, the title-character of *A King and No King*, in the conscientious agonies produced by his desire for his supposed sister Panthea. The 'whole story' is indeed, as he exclaims at the point of resolution, a 'wilderness to lose thyself / Forever' (5.4.287–8), and it is replete with the language of self-loss in numerous instances of self-speaking. As deeply subverted as he is by passion, however, Arbaces cannot lose himself in it; he can merely see himself as lost at a rhetorical distance:

> . . . I am left as far without a bound
> As the wild ocean that obeys the winds;
> Each sudden passion throws me as it lists
> And overwhelms all that oppose my will.
>   (4.4.67–70)

Similarly, although he can readily figure signs as arbitrary, he is incapable of acting on this perception:

> I have liv'd
> To conquer men and now am overthrown
> Only by words – 'brother' and 'sister'. Where
> Have those words dwelling? I will find 'em out
> And utterly destroy them, but they are
> Not to be grasp'd.
>   (4.4.116–21)

In fact, like reason itself ('The only difference betwixt man and beast' [4.4.65]), the signifying system is implanted within the self as a reflection of the transcendental discourse. When Panthea points out that ' 'tis not in the power of any force / Or policy to conquer' (127–8) the words in question, she speaks, as at other points, with the stronger of his own two voices – that of conscience. The subsumptive power of the transcendental discourse could not be clearer than in its ultimate incorporation of the counter-discourse of passion. What appeared to impose self-loss proves, in fact, the route to self-discovery, since Arbaces and Panthea are finally revealed to be unrelated. The signifiers 'brother' and 'sister' retain their standing but, in stark contrast with *'Tis Pity She's a Whore*, no longer apply. 'Tragic' subjectivity is appropriated on comedy's behalf.

A survey of the 'Beaumont and Fletcher canon' shows, however, that the discursive containment of aphanisis is similarly practised when the action no longer 'wants deaths' but rather proliferates them. Evadne in *The Maid's Tragedy*, the king's repentant mistress, moves swiftly in soliloquy from her sense of self-absence, which she situates in the past and surrounds by verbal ornament, to the daunting yet potentially liberating discovery of her 'true' self in conscience's mirror:

> Gods, where have I been all this time, how friended,
> That I should lose myself thus desperately,
> And none for pity show me how I wandered?
> There is not in the compass of the light
> A more unhappy creature; sure, I am monstrous,
> For I have done those follies, those mad mischiefs,
> Would dare a woman. O, my loaden soul,
> Be not so cruel to me, choke not up
> The way to my repentance.
>
> (4.1.178–86)

Her last words – more ominous for echoing Faustus ('My God, my God, look not so fierce on me!' [5.2.112]) – amount to a generic marker. They sway definitively towards her, and ultimately towards the circumstances of her pre-textual loss of maidenhood, the 'tragedy' that the title more superficially, but potentially more profoundly, accords to Aspatia, who, exiled from the 'self' defined as love, seeks and finds death at her unwitting lover's hands. The transcendental discourse conspicuously maintains itself by according Evadne an oversufficiency of rope in her despair, allowing her to fix quickly on vengeful regicide as a means of fashioning herself more damnably.

A useful perspective on Evadne is furnished by another semi-sympathetic regicide, Maximus in *The Tragedy of Valentinian*, who, of all the principal characters in Beaumont and Fletcher (though this play is Fletcher's alone), comes closest to tracing the standard discursive trajectory of the tragic subject. After the rape and suicide of his wife, Maximus takes refuge from self-loss in plotting revenge against Caesar. This, however, requires also killing his friend – his second self. His soliloquy insists on the aphanitic implications, yet the glimpse into the abyss is mitigated by melody:

> *Aecius* dies,
> Or I have lost my selfe: why should I kill him?
> Why should I kill my selfe? for tis my killing,
> *Aecius* is my roote, and whither him,
> Like a decaying branch, I fall to nothing.
>
> (3.3.17–21)

The same effect occurs even when, after these murders, he contemplates suicide – 'is ought else to be liv'd for?' (5.3.8) – but then, as it were, finds himself again in another plot. At first, his language is informed by a musical quality connoting the transcendental virtues he can still appreciate:

> Is there an other friend, an other wife,
> Or any third holds halfe their worthynesse,
> To linger here alive for? Is not vertue
> In their two everlasting soules departed,
> And in their bodies first flame fled to heaven?
>
> (9–13)

But the sense of self-absence resists incorporation into this rhetoric – 'Can any man discover this, and love me?' (14) – and his thoughts veer off in a surprising new direction:

> ... stay, I am foolish,
> Somewhat too suddaine to mine own destruction,
> This great end of my vengance may grow greater:
> Why may not I be *Caesar*, yet no dying?
> Why should not I catch at it?
>
> (23–7)

The resemblance to Marlowe's Barabas, hitting on revenge as an antidote to suicidal despair, points up the strange turn taken here – one that leads beyond the typical revenger's self-immolation in his self-fashioned success, the triumph over death through death. Maximus' sudden bid to avoid this fate in a grab for worldly power proves (like Barabas' final trick) to be his undoing and decisively tips the scale in the audience's perception of him: the grief-stricken madman is eclipsed by the mad villain. It is the equivalent of Evadne's move from promising penitence to impious murder. Such a second fall reveals, as a condition of tragedy, the instability of the discourse of conscience by which, in the tragicomedies, a mirror is infallibly held up to an idealized nature. Rhetorically softened though it is, the experience of aphanitic subjectivity, for both Evadne and Maximus, is encoded as profoundly dangerous – liable, in the absence of the tragicomic safety net, to generate the deepest evil, precisely to 'choke ... up' the 'way to ... repentance' by, Faustus-like, challenging the transcendental discourse's monopoly of meaning. Even in Beaumont and Fletcher's tragicomedy, the quasi-operatic effects keeping characters 'shallow' arguably involve a determined displacement, not a genial by-passing, of subjectivities 'always already' more fully realized: a trace of the dimension thereby placed *sous rature* continues to signal a vague but potent menace.

Notes to Chapter 6

1. On the relation of this speech to the general pattern, see my article, 'Meaning and Mortality'.
2. On mortality in the comedies, see also Garber.
3. This element in Shakespeare's comedy may be related to the 'Trickster function' (see my *Subversions*).
4. Burns may again undervalue 'nothing' when he observes that 'the deceit that Maria engineers foists the derangement of identifying signs on a man who has nothing within at all' (168).
5. *MND* is a key text, from the perspective of 'mimetic desire', for Girard (*passim*, esp. 29–56.). Greenblatt discusses Shakespeare's comic heroines as 'projected mirror images of masculine self-differentiation' ('Fiction' 92).
6. Esp. in *Problem Plays*.
7. The uncertain chronology, however, precludes any assessment of 'influence'.
8. This rubric, devised by Bowers for the collected edition, remains convenient when discussing the common features of these works, whose authorship, in fact, is variable, usually collaborative, and sometimes indeterminate.
9. Bliss (256–7) comments on the play's relation to *The Malcontent*, especially the satirical connection. It may have been composed earlier than has generally been held – perhaps as early as 1610 (Bliss 256n13).
10. Cf. the Duchess of Malfi, about to woo Antonio: 'I am going into a wilderness, / Where I shall find nor path, nor friendly clew / To be my guide' (1.1.359–61); the later dialogue between Antonio and the echo (5.3) is, of course, set amidst ancient ruins.
11. This is important background to the fact that, as Desmet observes, '[i]dentity crisis in *Cymbeline* involves moments of high comedy' (74).
12. This typically came, however, in support of action and at the expense of speech, including self-speaking; see Sprague, 'Shakespeare and Melodrama', who documents an 1809 adaptation of *Mac.* stripped of soliloquies (2).

7
(Off)Staging the Female Subject

That the Early Modern instances of dramatic self-speaking featured to this point have included a number of female characters ultimately reflects the extraordinary interest in the complex staging of women displayed by a predominantly commercial theatre whose authors and players (though not its audiences) were exclusively male. It appears, moreover, that certain discursive models of subjectivity were capable of crossing the gender barrier, even if stereotyping usually shaped the raw material with a heavy hand. I hope to have established a framework within which Belsey's claim that the dramatic subject in this period lacked the capacity to 'identify with the "I" of an utterance' (15) – a capacity on which aphanitic subjectivity depends, with its 'discovery' of the gap between the two *sujets* – conjures up the opposing testimony not only of Hamlet but of Juliet: 'I am not I, if there be such an ay' (*Rom.* 3.2.48). Conversely, I can locate no such subjectivity in either the male or female characters of, say, *A Women Killed with Kindness* or *Bussy D'Ambois* – or, for that matter, in Elizabeth Cary's woman-centred closet drama, *The Tragedy of Mariam*, whose heroine notably soliloquizes self-division, but along neo-classical lines whose intersection marks her double presence. This concluding chapter, however, aims at counteracting any tendency of my approach to elide gender difference. Here I would like to refocus the previous argument – to the extent of reviewing some of the same texts – by distinguishing certain figurations of specifically feminine subjectivity within larger discursive structures that remain thoroughly (if sometimes self-critically) patriarchal.

I

To begin with the patriarch *par excellence*, when Lear, having entered with the dead Cordelia in his arms, fondly recalls her as having a 'voice . . . soft, / Gentle, and low, an excellent thing in woman' (*Lr* 5.3.273–4), it is just possible to abstract the anti-feminist sentiment from its context and so to miss the paradoxical dramatic point. Certainly, Lear is nostalgically filtering the memory of his daughter through the stereotypical patriarchal fantasy – whose strongest testimony is its propensity for proliferating jokes – of the silent woman. Immediately, though, he is desperate to hear the silent Cordelia speak – 'What is't thou say'st?' (273) – and deluding himself as to why he cannot. The stereotype, complete with Lear's ambivalence, underlies the play's initiating incident. Cordelia first outrages her father by saying '[n]othing' (1.1.87), having resolved (in an aside) to '[l]ove, / And be silent' (62–3); when she affirms her 'duties' (97) with what might pass for becoming female reticence and modesty, he reacts as if she had spoken not too little but too much: 'So young, and so untender?' (106).

Already, the professions of Goneril and Regan to be, in effect, 'nothing' apart from their devotion to Lear have focused his ritual on identity as a function of discourse. The hypocritical sisters' volubility is counterpointed by Cordelia's second aside, in which she affirms that 'my love's / More ponderous than my tongue' (77–8), and when she picks up Regan's reference to a 'true heart' (70) to lament that she 'cannot heave / My heart into my mouth' (91–2), she confronts Lear with a disjunction between her 'tongue' and her 'true' love that is as destabilizing for him as 'that within which passes show' (*Ham.* 1.2.85) proves to be for Hamlet. In affirming continuity of signification between inward and outward – 'But goes thy heart with this?' (105) – Lear denies that the core of identity lies beyond discursive reach. The contingency of the self on the 'fallen' language of exchange-relations would vitiate his intended regression into prelinguistic plenitude by making the point (as will the 'true' voices of Goneril and Regan) that the corollary of that illusion of presence is the realization of absence. What Lear takes to be Cordelia's self-exemption from discourse enacts a shattering of the mirror-stage, an insistent Otherness reflecting, not the death he is willing '[u]nburthen'd' to 'crawl toward' (41), but the living condition that 'smells of mortality' (4.6.133). Lear may be making his other daughters his mothers, as the Fool will later observe (1.4.172–3), but, no less paradoxically, Cordelia's 'nothing', distilling the essence of her voice 'soft, / Gentle, and low', comes in the *Nom du Père*.

The discursive dynamic between Lear and Cordelia may fairly be taken as paradigmatic of the destabilizing menace of female silence. As the discourse that is 'not one' (to adapt Luce Irigaray's punning epithet for the female sex), such silence thus ranks with the evidence that, in terms of classical and Renaissance rhetorical theory, no less than according to Kristeva's nonessentialist concept of the 'semiotic', 'woman is associated with language's more disturbing effects' (Desmet 134).[1] Elsewhere, too, Shakespeare shows such menace lurking beneath the standard assumption of silence's desirability – apart from those instances (Silvia in *The Two Gentlemen of Verona*, Isabella in *Measure for Measure*) where silence betokening male power over the inmost self speaks to the audience with subversive ambiguity. Leontes' treatment of Hermione provides the closest parallel to Lear and Cordelia, but goes a step farther in staging the basic contradiction within the patriarchal attitude. For in *The Winter's Tale*, where the initial provocation to transgressive speech is separate from the public ritual staged by the king to disclose the 'true' state of the woman's love (according to his foregone conclusion), that ritual also aims directly at silencing her once and for all. This is the same paradox that Webster exploits in even more explicitly discursive terms, when, in effect, he rewrites Hermione's trial-scene for the far-from-innocent Vittoria. The proposal to try Vittoria in Latin would make her speech a version of silence, as she recognizes in refusing; yet by parrying the Cardinal's verbal assault with an adroit deployment of rhetoric, she preserves intact a potently disquieting silence at the presumptive core of identity.

On the other hand, there is reassurance in such superficially transgressive categories as 'shrew' and 'babbler' (a term, again, probably coloured by Babel), just as in the contemptuous stereotype of women's misuse of mirrors for specious self-fashioning. It is now common to read shrewish disobedience, like political rebellion, as playing into the hands of – indeed constructed by – authority. In the English drama, this pattern my be traced back to the cycle plays, whose comic figures of evil – mostly male but including Noah's wife, as she boisterously defies her husband and obstructs the church-prefiguring ark – establish verbal transgression as a sign of the transcendental preempting of subjectivity-as-voice. The later stereotype of the nonsensical woman who offends male ears with noise, such as Jonson's Lady Politic Would-be and 'Silent Women' her/himself, may then be seen as a back-formation from the doubtful privilege of aphanisis, offering a comfortable reflection of Otherness by assuming the burden of the post-Babel condition, in which identity is dissipated in a flux of receding signification. Hence, it is never enough, in a dramatic context, merely to impose silence on shrews and babblers; this would manifest patriarchal power on one level while sapping it on another. Rather, they must be recruited into the discourse that aspires to transcendence. Noah's wife, after all, is not beaten into submission but awed by God's power into active compliance with her husband's will. Shakespeare's Katherina, whose very labelling as 'shrew' restricts her potential subversiveness, is led first to accept the quasi-divine power of her husband as a matter of discourse ('What you will have it nam'd, even that it is' [*Shr.* 4.5.21]), then to ventriloquize patriarchal doctrine: 'Katherine, I charge thee tell these headstrong women / What duty they do owe their lords and husbands' (5.2.130–1).[2] Epicoene must be restored, not merely to meek womanhood, but to maleness.

Comic female babbling is a small step removed, discursively speaking, from that most poignant emblem of tragic subjectivity in women – madness, which is invariably engendered by the loss of, or longing for, a loved one. This tradition stretches back to the grief-stricken mothers in pageants of the Slaughter of the Innocents and the Crucifixion, as is effectively acknowledged by Shakespeare's Henry V, when he threatens the inhabitants of Harfleur that they shall see their

> . . . naked infants spitted upon pikes,
> Whiles the mad mothers with their howls confus'd
> Do break the clouds, as did the wives of Jewry
> At Herod's bloody-hunting slaughter-men.
>
> (*H5* 3.3.38–41)

The Medieval originals of this pattern are nonetheless positioned within the transcendental discourse of the divine will – as securely as if by the Doctor of the Brome *Abraham* (see Chapter 2). The key condition of psychotic speech in Lacanian terms, the disappearance of the 'existential subject of synchronic relations (*je*)' (Ragland-Sullivan 199), may be contrasted with the insistent use of 'I', as the *sujet de l'énonciation*, to contain their suffering – even, in the Wakefield *Herod the Great*, to delineate the skirting (pun intended) of madness: 'Out, I cry! I go near wood! / Alas! my hart is all on flood, / To se my chyld thus blede!' (Pollard and England, eds 376–8).

Only the Chester *Passion*'s Marian lament, to my knowledge –
and only, intriguingly, in a unique variant amongst the surviving
manuscripts[3] – notably anticipates later dramatic practice. In this
version, madness is not merely one bead on a string but the string
itself, and the effect, embodied in the shifting of the key verb between transitive and intransitive modes, is to highlight the vacilla-
tion of the self between object ('mowrning now madds me' [242][4])
and subject: 'Therfore I madd, both evon and morne, / to see my
byrth, that I have borne / this bitter bale to byde' (254–6). In one
stanza, the inward disjunction widens into delusional self-division,
signalled by 'methink', as Mary flees the self-image reflected by her
crucified son:

> Alas, the sorrow of this sight
> marrs my mynd, mayne and might,
> but aye my hart methink is light
> to looke on that I love.
> And when I looke anonright
> upon my child that thus is dight
> would death deliver me in height,
> then were I all above.
> (Lumiansky and Mills, eds *Passion*
> 256n., lines 9–16)

I have already (in Chapter 3) proposed that *Gorboduc*'s early Elizabethan adaptation of maternal lament foregrounds deviance from
the transcendental discourse. It would seem to have been Marlowe
who inaugurated the Elizabethan stage discourse of (sym)pathetic
female madness by first showing (in *Tamburlaine, Part 1*) a bereft
woman caught in the process by which '[m]ind . . . unravels into
the fragmented parts which previously functioned as a unity as
long as anchored by the sense of a cohesive self' (Ragland-Sullivan
199). In doing so, and in coding the experience as feminine, he
clearly tapped into the cycle play tradition. Tamburlaine may not
out-Herod Herod, but his slaughter of the virgins of Damascus
focuses the biblical allusion within the extraordinary suicide soliloquy, shortly afterwards, of the captive Turkish empress, Zabina.
Her discourse shifts radically when she discovers her husband dead:

> O Bajazeth, my husband and my lord,
> O Bajazeth, O Turk, O emperor – give him his liquor?

Not I. Bring milk and fire, and my blood I bring him again, tear
me in pieces, give me the sword with a ball of wild-fire upon it.
Down with him, down with him! Go to my child, away, away,
away. Ah, save that infant, save him, save him! I, even I, speak
to her. The sun was down. Streamers white, red, black, here,
here, here. Fling the meat in his face. Tamburlaine, Tamburlaine!
Let the soldiers be buried. Hell, death, Tamburlaine, hell! Make
ready my coach, my chair, my jewels, I come, I come, I come!
(5.1.308–19)

The fragmentation of Marlowe's 'mighty line' is even more striking
by contrast with Bajazeth's own verbal build-up to self-destruction
immediately before, which mechanically ventriloquizes the dominant heroic discourse ('O highest lamp of ever-living Jove, / Accursèd
day, infected with my griefs, / Hide now thy stainèd face in endless night' [290–2]). The disintegration of this discourse through
Zabina entails her subjectification through aphanisis, as her 'I' is
dispersed into a succession of intensely personal yet archetypically
female experiences of war. Finally, a fantasized recapture of her
imperial identity – a point picked up in Shakespeare's adaptation of
the lines for the suicide speech of Cleopatra[5] – manifests the triumph of Lacan's 'primordial ideal ego'. The psycho-rhetorical features, then, are essentially those employed by Kyd (and his
anonymous successor) in developing the mad Hieronimo (though
notably not Isabella).[6] The major difference in *Tamburlaine*, which
applies generally to the discourse of female madness, is that, instead
of turning outward as 'a mechanical god of power and destruction'
(Ragland-Sullivan 199), the subject turns inward, upon herself.

The tradition running from the Herod pageants through Zabina's
suicide ramifies after 1600 to include such diverse figures as Ophelia,
Cornelia in *The White Devil*, and – an exception in terms of social
class – the Jailer's Daughter in *The Two Noble Kinsmen* (by Shakespeare and Fletcher).[7] Consistently, however, female madness remains a reaction to male actions, either directly or by way of a
sexual love thwarted for patriarchal reasons. In principle, according
to contemporary ideas of love-melancholy, men are at least equally
susceptible, but in dramatic practice, Cupid is not *gender*-blind:
'Cupid is a knavish lad, / Thus to make poor females mad' (*MND*
3.2.440–1). So says, moreover, the male spirit who himself reduces
Helena and Hermia to desperate confusion over the behaviour of
the men in their lives. By contrast, the dangerous distraction of

Ariosto's love-sick Orlando Furioso is tempered (partly under the influence of Thomas Lodge) into the charming eccentricity of *As You Like It's* male lead, while Hamlet, that epitome of subjectifying self-absence, is not mad for Ophelia's love, if he is mad at all. Meanwhile, the distracted Ophelia, once forbidden to speak for herself, her language now teetering between grief for her father and a double betrayal by her lover, epitomizes female openness to discursive subjectivity through madness. Such subjectivity, which superficially transgresses the patriarchal ideal of the silent woman, simultaneously defuses the menace uneasily lurking in that ideal – the implicit female claim (from the male perspective) to be above or beyond language. With madness, the unitary image yields to patent fragmentation – hence, the attempt of Ferdinand to drive the Duchess of Malfi mad. The speech of madwomen, like that of babblers, confirms their entrapment in the fallenness of discourse, the excess of signification that imposes the impossibility of meaning.

At the same time, these effects are tied, in the cases of Ophelia, the Jailer's Daughter (who puts her father in danger for love of Palamon), and Cornelia (one of whose sons murders the other), to conflicting male allegiances – the embodiment of the patriarchal double-bind. And it is only fitting that patriarchy should find itself discursively 'hoist with [its] own petar' – stricken, like Ferdinand and Lear in the face of the ultimate silence, by the very submission it has produced. Female madness, far from confirming reason's control of meaning, interpellates would-be interpreters in the instability of signification:

> Her speech is nothing,
> Yet the unshaped use of it doth move
> The hearers to collection; they yawn at it,
> And botch the words up fit to their own thoughts,
> Which as her winks and nods and gestures yield them,
> Indeed would make one think there might be thought,
> Though nothing sure, yet much unhappily.
>
> *(Ham.* 4.5.7–13)

It is his encounter with the mad Ophelia that pushes Claudius beyond mere self-division, breaking down the binary system that, to this point, has contained his dialogue with the image reflected by his conscience ('My words fly up, my thoughts remain below . . .' [3.3.97]). Now a litany of 'sorrows', which 'come not single spies,

/ But in battalions' (4.5.78–9), strips away layers of the self till there is nothing left, thereby threatening to (re)produce Ophelia's tragic subjectivity in him: 'O my dear Gertrude, this, / Like to a murd'ring-piece, in many places / Gives me superfluous death' (94–6). Even the well-armoured Flamineo feels a deep shudder at his mother's self-absence ('I would I were from hence' [Webster, *White Devil* 5.4.91]) and is despatched on a downward spiral of self-reflection, counterpointed by his thirst for certainty as to 'the utmost of my fate' (116). He gropes for the names of what he finds in himself, as his journey leads him, not straightforwardly to 'conscience', but to the 'maze of conscience in my breast' (121). Finally, his pain slips out of his own interpretative reach: 'We think cag'd birds sing, when indeed they cry' (123).

II

Examples ranging from Desdemona and Hermione to Chapman's Cynthia and Eudora make the point that the threat to male identity posed by the image of female self-sufficiency tends to take a sexual form. This is, at least, the Lacanian perspective; classical psycho-analysis, cleaving more closely to Freud, would see things the other way round, situating the most profound threat at the sexual level. There is, no doubt, no way of settling the theoretical question of priority by practising on specific subjects, human or textual. Nevertheless, at this point I want to venture a reading of *Love's Labour's Lost* as, in effect, tracing male sexual anxiety to discursive roots. The play, I believe, is unique within the Early Modern dramatic canon in its capacity to do this because it subtextually attaches its preoccupation with language and identity, not simply to a general-ized sexuality, which may always lay claim to psychological origins, but to a specific sexual activity, shown in the process of becoming psychologically fraught. That activity (and I realize that I have a case to make here) is masturbation – a physical correlative of self-speaking. And indeed, what seem to me the play's insistent allu-sions to this practice encode a broad discursive difference, which Carolyn Asp has persuasively (if somewhat reductively) adapted to the analytical system of Lacan. In an argument dovetailing with much of my previous discussion, Asp proposes that the play's pri-mary male characters are, in effect, frozen in a form of immaturity corresponding to the mirror-stage, the imaginary register, while the female love-interests display a more fully realized subjectivity belonging to the symbolic order. I would further correlate these categories with the outstanding fact about the play's pattern of self-speaking – namely, that there is not a single female soliloquy, while the men do a great deal of talking to themselves, which conspicuously gets them nowhere.

'Fiction and Friction', a much-discussed chapter of Greenblatt's *Shakespearean Negotiations*, begins by citing Montaigne's account of a French female transvestite executed for using a dildo with the woman she had married. Greenblatt's argument moves from Early Modern ideas about natural and unnatural forms of sexual 'friction', as suggested by this anecdote, to a reading of dramatic 'fiction' in terms of the 'emergence of identity through the experience of erotic heat' (88). This characteristically daring leap into metaphor is made piggyback on a 'discovery' (88) attributed to Shakespeare personally: 'Shakespeare realized that if sexual chafing could not be presented literally onstage, it could be . . . chastened and hence *made fit* for the stage, by transforming it into the witty, erotically charged sparring that is the heart of the lovers' experience' (89, emphasis added).

Twelfth Night is the key text here, as it has been, understandably, for several recent critics concerned with sexual identity in general and especially with cross-dressing and the representation of homoerotic desire. And while sharp disagreements with Greenblatt's methodology and assumptions have been registered – in particular, he has been accused of essentialist tendencies (Traub, '[In]significance' 154) – most commentators would probably agree with him that this play encapsulates a major ideological project of Shakespearean comedy as a genre, namely, to contain and defuse the very homoerotic and gender-blurring elements with which it persistently flirts. This containment and defusing are accomplished by way of 'an imaginative heat that the plots promise will be realized offstage, in the marriage beds toward which they gesture' (Greenblatt, 'Fiction' 89). Indeed, alternative forms of 'heat', 'chafing', and 'friction' are normally (and normatively) subjected to exclusionary pressure in Early Modern English drama, as is effectively illustrated by Jean E. Howard's study of a partial exception to the rule: Moll Cutpurse, Middleton and Dekker's Roaring Girl, is a female transvestite who resists male attempts to eroticize her, scorns the marriage bed, and dreams, at least, in a discourse of autoeroticism associated with the playing of the viol (Howard 184 and n. 14).

I propose that Greenblatt's nebulous connection between physical and metaphorical 'heat', between literal 'chafing' and the 'sparring' of wit, is made a more tangible (so to speak) textual issue in
the most self-consciously witty – and notoriously bawdy – of all
Shakespearean comedies,[8] which not only does not end 'like an old
play' (*LLL* 5.2.874) but also does not conduct itself like one in several other respects, including the absence of a cross-dressing heroine. At the same time, these very departures from the pattern may
be seen as carrying transgressive resonances akin to those cluster-
ing around Moll Cutpurse – to the point of opposing to Greenblatt's
judgement about what is 'fit' for Shakespeare's stage an alternative
notion of the 'obscenely . . . fit' associated with Costard (4.1.143). To
the extent, however, that my reading entails a suggested staging
without, to my knowledge, recorded precedent, Greenblatt obviously has majority opinion on his side – including the view of one
character in the key scene in question.

With its ribald banter among Boyet, Costard, and the Princess's
ladies-in-waiting, Act 4, Scene 1, of *Love's Labour's Lost* presents one
of the surprisingly few occasions, for a play rife with linguistic
game-playing, when verbal 'sparring' involves substantial interchange across the sex boundary. Most of the play's displays of wit
either leave that boundary uncrossed or actively reinforce it, enacting the distance in sensibility and outlook between the visiting
women and their suitors, and so anticipating the final separate exits
that are seemingly signalled in the Folio text: 'You that way; we this
way' (5.2.931). Not only does an unusual proportion of the 'chafing'
dialogue, including most of Berowne's virtuoso performances, occur
among characters of the same sex, but even when the men and
women are talking to each other – and even when, as often, they
are lacing their speech with sexual innuendo – they are, as Ralph
Berry observes, 'only superficially sharing the same idiom' (80).[9]
Emblematically, the ladies' rebuff of the 'Muscovites' – who, having
redirected the initial project of self-conquest (1.1.8 ff.), have sallied
forth with aggressively phallic charm ('. . . upon them, lords; / Pell-
mell, down with them! but be first advis'd / In conflict that you get
the sun of them' [4.3.364–66])[10] – depends less on a sexually charged
matching of wits than on the identity-switching jest they share at
the men's expense. That jest squarely forestalls communication.

Boyet's equivocal role as a collaborating male within the female
camp is connected with his capacity to engage wittily with the
women as the suitors cannot. He is, in Berowne's bitter insinuation,

a ladies' man, traitor to his sex: 'Die when you will, a smock shall be your shroud' (5.2.479).[11] This insult comes after Boyet has abetted and aligned himself with the quasi-castrating female wit directed against the king and his courtiers: 'The tongues of mocking wenches are as keen / As is the razor's edge invisible' (256–7). The audience, however, is in a position to read this triumph as compensatory on Boyet's part. From his initial condescending direction of the women in sexually suggestive terms ('Now, madam, summon up your dearest spirits . . .' [2.1.1]), his wit takes a pronounced aggressive turn once he perceives the men's interest, with which he seeks to associate himself ('we lovers' [232]). Katherine's adroit parrying of his wish to pasture on her lips (220 ff.) sets the pattern for the end of this scene, as all three ladies-in-waiting unite in mocking him as 'an old love-monger' (254) and 'Cupid's grandfather' (255) – to the point where he pronounces them 'too hard for me' (261) as, apparently, they exit by separate ways.

In Act 4, Scene 1, the suggestion of Boyet's sexual rejection, exclusion, and inadequacy is extended by the women – here, too, in response to advances ('my continent of beauty' [109]) that insinuate their sexual openness and implicitly appropriate the men's love-cause. His first object this time is Rosaline, who in return, as Maria puts it, 'strikes at the brow' (117) with the standard accusation that he is cuckold material. He then lowers both the target and the tone in riposting, 'But she herself is hit lower. Have I hit her now?' (118), and the new motif (in keeping with shooting as the scene's nominal activity) opens into extensive *double entendre*, beginning with the catch, in which Rosaline taunts Boyet, 'Thou canst not hit it' (125), and he retorts, as she exits, 'And I cannot, another can' (128). Maria then sustains the sexual banter with Boyet for another ten lines, now with the participation of Costard, until a reprise of Boyet's earlier capitulation, followed again, it seems, by separate male and female exits:

> Costard She's too hard for you at pricks, sir, challenge her to
> bowl.
> Boyet I fear too much rubbing. Good night my good owl.
>
> (138–9)

In setting the seal on Boyet's defeat in this latest contest of 'vulgar wit' (142), Costard, left alone on stage, identifies himself with the female cause, arrogating both sexual and – with flagrant inversion – class superiority: 'By my soul, a swain, a most simple clown! / Lord, Lord, how the ladies and I have put him down!' (4.1.140–1).[12] The Clown's own contribution to this scene, which begins with asking for 'the head lady' (43) and misdelivering Armado's love-letter, thus specifically integrates his command of the idiom of female wit with his transgressive function in the play as a whole. That function consistently supports the 'realistic' outlook associated with the women against various forms of male self-delusion and irresponsibility,[13] and it is thoroughly sexualized from start to finish – from his escapade with Jacquenetta to his confrontation of Armado with the latter's (supposed) impregnation of her. Yet close to the end comes his own withdrawal behind the gender barrier, accompanied by symbolic sexual self-abnegation: abandoning the absurd phallic heroism of Pompey,[14] he steps forward to 'lay my arms before the legs of this sweet lass of France' (5.2.555). Thus the pageant, in confirming the separation of male and female ethos and idiom, extends the image of sexual inaccessibility. Finally, the somewhat surprising complicity of Boyet and Dumaine in mocking the inability of Armado, who at least has actually been to bed with Jacquenetta, to love the Princess 'by the yard' (669) ironically unites the courtly men in their own sexual exclusion.

I have taken some trouble to delineate the dramatic forces in play towards the end of Act 4, Scene 1, in order to frame the alternative staging that I wish to argue for. This staging, which involves the final ten lines of sexual banter referred to above, turns on the role of Costard and the question of whom Boyet is addressing. It is worth reproducing the full exchange, which begins with Costard and Maria (after Rosaline has exited); in praising the musicality of the catch, they implicitly harmonize the mutual sexual accusations of Boyet and Rosaline:

Costard By my troth, most pleasant. How both did fit it!
Maria A mark marvellous well shot, for they both did hit it.
Boyet A mark! O, mark but that mark! a mark, says my lady!
Let the mark have a prick in't, to mete at, if it may be.
Maria Wide a' the bow-hand! I'faith, your hand is out.
Costard Indeed 'a must shoot nearer, or he'll ne'er hit the clout.
Boyet And if my hand be out, then belike your hand is in.
Costard Then will she get the upshoot by cleaving the pin.
Maria Come, come, you talk greasily, your lips grow foul.

Costard She's too hard for you at pricks, sir, challenge her to
           bowl.
Boyet   I fear too much rubbing. Good night, my good owl.

                                                   (4.1.129–39)

It is notable that, instead of withdrawing gracefully from the
combat of wits, Boyet here turns his aggression on Maria, making
a sexual suggestion out of her word 'mark'. Her retort comments
on the strained quality of his wit, but Costard gives it a spin in the
familiar direction of Boyet's sexual inadequacy. What follows is the
key line, from my point of view. Boyet is universally presumed, as
far as I know, to be speaking to Costard, suggesting facetiously that
the latter may have an intimate relation with Maria. This, however,
is surely far from the natural reading: rather than defending himself, Boyet would thereby be conceding superior sexual prowess to
a peasant, and one whom he has hitherto not even addressed. It
makes more sense that Maria should continue to be the direct object
of his barbs, and if she is, the accusation that *her* 'hand is in' takes
on literal, not just metaphorical, bawdiness – moving from 'fiction'
back to 'friction', or, as the text has it, 'rubbing'. Boyet would then
be delivering a highly effective sexual insult, in his own terms: if he
cannot make a conquest of her, it is because she has relations with
no man and, for sexual satisfaction, masturbates herself. Costard's
follow-up works better, even on a grammatical level, if he seconds
Boyet's meaning: Maria will give herself the climactic 'upshoot' by
'cleaving the pin'. This reading is far from obscure. On the contrary,
it is perhaps too straightforward to have been admissible in the
past. Even Eric Partridge, in determined pursuit of 'Shakespeare's
bawdy', was equally determined to make sexual touching yet another manifestation of male control of female erotic experience.[15]
The current critical community may be ready, even eager, to register autoerotic allusions, but it remains difficult to imagine such a
staging today, especially at a theatre devoted to Shakespeare as a
cultural institution.

If I am right, the line must have carried shock value in its own
day as well. Then, as now, this area of sexuality was taboo: porno-
graphically (and comically) relished in Nashe's 'The Choise of Valentines' (probably pre-1594), which circulated only in manuscript; winked
at by Marston and Donne in the vein of Martial and Juvenal.[16] Even
the relentlessly bawdy Renaissance stage was hardly replete with
references to masturbation, much less female masturbation; we have

had to settle, until now, for Moll Cutpurse's ambiguous dreaming. Hence, perhaps, another anomalous feature of this scene: this is the only place in the Shakespearean canon (except for the comic prudery of Katherine in *Henry V* [3.4]) where a character specifically objects to ribald speech, throwing convention into metadramatic relief as surely as does Berowne, when he complains about the ending's transgression of genre. Maria is letting the men know – and she might appropriately convey embarrassment in performance – that they (and the play) have transgressed the bounds of *in*decency.

Boyet's last words in the scene call for a brief speculative digression. He may be taken as addressing either Maria or Costard as 'my good owl', and (although there is surprisingly little commentary on the part of editors) the expression is usually presumed to allude mockingly to the 'wisdom' of one or the other. This makes for a feeble parting-shot. From both a social and a dramatic point of view, the scene's dynamic tends to favour a split delivery of his line, with only the first half spoken in reply to Costard; the rest, then, would comprise a sardonic farewell to Maria. And if the epithet is meant for her, it may relate to the sexual means that he has just accused her of using to give herself a 'good night'. There is some corroborative evidence of this, given that the discourse of dildoes is not a rich one, in this or other periods.

In fact, the only substantial contemporary text in this category is 'The Choise of Valentines',[17] in which the narrator's prostitute-mistress has graphic recourse to a mechanical supplement when he proves inadequate to satisfy her. Her 'choice' of lover – the pivotal concept of *Love's Labour's Lost* itself – is neither one nor an*other*. Ruefully, knowingly, and bitterly (the mixture of tones is remarkably reminiscent of Boyet in Act 4, Scene 1), the failed lover blames the widespread use of dildoes not merely for women's resistance to male advances but for the very sort of artfulness deployed by the play's women:

> He [the dildo] wayte's on Courtlie Nimphs, that be so coye,
> And bids them skorne the blynd-alluring boye.
> . . . .
> He fortifies disdaine with forraine artes,
> And wanton-chaste deludes all louing hearts.
> If anie wight a cruell mistris serue's,
> Or in dispaire (unhappie) pine's and steru's
> Curse Eunuke dilldo, senceless, counterfet,
> Who sooth maie fill, but neuer can begett.

(255–64)

The dildo 'usurps in bed and bowre' (249), while 'sleep detaineth' (252) the unwary phallus. Nashe's pervasively parodic text is as self-conscious about its sexual politics as it is about its mock-Petrarchism. We are shown the persona, struck to the quick of his masculine ego, constructing the dildo as metonym for female sexual self-sufficiency, an alternative transcendental signifier to account for all behaviour that appears to break free from dependency upon men. The woman, in his eyes, enacts his castration by *having*, instead of merely *being*, the phallus.[18] Finally, the injunction to 'curse' is self-fulfilled in the line, 'God giue thee shame, thow blinde mischapen owle' (288), which seems to come, if not out of nowhere, at least out of the same discursive space as the scornful valediction of Boyet.

In Renaissance folklore and literature, the owl is not only, or even primarily, the emblem of Athenian wisdom. Rather, in Shakespeare and elsewhere, it is most often figured on the model of Ovid's *Metamorphoses*, as the ugly, solitary, and ill-boding bird of night: 'a filthie fowle, / A signe of mischiefe unto men, the sluggish skreching Owle' (5.681–2). Such associations suit Nashe's metaphor, but they do not fully account for it. That the owl may also be phallically coded is suggested by at least four non-Shakespearean instances. First, there is the salacious twisting of a familiar saying in the Induction to Fletcher's *Four Plays, or Moral Representations, in One*, where two courtiers regard an amorous couple:

> *Frigozo* Whist, Seignior; my strong imagination shews me Love (me thinks) bathing in milk, and wine in her cheeks: O how she clips him like a plant of Ivie.
>
> *Rinaldo* I; Could not you be content to be an owl in such an ivie-bush . . .?
>
> (105–12)

More specifically suggestive is a passage in Lyly's *Endymion*.[19] Tophas, absurdly in love with the foul Dipsas, recounts a dream that identifies the owl's cry with nocturnal self-stimulation, especially given the pun on 'account' ('a cunt') that Ellis (112–17) finds here, in *Love's Labour's Lost*, and elsewhere:

> *Tophas* There appeared in my sleep a goodly owl, who, sitting upon my shoulder, cried 'Twit, twit'; and before mine eyes presented herself the express image of Dipsas. I marvelled what the owl said, till at the last I perceived

'Twit, twit', 'To it, to it', only by contraction admonished
by this vision to make account of my sweet Venus.
Samias Sir Tophas, you have overslept yourself.
Tophas No, youth, I have but slept over my love.

(3.3.160–71)

Reference to an artificial phallus makes best sense, I think, of the
image used by Clod in Jonson's *The Gypsies Metamorphosed* to epitomize incredible ill-fortune: 'outcept I were with child of an owl (as
they say), I never saw such luck! It's enough to make a man a
whore' (837–8). If this expression was current (not merely Jonson's
invention), it evidently remained sub-proverbial, since it does not
appear to have been recorded elsewhere.[20]

Finally, a distinct hint of female self-gratification by means of a
phallus, artificial or otherwise, appears in the curious treatment by
William Adlington, the Elizabethan translator, of a passage in
Apuleius' *Metamorphoses* (*The Golden Ass*). Lucius aspires magically
to transform himself into an owl, and his mistress fears he will
abandon her. The original develops as follows his reassurance that
no other woman could tempt him:

> ... cum semel avem talem perunctus induero, domus omnes
> procul me vitare debere. Quam pulchro enim quamque festivo
> matronae perfuentur amatore bubone! Quid quod istas nocturnas
> aves, cum penetraverint larem quempiam, sollicite prehensas
> foribus videmus affigi, ut quod infaustis volatibus familiae
> minantur exitium suis luant cruciatibus?
> [... once I have anointed myself and costumed myself in that
> species of bird, I will have to stay far away from all houses. What
> a handsome and jolly lover housewives are going to enjoy in an
> owl! Aren't those nocturnal birds carefully caught whenever they
> get inside a home, and don't we see them nailed up on the door
> to expiate with their own sufferings the disaster threatened against
> the family by their ill-omened flight?]

(3.23; trans. Hanson 1:167–9)

In the second sentence, as all modern translations confirm, Lucius
sarcastically cites the ill-omened owl's improbability as a lover.
Adlington introduces continuity between lover and owl, adds a
prurient suggestion of too warm a welcome (with the help of the
familiar pun on 'handle'[21]), and turns Lucius' illustration of his point
into a separate reason for wariness:

. . . if by vertue of the ointment I shall become an Owle, I will take heede that I come nigh no mans house. For I am not to learne how these matrones would handle their louers if they knewe that they were transformed into Owles: moreouer when they are taken in any place, they are nayled upon postes, and so they are woorthely rewarded, because it is thought that they bringe euill fortune to the house.

(fol. 31ᵛ)

If Boyet's owl-reference indeed sustains obscenity so egregious as to provoke a unique rebuke, it is understandable that most other Shakespearean owls (they are not, for that matter, abundant) should be unequivocally non-sexual.[22] On the other hand, the owl surfaces suggestively in the discourse of two virginal madwomen, whose derangement has much to do with sexuality. Indeed, the Jailer's Daughter in *The Two Noble Kinsmen* can be cured only by supplying her with a sexual substitute for Palamon. As with Ophelia, her uninhibited mad discourse is made shockingly incongruous with maidenly purity. Hence, when she includes in her disjointed songs what has long been identified as the '[e]arliest known version of a popular nursery rhyme' (*TNK* n. to 3.5.67), she might plausibly be alluding to Nashe's 'Eunuke dildo', which he claims 'giue's yong guirls their gamesom sustenance' (257). Her theme, then, would be the male bewilderment and castration anxiety triggered by an emblem of female sexual self-sufficiency:

'There was three fools fell out about an howlet:
The one said it was an owl,
The other he said nay,
The third he said it was a hawk,
And her bells were cut away'.

(3.5.68–71)[23]

Far better known is the enigmatic remark of the distracted Ophelia, obviously a model for the figure in Shakespeare and Fletcher's later collaboration: 'They say the owl was a baker's daughter' (*Ham.* 4.5.42–3). Usually adduced in this connection is the legend of Christ's transforming a selfish woman. This rather thin explanation may be supplemented by a sexual one, given the Elizabethan use of 'baker's daughter' to mean prostitute.[24] Still, considering the associative pattern of Ophelia's speech, it would be strange if her words came out of nowhere, and, in fact, they do not:

King   How do you, pretty lady?
Ophelia Well, God dild you! They say the owl was a baker's
          daughter. . . .

                                                        (4.5.41–3)

Whether one reads 'God' with the First Quarto and Folio or 'good'
with the Second Quarto, the uncharacteristically colloquial formula
of thanks, which has only one rough parallel elsewhere in Shakespeare (*Mac.* 1.6.12–13), seems calculated to convey an obscene pun.
Ophelia would thus be subverting at once the innocent image of
'pretty lady' and the king's solicitude by taking 'do' in its crude
sexual sense, as if he had asked her how she was coping sexually,
given the lack of men in her life.

   Before pursuing the elusively signifying owl in the concluding
songs of *Love's Labour's Lost*, it is worth tracking the implications of
Boyet's proposition (as I take it) that Maria's 'hand is in'. First, in
the context of this community of 'mocking wenches', the accusation
gestures beyond autoeroticism to sexual activity between women.
The construction of narcissism as a link between these forms of
female sexuality has been regarded as a late nineteenth-century
phenomenon (Dijkstra 146–53), but the discourses of 'science' in the
latter period (notably including psychoanalysis) were arguably catching up with a long-standing association, which is evident, for instance, in Donne's lesbian love poem, 'Sapho to Philaenis':

> Likenesse begets such strange selfe flatterie,
>   That touching my selfe, all seemes done to thee.
> My selfe I'embrace, and mine owne hands I kisse,
>   And amorously thanke my selfe for this.
>
>   (51–4)

Arguably, the connection is solidified by the threat to masculine
sexual dominance posed by both lesbianism and masturbation.
Absent though the discourse of 'lesbian desire' may be from the Early
Modern record (Traub, '[In]significance' 150), there are substantial
late sixteenth-century French discussions of female-to-female sexual
relations, notably by the physician Ambrose Paré[25] and by Pierre de
Bourdeille, Seigneur de Brantôme. The latter, who purports to survey
lesbian practices amongst the courtly class, is preoccupied with the
question of whether women who engage in such activity remain
susceptible to men.[26] On the one hand, he reports, with surprise,

'Que j'en ay veu de ces lesbiennes qui, pour toutes leurs fricarelles et entre-frottemens, n'en laissent d'aller aux hommes! [How many of these lesbians have I seen, who, for all their rubbings and inter-strokings, still do not cease to frequent men!]' (193). On the other hand, he presents himself (in thinly disguised third-person) as having failed in an advantageous marriage suit because the 'fort honneste damoiselle [highly honourable young lady]' was kept by another woman 'en ses delices à pot et à feu [in her delights of the pot and the fire]' (194). This coy eroticizing of the homely *'pot-à-feu* [simmering pot]' may originate with Brantôme, as far as I know; in general, his vocabulary for lesbian practices is along the lines of the English term 'rubster', which is used by the late seventeenth-century translators of Bartholin's *Anatomy* (Eccles 34) – and effectively, I suggest, by Boyet. Brantôme also has a fair amount to say about dildoes, whose use he abhors as deleterious to the health, compared to other lesbian techniques.[27] Yet the dildo again becomes an emblematic link between lesbianism and self-gratification, as Brantôme moves into a discussion of 'de tres-belles and honnestes dames et damoiselles [some very beautiful and honourable ladies and young gentle-women]' (196) who suffer physically because they prefer dildoes to healthful heterosexual intercourse.

Love's Labour's Lost as a whole, if it allusively supplements Boyet's insinuations, resists his reductive reading of the courtly women's willingness to forego the men. In fact, the mixture of susceptibility and indifference, engagement and detachment, displayed by the women takes on a mystery akin to that which stymies Brantôme, as he tries to make sense of female sexual behaviour outside the patriarchally constituted heterosexual norm. At the outset, the women are obviously open to male charms, to the point where the Princess suspects her attendants of being in love (2.1.77–9). Once the men pursue their suits, however, the women appear to lose this erotic vulnerability; in proportion, they interact more intensely as a group. Their bawdy courtship with the men does not, according to convention, reflect seriously on their sexual behaviour. By contrast, the 'set of wit well played' (5.2.29) between Rosaline and Katherine at the beginning of the final scene cuts deeper, taking off from the destructive power of Cupid (''a kill'd your sister' [13]) to tease the audience with suggestions of 'light' behaviour in the 'dark' (15 ff.). Female erotic friction (to adapt Greenblatt) thus turns in on itself enigmatically; yet it also unfolds to include mortality as a condition of existence: 'Dead, for my life!' (720). The effect, as with Moll

Cutpurse's cross-dressing, is to valorize what begins as a scornful masculine accusation of transgression. To touch oneself, in this context, is to touch at once 'nothing' ('a fair thought to lie between maids' legs' [*Ham.* 3.2.118–19]) and everything.

On the other hand (so to speak), there is what Marston, after portraying a woman who gains satisfaction from 'her Monkey, & her instrument / Smooth-fram'd' (*Scourge* 3.32–3), terms 'the Cynick friction' (52) of male masturbation, the touching of *something* in the illusory guise of everything, the transcendental signifier made flesh. *Love's Labour's Lost* relentlessly (if subtextually) applies this model so as to satirize male language and behaviour – strong evidence against the argument that the text is finally complicit with Petrarchism because its deferral of consummation 'upholds a masculine structure of desire' (Breitenberg 437).[28] On the contrary, the encoded physicalizing of gendered discourses, including self-speaking (and the lack thereof), has the effect of exposing male desire, hence Petrarchism itself, to sceptical interrogation. In effect, the danger of the 'dangereux supplément [dangerous supplement]', as Derrida expounds Rousseau's addiction to masturbation,[29] is projected upon the desired objects, complete with the illusion of presence, which in turn presupposes and requires their absence.

Like the men's assaults on women throughout the play, Boyet's offensive redounds to the discredit of his own sex, as he inadvertently throws into relief the male masturbatory paradigm. While female autoeroticism is used to figure realism and self-sufficiency, its male counterpart illustrates precisely what the ladies perceive about their suitors: that their love is self-love, for which the women serve as objectified images – Lacan's 'objet [object] a'. According to Lacan's concept of 'la pulsion [the drive]', the '"object" providing satisfaction is not the object *of* the drive. It is always a divergence, a metonym, a lack of the real, displaced onto a substitute' (Grosz 75).[30] This matches Marston's exploration of autoerotic fantasy through the figure of Pygmalion (*Scourge* 3).[31] A similar insinuation attaches to Proteus, when he begs Silvia's portrait ('to your shadow will I make true love' [*TGV* 4.2.125]) and she acquiesces on the grounds that 'your falsehood shall become you well / To worship shadows and adore false shapes' (129–30) – an apt description of the 'Muscovites'' mistaken wooing.

It is in Act 4, Scene 3, however, with its multiple voyeuristic eavesdropping on soliloquized love raptures, which successively offer each eavesdropper a reflection of himself, that *Love's Labour's*

Lost comes closest to figuring its controlling sexual motif in (discursive) action.[32] This series of what amount to verbal masturbations is extended, in effect, when Boyet overhears the lovers planning the masque. His account eroticizes their self-satisfaction – to the point of according phallic overtones to the 'pretty knavish page' (5.2.97):

> With that all laugh'd, and clapp'd him on the shoulder,
> Making the bold wag by their praises bolder.
> One rubb'd his elbow thus, and fleer'd, and swore
> A better speech was never spoke before.
> Another, with his finger and his thumb,
> Cried, '*Via*! we will do't, come what will come'.
> The third he caper'd, and cried, 'All goes well'.
> The fourth turn'd on the toe, and down he fell.
> With that they all did tumble on the ground,
> With such a zealous laughter, so profound,
> That in this spleen ridiculous appears,
> To check their folly, passion's solemn tears.
>
> (107–18)

Thus the word 'rub' makes its only other appearance in the play.

The masturbatory subtext comes close to the surface in the masque itself. Berowne, whose self-indulgent wit, regularly presented in monologue or soliloquy, makes for particularly 'Cynick friction', reprises Proteus' plea for Silvia's 'shadow' – except that he knows enough to claim the truth of 'sunshine':

> We number nothing that we spend for you;
> Our duty is so rich, so infinite,
> That we may do it still without accompt.
> Vouchsafe to show the sunshine of your face,
> That we (like savages) may worship it.
>
> (5.2.198–202)

The pun in 'accompt' sets the seal on concentrated *double entendre*, which develops the familiar notion of ejaculation as 'expense of spirit' (Shakespeare, *Son.* 129, 1).[33] Striking, too, is the economic metaphor, which, by pointedly engaging the title, engages it also in the discourse of autoeroticism. This is the obvious physical way in which 'love's labour(s)'[34] may be 'lost', and the Elizabethan use of 'labour' for male sexual activity, as well as for the birth-process, supports the point.[35]

Holofernes, extemporizing on the Princess's killing of a 'pricket' (4.2.56 ff.) and boasting that he will 'put it to' (80) the parish's daughters, is backhandedly linked with Berowne by his own effusion of 'spirit' – the result of pseudo-intellectual 'friction', rather than, as he claims, conception and birth:

> This is a gift that I have, simple; simple, a foolish extravagant spirit, full of forms, figures, shapes, objects, ideas, apprehensions, motions, revolutions. These are begot in the ventricle of memory, nourish'd in the womb of pia mater, and delivered upon the mellowing of occasion.
>
> (65–70)

Also made a foil to the suitors by the masturbatory route (as by others) is Don Armado, whose union with Jacquenetta will require him to 'hold the plough for her sweet love three year' (5.2.883–4). (To 'labour' originally meant to 'plough' [OED], as the French *labourer* still does.)

He will, of course, be holding his 'plough' in his hands, and the image rudely picks up that chosen by the Princess:

> Come challenge me, challenge me by these deserts,
> And by this virgin palm now kissing thine,
> I will be thine; . . .
> If this thou do deny, let our hands part,
> Neither intitled in the other's heart.
>
> (5.2.805–12)

Romantically elevated as this moment is, and conventional as is the 'hand' as metonymy for marriage, this is a text that refuses to let go of the question, focused in Boyet's encounter with Maria, of what men and women are literally doing with their hands – and not doing with each others'. Berowne's love-letter to Rosaline is to be delivered by Costard 'to her white hand' (3.1.168); at Holofernes' command, it is returned from female to male – diverted from the 'snow-white hand' (4.2.132) specified in the address to the 'royal hand of the King' (141–2). The conclusion of the Muscovite adventure, with its overtones of the Rape of the Sabine Women, is conceived by Berowne in terms suggesting not only possession but arrest: 'Then homeward every man attach the hand / Of his fair mistress' (4.3.372–3). Yet ultimately, he must allow the spotless purity of the hand beneath the glove to retain the mystery of an article of faith: 'By this white glove (how white the hand, God knows!) . . .' (5.2.411). Certainly, neither we nor they ever know whose hand may be 'in'.

The final songs in *Love's Labour's Lost* have held great appeal for post-Barber adherents of what might be thought of as the school of idealist festivity. The songs have been almost gratefully seized upon as a supplement to the action, swaying towards affirmation the ambiguity inherent in the 'promise of marriage' (Rose 36). As Louis Adrian Montrose put it (writing, it is clear, before New Historicism), 'The sweetness and adversity so radically disjoined in the play's dramatic fiction are reintegrated by the songs' (167). Rejecting the previous emphasis on the undercutting of illusion by reality – spring love by the menace of cuckoldry, spring itself by winter – such readings have emphasized the songs' symmetry and syncretism, the 'interrelatedness of apparent opposites' (Carroll 174).[36] Another lack was thereby also being supplied – the absence of the transvestite heroine, who, for recent psychological critics, as well as for Greenblatt ('Fiction' 91–2), serves in Shakespearean comedies to figure the formation of socially sanctioned subjectivity from a liminal stage of sexual non-differentiation. Given the limited 'chafing' of the Princess's 'virgin palm' in momentary contact with Navarre's 'royal hand', the simmering pot of 'greasy Joan' (5.2.920,929) suggests the only substantial antidote to winter – to the point of making the normally lugubrious owl sound 'a merry note' (919,928) (Montrose 166).

Still, the owl and the greasiness both carry baggage from the 'obscenely . . . fit' exchange of Act 4, Scene 1 – however one reads it, and elusive as specific significance may be. The readings I have proposed suggest that Joan may be more than physically 'greasy' for practising what Maria considers to be 'greasily' alluded to. Although a pot may be 'keeled' (that is, 'cooled . . . in order to prevent it from boiling over' [*OED* 1.b]) by adding cold liquid, the usual method – and the one that involves continual action – is stirring. Hence, the *OED* records an association between 'keeling the pot' and ladles that goes back to Langland and lasts into the nineteenth century in a children's game: 'a girl says, "Mother, the pot's boiling over"; and the answer is, "Get a ladle and keel it"' (*OED* 1.b). If masturbation is indeed in the textual air, the image would graphically (like Brantôme's 'delices à pot et à feu') convey a 'friction' paradoxically aimed at cooling excess sexual heat. The symmetrical songs would thus recapitulate the earlier exchange, which similarly offers female autoeroticism as an 'answer' to the women's charge of male sexual inadequacy – Boyet's 'horns'. In the play's action, too, the men are left out in the cold. Here, only 'greasy Joan' seems immune to the weather that causes the 'blood' of Dick and Tom to be 'nipp'd' (916) and freezes the milk – an obvious emblem of female fecundity – that they are carrying.

The owl's 'merry note', which includes the same 'Tu-whit' (918, 927) taken as sexually provocative by Tophas in *Endymion*, specifically occurs 'nightly' (917,926) as accompaniment to Joan's keeling of the pot. Given that this activity, if it is obscenely suggestive, hints at a mechanical implement, it is worth turning briefly from Shakespeare's 'staring owl' (917,926) to Nashe's 'blinde, mischapen' one. What we find tends to confirm 'The Choise of Valentines' as a significant intertext for the play, regardless of chronological priority. The outburst of Nashe's persona against the dildo-as-owl marks the climax at once of his description and of the woman's sexual experience, reinforcing the point that he himself has been left far behind:

> In clammie waies he treaddeth by and by,
>> And plasheth and sprayeth all that be him nye.
> So fares this iollie rider in his race,
>> Plunging, and soursing forward in lyke case,
> Bedasht, bespurted, and beplodded foule,
>> God giue thee shame, thow blind mischapen owle.
>> (283–8)

In Winter's song, of course, the owl sings when 'ways be foul' (916), and the rhyme (an obvious one, but also used in the fourth-act obscene exchange [4.1.137–9]) is the same. Still more striking are Nashe's next lines, which associate the owl-epithet with the ecstatic crying-out that threatens to betray what Cicelie – an all-purpose name like Joan – is up to:

> Fy – fy for grief; a ladies chamberlaine,
>> And canst not thow thy tatling tongue refraine?
> I reade thee beardles blab, beware of stripes,
>> And be aduised what thow vainelie pipes.
> Thow wilt be whipt with nettles for this geare
>> If Cicelie shewe but of thy knauerie heere.
>> (289–94)

Ovid may, it seems, be relevant after all: Ascalaphus was transformed into an owl as punishment 'for his lavas tongue and telling
tales' (*Metamorphoses* 5.683) in 'blabbing' (672) Persephone's secret
and forbidden indulgence of her appetite: 'She gathering from a
bowing tree a ripe Pownegarnet, tooke / Seven kernels out and
sucked them. None chaunst hereon to looke, / Save onely one
Ascalaphus . . .' (667–9).

If we admit such a down-to-earth insinuation regarding the
marvellous metamorphosis of the owl's note from dire to 'merry',
there is indeed plenty of 'chafing' in the conclusion of *Love's Labour's
Lost*, though of a kind usually thought of as producing no light to
accompany its heat. Lacan, however, thinks differently: 'Woman
experiences a *jouissance beyond the phallus* . . . outside of articulation
and . . . *unknowable*' (Grosz 139). This is to free women from the
traditional idea (Freudian but surely also pre-Freudian) that they
are 'necessarily bound to male sexuality' (Grosz 139). Yet the fact
that Lacan has been faulted for thereby putting women 'backhandedly . . . in a dependent position' (Grosz 139) emphasizes the
masculinity of such a point of view: the songs are, after all, the
composition of 'the two learned men' (*LLL* 5.2.886); the fantasy of
Nashe's rejected Valentine belongs to its author. And the play is
Shakespeare's.

That *jouissance* should loom ruefully as the loss of love's labour(s)
within the songs' much-discussed affirmation of natural balance
and accommodation matches the trajectory of the plot and the separate exits that immediately follow. The picture of male and female
sexual isolation within the apparently harmonious household – the
very image of the Lacanian principle that 'il n'y a pas de rapport
sexuel [there is no sexual relation]' (Gérard Miller 79; Grosz 137) –
restates as generically transgressive the absence of the figure of
androgyny, uniting male and female so that they may be redistin-
guished as (to adapt Nathaniel's sexually resonant praise of Holofernes) 'good member[s] of the commonwealth' (4.2.76–7). Yet that
picture may also be read as redefining, not merely subverting, the
songs' affirmative promise. The immature suitors have a year, a
spring and a winter, free from erotic fantasy projected upon 'shadows' as if they were 'sunshine', to grow 'fit' for the women, whose
more fully integrated subjectivity can 'do' without them in the
meantime. That such self-transformation, figured as the challenge
'[t]o move wild laughter in the throat of death', is not 'impossible'
(5.2.855–6), as Berowne fears, is suggested by the change in the

owl's death-boding 'note' to one associated with a more pleasurable form of dying. Yet the process must take place within 'real' time, without the magic of the theatre ('That's too long for a play' [5.2.878]), for that magic is ultimately bounded by language: the hand is inevitably quicker than the 'I'.

III

In concluding at once this chapter and this book, I wish to return to the representation of male subjectivity by way of the 'feminine'. Notoriously, 'manhood' has defined itself in opposition to qualities stereotypically assigned to women. Such binarism obviously pervades Early Modern drama, chiefly in the form of countless male repudiations of 'womanish' weakness. This stark model is sometimes varied, however – especially in Shakespeare – by productive cross-fertilization between genders (as in the cross-dressing comedies), even by quasi-mystical synthesis (notably in *Antony and Cleopatra*, according to some recent readings[37]). And in plenty of other instances, ranging from treatments of male political behaviour to Posthumus' misguided attack on the 'woman's part in me' (*Cym.* 2.5.20), there are intimations of the cost to men themselves of the exclusion of the feminine.

Macbeth is the text in which 'manhood' as such is most relentlessly at issue, closely – and illuminatingly – followed by *Coriolanus*, where the transfer of the goading function from wife to mother points to the child's attempt to span the gap between itself and the '(m)other' by means of 'an identificatory image of its own stability and permanence' (Grosz 35). In Macbeth's case, the emphasis is rather on resistance to 'splitting' as a 'mode of being', the 'ontological rift with nature' (Grosz 35), but such splitting is gender-coded by the exchange between Malcolm and Macduff, when the latter learns of the murder of his wife and children. In reaction to his grief, which is registered in disjunctive discourse ('Did you say all? O hell-kite! All?' [*Mac.* 4.3.217]), Malcolm urges, 'Dispute it like a man' (220). At first, Macduff not only incorporates 'feminine' emotion into manhood ('I shall do so; / But I must also feel it as a man' [220–1]) but attaches it to a process of aphanisis. As when Hermione details her successive privations of husband and children, Macduff's loss of loved ones produces, through the mechanism of memory, a realization of self-absence: from 'I cannot but remember such things were, / That were most precious to me' (222–3), he descends into despairing self-blame, whose nadir is 'naught that I am' (225). His subsequent refashioning of a 'whole' self through anticipation of revenge is quite conventional, except that it conspicuously recuperates a binary conception of gender, and in extreme terms: 'O, I could play the woman with mine eyes, / And braggart with my tongue' (230–1).

This brief but definitive encounter with the feminine in the course of masculine self-speaking suggests that a semiotics of gender figures broadly, if usually less actively, in the production of dramatic presence through self-absence. That semiotics cuts both ways. There is more than conventional stereotyping at work when Webster's Vittoria, playing the bullfighter with her persecutors, gestures tauntingly toward a secure identity located in 'modesty / And womanhood' (*White Devil* 3.2.132–3), but then interposes, 'like Perseus' indeed, a mirroring shield: 'my defence of force like Perseus, / Must personate masculine virtue' (135–6).[38] Behind that shield, ironically, resonates the laugh of a Medusa[39] who has no intention of letting them 'sever head from body' (137). More commonly, however, the feminine element serves more straightforwardly to open the door to tragic subjectivity by destabilizing masculine self-fashioning, if only momentarily. This process is, I believe, most fully developed in *Hamlet*, which thus earns by this route, too, its pivotal status in the representational history of aphanitic subjectivity.

Before returning to that text, however, it is worth observing that such a treatment of the feminine has, like the discourse of female madness, a significant Marlovian precedent – one indirectly linked, in fact, with the experience of Zabina. It is the tender-hearted sorrow of Zenocrate over Tamburlaine's injuries to her father and country (not that she adores the brute any the less) that inspires that hero's first and only soliloquy – indeed, the only self-speaking on his part that is not publicly performative. In a subsequent soliloquy of her own, Zenocrate vividly extends her pity to the slaughtered virgins, then to the dead emperor and his wife: 'Ah wretched eyes, the enemies of my heart, / How are ye glutted with these grievous objects, / And tell my soul more tales of bleeding ruth!' (*Tamburlaine, Part 1* 5.1.341–3). Zenocrate's self-speaking remains binary, however; even the killing of the maidens, mirror-images of herself, merely mingles her love with horror:

> Ah Tamburlaine, wert thou the cause of this,
> That termest Zenocrate thy dearest love –
> Whose lives were dearer to Zenocrate
> Than her own life, or aught save thine own love?
>
> (336–9)

Zenocrate thereby at once encourages pity for Tamburlaine's victims and helps to contain it within his awesome grandeur – a double effect akin to that of most climactic revenges.

By contrast, Tamburlaine's soliloquy offers a fleeting glimpse of aphanitic experience through the obtrusion of feminine beauty and sentiment upon warlike thoughts, then shows the heroic self-image foreclosing that experience. The crucial step beyond the binary opposition of beauty and heroism is taken by way of the inadequacy of language, as epitomized even in the 'immortal flowers of poesy, / Wherein as in a mirror we perceive / The highest reaches of a human wit' (166–8). For with the Platonic idealism goes, as befits Marlowe's (if not Tamburlaine's) scholarly understanding, a painful sense of human shortcoming. On close inspection, the mirror-image fades as a figuration of perfect signification and, therefore, of immortality. The utmost stretch of poets' capacity to put ideas into language is not sufficient: 'Yet should there hover in their restless heads / One thought, one grace, one wonder at the least, / Which into words no virtue can digest' (171–3). This realization of the fallenness of language sends Tamburlaine fleeing – his anxiety is strongly communicated – into an essential masculine 'nature' and 'name':

> But how unseemly is it for my sex,
> My discipline of arms and chivalry,
> My nature, and the terror of my name,
> To harbour thoughts effeminate and faint!
>
> (174–7)

His next step is to rationalize susceptibility to beauty, appropriating such thoughts as fit for 'every warrior that is rapt with love / Of fame, of valour, and of victory' (180–1). Tamburlaine thus resituates himself within discursive binarism; his assimilative mastery of beauty proves him superior to the gods, validating his transcendental self-fashioning and self-naming:

> I thus conceiving and subduing, both,
> That which hath stopped the tempest of the gods,

Even from the fiery spangled veil of heaven,
To feel the lovely warmth of shepherds' flames
And march in cottages of strewèd weeds,
Shall give the world to note, for all my birth,
That virtue solely is the sum of glory
And fashions men with true nobility.

(183–90)

Far from rhetorically mystifying the dynamics of power, as Shepherd maintains (21–2), this soliloquy's unique discursive figuration of Tamburlaine as subject dispassionately dissects them. It is, after all, conspicuously 'out of character'.

IV

In dealing, for the last time, with *Hamlet*, I will also return to the intertextual presence of Montaigne, but by way of a supplementary intertext. This second work is likely to be obscure for English readers – the 'Préface' written by Marie le Jars de Gournay for the 1595 edition of Montaigne's essays. Without insisting on Shakespeare's knowledge of this rare instance of female self-writing (though such knowledge is hardly an impossibility), I will use it to shed light on Hamlet's representation (and repression) of aphanitic experience. From this perspective, Hamlet's intense and conflicted misogyny proves to be a matter, less of complexity of character, involving the illusion of 'separation of role from self' (Leverenz 113),[40] than of character's discursive production.

I wish to tease out some implications of one of the few of Hamlet's statements that has not come in for much commentary, no doubt because it has seemed so 'natural' – at least, for a conflicted misogynist. In the final scene, Hamlet confides to Horatio 'how ill all's here about my heart' (5.2.212–13), but with the same self-withholding as in his initial declaration of 'that within which passes show' (1.3.85); he then shunts his anxiety aside: 'It is but foolery, but it is such a kind of gain-giving, as would perhaps trouble a woman' (5.2.215–16). The rare term 'gain-giving' (thus in the First Folio; both Quartos read 'gam[e]-giving', which is not attested elsewhere), refocuses the well-established 'misgiving' on a spirit divided *against* itself; to judge from its earliest usage, it may also carry overtones of reciprocity (*OED* 1).

Of course, Hamlet shows himself in a misogynistic light from one end of the play to the other, virtually from his first words, but his violent reproaches of Gertrude, as well as Ophelia, have to do exclusively with the supposed weakness of women with respect to their passions and vanity: 'Frailty, thy name is woman!' (1.2.146). Along the same lines, he compares himself in soliloquy to a vituperative 'whore' because he seems able only to 'unpack my heart with words' (2.2.585), thereby traducing the 'masculine' self-restraint that he had affirmed (albeit out of necessity) in concluding the first soliloquy: 'But break my heart, for I must hold my tongue' (1.2.159). Of course, Hamlet's contempt for feminine weakness is no less present in the avowal he makes to Horatio. Yet here that weakness is not merely one term in a binary system: 'woman' enters Hamlet's mind for the last time as a complex entity endowed, like himself, with contradictory voices, hence, despite himself, as a focus for identification, even empathy. This multivocity, after all, is the inner voice that seeks to save his life. In this light, Hamlet's transitory comparison emerges as less conventional, as well as less negative, and stands out within his misogynistic discourse as an 'ungrammaticality' – the sign of the intertext.

The feminine is thus integrated into issues of identity and subjectivity in a more complex way than is recognized by standard psychological readings of Hamlet's resentment of women, beginning with his mother. Such complexity may itself be read as 'ungrammatical' *vis-à-vis* the rudiments of the revenge play genre – another aspect of Shakespeare's radical investment of this old-fashioned form with new content. For much traditional criticism, concerned with Hamlet as revenger-philosopher, the most notable such content has been intellectual and, as was discussed in Chapter 4, has often been attributed to the influence of Montaigne. At the risk of proliferating Montaignian echoes, I would like here to introduce an intertext from the *Essais* bearing on subjectivity, particularly as that topic figures in Hamlet's soliloquy:

> To be, or not to be, that is the question:
> Whether 'tis nobler in the mind to suffer
> The slings and arrows of outrageous fortune,
> Or to take arms against a sea of troubles,
> And by opposing, end them.
>   (3.1.55–9)

Almost tediously familiar as this 'question' is, its ultimately rhetorical status sometimes escapes notice. The option of endurance fades into the background as the speech unfolds, and the conclusion leaves no doubt as to which is the 'nobler' course, whether Hamlet likes the fact or not. It is the stasis of excessive contemplation that makes 'enterprises of great pitch and moment / ... their currents turn awry, / And lose the name of action' (85–7). Thus Hamlet is inexorably aligned with Montaigne's claim that 'estre consiste en mouvement et action [Being consisteth in moving and action]' (2:59; trans. Florio 2:67) and that passivity is contemptible.

More extensively, albeit obliquely, comparable are the following passages – Montaigne's taken from the same essay (Bk. 2, Ch. 8) – which were first associated by Robertson (61–2):[41]

> Puisqu'il a pleu à Dieu nous doüer de quelque capacité de discours, affin que, comme les bestes, nous ne fussions pas servilement assujectis aux lois communes, ains que nous nous appliquassions par jugement et liberté volontaire, nous devons bien prester un peu à la simple authorité de nature, mais non pas nous laisser tyranniquement emporter à elle; la seule raison doit avoir la conduite de nos inclinations.
> [Since it hath pleased God to endow us with some capacitie of discourse, that as beasts we should not servily be subjected to common lawes, but rather with judgement and voluntary liberty apply our selves unto them; we ought somewhat to yeeld unto the simple auctoritie of Nature: but not suffer her tyrannically to carry us away: only reason ought to have the conduct of our inclinations.]
>
> (2:60; trans. Florio 2:67–8)

> What is a man,
> If his chief good and market of his time
> Be but to sleep and feed? a beast, no more.
> Sure He that made us with such large discourse,
> Looking before and after, gave us not
> That capability and godlike reason
> To fust in us unus'd.
>
> (4.4.33–9)

Hamlet's final soliloquy on the courageous example of Fortinbras thereby echoes his initial condemnation of his 'frail' mother:

'O God, a beast that wants discourse of reason / Would have mourn'd longer' (1.2.150–1). Hence, it is all the more impressive that the *Essai* in question is 'De l'affection des pères aux enfans [Of the Affection of Fathers to their Children]'.

In this piece, Montaigne, after affirming that the love of fathers for their children is stronger by nature than the inverse, advises fathers to moderate their affection and to judge their children on the basis of demonstrated merit. For his part, of course, Hamlet is in the midst of reproaching himself for a lack of passionate devotion to his father, who, moreover, has established the act of revenge as a veritable touchstone of filial affection: 'If thou didst ever thy dear father love –' (1.5.23). The overlapping language of the two texts throws into relief the radically divergent perspectives: the judgemental father contrasts with the son, who feels himself constantly under his father's eyes, and whose very 'being' is threatened by his incapacity to act. As an intertext, the essay offers little more than points of verbal and thematic contact. And this is arguably true for the *Essais* in general, even when it comes to the author's relations with his terrestrial and divine fathers.[42] For while Montaigne's techniques of self-portraiture shed much light on the play's representation of aphanisis, as I argued earlier, the *Essais* are far from anticipating its transformation of the family situation into subjectivity's testing-ground. Besides, there is as yet no woman in the picture.

At this point, the 'Préface' of Marie de Gournay imposes itself as a supplementary intertext. Cathleen M. Bauschatz has recently argued that this piece, written before the author's overtly feminist work, serves as a sort of female supplement to the *Essais*, insofar as the latter deal from a specifically masculine perspective with a 'struggle for self-definition in relation to the father, who is revered and yet who causes anxiety' (349). Prior to Bauschatz, the valuable commentary of François Rigolot had already established the 'double discours [double discourse]' of the 'Préface' as enacting a family drama for the self-styled 'fille d'alliance [adoptive daughter]' of Montaigne: on the one hand, 'la voix féminine ne saurait s'exprimer sans avoir constamment à se justifier aux yeux de ses lecteurs virtuels [the female voice cannot express itself without having constantly to justify itself in the eyes of its presumed readers]'; on the other hand, since 'le "père" demande à sa "fille" de parler pour *lui* et non pour *elle*, c'est seulement à travers les intérêts du surmoi paternel que peut se faire reconnaître l'identité de la "fille d'alliance" [the "father" asks his "daughter" to speak for *him*, and not for *her*, the identity of the "adoptive daughter" can gain recognition only by cutting across the interests of the paternal superego]' (Introd. 17). This is indeed 'such a kind of gain-giving, as would perhaps trouble a woman', and it recalls the double-bind of Hamlet, who feels unable either to fulfil or to abandon the role imposed by his father. Even the double dimension of that role, which mingles public justice with private vengeance, has its equivalent in the defence initially undertaken by Marie de Gournay at once against the detractors of the *Essais* and, more personally, against those of her own readers who disdain women on the pretext of their weakness. In her imagination, too, a mission of double vindication – both of her dead 'father' and of herself – has been conferred upon her by that father's spirit. Rigolot's formulation is especially evocative of Hamlet's situation: 'Cette "liaison", qui se poursuit au delà de la mort du père pour déterminer l'identité de la fille, constitue ainsi à la fois une promesse de plénitude et un danger d'aliénation [This "relationship", which perpetuates itself beyond the father's death to determine the identity of the daughter, thus constitutes at once a promise of plenitude and a danger of alienation]' (Introd. 17).

Nothing in the representation of parent-child relations in Montaigne corresponds to the personal intensity of Marie de Gournay's tribute to the widow of Montaigne for having 'voulu r'embrasser et r'échauffer en moy les cendres de son mary, et non pas l'espouser mais se rendre une autre luy-mesme [wished to rekindle and rewarm in me the ashes of her husband, and, not to marry him, but to make of herself another him]' (26). Equally, nothing in the *Essais*, whose declared purpose is self-portrayal, prepares us for Marie de Gournay's self-effacement – 'je ne suis moy-mesme que par où je suis sa fille [I am not myself except insofar as I am his daughter]' (25) – even when she most strongly asserts herself:

la nature m'ayant faict tant d'honneur que, sauf le plus et le moings, j'etois toute semblable à mon Pere, je ne puis faire un pas, soit escrivant ou parlant, que je ne me trouve sur ses traces; et croy qu'on cuide souvent que je l'usurpe.
[nature having done me so much honour that, except in the greatest and the least respects, I was wholly like my Father, I cannot take a step, whether in writing or speaking, without finding myself in his footsteps; and I believe that I am often supposed to usurp him.]

(45–6)

In terms of literary influence, certain extreme expressions used by Marie de Gournay to describe the dependence of her identity on her 'father' are indebted to the *Essais*. As Rigolot makes clear (Introd. 16n18; 'L'amitié intertextuelle'), she draws heavily on Montaigne's account of his perfect friendship with La Boétie and of his mourning after the latter's death. In fact, Marie de Gournay appears to model herself on both parties in that relation: while she came, at the end of Montaigne's life, to hold the place in his affections that La Boétie had occupied in his youth, she now suffers as Montaigne once did. Indeed, her pain leads her to claim, not merely that '[e]stre seul c'est n'estre que demy [(t)o be alone is only to half-exist]', but that the survivor of such a pair 'n'est plus que par son mal-heur [no longer exists, except through his misery]' (50).

Such an affirmation of subjectivity through total self-loss may be radically differentiated from Montaigne's grieving, which stops at half-existence ('il me semble n'estre qu'à demy [me thinks I am but halfe my selfe]') and acknowledges present pleasure, even if that pleasure increases his pain: 'les plaisirs mesmes qui s'offrent à moy, au lieu de me consoler, me redoublent le regret de sa perte [even those pleasures, all things present me with, in stead of yeelding me comfort, doe but redouble the griefe of his loss]' (1:210; trans. Florio 1:207). What complicates the picture for Marie de Gournay is that having been Montaigne's friend is inextricable from still being his daughter:

> Estre amy c'est n'estre que depositaire de soy-mesme. La plus grande infelicité du monde c'est d'avoir la plus grande felicité; je l'avois en ce tres-grand Pere, puis qu'il en fault achepter la possession terminée au prix de la privation perpetuelle.
> [To be a friend is to exist only as the depositary of oneself. The greatest unhappiness in the world is to have the greatest happiness; I had this in that greatest of Fathers, since I must pay for my expired possession of him with perpetual deprivation.]
>
> (51)

Paradoxically, the intertextual effect of the *Essais* on the 'Préface' includes destabilizing such a mixed concept of the self. Montaigne actually begins his eulogy of La Boétie by distinguishing sharply between friendship and the emotional attachment of a child for a parent, which he characterizes as at best limited to respect and liable to degenerate (as in *King Lear*) because of competing interests and identities:

Il s'est trouvé des nations où, par usage, les enfans tuoyent leurs peres, et d'autres où les peres tuoyent leurs enfans, pour eviter l'empeschement qu'ils se peuvent quelquefois entreporter, et naturellement l'un depend de la ruine de l'autre.

[There have nations beene found, where, by custome, children killed their parents, and others, where parents slew their children, thereby to avoid the hindrance of enter-bearing one another in aftertimes: for naturally one dependeth from the ruine of another.]

(1:199; trans. Florio 1:197)

This bleak assessment of filiality obtrudes intertextually as Marie de Gournay appropriates Montaigne's celebration of friendship: 'Sa conservation n'est autre chose que celle de ceste chere teste; car il s'est perdu en soy, pour se recouvrer en autruy [Preserving himself means nothing but preserving that precious life; for he has lost himself in himself to recover himself in another]' (de Gournay 51).[43] The effect is to adumbrate the ambivalence attaching to the loss of such a self-repository – an ambivalence prominent in the filial mourning of Hamlet, of whom it might be equally said, at least before his task is imposed, that he 'n'est plus que par son mal-heur'.

The reworking by his 'daughter' of the mourning of Montaigne (which, of course, occupies a very small portion of the *Essais*) highlights a more general distinction between them – one that again draws together the Préface and the play. By way of both La Boétie and Montaigne, Marie de Gournay actively engages in the construction of her identity by self-comparison with others – an element not contained in Montaigne's tribute, at least not in the same form. As I mentioned in Chapter 4, some important recent criticism concerns the construction of the subject in Montaigne, applying the idea of the text as a mirror (or, rather, as a series of mirrors). Self-comparisons with figures drawn from personal knowledge, from history, and from mythology play an important role in this dynamic. The notion of 'playing' is key, however; Montaigne's text naturally arrogates the privilege of improvisation, suspending an identity well established in the eyes of others so that it may be recreated, fragment-by-fragment. This presumes, if not the stability of writing itself, at least a fundamental confidence in the right to write. For Marie de Gournay, the agonizing question, equivalent to Hamlet's dilemma concerning action, has to do, in the first instance, with the act of filling up the page:

Mon ame a refusé cent fois obeyssance à ce mien dessein d'escrire un mot sur les *Essays*. . . . Lecteur, n'accuse pas de temerité le favorable jugement qu'il a faict de moy, quand tu considereras, en cet escrit icy, combien je suis loing de le meriter.
[My soul has a hundred times refused to comply with this intention of mine to write a word about the *Essais*. . . . Reader, do not accuse of rashness the favourable judgement that he made of me, when you consider, in what is written here, how far I am from deserving it.]

(51)

Given the contingency of the very medium of self-construction, the act of comparison becomes the site of existential contestation. So it does for Hamlet, whose struggle at once on behalf of and against his father is often represented, moreover, by means of 'scriptive gestures' (Goldberg 311).

From this perspective, it becomes significant that Montaigne's widow is treated by Marie de Gournay in a psychologically complex way, in contrast to the widow, Madame d'Estissac, to whom Montaigne dedicates his essay, 'De l'affection des pères aux enfans'. Montaigne follows a conventional formula in praising Madame D'Estissac as an exemplar of noble widowhood and 'affection maternelle [motherly affection]' – a status that apparently depends on her refusal of 'les grands et honorable partis qui vous ont esté offerts [the great and honorable matches have beene offered you]' (2:58–9; trans. Florio 2:66). This agrees with the judgement of Hamlet, for whom Gertrude's marriage involves a betrayal both of his father and of himself. Marie de Gournay, however, actually projects intense and conflicted emotion upon the widow, who represents her only link with an idealized 'father', yet whose privileged intimacy with the latter inevitably makes for a certain jealousy. In establishing the absolute devotion of Madame de Montaigne, who has 'rendu les offices d'une tres-ardente amour conjugale à la memoire de son mary [rendered all the offices of an ardent conjugal love to the memory of her husband]' (25), the author anticipates the description (cited above) of her own feelings as at once friend and daughter. She begins with the image of tears – also the preoccupation of Hamlet, whose mother had at first behaved '[l]ike Niobe, all tears' (1.2.149) before revealing those tears as 'unrighteous' (154):

Qualifierons nous ces larmes odieuses ou desirables? veu que, si Dieu l'a reservée au plus lamentable des veufvages, il luy a pour le moins assigné quand et quand en luy le plus honnorable tiltre qui soit entre les femmes? Et n'est Dame de merite et de valeur, qui n'aymast mieux avoir eu son mary, qu'en avoir nul autre, tel qu'il soit. Haut et glorieux advantage que le pis, dont Dieu l'ait estimée digne, reste encore achetable au pris de toute autre felicité. [Shall we account those tears hateful or desirable, seeing that, if God has destined her for the most miserable of widowhoods, he has at least concurrently conferred upon her the most honourable title that a woman may hold? And there is no Lady of merit and worth who would not rather have had her husband than have any other, whoever he might be. It is a great and glorious benefit that the worst of which God has judged her to be worthy still rates at the value of all other happiness.]

(26)

Here, too, *Hamlet* stands at the intertextual intersection of Marie de Gournay and Montaigne: the latter's essay 'De la tristesse [Of Sadnesse or Sorrowe]' follows Ovid in citing Niòbe as petrified by grief at the loss of her children, not as a weeping widow (1:8; trans. Florio 1:22).[44] That reference, however, follows from the very (non)image of aphanisis: Montaigne cites the ancient painter's decision not to depict the face of Iphigenia's father, 'comme si nulle contenance ne pouvoit representer ce degré de deuil [as if no countenance were able to represent that degree of sorrow]' (1:8; trans. Florio 1:22).

Once again, identification with others draws Marie de Gournay in two directions, here in a close anticipation of Hamlet's simultaneous self-imaging in the positions of his mother and of his father. Thanks to the pure and devoted sentiments of Madame de Montaigne, however, Marie de Gournay comes closer to taking the place of the lost husband. I have already noted her gratitude to the widow 'd'avoir voulu r'embrasser et r'échauffer en moy les cendres de son mary, et non pas l'espouser mais se rendre une autre luy-mesme'. She develops this idea by portraying the lady as 'ressuscitant en elle à son trespas une affection où jamais elle n'avoit participé que par les oreilles [reviving in herself at his death an affection in which she had never participated except by hearing of it]', so as, in effect, to 'luy restituer un nouvel image de vie par la continuation de l'amitié qu'il me portoit [restore to him a new appearance of life by the continuation of the friendship that he bore me]' (26). Such passages establish the credentials of the 'Préface' as an intertextual catalyst capable of rendering psychologically more potent several thematic correspondences between Montaigne and Shakespeare's play. It is nonetheless remarkable that at the heart of Marie de Gournay's text lies the central question for both Montaigne and Hamlet – the nature of being. Moreover, that question is addressed by way of mirror-imaging. Marie de Gournay applies Montaigne's principle that 'estre consiste en mouvement et action' to her position as his 'semblable', on which she bases her entitlement to write – the equivalent for her of acting, hence of being: 'les grands esprits sont desireux, amoureux, et affolez des grands esprits: comme tenans leur estre du mouvement, et leur prime mouvement de la rencontre d'un pareil [great minds desire, love, are mad for great minds, as if deriving their being from movement, and their prime movement from meeting one like them]' (47). A little further on, she writes, 'Estre incognu c'est aucunement n'estre pas; car estre se refere à l'agir; et n'est point, ce semble, d'agir parfaict, vers qui n'est pas capable de le gouster [To be unknown is, in a way, not to be; for being has reference to acting, and action can hardly be brought to perfection, it seems, when directed towards someone who cannot relish it]' (48). Twice more in close proximity Marie de Gournay uses the term 'semblable', first in noting 'la volupté de l'esprit qui naist principalement en ce commerce d'un semblable [the mental pleasure that is born principally in this interchange with a soulmate]', then in affirming the need of 'quelque suffisance semblable [someone of like sufficiency]' to share 'belles conceptions [beautiful conceptions]' (48).

Montaigne himself employs 'semblable' sparingly in the *Essais*: as a substantive, only three times and never in the singular. Attested in English from the fifteenth century, the word appears twice in Shakespeare. In the soliloquy opening his stint in the woods, the newly misanthropic Timon confirms that, just as fully as in his self-aggrandizing days, he mirrors himself in others: 'His semblable, yea, himself, Timon disdains' (*Tim.* 4.3.22). An earlier usage is by Hamlet, when he scornfully turns Osric's affectation back on him in praising Laertes: 'his semblable is his mirror' (5.2.118–19). In fact, Marie de Gournay's defence of Montaigne's language contains a portrait of Osric's type – 'quelques jeunes courtisans [certain young courtiers]' who

ne cherchent pas d'innover pour amender, mais d'empirer pour innover: et, qui pis est, avec condemnation des vieux vocables, qui sont ou meilleurs ou, s'ils sont egaux, doivent encore estre preferez par l'usage.

[seek, not to innovate in order to improve, but to degrade in order to innovate – and, what is worse, while condemning old expressions that either are better or, if of equal quality, ought still to be preferred on account of usage.]

(30–1)

These self-styled linguistic reformers are irrepressible: 'on se mocquera bien de nostre sottise à nous autres [the stupidity of the rest of us will be mocked]' if standard language is used 'au lieu de leurs nouveaux termes [instead of their new terms]' (31). Her own irony anticipates Hamlet's mocking spirit.

Despite that mockery, the idea of the 'semblable', important from the outset, has by this point become increasingly urgent for Hamlet. He has just told Horatio that he recognizes Laertes' 'cause' by the 'image' of his own (5.2.77). Earlier, it was Fortinbras by whom he measured himself – another would-be revenger of a father, who will finally take both the measure of Hamlet and his place on the throne. But it is above all Horatio that Hamlet seeks to transform into a 'semblable' in Marie de Gournay's sense: 'Since my dear soul was mistress of her choice / And could of men distinguish her election, / Sh' hath seal'd thee for herself' (3.2.63–5). In elevating that bland young man into a 'grand esprit' who is not 'passion's slave' (72), he distances himself from his own lack of due passion.

It follows from the construction of Horatio as foil that, just before the prospect of immediate action calls forth Hamlet's 'gain-giving', the latter calls on him to witness the justice of his (supposed) vengeful resolution: 'is't not perfect conscience / To quit him with this arm?' (5.2.67–8). One of the marks of an 'homme parfaict [perfect man]', according to Marie de Gournay, is 'sçavoir où la vengeance est licite [to know where revenge is allowable]' (37). In his self-fashioning, Hamlet virtually traces her model: 'un sage languit si'l ne peult rendre un homme de bien tesmoign de la pureté de sa conscience [a wise man languishes if he cannot make someone honourable a witness to the purity of his conscience]' (48). Finally, Hamlet counts on Horatio to tell his story after his death: 'O God, Horatio, what a wounded name, / Things standing thus unknown, shall I leave behind me!' (5.2.344–5). Indeed, for him, at this moment, '[e]stre incognu c'est aucunement n'estre pas'. He condemns Horatio to '[l]a plus grande infelicité du monde':

If thou didst ever hold me in thy heart,
Absent thee from felicity a while,
And in this harsh world draw thy breath in pain
To tell my story.

(346–9)

And if, as Marie de Gournay admits, such an impulse of the 'belle ame [rare spirit]' to 'se faire cognoistre [make itself known]' may be accounted 'ambition' (47–8), the intertext reflects even on Hamlet's earlier evasive discussions with Rosencrantz and Guildenstern (2.2.252 ff., 3.2.340 ff.).

The mention of his 'wounded name' recalls the lines in which Hamlet, then incapable of communicating the secret of his affair, posits a 'conscience' that interferes with the movement in which being consists, so that daring projects 'lose the name of action'. It has perhaps been underrecognized that 'name' here, as often in Elizabethan English, means 'renown' (French 'renommée'). This amounts to a semantic sandbagging of 'conscience' so as to sustain its moral meaning, hence its repressive efficacy, against the potential deluge of 'consciousness' and its undercurrents. In the final analysis, the key intertextual contribution of the 'Préface' to *Hamlet* may be precisely to introduce the mediation of 'renommée' into the equation between 'estre' and 'action' proposed by Montaigne. The effect, however, is hardly to narrow and fix signification, but rather to destabilize it. Paradoxically, Marie de Gournay must begin to champion Montaigne by opposing his own opinion that 'la renommée de ce livre suffit à son merite [that the renown of this book is sufficient to its merit]' (23). Her subsequent argument establishes that, for her, 'renommée' has little in common with the inert ideal of Medieval and Renaissance ideology; rather, it is produced collaboratively in a process depending on 'l'alliance d'une autre [belle ame] [the alliance of another (rare spirit)]' (47–8). As 'alliance' indicates, she is above all defining her own role as 'fille d'alliance' in the drama unfolding around the memory of her 'père'. In increasing his 'renommée', she literally renames herself – and thereby exempts herself from naming in terms of Hamlet's misogynistic equation: 'Frailty, thy name is woman!'

Such 'renommée' gestures, with Neoplatonic grandeur, towards the extravagant promise of the mirror-stage but also coveys its contrary warning that such a semblable, always 'autre', must prove unstable and fleeting. In Hamlet's self-speaking, the 'semblable' makes its first appearance negatively, when he abuses his new 'father' (and himself) by means of another soliloquized equation: 'no more like my father / Than I to Hercules' (1.2.152–3). Yet even Hercules – the archetype of masculinity, seamlessly eliding the gap between constative and performative – was conquered by a woman, as Marie de Gournay is well aware in ridiculing the 'foiblesse [weakness]' (27) of boasting anti-feminists: 'Cet autre, en fin, bravant une femme, fera cuider à sa grand'mere que, s'il n'estoit pitoyable, Hercules ne vivroit pas [This other, finally, boldly challenging a woman, will make his grandmother believe that, if he did not take pity, Hercules would not come out alive]' (28). Omphale ineluctably belongs to the story.[45] Inevitably, a female intertext spoils the rigid masculine equations, insisting on the confused and contradictory currents of human existence, if only as 'gain-giving' – a voice 'soft, / Gentle, and low'. The perfect 'semblable', who will guarantee 'renommée', being as presence, must remain unrealized, given that, as the 'fille' heard resonating within the *Nom/non* of her 'père', 'la vie mesme n'est qu'une contexture de punctilles [life itself is merely a composite of little details]' (42). Hamlet's being could have been prolonged, had he listened, only at the universal cost of its evanescence.

Notes to Chapter 7

1. That those effects extended to religion appears from the Geneva Bible's rather cryptic gloss on Paul's injunction against women speaking in church (1 *Cor.* 14:34): 'Because this disordre was in the Church, that women vsurped that which was peculiar to men. . . .' As I noted in Chapter 1, Paul's stricture is juxtaposed with his wariness about speaking in tongues: 'let him speake to him self, and to God' (14:28).
2. See my *Subversions* 24–38.
3. That of British Library MS Harley 2124, which I cite from the textual notes of Lumiansky and Mills.
4. In itself this is one variant of a conventional formula, used, e.g., *en passant* by Mary in the Wakefield *Crucifixion* (England and Pollard, eds. 383) and by Andrew in the same cycle's pageant of *The Lord's Ascension* (166).
5. 'Give me my robe, put on my crown, I have / Immortal longings in me . . . / . . . / . . . Husband, I come! (*Ant.* 5.2.280–7).
6. While Isabella's destruction of the garden signals irrational fury, the soliloquy preceding her suicide resembles that of Bajazeth in its conventional formality. See Chapter 4, 123.

7. I agree with Bruster that 'with madness the Jailer's Daughter inherits a complex subjectivity we typically associate with aristocrats, often male, of late Elizabethan tragedy' (289), although the line surely starts with the socially problematic Hieronimo. Similarly, the discourse of sexually-charged female madness, although undoubtedly 'a convention of the early modern theater' (281), needs to be recognized as an inflection of an older female discourse of subjectivity.

8. Only *LLL*, as far as I know, has attracted such concentrated attention to its obscene wordplay as is provided by Ellis, who (sometimes inadvertently) demonstrates not only the richness but the elusiveness of the sexual suggestions; see, e.g., his discussion of 'wit' itself as *double entendre* (103–10).

9. Cf. Breitenberg 440 (who adapts Greenblatt's image of 'chafing') and Asp.

10. On the use of military imagery to depict '[t]he young men's attitude towards the women' as 'at once aggressive and anxious', see Bevington 8.

11. Holdsworth (351) perceives in Berowne's abuse of Boyet here a series of sexual innuendos anchored in the slang use of 'squier' in the sense of 'pimp'.

12. It is notoriously hard to read the conclusion of his speech – the state of the text is sometimes blamed – but he arguably anticipates Berowne's scornful remarks by characterizing Boyet as a composite figure resembling at once the effeminately courtly Armado ('O, a most dainty man! / To see him walk before a lady and to bear her fan!' [144–5]) and ('a' t' other side') Moth, 'that handful of wit' (147).

13. I develop this view in *Subversions* 89–97.

14. On the phallic implication, see Ellis 179–80.

15. Hence Partridge glosses 'rubbing' here as '[a] fricative sexual caress, especially of the male by the female' (176) and in his Introduction explains that Shakespearean caressing is normally done by men to women (less often by women to men). This supports a fantasy of Shakespeare's *sexual* genius, with which Partridge palpably identifies – up to an (unmentionable) point:

    ... we – inevitably, I think – form the opinion that Shakespeare was an exceedingly knowledgeable amorist, a versatile connoisseur, and a highly artistic, an ingeniously skilful, practitioner of love-making, who could have taught Ovid rather more than that facile doctrinaire could have taught him; he evidently knew of, and probably he practised, an artifice accessible to few – one that I cannot becomingly mention here, though I felt it obligatory to touch on it [*sic*], very briefly, in the Glossary.

    (25)

    In fact, both 'fricative' (as least in French cognates) and 'rub' were applied by Early Modern writers to female homoeroticism.

16. Marston's references in *The Scourge of Villanie* (3 and 8) are placed in the context of fetishism by McLuskie 112. Donne, in 'The Anagram', abuses an ugly woman 'Whom Dildoes, Bedstaves, and her Velvet

Glasse / Would be as loath to touch as Joseph was' (53–4). This 'Velvet Glasse' seems less likely to be a 'velvet-backed mirror' (Shawcross, ed. n. to 53), given Marston's 'glassie instrument' (*Scourge* 3.123) and Nashe's dildo

> Attired in white veluet or in silk,
> And nourisht with whott water or with milk;
> Arm'd otherwhile in thick congealed glass,
> When he more glib to hell be lowe would passe.
> (273–6)

17. Given the uncertain dating of both texts, there is no question of tracing 'influence' in the traditional sense; intertextually speaking, it is important merely that both participate in the same discourse of sexuality.

18. Cf. Grosz on 'Lacan and romantic love' (131–7).

19. The Lylyan quality of *LLL* has been much-discussed; Bevington compares *Sappho and Phao* as similarly concerned with the sexual anxieties and fantasies of young males.

20. Analogues supporting an allusion to bewitching by owls (Percy and Simpson, ed. 10: n. to 913) do not refer to pregnancy or sexuality.

21. Cf. *H5* 2.3.37.

22. One equivocal reference figures in Titania's charge to her fairies as she prepares for sleep: 'some keep back / The clamorous owl, that nightly hoots and wonders / At our quaint spirits' (2.2.5–7). She has 'forsworn [Oberon's] bed and company' (*MND* 2.1.62) but is, of course, about to experience an erotic adventure reminiscent of *The Golden Ass*. 'Quaint' and 'spirits' are words often endowed with sexual import.

23. See *The Oxford Dictionary of Nursery Rhymes* 421–3. The only variant cited that includes the owl and the hawk reads, 'her Bels were falne away' (422). For Bruster, '[t]hese cut-away bells point to a trope of cutting that underlies how the Jailer's Daughter explains gender difference' (295).

24. See Tracy (83–6), who also cites the Welsh folk-belief that the owl hoots when a maiden loses her virginity. Relevant, too, may be Apuleius' account of the baker whose death is caused by his adulterous wife and whose daughter falls into distracted mourning after her father's burial (9.30–1; ed. Hanson 2:182–5).

25. See Traub, '(In)significance' n. 9.

26. Cf. the similar perspective of the seventeenth-century writer on midwifery, Pierre Dionis, as cited by Eccles 34.

27. Brantôme's discussion makes it difficult to justify extrapolating from Greenblatt's evidence an absolute principle that in France the 'prosthetic supplementation of [a woman's] body was grounds for execution' (Traub, '[In]significance' 153). Certainly, a distinction is made by Estienne between a similar case, in which a women sought to impersonate a male within marriage, and the practice of 'quelques vilaines qu'on appeloit anciennement tribades [certain base women who in ancient times were called *tribades*]' (1:178) – a word whose

Greek root means 'rub'. Class may also have been a mitigating factor. Brantôme tells of a 'grand prince [great prince]' (195) who surprised two women using a dildo and, out of curiosity, ordered them to continue. The same writer relates the discovery amidst a court-woman's personal effects of four dildoes, 'gentiment façonnez, qui donnerent bien de la risée au monde [nicely made, which gave rise to much ridicule on the part of society]' (196). The woman is apparently still living but does not look well – the consequence of self-abuse. On the other hand, a medical text recommends female masturbation in moderation (even with the aid of a midwife) in the absence of 'normal' sexual outlets (Hilda Smith 104). Montaigne instances the inhibition against public masturbation, both male and female, as contingent on custom (2:294; trans. Florio 2:303). All in all, given Early Modern views of sexuality in general, it is plausible that, compared with Victorian attitudes, 'Stuart opinion was less censorious and guilt-ridden about [masturbation and lesbianism]' (Eccles 34).

28. Breitenberg deems the theatre itself 'resolutely masculine in its structuring of desire, as Greenblatt argues' (440) – a view irrefutable in terms of plot. Thus *LLL*'s transgressive ending makes shaky evidence for female empowerment. Discursive analysis yields a stronger case, as Breitenberg implicitly recognizes, though he is understandably wary of conferring 'a status transcendent of those structures of desire and representation available in the late sixteenth century' (436). I simply consider further structures to have been available.

29. See *De la grammatologie* 203–34; *Of Grammatology* 141–64.

30. See also Grosz 137–8:

> For Lacan, love . . . is always structured with reference to the phallus, which, in a sense is the third term coming between two lovers. The subject demands a wholeness, unity, and completion which it imagines the other can bestow on it. The symbolic, on the other hand, requires a subject irrevocably split, divided by language, governed by the phallus and the Other. . . .
> Courtly love is a masculine way of refusing to recognize this fundamental rupture. It is a (spurious) attempt to put the Other in place of the other.

31. See Davenport, ed. n. to 3.35; also Marston's 'The Metamorphosis of Pigmalions Image', where, as McLuskie observes, the 'image of matching perfection between Pygmalion's and his lover's body . . . glosses over sexual difference' (111).

32. Cf. Malvolio's erotic fetishizing of Olivia's supposed letter (*TN* 2.5), as the dupers look on.

33. See Ellis 112, who does not, however, appear to realize what it would actually mean to 'do it still without accompt'. But then the masturbatory paradigm has hovered just out of commentators' reach, despite general sensitivity to the lovers' 'plunging from one crude male immaturity to another' (Tillyard, *Comedies* 145). Even Rose fails to mention masturbation – surprisingly, given her title (*The Expense of Spirit*), her focus on the dramatic uses and abuses of sexual desire,

金閣寺 Kinkaku-ji

Dear Sandra,

Thank you for your beautiful card from Canada. I am pleased you have had a relaxed holiday there after too busy days.

I am writing a book in this summer, she lonely opportunity to have my own time. But in October when I attend the conference at New York, I intend to have my holiday there after the conference.

Shin-Ichi will leave for Geneva and Vienna next week for a conference.

With best regards,
Yoshiko Ueno

JAL
(Japan Airlines)
Pavilion in Kyoto?

PRINTED IN JAPAN
JG AB AJ

POST CARD

Yoshiko Ueno
1-6-21 Kamirenjaku
Mitaka-shi, 181
Tokyo, Japan

Dr. Sandra CLARK
2 Lynton Rd.
London N8 8SL
U.K. (イギリス)

Air Mail

NIPPON
70

Cherry Salmon Dog

and her portrayal of the 'sophomoric callowness' of the lovers in *LLL* as involving 'an infatuation with verbal wit, an enchantment with their own cleverness', and 'narcissistic posturing', as opposed to 'a plain style and shared experience' (35–6). Nor does *LLL* appear in the index of Traub's recent Shakespearean study, despite her perception of masturbatory overtones in the 'young man' sonnets and her hypothesis that the 'anxiety about reproduction' thus expressed informs *AYL* and *TN* (*Desire* 139).

34. The aural suggestion of the plural, whether 'labour's' is written with an apostrophe (as in the First Folio text) or without (as in the First Quarto), is significant in this regard.

35. Cf. Donne's elegy, 'Going to Bed': 'Until I labour, I in labour lie' (2).

36. The wheel has come full circle, as Breitenberg's reading testifies. Strangely, since he cites Carroll's survey of previous criticism, Breitenberg professes himself unaware of any previous non-syncretic reading of the Cuckoo Song (n. 11); it is precisely the 'traditional reading' in terms of conflict between 'Winter-Reality' and 'Spring-Illusion' to which Carroll opposes his 'interplay of dualistic forces' (172–3).

37. Including my own – see *Subversions* 206–19.

38. Commentators have seen in Perseus here only one of the 'types of "brave and masculine Vertue"' (Brown, ed. n. to 3.2.132, citing a marginal note in Jonson's *The Masque of Queens*). 'Defence' and 'personate' surely evoke the mythological hero's ruse for defeating the snake-haired Gorgon, with whom Vittoria thus implicitly identifies her auditors, boldly reflecting upon them the gaze by which they construct her monstrosity.

39. I borrow this image from Cixous, who puts it to a broadly compatible (but anti-Lacanian) use.

40. Leverenz's application of 'interpersonal' psychological analysis illustrates the essentializing tendency of early feminist analysis, both in presuming Hamlet's division from his 'heart' and 'self' and in identifying these elements as feminine. As a sustained exploration of 'The Woman in Hamlet', however, the essay sometimes intersects with my own discussion.

41. See also Robertson 46–8 on 'discours' / 'discourse' in Montaigne and Shakespeare.

42. See Bauschatz 348–9.

43. On her use of Montaigne's terms, see Rigolot, Introd. 51n80.

44. I am grateful to Professor François Rigolot for alerting me to this passage, in which Montaigne may be figuring his grief for La Boétie (see Rigolot, *Les métamorphoses* 222–3).

45. Rigolot (Introd. 28n19) cites the allusion to Omphale in Marie de Gournay's 1622 treatise, *Égalité des hommes et des femmes* 122; there she similarly derides male derogators of female 'faiblesse' as 'plus braves qu'Hercule [braver than Hercules]' (113–14).

Works Cited

Adelman, Janet. *Suffocating Mothers: Fantasies of Maternal Origin in Shakespeare's Plays*, Hamlet *to* The Tempest. New York: Routledge, 1992.

Aers, David. *Community, Gender, and Individual Identity: English Writing 1360–1430*. London: Routledge, 1988.

Aggeler, Geoffrey. 'The Eschatological Crux in *The Spanish Tragedy*'. *Journal of English and Germanic Philology* 86 (1987): 319–31.

Alanus De Insulis (Alain de Lille). *The Art of Preaching*. Trans. Gillian R. Evans. Cistercian Studies 23. Kalamazoo, MI: Cistercian Publications, 1981.

———. *Summa de Arte Praedicatoria. Patrilogiae Cursus Completus Series Latina (Patrilogia Latina)*. Ed. J.-P. Migne. 221 vols. in 222. Paris: Garnier, 1878–90. 210: col. 109–98.

Angenot, Marc. 'L'"intertextualité": enquête sur l'émergence et la diffusion d'un champ notionnel'. *Revue des sciences humaines* 60.189 (1983): 121–35.

Apuleius. *The xi bookes of the Golden asse, with the mariage of Cupide and Psiches (Metamorphoses)*. Trans. William Adlington. London: H. Wykes, 1566. STC 718.

———. *Metamorphoses*. Ed. and trans. J. Arthur Hanson. 2 vols. Loeb Classical Library 44. Cambridge, MS: Harvard UP, 1989.

Ardolino, Frank R. 'Hieronimo as St. Jerome in *The Spanish Tragedy*'. *Études anglaises* 36 (1983): 435–7.

———. '"Now Shall I See the Fall of Babylon": *The Spanish Tragedy* as a Reformation Play of Daniel'. *Renaissance and Reformation/Renaissance et Réforme* ns 14 (1990): 49–55.

Arnold, Morris Leroy. *The Soliloquies of Shakespeare: A Study in Technic*. Columbia University Studies in English. New York: Columbia UP, 1911.

Asp, Carolyn. '*Love's Labour's Lost*: Language and the Deferral of Desire'. *Literature and Psychology* 35.3 (1989): 1–21.

Assarsson-Rizzi, Kerstin. Friar Bacon and Friar Bungay: *A Structural and Thematic Analysis of Robert Greene's Play*. Lund Studies in English 44. Ed. Claes Schaar and Jan Svartvik. Lund: Gleerup, 1972.

Augustine, Saint. *De Civitate Dei Libri 22*. Ed. Bernardus Dombart and Alphonsus Kalb. *Aurelii Augustini Opera*. Part 14. *Corpus Christianorum Series Latina*. Vols. 47–8. Turnhout: Brepols, 1955.

———. *De Spiritu et Littera. Patrilogiae Cursus Completus Series Latina (Patrilogia Latina)*. Ed. J.-P. Migne. 221 vols. in 222. Paris: Garnier, 1878–90. 44: col. 199–246.

———. *De Trinitate Libri 15*. Ed. W. J. Mountain and Fr. Glorie. *Aurelii Augustini Opera*. Part 16. *Corpus Christianorum Series Latina*. Vols. 50–50a. Turnhout: Brepols, 1968.

———. *On the Spirit and the Letter. Saint Augustine's Anti-Pelagian Works*. Trans. Peter Holmes and Robert Ernest Wallis (rev. Benjamin B. Warfield). A Select Library of the Nicene and Post-Nicene Fathers of the Christian

Church, ed. Philip Schaff *et al.*, Vol. 5. Buffalo, NY: The Christian Literature Company, 1887.

——. *On the Trinity*. Trans. Arthur West Haddan. Rev. and annotated William G. T. Shedd. A Select Library of the Nicene and Post-Nicene Fathers of the Christian Church, ed. Philip Schaff *et al.*, Vol. 3. Buffalo, NY: The Christian Literature Company, 1887.

——. *St. Augustine's City of God*. Trans. Marcus Dods. A Select Library of the Nicene and Post-Nicene Fathers of the Christian Church, ed. Philip Schaff *et al.*, Vol. 2. Buffalo, NY: The Christian Literature Company, 1887. 1–511.

Aurenhammer, Hans. *Lexikon der christlichen Ikonographie*. Vol. 1. Vienna: Hollinek, 1959.

Axton, Richard. *European Drama of the Early Middle Ages*. London: Hutchinson University Library, 1974.

Bacon, Francis. *Novum Organum (Instauratio Magna, Part 2)*. The Works of *Francis Bacon, Baron of Verulam, Viscount St. Alban, and Lord High Chancellor of England*. Ed. James Spedding, Robert Leslie Ellis, and Douglas Denon Heath. New ed. Vol. 1 (Philosophical Works, Vol. 1). London: Longmans, 1889, 149–365.

——. 'Of Death'. *Essays or Counsels Civil and Moral*. The Works of Francis *Bacon, Baron of Verulam, Viscount St. Alban, and Lord High Chancellor of England*. Ed. James Spedding, Robert Leslie Ellis, and Douglas Denon Heath. New ed. Vol. 6. London: Longmans, 1890. 379–80.

Bacon, Roger. *An excellent discourse of the admirable force and efficacie of Art and Nature. The Mirror of Alchimy....* London: (T. Creede) for R. Oliue, 1597. STC 1182.

——. *The Opus Majus of Roger Bacon*. Ed. John Henry Bridges. 2 vols. 1897; rpt. Frankfurt am Main: Minerva, 1964.

——. *The Opus Majus of Roger Bacon*. Trans. Robert Belle Burke. 2 vols. 1928; rpt. New York: Russell, 1962.

Bakhtin, Mikhail. *Rabelais and His World*. Trans. Helene Iswolsky. Cambridge, MA: M.I.T. Press, 1968.

Barber, C. L. *Shakespeare's Festive Comedy: A Study of Dramatic Form and Its Relation to Social Custom*. Princeton, NJ: Princeton UP, 1959.

Barker, Francis. *The Tremulous Private Body: Essays on Subjection*. London: Methuen, 1984.

Bartsch, Karl. 'Über ein geistliches Schauspiel des XV. Jahrhunderts'. *Germania: Vierteljahrschrift für Deutsche Alterthumskunde* 3 (1858): 267–97.

Bauschatz, Cathleen M. 'Imitation, Writing, and Self-Study in Marie de Gournay's 1595 "Préface" to Montaigne's *Essais*'. *Contending Kingdoms: Historical, Psychological, and Feminist Approaches to the Literature of Sixteenth-Century England and France*. Ed. Marie-Rose Logan and Peter L. Rudnytsky. Detroit, MI: Wayne State UP, 1991. 346–64.

Beadle, Richard, ed. *The York Plays*. London: Arnold, 1982.

Beaujour, Michel. *Miroirs d'encre: Rhétorique de l'autoportrait*. Paris: Seuil, 1980.

Beaumont, Francis, and John Fletcher. *A King and No King*. Ed. Robert K. Turner Jr. Regents Renaissance Drama Series. Lincoln: U of Nebraska P, 1963.

——. *The Maid's Tragedy*. Ed. T. W. Craik. The Revels Plays. Manchester: Manchester UP, 1988.

——. *Philaster: or, Love Lies A-bleeding*. Ed. Andrew Gurr. The Revels Plays. London: Methuen, 1969.

Beckwith, Sarah. 'A Very Material Mysticism: The Medieval Mysticism of Margery Kempe'. *Medieval Literature: Criticism, Ideology, and History*. Ed. David Aers. Brighton: Harvester; New York: St. Martin's, 1986. 34–57.

Bedford Missal (Book of Hours). British Library MS Add. 18850.

Belsey, Catherine. *The Subject of Tragedy: Identity and Difference in Renaissance Drama*. London: Methuen, 1985.

——. 'Subjectivity and the Soliloquy'. *Macbeth: William Shakespeare*. Ed. Alan Sinfield. New Casebooks. Basingstoke, Hampshire: Macmillan Education, 1992. 79–91.

Benveniste, Émile. *Problèmes de linguistique générale*. 2 vols. Vol. 1. Paris: Gallimard: 1966.

——. *Problems in General Linguistics*. Trans. Mary Elizabeth Meek. Miami Linguistics Series 8. Coral Gables, FLA: U of Miami P, 1971.

Berry, Ralph. *Shakespeare's Comedies: Explorations in Form*. Princeton, NJ: Princeton UP, 1972.

Bevington, David. ' "Jack hath not Jill": Failed Courtship in Lyly and Shakespeare'. *Shakespeare Survey*, 42 (1990): 1–13.

——, ed. *Medieval Drama*. Boston: Houghton Mifflin, 1975.

Bèze, Théodore de. *A Tragedie of Abraham's Sacrifice*. Trans. Arthur Golding. Ed. Malcolm W. Wallace. University of Toronto Studies Philological Series. Toronto: U of Toronto Library, 1906.

The Bible (Bishops'). London: by the assignment of Christopher Barker, 1578. STC 2124.

—— (Geneva). *The Geneva Bible: A Facsimile of the 1560 Edition*. With an introd. by Lloyd E. Berry. Madison: U of Wisconsin P, 1969.

—— (Vulgate). Madrid: Biblioteca de Autores Cristianos, 1965.

Bliss, Lee. 'Pastiche, Burlesque, Tragicomedy'. *The Cambridge Companion to English Renaissance Drama*. Ed. A. R. Braunmuller and Michael Hattaway. Cambridge: Cambridge UP, 1990. 237–61.

Boas, Frederick S., ed. *The Works of Thomas Kyd*. Oxford: Clarendon, 1901.

Boccaccio, Giovanni. *De Casibus Virorum Illustrium. Tutte le Opere di Giovanni Boccaccio*. Ed. Vittore Branca. 12 vols. Vol. 9. Milan: Mondadori, 1983.

Borst, Arno. *Der Turmbau von Babel: Geschichte der Meinungen über Ursprung und Vielfalt der Sprachen und Völker*. 4 vols. Stuttgart: Hiersemann, 1957–63.

Bost, Hubert. *Babel: Du texte au symbole*. Geneva: Labor et Fides, 1985.

Boswell-Stone, W. G., ed. *Shakespeare's Holinshed: The Chronicle and the Plays Compared*. 2nd ed. 1907; rpt. New York: Dover, 1968.

Bowers, Fredson, gen. ed. *The Dramatic Works in the Beaumont and Fletcher Canon*. 8 vols. Cambridge: Cambridge UP, 1966–92.

Bradley, Ritamary. 'Backgrounds of the Title *Speculum* in Mediaeval Literature'. *Speculum* 29 (1954): 100–15.

Bradshaw, Graham. *Misrepresentations: Shakespeare and the Materialists*. Ithaca, NY: Cornell UP, 1993.

Brantôme, Pierre de Bourdeille, Seigneur de. *Les dames galantes*. Ed. Pascal Pia. Paris: Gallimard, 1981.

Braunmuller, A. R. 'The Arts of the Dramatist'. *The Cambridge Companion to English Renaissance Drama*. Ed. A. R. Braunmuller and Michael Hattaway. Cambridge: Cambridge UP, 1990. 53–90.

Breitenberg, Mark. 'The Anatomy of Masculine Desire in *Love's Labor's Lost*'. *Shakespeare Quarterly* 43 (1992): 430–49.

Bridges, John Henry. Introduction. *The Opus Majus of Roger Bacon*. Ed. John Henry Bridges. 2 vols. 1897; rpt. Frankfurt am Main: Minerva, 1964. 1: xxi–xcii.

Bruster, Douglas. 'The Jailer's Daughter and the Politics of Madwomen's Language'. *Shakespeare Quarterly* 46 (1995): 277–300.

Bullough, Geoffrey, ed. *Narrative and Dramatic Sources of Shakespeare*. 8 vols. London: Routledge; New York: Columbia UP, 1957–75.

Burckhardt, Jacob. *The Civilization of the Renaissance in Italy*. Trans. S. G. C. Middlemore. 2 vols. 1929; rpt. New York: Harper Torchbooks, 1958.

Burns, Edward. *Character: Acting and Being on the Pre-Modern Stage*. Basingstoke, Hampshire: Macmillan; New York: St. Martin's, 1990.

Bynum, Caroline W. *Jesus as Mother: Studies in the Spirituality of the High Middle Ages*. Berkeley: U of California P, 1982.

Cabrol, Fernand, H. Leclercq, *et al. Dictionnaire d'archéologie chrétienne et de liturgie*. 15 vols. Paris: Letouzey et Ané, 1903–53.

Calvin, Jean. *Institutio Christianae Religionis* (1559 ed.). *Ioannis Calvini Opera Quae Supersunt Omnia*. Ed. Wilhelm Baum, Edward Cunitz, and Edward Reuss. Vol. 2. Corpus Reformatorum 30. Brunswick: Schwetschke, 1864.

——. *The Institution of Christian Religion*. Trans. Thomas Norton. London: R. Wolfe and R. Harison, 1561. STC 4415.

Carroll, William C. *The Great Feast of Language in* Love's Labour's Lost. Princeton, NJ: Princeton UP, 1976.

The Castle of Perseverance. *The Macro Plays: The Castle of Perseverance, Wisdom, Mankind*. Ed. Mark Eccles. Early English Text Society 262. London: Oxford UP for the Early English Text Society, 1969.

Cawley, A. C. Introduction. *The Wakefield Pageants in the Towneley Cycle*. Ed. A. C. Cawley. Manchester: Manchester UP, 1958. xi–xxxiii.

Cave, Terence. *The Cornucopian Text: Problems of Writing in the French Renaissance*. Oxford: Clarendon, 1979.

Chapman, George. *Bussy D'Ambois*. Ed. Nicholas Brooke. The Revels Plays. London: Methuen, 1964.

——. *The Revenge of Bussy D'Ambois*. Ed. Robert J. Lordi. *The Plays of George Chapman: The Tragedies with* Sir Gyles Goossecappe: *A Critical Edition*. Gen. ed. Allan Holaday. Cambridge: Brewer, 1987.

——. *The Tragedy of Charles Duke of Byron*. *The Conspiracy and Tragedy of Charles Duke of Byron*. Ed. John Margeson. Manchester: Manchester UP, 1988.

——. *The Widow's Tears*. Ed. Akihiro Yamada. The Revels Plays. London: Methuen, 1975.

Chappell, William, and J. W. Epsworth, eds. *The Roxburghe Ballads*. 6 vols. 1871–99; rpt. New York: AMS, 1966.

Chaucer, Geoffrey. *The Riverside Chaucer*. Gen. ed. Larry D. Benson. 3rd ed. Boston: Houghton Mifflin, 1987.

Cixous, Hélène. 'The Laugh of the Medusa'. Trans. Keith Cohen and Paula Cohen. *New French Feminisms: An Anthology*. Ed. Elaine Marks and Isabelle de Courtivron. New York: Schocken, 1981. 245–64.

Clemen, Wolfgang. *English Tragedy before Shakespeare: The Development of Dramatic Speech*. Trans. T. S. Dorsch. Orig. title *Die Tragödie vor Shakespeare: ihre Entwicklung im Spiegel der dramatischen Rede* (1955). London: Methuen, 1961.

——. *Shakespeare's Soliloquies*. Trans. Charity Scott Stokes. London: Methuen, 1987.

Colish, Marcia L. *The Mirror of Language: A Study in the Medieval Theory of Knowledge*. Yale Historical Publications Miscellany 88. New Haven, CT: Yale UP, 1968.

Cottet, Serge. 'Je pense où je ne suis pas, je suis où je ne pense pas'. *Philosophie présente Lacan*. By Marie-Hélène Brousse, Serge Cottet, Claude Léger, Jean-Daniel Matet, Gérard Miller, Dominique Miller, François Regnault, Danièle Silvestre, Michel Silvestre, Colette Soler, and Marc Strauss, under the direction of Gérard Miller. Paris: Bordas, 1987. 11–29.

Craig, Hardin. *English Religious Drama*. Oxford: Clarendon, 1955.

——. 'Hamlet's Book Cardan's *De Consolatione*'. *Huntington Library Bulletin* November 1934: 17–37.

Craik, T. W. *The Tudor Interlude: Stage, Costume, and Acting*. Leicester: Leicester UP, 1958.

Curtius, Ernst Robert. *European Literature and the Latin Middle Ages*. Trans. Willard R. Trask. Bollingen Series 36. New York: Pantheon Books for the Bollingen Foundation, 1953.

Dahl, Liisa. *Nominal Style in the Shakespearean Soliloquy with Reference to the Early English Drama, Shakespeare's Immediate Predecessors, and His Contemporaries*. Turun Yliopiston Julkaisuja / Annales Universitatis Turkuensis, Series B, Vol. 112. Turku: Turun Yliopisto, 1969.

Daniel, Samuel. *The Complaint of Rosamond. Poems and A Defence of Ryme*. Ed. Arthur Colby Sprague. London: Oxford UP; Cambridge, MA: Harvard UP, 1930.

——. 'To my deere friend M. *Iohn Florio*, concerning *his translation of Montaigne*'. *Montaigne's Essays*. Trans. John Florio. With an Introduction by L. C. Harmer. 3 vols. Everyman's Library. London: Dent; New York: Dutton, 1965. 1: 12–14.

Davis, Norman, ed. *Non-Cycle Plays and Fragments*. E.E.T.S. Supplementary Text 1. London: Oxford UP for the Early English Text Society, 1970.

Davis, Tenney L., ed. and trans. *Roger Bacon on the Nullity of Magic*. 1923; rpt. New York: AMS, 1982.

Dawson, Anthony B. '*Women Beware Women* and the Economy of Rape'. *Studies in English Literature 1500–1900* 27 (1987): 303–20.

Delany, Paul. *British Autobiography in the Seventeenth Century*. London: Routledge; New York, Columbia UP, 1969.

Demonet, Marie-Luce. *Les voix du signe: Nature et origine du langage à la Renaissance (1480–1580)*. Bibliothèque Littéraire de la Renaissance, Series 3, Vol. 29. Paris: Champion; Geneva: Slatkine, 1992.

Derrida, Jacques. *Aporias*. Trans. Thomas Dutoit. Stanford, CA: Stanford UP, 1993.

——. 'Apories: Mourir – s'attendre aux "limites de la vérité" '. *Le passage des frontières: Autour du travail de Jacques Derrida* (Colloque de Cerisy). Ed. Marie-Louise Mallet. Paris: Galilée, 1994. 309–38.

——. *De la grammatologie*. Paris: Les Editions de Minuit, 1967.

——. 'Des Tours de Babel'. *Difference in Translation*. Ed. Joseph F. Graham. Ithaca, NY: Cornell UP, 1985. 209–48.

——. 'Des Tours de Babel'. Trans. Joseph F. Graham. *Difference in Translation*. Ed. Joseph F. Graham. Ithaca, NY: Cornell UP, 1985. 165–207.

——. *Of Grammatology*. Trans. Gayatri Chakravorty Spivak. Baltimore, MD: Johns Hopkins UP, 1974.

Desan, Philippe. 'The Book, the Friend, the Woman: Montaigne's Circular Exchanges'. Trans. Brad Bassler. *Contending Kingdoms: Historical, Psychological, and Feminist Approaches to the Literature of Sixteenth-Century England and France*. Ed. Marie-Rose Logan and Peter L. Rudnytsky. Detroit, MI: Wayne State UP, 1991. 225–62.

Desmet, Christy. *Reading Shakespeare's Characters: Rhetoric, Ethics, and Identity*. Massachusetts Studies in Early Modern Culture. Amherst: U of Massachusetts P, 1992.

A Dictionary of Biblical Tradition in English Literature. Gen. ed. David Lyle Jeffrey. Grand Rapids, MI: Eerdmans, 1992.

Dijkstra, Bram. *Idols of Perversity: Fantasies of Feminine Evil in Fin-de-Siècle Culture*. New York: Oxford UP, 1986.

Diller, Hans-Jürgen. *The Middle English Mystery Play: A Study in Dramatic Speech and Form*. Trans. Frances Wessels. European Studies in English Literature. Cambridge: Cambridge UP, 1992.

Dollimore, Jonathan. *Radical Tragedy: Religion, Ideology and Power in the Drama of Shakespeare and His Contemporaries*. 2nd ed. New York: Harvester, 1989.

——. 'Subjectivity, Sexuality, and Transgression: The Jacobean Connection'. *Renaissance Drama* ns 17 (1986): 53–79.

Donne, John. *The Complete Poetry of John Donne*. Ed. John T. Shawcross. Garden City, NY: Doubleday Anchor, 1967.

Drayton, Michael. *The Works of Michael Drayton*. Ed. J. William Hebel. 5 vols. Corrected ed. Oxford: Blackwell, 1961.

Dubois, Claude-Gilbert. *Mythe et langage au seizième siècle*. Bordeaux: Ducros, 1970.

Eccles, Audrey. *Obstectrics and Gynaecology in Tudor and Stuart England*. London: Croom Helm, 1982.

Edgerton, Samuel Y. Jr. 'Maniera and the Mannaia: Decorum and Decapitation in the Sixteenth Century'. *The Meaning of Mannerism*. Ed. Franklin W. Robinson and Stephen G. Nichols Jr. Hanover, NH: UP of New England, 1972. 67–103.

——. *The Renaissance Rediscovery of Linear Perspective*. New York: Basic, 1975.

Edwards, Philip. Introduction. *The Spanish Tragedy*. Ed. Philip Edwards. The Revels Plays. London: Methuen, 1959.

Ellis, Herbert A. *Shakespeare's Lusty Punning in Love's Labour's Lost*. The Hague: Mouton, 1973.

Ellrodt, Robert. 'Self-Consciousness in Montaigne and Shakespeare'. *Shakespeare Survey* 28 (1975): 37–50.

Empson, William. *'The Spanish Tragedy'. Elizabethan Drama: Modern Essays in Criticism*. Ed. R. J. Kaufmann. New York: Oxford UP, 1961. 60–80.

England, George, and Alfred W. Pollard, eds. *The Towneley Plays*. Early English Text Society Extra Series 71. London: Kegan, Paul, Trench, Trübner, 1897.

Estienne, Henri. *Apologie pour Hérodote: Satire de la société au xvie siècle*. New ed. Ed. P. Ristelhuber. 2 vols. 1879; rpt. Geneva: Slatkine, 1969.

Everyman. Ed. A. C. Cawley. Manchester: Manchester UP, 1961.

Faber, M. D., and Colin Skinner. *'The Spanish Tragedy*: Act IV'. *Philological Quarterly* 49 (1970): 444–59.

The Famous History of Fryer Bacon, etc. London: T. C[otes], [1640?]. STC 1184.5.

Farce . . . de Pernet qui va au vin. Ancien théâtre françois; ou, Collection des ouvrages dramatiques les plus remarquables depuis les mystères jusqu'à Corneille. Ed. Emmanuel Louis Nicholas Viollet-le-Duc. Vol. 1 (ed. A. de Courde de Montaiglon). 1854; rpt. Nendeln, Liechtenstein: Kraus, 1972.

La Farce du pasté. Receuil de farces françaises inédites du xve siècle. Ed. Gustave Cohen. Mediaeval Academy of America Publications 47. Cambridge, MA: Mediaeval Academy of America, 1949.

Felman, Shoshana. *The Literary Speech Act: Don Juan with J. L. Austin, or Seduction in Two Languages*. Trans. Catherine Porter. Orig. title *Le scandale du corps parlant*. Ithaca, NY: Cornell UP, 1983.

Ferry, Anne. *The 'Inward' Language: Sonnets of Wyatt, Sidney, Shakespeare, Donne*. Chicago: U of Chicago P, 1983.

Fineman, Joel. *Shakespeare's Perjured Eye: The Invention of Poetic Subjectivity in the Sonnets*. Berkeley: U of California P, 1986.

Fletcher, John. *Four Plays, or Moral Representations, in One*. Ed. Cyrus Hoy. *The Dramatic Works in the Beaumont and Fletcher Canon*. Gen. ed. Fredson Bowers. Vol. 8. Cambridge: Cambridge UP, 1992.

——. 'To the Reader'. *The Faithful Shepherdess*. Ed. Cyrus Hoy. *The Dramatic Works in the Beaumont and Fletcher Canon*. Gen. ed. Fredson Bowers. Vol. 3. Cambridge: Cambridge UP, 1966.

——. *The Tragedy of Valentinian*. Ed. Robert K. Turner. *The Dramatic Works in the Beaumont and Fletcher Canon*. Gen. ed. Fredson Bowers. Vol. 4. Cambridge: Cambridge UP, 1979.

Ford, John. *The Broken Heart*. Ed. T. J. B. Spencer. The Revels Plays. Manchester: Manchester UP, 1980.

——. *The Chronicle History of Perkin Warbeck: A Strange Truth*. Ed. Peter Ure. The Revels Plays. London: Methuen, 1968.

——. *Love's Sacrifice. The Collected Works of John Ford*. Ed. William Gifford and Alexander Dyce. 3 vols. 1895; rpt. New York: Russell, 1965. Vol. 2.

——. *'Tis Pity She's a Whore*. Ed. Derek Roper. The Revels Plays. London: Methuen, 1975.

Foxe, John. *Acts and Monuments* (1563 ed.). Ed. George Townsend. 8 vols. 1843–49(?); rpt. New York: AMS, 1965.

——. *The seconde Volume of the Ecclesiasticall Historie, conteyning the Acts and Monvments of Martyrs*, etc. Newly recognised and inlarged by the Authour. London: P. Short, 1597. (Variant of 1596 ed.; STC 11226a.)

Foucault, Michel. *Discipline and Punish: The Birth of the Prison.* Trans. Alan Sheridan. New York: Pantheon, 1977.

——. *Folie et déraison: Histoire de la folie à l'âge classique.* Abridged by the author. Plon 10/18 series. Paris: Union Générale d'Éditions, 1964.

——. *Madness and Civilization: A History of Insanity in the Age of Reason.* Trans. Richard Howard. Plon 10/18 ed. supplemented by the author with material from the 1st ed. New York: Vintage, 1973.

——. *Les mots et les choses: Une archéologie des sciences humaines.* Paris: Gallimard, 1966.

——. *The Order of Things: An Archaeology of the Human Sciences.* Trans. of *Les mots et les choses: Une archéologie des sciences humaines.* World of Man series. New York: Vintage, 1973.

——. 'La Prose d'Actéon'. *La nouvelle revue française* 23 (1964): 444–59.

——. 'Qu'est-ce qu'un auteur?' 'Qu'est-ce qu'un auteur? Séance du 22 février 1969'. By Michel Foucault *et al. Bulletin de la Société française de philosophie.* 63.3 (1969): 73–104. 75–95.

——. *Surveiller et punir: Naissance de la prison.* Paris: Gallimard, 1975.

Franz, Adolph. *Die kirchlichen Benedicktionen im Mittelalter.* 2 vols. Freiburg im Breisgau: Herdersche Verlagshandlung, 1909.

Freedman, Barbara. *Staging the Gaze: Postmodernism, Psychoanalysis, and Shakespearean Comedy.* Ithaca, NY: Cornell UP, 1991.

Frieden, Ken. *Genius and Monologue.* Ithaca, NY: Cornell UP, 1985.

Frye, Northrop. *A Natural Perspective: The Development of Shakespearean Comedy and Romance.* New York: Columbia UP, 1965.

Furness, Horace Howard, ed. *Richard III.* By William Shakespeare. Variorum ed. Philadelphia, PA: Lippincott, 1908.

Fuss, Diana. *Essentially Speaking: Feminism, Nature and Difference.* New York: Routledge, 1989.

Gair, W. Reavley. Introduction. *Antonio's Revenge.* By John Marston. Ed. W. Reavley Gair. The Revels Plays. Manchester: Manchester UP; Baltimore, MD: Johns Hopkins UP, 1978. 1–46.

——. Introduction. *Antonio and Mellida.* By John Marston. Ed. W. Reavley Gair. The Revels Plays. Manchester: Manchester UP, 1991. 1–51.

Garber, Marjorie. ' "Wild Laughter in the Throat of Death": Dark Purposes in Shakespearean Comedy'. *Shakespearean Comedy.* Ed. Maurice Charney. New York: New York Literary Forum, 1980. 121–6.

Gardiner, Harold C. *Mysteries' End: An Investigation of the Last Days of the Medieval Religious Stage.* Yale Studies in English 103. New Haven, CT: Yale UP, 1946.

Gasché, Rodolphe. *The Tain of the Mirror: Derrida and the Philosophy of Reflection.* Cambridge, MA: Harvard UP, 1986.

Gauvin, Claude. *Un cycle du théâtre religieux anglais du moyen âge: Le jeu de la ville de 'N'.* Paris: Centre National de la Recherche Scientifique, 1973.

Girard, René. *A Theater of Envy: William Shakespeare.* New York: Oxford UP, 1991.

Goldberg, Jonathan. 'Hamlet's Hand'. *Shakespeare Quarterly* 39 (1988): 307–27.

Goldin, Frederick. *The Mirror of Narcissus in the Courtly Love Lyric.* Ithaca, NY: Cornell UP, 1967.

Goodstein, Peter. 'Hieronimo's Destruction of Babylon'. *English Language Notes* 3 (1966): 172–3.

Gournay, Marie le Jars de. *Égalité des hommes et des femmes. Fragments d'un discours féminin*. Ed. Elyane Dezon-Jones. [Paris]: Corti, 1988. 109–27.

——. 'Préface à l'édition des *Essais* de Montaigne'. Ed. François Rigolot. *Montaigne Studies: An Interdisciplinary Forum* 1 (1989): 7–60.

Gower, John. *The Complete Works of John Gower*. Ed. G. C. Macaulay. 4 vols. Oxford: Clarendon, 1901.

——. *Jo. Gower de confessione amantis*. London: T. Berthelette, 1554. STC 12144.

Grabes, Herbert. *The Mutable Glass: Mirror-imagery in Titles and Texts of the Middle Ages and English Renaissance*. Trans. Gordon Collier. Cambridge: Cambridge UP, 1982.

Greenblatt, Stephen. 'Fiction and Friction'. *Shakespearean Negotiations: The Circulation of Social Energy in Renaissance England*. Berkeley: U of California P, 1988. 66–93.

——. *Renaissance Self-Fashioning: From More to Shakespeare*. Chicago: U of Chicago P, 1980.

Greene, Robert. *Friar Bacon and Friar Bungay*. Ed. J. A. Lavin. The New Mermaids. London: Benn, 1969.

Greene, Thomas M. *The Light in Troy: Imitation and Discovery in Renaissance Poetry*. New Haven, CT: Yale UP, 1982.

Grosz, Elizabeth. *Jacques Lacan: A Feminist Introduction*. London: Routledge, 1990.

Guichard-Tesson, Françoise. 'Le pion souvenir et les miroirs déformants dans l'allégorie d'amour'. *Jeux de mémoire: Aspects de la mnémotechnie médiévale*. Ed. Bruno Roy and Paul Zumthor. Études Mediévales. Montréal: Presses de l'Université de Montréal; Paris: Vrin, 1985. 99–108.

Gusdorf, Georges. *La découverte du soi*. Bibliothèque de Philosophie Contemporaine. Paris: Presses Universitaires de France, 1948.

Hallett, Charles A., and Elaine S. Hallett. *The Revenger's Madness: A Study of Revenge Tragedy Motifs*. Lincoln: U of Nebraska P, 1980.

Hanning, Robert W. *The Individual in Twelfth-Century Romance*. New Haven, CT: Yale UP, 1977.

Harrad of Hohenbourg. *Hortus Deliciarum*. Ed. Rosalie Green *et al*. Studies of the Warburg Institute 36. 2 vols. London: Warburg Institute and U of London; Leiden: Brill, 1978.

Henryson, Robert. *The Poems of Robert Henryson*. Ed. Denton Fox. Oxford: Clarendon, 1981.

Heywood, John. *A Mery Play Betwene Johan Johan the Husbande, Tib His Wife, and Sir Johan the Preest*. *Medieval Drama*. Ed. David Bevington. Boston: Houghton Mifflin, 1975.

Hieatt, A. Kent. 'The Alleged Early Modern Origin of the Self and History: Terminate or Regroup?' *Spenser Studies: A Renaissance Poetry Annual* 10 (1989): 1–35.

Hillman, Richard. '*Everyman* and the Energies of Stasis'. *Florilegium* (Carleton University Annual Papers on Classical Antiquity and the Middle Ages) 7 (1985): 206–26.

——. *Intertextuality and Romance in Renaissance Drama: The Staging of*

Nostalgia. Basingstoke, Hampshire: Macmillan; New York, St. Martin's, 1992.

———. 'Meaning and Mortality in Some Renaissance Revenge Plays'. *University of Toronto Quarterly* 49 (1979): 1–17.

———. *Shakespearean Subversions: The Trickster and the Play-text*. London: Routledge, 1992.

———. *William Shakespeare: The Problem Plays*. Twayne's English Authors Series. New York: Twayne, 1993.

Hoeniger, F. D. Introduction. *Pericles*. By William Shakespeare. Ed. F. D. Hoeniger. The Arden Shakespeare. London: Methuen, 1963. xiii–xci.

Holdsworth, R. V. 'Sexual Allusions in *Love's Labour's Lost, The Merry Wives of Windsor, Othello, The Winter's Tale*, and *The Two Noble Kinsmen*'. *Notes and Queries* 33 (1986): 351–53.

Howard, Jean E. 'Sex and Social Conflict: The Erotics of *The Roaring Girl*'. *Erotic Politics: Desire on the Renaissance Stage*. Ed. Susan Zimmerman. New York: Routledge, 1992. 170–90.

Hunter, G. K. Introduction. *Antonio's Revenge: The Second Part of Antonio and Mellida*. By John Marston. Ed. G. K. Hunter. Regents Renaissance Drama Series. Lincoln: U of Nebraska P, 1965. ix–xxi.

Irigaray, Luce. *This Sex Which Is Not One*. Trans. Catherine Porter with Carolyn Burke. Ithaca, NY: Cornell UP, 1985.

Jenkins, Harold, ed. *Hamlet*. By William Shakespeare. The Arden Shakespeare. London: Methuen, 1982.

Johnson, S. F. '*The Spanish Tragedy*, or Babylon Revisited'. *Essays on Shakespeare and Elizabethan Drama in Honour of Hardin Craig*. Ed. Richard Hosley. London: Routledge, 1963. 23–36.

Jonson, Ben. *Bartholomew Fair*. Ed. E. A. Horsman. The Revels Plays. London: Methuen, 1960.

———. *The Complete Poetry of Ben Jonson*. Ed. William B. Hunter Jr. New York: Norton, 1963.

———. *The Gypsies Metamorphosed. Ben Jonson: The Complete Masques*. Ed. Stephen Orgel. The Yale Ben Jonson. New Haven, CT: Yale UP, 1969.

———. *Sejanus His Fall*. Ed. Philip J. Ayres. The Revels Plays. Manchester: Manchester UP, 1990.

———. *Volpone or, The Fox*. Ed. R. B. Parker. The Revels Plays. Manchester: Manchester UP, 1983.

Joseph, B. L. *Elizabethan Acting*. 2nd ed. London: Oxford UP, 1964.

Kahrl, Stanley J. *Traditions of Medieval English Drama*. London: Hutchinson; Pittsburgh, PA: U of Pittsburgh P, 1975.

Keefer, Michael. Introduction. *Christopher Marlowe's Doctor Faustus: A 1604–Version Edition*. Ed. Michael Keefer. Peterborough, Ontario; Lewiston, NY: Broadview, 1991. xi–xcii.

Kirschbaum, Engelbert, Günter Bandmann, *et al.*, eds. *Lexikon der christlichen Ikonographie*. 8 vols. Vols. 5–8 ed. Wolfgang Braunfels. Freiburg: Herder, 1968–76.

Knowles, Richard, and Evelyn Joseph Mattern, eds. *As You Like It*. By William Shakespeare. *A New Variorum Edition of Shakespeare*. New York: MLA, 1977.

Kristeva, Julia. 'The Bounded Text'. *Desire in Language: A Semiotic Approach to Literature and Art*. Ed. Leon S. Roudiez. Trans. Thomas Gora, Alice Jardine, and Leon S. Roudiez. New York: Columbia UP, 1980. 36–63.

——. *La révolution du langage poétique: L'avant-garde à la fin du xixe siècle: Lautréamont et Mallarmé*. Paris: Seuil, 1974.

——. *Revolution in Poetic Language*. Trans. Margaret Waller. Introd. by Leon S. Roudiez. New York: Columbia UP, 1984.

——. 'Le texte clos'. *Σημειωτικὴ: Recherches pour une sémanalyse*. Paris, Seuil, 1969. 113–42.

Kretzmann, Paul Edward. *The Liturgical Element in the Earliest Forms of the Medieval Drama with Special Reference to the English and German Plays*. University of Minnesota Studies in Language and Literature 4. Minneapolis: Bulletin of the University of Minnesota, 1916.

Kyd, Thomas. *The Spanish Tragedy*. Ed. J. R. Mulryne. 2nd ed. The New Mermaids. London: Black; New York: Norton, 1989.

Lacan, Jacques. 'Desire and the Interpretation of Desire in *Hamlet*'. Trans. James Hulbert. *Yale French Studies* 55/56 (1977): 11–52.

——. *The Four Fundamental Concepts of Psycho-Analysis*. Ed. Jacques-Alain Miller. Trans. Alan Sheridan. The International Psycho-Analytical Library 106. London: Hogarth Press and the Institute of Psycho-Analysis, 1977.

——. 'The Mirror Stage as Formative of the Function of the I'. *Écrits: A Selection*. Trans. Alan Sheridan. London: Tavistock, 1977. 1–7.

——. Response to Michel Foucault. 'Qu'est-ce qu'un auteur? Séance du 22 février 1969'. By Michel Foucault *et al*. *Bulletin de la Société française de philosophie* 63.3 (1969): 73–104. 104.

——. *Le Séminaire de Jacques Lacan, Livre VII*. Ed. Jacques-Alain Miller. Paris: Seuil, 1986.

——. *Le Séminaire de Jacques Lacan, Livre XI (Les quatre concepts fondamentaux de la psychanalyse)*. Ed. Jacques-Alain Miller. Paris: Seuil, 1973.

——. *The Seminar of Jacques Lacan, Book VII: The Ethics of Psychoanalysis 1959–60*. Ed. Jacques-Alain Miller. Trans. with notes by Dennis Porter. New York: Norton, 1992.

——. 'Le stade du miroir comme formateur de la fonction du Je . . .'. *Écrits*. Le Champ Freudien. Paris: Seuil, 1966. 93–100.

Lamb, Charles. 'On the Tragedies of Shakespeare, Considered with Reference to Their Fitness for Stage Representation'. 1811. *Shakespeare Criticism: A Selection*. Ed. D. Nicol Smith. London: Oxford UP, 1916. 215–40.

Lebègue, Raymond. *Le mystère des actes des apôtres: Contribution à l'étude de l'humanisme et du protestantisme français au xvie siècle*. Paris: Champion, 1929.

Lee, Sidney. *The French Renaissance in England: An Account of the Literary Relations of England and France in the Sixteenth Century*. Oxford: Clarendon, 1910.

Léger, Claude. 'Quel est donc cet autre auquel je suis plus attaché qu'à moi?' *Philosophie présente Lacan*. By Marie-Hélène Brousse, Serge Cottet, Claude Léger, Jean-Daniel Matet, Gérard Miller, Dominique Miller, François Regnault, Danièle Silvestre, Michel Silvestre, Colette Soler, and Marc Strauss, under the direction of Gérard Miller. Paris: Bordas, 1987. 31–57.

Leggatt, Alexander. *Jacobean Public Theatre*. Theatre Producion Studies. London: Routledge, 1992.

Lehnen, Brigitte. *Das Egerer Passionspiel*. Frankfurt-am-Main: Peter Lang, 1988.

Leo, Friedrich. *Der Monolog im Drama: Ein Beitrag zur griechisch-römischen Poetik*. Abhandlungen der Königlichen Gesellschaft der Wissenschaften zu Göttingen, Philologisch-Historische Klasse, ns 10, No. 5. Berlin: Weidmannsche Buchhandlung, 1908.

Leverenz, David. 'The Woman in Hamlet: An Interpersonal View'. *Representing Shakespeare: New Psychoanalytic Essays*. Ed. Murray M. Schwartz and Coppélia Kahn. Baltimore, MD: Johns Hopkins UP, 1980. 110–28.

Levin, Richard. 'Bashing the Bourgeois Subject'. *Textual Practice* 3 (1989): 76–86.

———. 'Unthinkable Thoughts in the New Historicizing of English Renaissance Drama'. *New Literary History* 21 (1990): 433–47.

Little, A. G. 'On Roger Bacon's Life and Works'. *Roger Bacon: Essays Contributed by Various Writers on the Occasion of the Commemoration of the Seventh Centenary of his Birth*. Ed. A. G. Little. Oxford: Clarendon, 1914. 1–31.

Lorris, Guillaume de, and Jean de Meun. *The Romaunt of the Rose*. Trans. Geoffrey Chaucer (?). *The Riverside Chaucer*. Gen. ed. Larry D. Benson. 3rd ed. Boston: Houghton Mifflin, 1987.

Lumiansky, R. M., and David Mills, eds. *The Chester Mystery Cycle*. 2 vols. Early English Text Society ss 3. London: Oxford UP for the Early English Text Society, 1974.

Lydgate, John. *Lydgate's Fall of Princes*. Ed. Henry Bergen. Part 1 (Books 1 and 2). Washington, DC: The Carnegie Institute of Washington, 1923.

Lyly, John. *Endymion*. *English Drama 1580–1642*. Ed. C. F. Tucker Brooke and Nathaniel Burton Paradise. Lexington, MA: Heath, 1933.

Machiavelli, Niccolò. *Discorsi sopra la prima deca di Tito Livio*. *Opere di Noccolò Machiavelli*. Ed. Ezio Raimondi. 6th ed. Milan: Mursia, 1973.

———. *The Discourses of Niccolò Machiavelli*. Trans. and ed. Leslie J. Walker. 2 vols. 1950; rpt. with a new Introduction and appendices by Cecil H. Clough. London: Routledge, 1975.

McLuskie, Kathleen. ' "Lawless desires well tempered" '. *Erotic Politics: Desire on the Renaissance Stage*. Ed. Susan Zimmerman. New York: Routledge, 1992. 103–26.

McMillin, Scott. 'The Figure of Silence in *The Spanish Tragedy*'. *ELH* 39 (1972): 27–48.

Mâle, Émile. *Religious Art in France: The Twelfth Century: A Study of the Origins of Medieval Iconography*. Ed. Harry Bober. Trans. Marthiel Mathews. Bollingen Series 90.1. Princeton, NJ: Princeton UP, 1978.

Marcus, Leah S. *Puzzling Shakespeare: Local Reading and Its Discontents*. The New Historicism: Studies in Cultural Poetics 6. Berkeley: U of California P, 1988.

Marlowe, Christopher. *Christopher Marlowe's* Doctor Faustus: *A 1604-Version Edition*. Ed. Michael Keefer. Peterborough, Ontario, and Lewiston, NY: Broadview, 1991.

———. *The Jew of Malta*. Ed. N. W. Bawcutt. The Revels Plays. Manchester: Manchester UP, 1978.

———. *Tamburlaine the Great* (Part One). Ed. J. S. Cunningham. The Revels Plays. Manchester: Manchester UP; Baltimore, MD: Johns Hopkins UP, 1981.

Mary Magdalen. The Late Medieval Religious Plays of Bodleian MSS Digby 133 and e Museo 160. Early English Text Society 283. Ed. Donald C. Baker, John L. Murphy, and Louis B. Hall Jr. Oxford: Oxford UP for the Early English Text Society, 1982.

Marston, John. *Antonio and Mellida.* Ed. W. Reavley Gair. The Revels Plays. Manchester: Manchester UP, 1991.

———. *Antonio's Revenge.* Ed. W. Reavley Gair. The Revels Plays. Manchester: Manchester UP; Baltimore, MD: Johns Hopkins UP, 1978.

———. *The Malcontent.* Ed. G. K. Hunter. The Revels Plays. London: Methuen, 1975.

———. 'The Metamorphosis of Pigmalions Image'. *The Poems of John Marston.* Ed. Arnold Davenport. Liverpool: Liverpool UP, 1961.

———. *The Scourge of Villanie. The Poems of John Marston.* Ed. Arnold Davenport. Liverpool: Liverpool UP, 1961.

Maus, Katharine Eisaman. *Inwardness and Theater in the English Renaissance.* Chicago: U of Chicago P, 1995.

Maxwell, Ian. *French Farce and John Heywood.* Melbourne and London: Melbourne UP in assoc. with Oxford UP, 1946.

Meredith, Peter. Introduction. *The Mary Play from the N.town Manuscript.* Ed. Peter Meredith. London: Longman, 1987. 1–23.

Middleton, Thomas. *Women Beware Women.* Ed. J. R. Mulryne. The Revels Plays. London: Methuen, 1975.

———, and William Rowley. *The Changeling.* Ed. N. W. Bawcutt. The Revels Plays. Manchester: Manchester UP, 1958.

Miller, Gérard. 'L'acte manqué par excellence, c'est l'acte sexuel'. *Philosophie présente Lacan.* By Marie-Hélène Brousse, Serge Cottet, Claude Léger, Jean-Daniel Matet, Gérard Miller, Dominique Miller, François Regnault, Danièle Silvestre, Michel Silvestre, Colette Soler, and Marc Strauss, under the direction of Gérard Miller. Paris: Bordas, 1987. 77–90.

Miller, Jacques-Alain. 'Language: Much Ado About What?' *Lacan and the Subject of Language.* Ed. Ellie Ragland-Sullivan and Mark Bracher. New York: Routledge, 1991. 21–35.

Minnis, A. J. *Medieval Theory of Authorship: Scholastic Literary Attitudes in the Later Middle Ages.* London: Scolar Press, 1984.

The Mirror for Magistrates. Ed. Lily B. Campbell. Huntington Library Publications. Cambridge: Cambridge UP, 1938.

Le mistère du viel testament. Ed. James de Rothschild. 6 vols. Paris: Didot (Société des anciens textes français): 1878–91.

Montaigne, Michel Eyquem de. *Essais.* Ed. Maurice Rat. 3 vols. Paris: Garnier, [1957].

———. *Montaigne's Essays.* Trans. John Florio. With an Introduction by L. C. Harmer. 3 vols. Everyman's Library. London: Dent; New York: Dutton, 1965.

Montrose, Louis Adrian. *'Curious-Knotted Garden': The Form, Themes, and Contexts of Shakespeare's Love's Labour's Lost.* Salzburg: Institut für Englische Sprache und Literatur, Universität Salzburg, 1977.

Moretti, Franco. 'The Great Eclipse: Tragic Form as the Deconsecration of Sovereignty'. Trans. David Miller. *Signs Taken for Wonders: Essays in the Sociology of Literary Forms.* Trans. Susan Fischer, David Forgacs, and David Miller. Rev. ed. London: Verso, 1988. 42–82.

Mullaney, Steven. *The Place of the Stage: License, Play, and Power in Renaissance England*. Chicago: U of Chicago P, 1988.

Müller, Wolfgang G. 'Das Ich im Dialog mit sich selbst: Bemerkungen zur Struktur des dramatischen Monologs von Shakespeare bis zu Samuel Beckett'. *Deutsche Vierteljarhrsschrift für Literaturwissenschaft und Geistesgeschichte* 56 (1982): 314–33.

Mulryne, J. R. Introduction. *The Spanish Tragedy*. By Thomas Kyd. Ed. J. R. Mulryne. 2nd ed. The New Mermaids. London: Black; New York: Norton, 1989. xi–xxxiv.

Nashe, Thomas. 'The Choise of Valentines'. *The Works of Thomas Nashe*. Ed. Ronald B. McKerrow. 5 vols. Rev. ed. by F. P. Wilson. Oxford: Blackwell, 1958. Vol. 3.

Nelson, Alan H. *The Medieval English Stage: Corpus Christi Pageants and Plays*. Chicago: U of Chicago P, 1974.

Neuss, Paula. Introduction. *Magnificence*. By John Skelton. Ed. Paula Neuss. The Revels Plays. Manchester: Manchester UP; Baltimore, MD: Johns Hopkins UP, 1980. 1–64.

Newell, Alex. *The Soliloquies in* Hamlet: *The Structural Design*. Rutherford, NJ: Fairleigh Dickinson UP; London: Associated University Presses, 1991.

Oppenheimer, Paul. *The Birth of the Modern Mind: Self, Consciousness, and the Invention of the Sonnet*. New York: Oxford UP, 1989.

Ordo Repraesentationis Adae. *Medieval Drama*. Ed. David Bevington. Boston: Houghton Mifflin, 1975.

Ovid. *Shakespeare's Ovid: Being Arthur Golding's Translation of* The Metamorphoses. Ed. W. H. D. Rouse. Centaur Classics. Carbondale: Southern Illinois UP, 1961.

The Oxford Dictionary of Nursery Rhymes. Ed. Iona and Peter Opie. Oxford: Clarendon, 1952.

Partridge, Eric. *Shakespeare's Bawdy: A Literary and Psychological Essay and a Comprehensive Glossary*. Rev. ed. New York: Dutton, 1969.

Patterson, Lee. *Chaucer and the Subject of History*. Madison: U of Wisconsin P, 1991.

Percy, C. H. Herford, and Evelyn Simpson, eds. *Ben Jonson* (Complete Works). Vol. 10 (Play Commentary, Masque Commentary). Oxford: Clarendon, 1950.

Plutarch. *Plutarch's Lives of the Noble Grecians and Romanes*. Trans. Thomas North. *Narrative and Dramatic Sources of Shakespeare*. Ed. Geoffrey Bullough. Vol. 5. London: Routledge; New York: Columbia UP, 1964. 58–140.

Ragland-Sullivan, Ellie. *Jacques Lacan and the Philosophy of Psychoanalysis*. Urbana: U of Illinois P, 1986.

Ralegh, Walter. *The History of the World*. Ed. C. A. Patrides. London: Macmillan, 1971.

Réau, Louis. *Iconographie de l'art chrétien*. 3 vols. Paris: Presses Universitaires de France, 1956.

Redford, John. *Wit and Science*. *Medieval Drama*. Ed. David Bevington. Boston: Houghton Mifflin, 1975.

Regan, Mariann Sanders. *Love Words: The Self and the Text in Medieval and Renaissance Poetry*. Ithaca, NY: Cornell UP, 1982.

Regosin, Richard L. *The Matter of My Book: Montaigne's Essais as the Book of the Self*. Berkeley: U of California P, 1977.

Rider, Frederick. *The Dialectic of Selfhood in Montaigne.* Stanford, CA: Stanford UP, 1973.

Riffaterre, Michael. 'Syllepsis'. *Critical Inquiry* 6 (1980): 625–38.

Rigolot, François. 'L'amitié intertextuelle: Étienne de La Boétie et Marie de Gournay'. *L'esprit et la lettre: Mélanges offerts à Jules Brody.* Ed. Louis van Delft. Tübingen: Narr, 1991. 57–66.

——. Introduction. 'Préface à l'édition des *Essais* de Montaigne'. By Marie le Jars de Gournay. Ed. François Rigolot. *Montaigne Studes: An Interdisciplinary Forum* 1 (1989): 8–20.

——. *Les métamorphoses de Montaigne.* Paris: Presses Universitaires de France, 1988.

Robertson, John M. *Montaigne and Shakespeare, and Other Essays on Cognate Questions.* 2nd ed. London: Black, 1909.

Rose, Mary Beth. *The Expense of Spirit: Love and Sexuality in English Renaissance Drama.* Ithaca, NY: Cornell UP, 1988.

Rothschild, James de. Introduction. *Le mistère du viel testament.* Ed. James de Rothschild. Vol. 1. Paris: Didot (Société des anciens textes français), 1878. i–xcii.

Sacks, Peter. 'Where Words Prevail Not: Grief, Revenge, and Language in Kyd and Shakespeare'. *ELH* 49 (1982): 576–601.

Sackville, Thomas. 'The Induction' and 'The complaynt of Henrye duke of Buckingham'. *The Mirror for Magistrates.* Ed. Lily B. Campbell. Huntington Library Publications. Cambridge: Cambridge UP, 1938. 298–345.

——, and Thomas Norton. *Gorboduc, or Ferrex and Porrex. Drama of the English Renaissance I: The Tudor Period.* Ed. Russell A. Fraser and Norman Rabkin. New York: Macmillan, 1976.

Safouan, Moustapha. 'Representation and Pleasure'. Trans. Ben Brewster. *The Talking Cure: Essays in Psychoanalysis and Language.* Ed. Colin MacCabe. London: Macmillan, 1981. 75–89.

Sandys, John Edwin. 'Roger Bacon in English Literature'. *Roger Bacon: Essays Contributed by Various Writers on the Occasion of the Commemoration of the Seventh Centenary of his Birth.* Ed. A. G. Little. Oxford: Clarendon, 1914. 359–72.

Shakespeare, William. *The Riverside Shakespeare.* Gen. ed. G. Blakemore Evans. Boston: Houghton Mifflin, 1974.

Shepherd, Simon. *Marlowe and the Politics of Elizabethan Theatre.* Brighton, Sussex: Harvester; New York: St. Martin's, 1986.

Silverman, Kaja. *The Subject of Semiotics.* New York: Oxford UP, 1983.

Skelton, John. *Magnificence.* Ed. Paula Neuss. The Revels Plays. Manchester: Manchester UP; Baltimore, MD: Johns Hopkins UP, 1980.

Smith, Hilda. 'Gynecology and Ideology in Seventeenth-Century England'. *Liberating Women's History: Theoretical and Critical Essays.* Ed. Berenice A. Carroll. Champagne: U of Illinois P, 1976. 97–114.

Smith, Lacey Baldwin. 'English Treason Trials and Confessions in the Sixteenth Century'. *Journal of the History of Ideas* 15 (1954): 471–98.

Smith, Molly. 'The Theater and the Scaffold: Death as Spectacle in *The Spanish Tragedy*'. *Studies in English Literature 1500–1900* 32 (1992): 217–32.

Smith, Paul. *Discerning the Subject.* Foreward by John Mowitt. Theory and History of Literature 55. Minneapolis: U of Minnesota P, 1988.

Soellner, Rolf. *Shakespeare's Patterns of Self-Knowledge*. Columbus: Ohio State UP, 1972.

Spector, Stephen, ed. *The N-Town Play: Cotton MS Vespasian D.8*. 2 vols. Early English Text Society ss 11. Oxford: Oxford UP for the Early English Text Society, 1991.

Spierenburg, Pieter. *The Spectacle of Suffering: Executions and the Evolution of Repression: From a Preindustrial Metropolis to the European Experience*. Cambridge: Cambridge UP, 1984.

Sprague, Arthur Colby. 'Shakespeare and Melodrama'. *Essays and Studies* ns 18 (1965): 1–12.

——. *Shakespeare and the Audience: A Study in the Techniques of Exposition*. Cambridge, MA: Harvard UP, 1935.

Stearns, Marshall W. *Robert Henryson*. New York: Columbia UP, 1949.

Steiner, George. *After Babel: Aspects of Language and Translation*. New York: Oxford UP, 1975.

Strauss, Marc. 'La vraie fonction du père, c'est d'unir un désir à la loi'. *Philosophie présente Lacan*. By Marie-Hélène Brousse, Serge Cottet, Claude Léger, Jean-Daniel Matet, Gérard Miller, Dominique Miller, François Regnault, Danièle Silvestre, Michel Silvestre, Colette Soler, and Marc Strauss, under the direction of Gérard Miller. Paris: Bordas, 1987. 59–76.

Taylor, George C. 'The English "Planctus Mariae"'. *Modern Philology* 4 (1907): 605–37.

Tillyard, E. M. W. *The Elizabethan World Picture*. London: Chatto, 1943.

——. *Shakespeare's Early Comedies*. London: Chatto, 1965.

Tourneur, Cyril. *The Atheist's Tragedy, or, The Honest Man's Revenge*. Ed. Irving Ribner. The Revels Plays. London: Methuen, 1964.

—— (?). *The Revenger's Tragedy*. Ed. R. A. Foakes. The Revels Plays. London: Methuen, 1966.

Tracy, Robert. 'The Owl and the Baker's Daughter: A Note on *Hamlet* IV.v.42–43'. *Shakespeare Quarterly* 17 (1966): 83–6.

Traub, Valerie. *Desire and Anxiety: Circulations of Sexuality in Shakespearean Drama*. London: Routledge, 1992.

——. 'The (In)significance of "Lesbian" Desire in Early Modern England'. *Erotic Politics: Desire on the Renaissance Stage*. Ed. Susan Zimmerman. New York: Routledge, 1992. 150–69.

Trilling, Lionel. *Sincerity and Authenticity*. Cambridge, MA: Harvard UP, 1974.

Tripet, Arnaud. *Pétrarque; ou, La conaissance de soi*. Travaux d'Humanisme et Renaissance 91. Geneva: Droz, 1967.

The True Tragedy of Richard III. *Narrative and Dramatic Sources of Shakespeare*. Ed. Geoffrey Bullough. Vol. 3. London: Routledge; New York: Columbia UP, 1966. 317–45.

Untersteiner, Mario. *The Sophists*. Trans. Kathleen Freeman. Oxford: Blackwell, 1954.

Ure, Peter. Introduction. *The Chronicle History of Perkin Warbeck: A Strange Truth*. By John Ford. Ed. Peter Ure. The Revels Plays. London: Methuen, 1968. xvii–lxxxix.

Vandekerchove, Christian. 'L'iconographie médiévale de la construction'. *Les batisseurs des cathédrales gothiques*. Ed. Roland Recht. Strasbourg: Les musées de la ville de Strasbourg, 1989. 61–80.

Villey, Pierre. *Montaigne et François Bacon.* 1913; rpt. Geneva: Slatkine, 1973.

Wallace, Malcolm W. Introduction. *A Tragedie of Abraham's Sacrifice.* By Théodore de Bèze. Trans. Arthur Golding. Ed. Malcolm W. Wallace. University of Toronto Studies Philological Series. Toronto: U of Toronto Library, 1906. xi–lxi.

Wayne, Don E. 'Drama and Society in the Age of Jonson: Shifting Grounds of Authority and Judgment in Three Major Comedies'. *Renaissance Drama as Cultural History: Essays from* Renaissance Drama *1977–1987.* Ed. Mary Beth Rose. Evanston, ILL: Northwestern UP and The Newberry Library Center for Renaissance Studies, 1990. 3–29.

Webster, John. *The Devil's Law-Case.* Ed. Elizabeth M. Brennan. The New Mermaids. London: Benn, 1975.

——. *The Duchess of Malfi.* Ed. John Russell Brown. The Revels Plays. London: Methuen, 1964.

——. *The White Devil.* Ed. John Russell Brown. 2nd ed. The Revels Plays. London: Methuen, 1966.

Weimann, Robert. *Shakespeare and the Popular Tradition in the Theater: Studies in the Social Dimension of Dramatic Form and Function.* Ed. Robert Schwartz. Orig. title *Tradition des Volkstheaters* (1967). Baltimore, MD: Johns Hopkins UP, 1978.

Wilden, Anthony. 'Lacan and the Discourse of the Other'. *The Language of the Self: The Function of Language in Psychoanalysis.* By Jacques Lacan. Trans. with notes by Anthony Wilden. Baltimore, MD: Johns Hopkins UP, 1968. 159–310.

Williams, Raymond. 'On Dramatic Dialogue and Monologue (Particularly in Shakespeare)'. *Writing in Society.* London: Verso, 1983. 31–64.

Woolf, Rosemary. *The English Mystery Plays.* London: Routledge; Berkeley: U of California P, 1972.

Wright, Herbert G. *Boccaccio in England from Chaucer to Tennyson.* London: Athlone, 1957.

Yamada, Akihiro, ed. *The Widow's Tears.* By George Chapman. The Revels Plays. London: Methuen, 1975.

Young, Karl. *The Drama of the Medieval Church.* 2 vols. Oxford: Clarendon, 1933.

Zumthor, Paul. 'Le Carrefour des rhétoriqueurs: Intertextualité et rhétorique'. *Poétique* 27 (1976): 317–37.

——. *Langue, texte, énigme.* Paris: Seuil, 1975.

Zwingli, Ulrich. *Of the Clarity and Certainty of the Word of God. Zwingli and Bullinger.* Trans. and ed. G. W. Bromiley. The Library of Christian Classics 24. Philadelphia, PA: Westminster, 1953. 59–95.

——. *Von Klarheit und Gewißheit des Wortes Gottes. Huldreich Zwinglis Sämtliche Werke.* Ed. Emil Egli and Georg Finsler. 14 vols. Vol. 1. Corpus Reformatorum 88. Berlin: Schwetschke, 1905.

Index